★ABOUT THIS BOOK

This year's principal font is Georgia, the first seriffed typeface to be used as body copy in *Guinness World Records* for more than 15 years. (Serifs are the small slabs or hooks at the ends of the letters; historically, type designers believed that they increased the readability of text.) Matthew Carter of Microsoft created Georgia in order that a seriffed font could be read more easily on a computer screen, where certain fonts were considered more difficult to read.

The overwhelming body of evidence – researched since the 1930s – reveals, however, that serifs do nothing to improve readability. This year's font choice, then, is purely an aesthetic one.

The display font is **BLACKSTOCK**, created by Aerotype of Glendale, California, USA. Reproduced "warts and all" from a source dating to the 1820s, this distressed face is reminiscent of old letterpressed or screen-printed circus and "wanted" posters. This chunky and bold feel is extended into the design of the pages, and lends the book a fun, nostalgic, vaudeville vibe.

The cover uses a laser-cut holographic flame effect – designed in the UK and rendered in metallic foil in California, USA – with a photographic fire printed on top. Incorporated into the foil is a holographic lens with the new-look spherical Guinness World Records text block.

INTRODUCTION
FIRE!

★ ★ ★ ★ ★ ★ ★ ★ ★

HIT!
THE RECORD FOR THE MOST FLAMING TORCHES JUGGLED AT THE SAME TIME IS HELD BY ANTHONY GATTO (USA), WHO JUGGLED SEVEN TORCHES IN 1989.

MISS!
DELIBERATELY STARTED FOREST FIRES MADE 1997 THE WORST YEAR IN RECORDED HISTORY FOR THE DESTRUCTION OF THE ENVIRONMENT BY FIRE.

FARTHEST DISTANCE FIREWALKING

Trever McGhee (Canada) walked 597 ft (181.9 m) over embers with temperatures in excess of 1,215.80°F (657.67°C) at Symons Valley Rodeo Grounds in Calgary, Alberta, Canada, on November 9, 2007.

★LONGEST RUN DURING A FULL-BODY BURN

The greatest distance run while performing a full-body burn is 259 ft (78.9 m) and was achieved by professional stunt performer Keith Malcolm (UK) of The Stannage International Stunt Team at the Alton Show in Hampshire, UK, on July 5, 2009.

LONGEST-BURNING FIRE

A burning coal seam lying beneath Mount Wingen in New South Wales, Australia, is thought to have started around 5,000 years ago when lightning struck the coal seam at the point where it reached the Earth's surface. The fire is still burning, around 100 ft (30 m) underground, as it has slowly eaten away at the seam.

LARGEST FIREWORKS DISPLAY

A fireworks display featuring 66,326 fireworks was achieved by Macedo's Pirotecnia, Lda. in Funchal, Madeira, Portugal, on December 31, 2006. The display, which was part of the New Year celebrations on the island of Madeira, was launched from 40 different sites and was over in just eight minutes.

WORST FIREWORKS DISASTER

An estimated 800 people died as a result of an accident during a fireworks display staged beside the river Seine in Paris, France, on May 16, 1770 to mark the marriage of the future Louis XIV.

MOST PEOPLE BURNED AT THE STAKE

The burning of "witches" at the stake reached its greatest intensity in Germany in the 16th and 17th centuries. At Quedlinburg, near Leipzig, 133 witches were burned in one day in 1589. Elsewhere, in the towns of Wurzburg and Bamberg, at least 1,500 witches were burned in less than a decade during the mid-17th century.

★LARGEST BURNING MAN FESTIVAL

The annual Burning Man festival staged in the Black Rock Desert in Nevada, USA, attracted a record 49,599 visitors to the 2008 event. The week-long festival is named after the giant wooden effigy that is burned during the Saturday of Labor Day weekend. The event dates back to 1986.

DID YOU KNOW?
THE LONGEST MOTORCYCLE RIDE THROUGH A TUNNEL OF FIRE WAS BY CLINT EWING (USA) AND MEASURED 200 FT (60.9 M) LONG ON JANUARY 27, 2008.

The earliest use of fire by humans has been traced back approximately 1.5 million years to locations in East Africa.

TRIVIA

★ LONGEST FULL-BODY BURN (NO OXYGEN)

On February 25, 2010, stuntman Ted A Batchelor (USA) endured a full-body burn without oxygen for 2 min 57 sec on the set of *Lo Show dei Record* in Rome, Italy. Previously, on September 19, 2009, Ted had led a group of 17 in the **largest simultaneous body burn**, when members of his team and the "Ohio Burns Unit" (USA) set themselves alight for 43 seconds in South Russell, Ohio, USA.

HIGHEST FLAME BLOWN BY A FIRE BREATHER

Tim Black (Australia) blew a 23-ft 7-in-high (7.2-m) flame for *Zheng Da Zong Yi – Guinness World Records Special* in Beijing, China, on September 15, 2007.

★ MOST PEOPLE SPINNING FIRE

On August 15, 2009, in an event organized by The Arts Factory Lodge in New South Wales, Australia, 102 participants span fire brands for a total of six-and-a-half minutes. The high-temperature twirling was accompanied by a group of drummers, who kept track of time by beating on their instruments. A crowd of more than 300 people cheered on the fire spinners.

★ TALLEST VOLCANIC FIRE FOUNTAIN

When the Izu-Oshima volcano, Japan, erupted in November 1986, it launched a fountain of fire into the air that was recorded as reaching 5,250 ft (1,600 m) in height. A volcanic fire fountain is characterized by a violent, geyser-like eruption of incandescent lava, rather than an ash column.

★ LARGEST GATHERING OF FIRE BREATHERS

On October 15, 2008, 269 people got hot under the collar together in Eindhoven, the Netherlands, when they set the record for the largest gathering of fire breathers. The event was coordinated by the Dutch student association Intermate.

★ LARGEST FLAMING IMAGE USING CANDLES

On December 10, 2009, 118 employees of the Sandoz (Pakistan) company created a flaming image with 35,478 candles at the Hotel Serena in Faisalabad, Pakistan. The image depicted the Sandoz logo and motto and had an area of 9,800 ft² (910.45 m²).

WORST TUNNEL FIRE

On November 12, 2000, 155 skiers died in a tunnel fire on the Kaprun railway, which took passengers up the Kitzsteinhorn Glacier in the Austrian Alps. The fire occurred when a blocked heating ventilator caused leaking hydraulic oil to ignite.

★ LONGEST WALL OF FIRE

A wall of fire measuring 10,178 ft 3 in (3,102.3 m) long was created by the Marine Corps Community Services (USA) during the 2009 MCAS Yuma Air Show in Yuma, Arizona, USA, on March 14, 2009.

FASTEST JET-POWERED FIRE TRUCK

On July 11, 1998, in Ontario, Canada, the jet-powered *Hawaiian Eagle*, owned by Shannen Seydel of Navarre, Florida, USA, attained a speed of 407 mph (655 km/h). The truck is a red 1940 Ford, powered by two Rolls-Royce Bristol Viper engines boasting 6,000 hp (4,470 kW) per engine and generating 12,000 lb (5,443 kg) of thrust.

LARGEST BONFIRE

A bonfire with a volume of 60,589 ft³ (1,715.7 m³) was built by ŠKD Mladi Boštanj and lit on April 30, 2007 in Boštanj, Slovenia, to celebrate Labour Day. Its 142-ft 6.2-in (43.44-m) height also qualifies the conflagration as the **tallest bonfire**.

INSTANT EXPERT

✪ FIRE RESULTS FROM A CHEMICAL REACTION BETWEEN OXYGEN AND A SOURCE OF FUEL THAT HAS BEEN HEATED TO ITS IGNITION TEMPERATURE.

✪ THE HOTTEST FLAME CREATED IN A LABORATORY IS PRODUCED BY CARBON SUBNITRIDE (C_4N_2). AT 1 ATMOSPHERE PRESSURE, IT BURNS WITH A FLAME CALCULATED TO REACH 9,010°F (4,988°C).

✪ "GREEK FIRE" WAS CREATED IN THE 7TH CENTURY AD. PROJECTED AS BURNING LIQUID JETS, IT COULD BURN ON, OR EVEN UNDER, WATER. THE FORMULA FOR ITS CREATION HAS BEEN LOST FOR CENTURIES.

Dedicated to
Michael Jackson
(1958–2009) &
He Pingping
(1988–2010)

British Library Cataloguing-in-Publication Data:
A catalogue record for this book is available from the British Library

ISBN: 978-1-897553-05-3

For a complete list of credits and acknowledgements, turn to p.278.

If you wish to make a record claim, find out how on p.18. Always contact us before making a record attempt.

Check the official website **www.guinnessworldrecords.com** regularly for record-breaking news, plus video footage of record attempts. You can also join and interact with the GWR online community.

Sustainability
The trees that are harvested to print *Guinness World Records* are carefully selected from managed forests to avoid the devastation of the landscape. For every tree harvested, at least one other is planted.

The paper contained within this edition is manufactured by UPM Kymi, Finland. The production site has been awarded the EU Flower Licence, is Chain-of-Custody certified, and operates environmental systems certified to both ISO 14001 and EMAS in order to ensure sustainable production.

The European Eco-label distinguishes products that meet high standards of both performance and environmental quality. Every product awarded the European Eco-label must pass rigorous environmental fitness trials, with results verified by an independent body.

Made of paper awarded the European Union Eco-label
reg.nr FI/11/1

Pictured opposite is Francisco Domingo Joaquim – aka Mr Bongo – of Angola. He rose to fame in the past few years thanks to his appearance on YouTube demonstrating his record for the **widest mouth**. Find out just how far apart he can stretch his lips on pp.74–75.

EDITOR-IN-CHIEF
Craig Glenday

MANAGING EDITORS
Matt Boulton, Ben Way

EDITORIAL TEAM
Chris Bernstein (index), Rob Cave, Rob Dimery, Carla Masson, Joel Meadows, Matthew White

DESIGN
Keren Turner and Lisa Garner at Itonic Design Ltd, Brighton, UK

COVER PRODUCTION
API; Simon Thompson

COVER DESIGN
Simon Jones

DIRECTOR OF PUBLISHING
Mina Patria

PRODUCTION MANAGER
Jane Boatfield

PRODUCTION ASSISTANT
Erica Holmes-Attivor

PRODUCTION CONSULTANTS
Patricia Magill, Roger Hawkins, Esteve Font Canadell, Salvador Pujol, Julian Townsend

PRINTING & BINDING
Printer Industria Gráfica, Barcelona, Spain

ORIGINAL COMIC ART
Jimmy Rumble

PICTURE EDITOR
Michael Whitty

DEPUTY PICTURE EDITOR
Laura Jackson

PICTURE RESEARCHER
Fran Morales

ORIGINAL PHOTOGRAPHY
Tim Anderson, Richard Bradbury, Jacob Chinn, Maria Elisa Duque, Paul Michael Hughes, Jonathan Lewis, Ranald Mackechnie, John Wright

COLOUR ORIGINATION
Resmiye Kahraman at FMG, London, UK

EDITORIAL CONSULTANTS
Earth, Science & Technology: David Hawksett

Life on Earth: Dr Karl Shuker

Human Body: Dr Eleanor Clarke; Robert Young (gerontology)

Adventure/Exploration: Ocean Rowing Society; World Speed Sailing Records Council

Weapons & Warfare: Stephen Wrigley

Arts & Entertainment: Dick Fiddy (TV); Thomasina Gibson

Society: Mike Flynn

Music: Dave McAleer

Sports & Games: Christian Marais; David Fischer (US sports)

GUINNESS WORLD RECORDS
Managing Director:
Alistair Richards

SVP Finance: Alison Ozanne
Finance Managers:
UK: Neelish Dawett
USA: Jason Curran
Accounts Payable Manager:
Kimberley Dennis/Laura Hetherington
Accounts Receivable Manager/ Contracts Administrator:
Lisa Gibbs
Legal and Business Affairs:
Raymond Marshall
Global Director of HR: Kelly Garrett

RECORDS MANAGEMENT
VP OF RECORDS
Marco Frigatti (Italy)

HEAD OF ADJUDICATIONS
Andrea Bánfi (Hungary)

ADJUDICATIONS TEAM
Jack Brockbank (UK)
Danny Girton, Jr (USA)
Amanda Mochan (USA)
Talal Omar (Yemen)
Tarika Vara (UK)
Lucia Sinigagliesi (Italy)

HEAD OF RECORDS MANAGEMENT
UK: Mariamarta Ruano-Graham (Guatemala)
USA: Carlos Martínez (Spain)

RECORDS MANAGEMENT
Gareth Deaves (UK)
Ralph Hannah (UK)
Louise Ireland (Wales)
Kaoru Ishikawa (Japan)
Mike Janela (USA)
Olaf Kuchenbecker (Germany)
Kimberly Partrick (USA)
Chris Sheedy (Australia)
Kristian Teufel (Germany)
Louise Toms (UK)
Aleksandr Vipirailenko (Lithuania)
Wu Xiaohong (China)

Director of IT: Katie Forde
Web Developer: Daniel Sharkey
IT Analyst: Paul Bentley
Developer: Imran Javed
System Analyst: Jawad Ahmed Butt
Director of Television: Rob Molloy
Digital Content Manager:
Denise Anlander
Television Assistant: Jimmy Rumble
Director of GWR LIVE!: Paul O'Neill

SALES AND MARKETING
Senior VP Sales & Marketing:
Samantha Fay
US Marketing Director:
Laura Plunkett
US PR Executive:
Jamie Panas
US PR & Marketing Assistant:
Sara Wilcox
English Language Sales & Marketing Director:
Nadine Causey

Licensing Director:
Frank Chambers
Senior National Accounts Manager:
John Pilley
National Accounts Executive:
Lisa Gills
English Language Marketing Executive:
Tom Harris

PR Manager:
Amarilis Espinoza
International Licensing Manager:
Beatriz Fernandez
US Licensing Manager:
Jennifer Gilmour
Business Development Managers:
USA: Stuart Claxton
Japan: Erika Ogawa
International Marketing Manager:
Justine Bourdariat
PR Manager: Karolina Davison
PR Executive: Damian Field

Office Administrators/Reception:
Jennifer Robson (UK)
Morgan Wilber (US)

INTRODUCTION
CONTENTS

EXTRA! NAVIGATE YOUR WAY THROUGH THIS YEAR'S BOOK USING HANDY CROSS REFERENCES.

TRIVIA SCATTERED THROUGHOUT THE BOOK ARE THESE FUN, FACT-FILLED NUGGETS OF RECORD-RELATED TRIVIA.

RECORDS BY CITY

51°28'N 0°00'E

At the foot of every page, you'll find records associated with different cities. Starting in the UK, from London's Greenwich meridian at 0°00'E, these cities are arranged in order of their longitude (distance from the meridian), so as you read the book, you can read your way around the world, eastward, city by city.

GUINNESS WORLD RECORDS 2011

QUIZ! WHAT ARE THESE? THEY'RE SIMPLE QUIZ QUESTIONS TO TEST YOUR FAMILY AND FRIENDS.
SEE P.278 FOR ALL THE ANSWERS.

INTRODUCTION
EDITOR'S LETTER

★ ★ ★ ★ ★ ★ ★ ★ ★ ★ ★ ★ ☆

WELCOME TO THE EXPLOSIVE NEW EDITION OF THE WORLD'S BIGGEST-SELLING COPYRIGHT BOOK. WHAT A YEAR IT'S BEEN – WE'VE LITERALLY GONE FROM ONE EXTREME TO ANOTHER TO BRING YOU MORE PICTURES, MORE RECORDS AND MORE INCREDIBLE ACHIEVEMENTS THAN EVER...

GOING FOR GOLDS

Finally claiming home advantage, Canada won a record 14 gold medals at the XXI Winter Olympiad held at Vancouver, British Columbia in February 2010 – by far the country's most impressive haul as host nation. Pictured below are just some of Canada's golden athletes.

Left to right: Kaillie Humphries and Heather Moyse (women's bobsleigh); Charles Hamelin of Canada competes in the men's 500 m relay short track speed skating; and Jasey Jay Anderson (snowboard men's parallel giant slalom).

★MOST OLYMPIC ICE HOCKEY GOLDS (MALE)

The 2010 Winter Olympics saw Canada match the USSR's achievement of eight Olympic gold medals in the men's ice hockey event, adding to Canada's previous wins in 1920, 1924, 1928, 1932, 1948, 1952, and 2002.

It's been a roller coaster of a year here at Guinness World Records (for actual **roller coaster** records, see p.198). We've witnessed some incredible highs and experienced some poignant lows, but we've survived the ride for another year and the result is *Guinness World Records 2011*, the first edition of the new decade.

As ever, the **biggest-selling copyright book** is crammed with record-breaking facts and feats from across North America and all around the world. Once again, Canada has made a major contribution with 2,256 record claims resulting in 62 successful attempts. We've tried to include as many of these records as physically possible into these pages, so congratulations to everybody who succeeded in making it into the book – and a big thank

you to those who didn't make it and to anyone else who tried to break or set a world record – you make the book what it is!

To mark North America's contribution to the world of record breaking, we've given this edition a special North American focus – lookout for **American Heroes** (p.136), **American Wildlife** (p.68), and **Route 66** (p.148)! Also, sports fans can enjoy extended coverage of football, baseball, and basketball records in the Sports section, which begins on p.220.

EXTRA!
FOR SENSATIONAL STRONGMAN FEATS AND BREATH-TAKING BALANCING, SEE P.90.

'APPY TALK
GWR HAS GONE APP MAD, CREATING UNIQUE DIGITAL CONTENT FOR THE IPAD AND IPHONE PLATFORMS – CHECK US OUT ON APPLE'S APP STORE.

DID YOU KNOW?

THE BAY OF FUNDY IN NOVA SCOTIA, CANADA, HAS THE HIGHEST MEAN SPRING TIDE RANGE – 14.5 M (47 FT 6 IN) BETWEEN LOW AND HIGH TIDE.

At exactly 1,178.3 miles (1,896.3 km), Yonge St in Ontario is the **longest street** in the world!

TRIVIA

★ LONGEST-SERVING WEATHER FORECASTER

Dave Devall (Canada) served as the weather forecaster for Toronto's CTV for 48 years, 2 months, and 27 days, from the station's launch on January 7, 1961 to his retirement on April 3, 2009.

LONG GAME: Martin Phillips-Hing, Mark Hing, David Ediger, Sam Dyck, Dave Northey and George Sawatzky Jr. (all Canada) played a record 50-hour game of *Settlers of Catan: Cities and Knights* in January 2009.

So, what are our big stories of this year? Firstly, Ashrita Furman of Queens, New York, USA – the man with the record for having the most records – celebrated his 100th concurrent Guinness World Records achievement – the first person ever to do so. Find out more about Ashrita's truly awe-inspiring total (now more like 114 records at time of going to press!) on p.86.

What else? Well, as ever, Guinness World Records spent the year criss-crossing North America to attend some key events in the record-breaking calendar, including both the Summer and Winter X Games (see pp.264–267), and the **NBA Jam** (p.248). Our man on the road, Stuart Claxton,

has worked tirelessly to bring record breaking to the public at these events, so look out for your name if you took part!

Globally, our teams of adjudicators and consultants have been busier than ever dealing with claims from every country – making my job as Editor even more difficult by unearthing ever more fascinating records. Find out what these two important teams do for Guinness World Records on pp.12–13.

A BIGGER BEARD?

Pictured here in front of the CN Tower (the **tallest tower**, see p.216) Sarwan Singh (Canada) travelled to Rome, Italy, to appear on *Lo Show dei Record* on March 4, 2010 – how did it measure up on set? Turn to pp.80–81 to find out the hair-raising details.

COMICS LEGEND

TURN TO P.166 FOR ALL THE BEST COMICS & GRAPHIC NOVELS RECORDS. CHECK OUT THE SPECIAL HEADER CREATED FOR US BY LETTERING GURU TODD KLEIN. THANKS TODD!

INTRODUCTION
EDITOR'S LETTER

★MOST DOGS WALKED SIMULTANEOUSLY

Melissa Crispin Piche (Canada) took a total of 27 dogs for a for a 43-minute walk at the Kinsmen Park, Strathmore, Alberta, Canada, and on September 13, 2008. The event started with 31 dogs on the leash, however, one dog got loose and three others were too tired to finish.

GET YOUR GAME ON:
605 staff from video games company EA demonstrated how to get fit using their *EA Sports Active* game at the EA Burnaby Campus Sports Field, BC, in May 2009.

And now there's a new way to get *your* name into the records books – it's called *GWR Live!* You can find out about this hands-on record-breaking roadshow on p.16.

Oh, and there's yet another way to get your name listed here -- by setting or breaking a record on one of our global TV shows. For a round-up of global GWR TV output this year, see p.14.

With all these exciting new ways to source world records, it's been a job and half trying to squeeze them all in. Still, it's allowed me to create some exciting new sections for this year's book:
• Did you miss the very first spread on *Fire!*? If so, turn back to pp.2–3 now for an explosive start to *GWR 2011*.
• We say goodbye to the *Space Shuttles* on p.28, as NASA confirms the end of an era for reusable space craft.
• Find out how the **tallest man**'s world tour went in our picture feature on p.72 (and check out the latest news on the **shortest living mobile man** on p.77).
• We've dedicated entire chapters to two of your favorite subect areas: *Living Planet* on pp.46–69, and *Animal Magic* on pp.150–159.
• Get the lowdown on your top *Cop & Crime Shows* (p.170) and *Sci-Fi & Fantasy TV* (p.172).
• Thanks to James Cameron's *Avatar* (see p.160), the world's gone mad for *3D Cinema*, so don't miss our special feature on p.182.
• Along the bottom of every page you'll find our *Records GPS* feature: go on a city-by-city tour of world records, starting at 0° on the map and traveling east around the world to various cities in order of longitude.
• And as usual, you'll find every major sporting record listed in our *Sports Reference* section starting on p.268.

A PIECE OF CAKE:
Casino de Charlevoix of Quebec organized the ★largest cake decoration lesson with 1,293 participants on June 24, 2009. That's a lot of spoons to lick at the end!

A LONG CURL:
A group of 10 players from The Nipigon Curling Club in Nipigon, Ontario, performed a record curling marathon that lastest 50 hr 3 min between March 12 and 15, 2009.

★ **NEW RECORD**
★ **UPDATED RECORD**

WALKING TALL:
Cirque du Soleil celebrated its 25th anniversary by organizing a record-breaking gathering of 737 stilt walkers in Montreal, Quebec, on June 16, 2009.

OBITUARY

He might have been small in stature, but He Pingping (right) had the personality of a giant. The news of his passing made headlines around the world; Pingping was adored by millions of people, many of whom wrote to us to express their sadness.

Many of you also asked who would be the new **shortest living mobile man**. The answer is Edward Niño Hernandez (left) of Colombia -- *read his story on p.77.*

> *"There are few jobs in which you end the day teaching the world's smallest man how to play the drums!"*
>
> **Craig Glenday,
> GWR Editor-in-Chief**

IN MEMORIA

This year's edition is a particularly poignant one for us at Guinness World Records, as it is our tribute to two very special record holders we lost in the past year: the USA's Michael Jackson (p.189) and China's He Pingping (p.76).

Michael Jackson was always a big fan of the book, and always willing to give up his time for us, whether it was to open a new GWR Museum, or just to pop into the office to say hello. I was honored to be considered a friend of Michael, and I'll always cherish the memories of his visit to the London office in 2006, and presenting him his award for *Thriller* at that year's World Music Awards alongside Beyoncé Knowles.

A more recent addition to the GWR family was He Pingping, the world's **shortest living mobile man**. The cheeky, impish Pingping first lit up our lives in 2009 when he made the pages of our book, before going on to become an international superstar.

I was the lucky one who got to fly out to Inner Mongolia to measure the little man for the first time.

As we traveled together, one thing became clear -- his short stature was always going to have health implications. Yet, he never let his size get in the way of having a good time, and he refused to be treated as an invalid. He wrung all he could out of the precious time he had, and made a major impact on the world, inspiring around him.

So, what better a message to take into the new decade than this: Life is there to be lived! Enjoy every frightening bank and turn of that roller coaster of life, and feel the thrill of the unknown highs and lows ahead of you as they happen. And if you break some records along the way, so much the better! Have a fantastic 2011 -- now get out there and let's break some world records!

Craig Glenday
Editor-in-Chief

PULLING A FAST ONE

Canadian superstar Rev. Kevin Fast really excelled himself this year. He attempted to better his **heaviest vehicle pulled over a level 100 ft** (30.48 m) and **heaviest truck pulled by arm** achievements by trying to pull a CC-177 Globemaster III operated by the Canadian Forces Air Command. Was he successful? Find out on p.89.

701

INTRODUCTION
ADJUDICATORS & CONSULTANTS

★ ★ ★ ★ ★ ★ ★ ★ ★ ★ ★ ★ ★

MEET THE TWO TEAMS THAT CAN TURN YOUR DREAMS INTO REALITY... THE <u>RECORDS ADJUDICATORS</u>, WITH THE POWER TO SAY "YES" OR "NO" TO YOUR CLAIM, AND THE <u>CONSULTANTS</u>, WHO USE THEIR SPECIALIST KNOWLEDGE TO FIND WORLD RECORD FACTS AND SUPERLATIVES ALL YEAR ROUND.

Information flows into the *Guinness World Records* office in one of two main ways. The first is via our **Adjudicators** – these are the records managers who process the 65,000 claims we receive from the public each year.

This multilingual team divides itself between the various international GWR offices and visiting record attempts all around the world. As each record application comes in, it is assigned to one of the team, who will work on approving or rejecting the claim. These are the guys who also write the official rules – often in conjunction with a relevant governing body or acknowledged expert or consultant (*see next page*).

You might recognize some of these faces; they are often judges on GWR TV shows!

ADJUDICATOR ON SITE

Here's GWR Adjudicator Carlos Martínez (Spain) assessing a record claim for the **highest gas pipeline** in Peru. To find out how you can apply to have a judge on site, visit **www.guinnessworldrecords.com**.

The Adjudicators
1. Louise Toms (UK)
2. Lucia Sinigagliesi (Italy)
3. Ralph Hannah (UK)
4. Louise Ireland (UK)
5. Aleksandr Vypirailenko (Ukraine)
6. Andrea Bánfi (Hungary)
7. Talal Omar (Yemen)
8. Marco Frigatti (Italy)
9. Jack Brockbank (UK)
10. Mariamarta Ruano-Graham (Guatemala)
11. Kristian Teufel (Germany)
12. Gareth Deaves (UK)
13. Amanda Mochan (USA)
14. Tarika Vara (UK)

WE SEEK
GWR FOUNDING EDITOR NORRIS McWHIRTER ONCE DESCRIBED HIS JOB AS "FINDING THE -ESTS FROM THE -ISTS" – THAT IS, FINDING SUPERLATIVES FROM THE EXPERTS.

WE SPEAK
ENGLISH, SPANISH, JAPANESE, GERMAN, DUTCH, PORTUGUESE, FRENCH, RUSSIAN, UKRAINIAN, HUNGARIAN, ROMANIAN, ITALIAN, KOREAN, ARABIC, CHINESE, AND WELSH.

THE ADJUDICATORS

YOUNG AND OLD

Among those missing from the group photo below are Robert Young (left), pictured here with last year's **oldest woman** Gertrude Baines (USA, 1894–2009) in Los Angeles, California, USA, and our TV historian Dick Fiddy (inset) of the British Film Institute.

Without all of these people – and feedback from you, the public – we wouldn't be able to produce such a compelling and diverse snapshot of our record-breaking year. So thanks to everyone who contributes to making the book – it's because of *you* that it continues to be the planet's **biggest-selling copyright book**!

Supporting the Adjudications team – and playing a crucial role as part of the Publishing team that actually designs and edits the book – are the **Consultants**. This is the international panel of experts who use their expert knowledge to proactively research records on behalf of Guinness World Records.

The spectrum of topics covered by the Consultants is what gives Guinness World Records its unique appeal -- from the latest scientific breakthroughs, via all the most important sporting achievements to the very latest gossip and showbiz news from the entertainment industry. In between, we have medical expertise from a range of specialists (including a gerontologist who researches old age and longevity, a trichologist – that's a "hair doctor"! – and an endocrinologist who advises us on giants and dwarves), as well as engineers, mountain climbers, retired Air Force officers, sailors, musicians, a couple of very on-the-ball sports experts – one of whom specializes in US sports – and a TV historian from the British Film Institute.

Rounding off the list of experts are the countless (and often uncredited) academics, scientists, researchers, and inventors who help us ratify records across our wide range of topics.

The Consultants

1. Kenneth (and Tatiana, not in shot) Crutchlow: Ocean Rowing Society
2. Thomasina Gibson: showbiz, movies, entertainments
3. Christian Marais: world sports, gambling, games
4. Craig Glenday: Editor-in-Chief, Guinness World Records
5. David Hawksett: planets, science, technology, engineering
6. Stephen Wrigley: aircraft, military, crime, judiciary, society
7. Dr Eleanor Clarke: anatomy, medicine, human body
8. Dave McAleer: music
9. Mike Flynn: journeys, adventuring.

SHUKER
ALSO MISSING FROM THE GROUP SHOT IS OUR ZOOLOGY CONSULTANT (AND CRYPTOZOOLOGIST) DR KARL SHUKER, WHO WAS ON A FIELD TRIP TO JAPAN AT THE TIME.

THE CONSULTANTS

SHOOT
ALAS, THE WEEK IN WHICH WE PLANNED TO PHOTOGRAPH ALL OUR ADJUDICATORS AND CONSULTANTS WAS THE WEEK IN WHICH THE ICELANDIC VOLCANO EYJAFJALLAJÖKULL ERUPTED, SO SOME OF THEM COULDN'T MAKE IT.

INTRODUCTION
GWR TV

★ ★ ★ ★ ★ ★ ★ ★ ★ ★ ★ ★ ★ ★ ★

THE LAST 12 MONTHS HAVE SEEN US FILMING BREATHTAKING FEATS IN 17 COUNTRIES, PUTTING TOGETHER 120 HOURS OF DYNAMIC, PRIMETIME ENTERTAINMENT FOR SHOWS SEEN IN 85 COUNTRIES, AND FEATURING MORE THAN 250 RECORD ATTEMPTS.

★OLDEST BODYBUILDER

On *Lo Show dei Record* in Italy on March 18, 2010, Ernestine Shepherd (USA, b. June 16, 1936) set a record for the **oldest competitive female bodybuilder**. She was 73 years 9 months and 2 days old at that time, and still competes in international bodybuilding competitions.

JAPAN

In Japan we have a series called *Guinness World Records Special* featuring the feats of a fair few talented individuals such as competitive eater extraordinaire Takeru Kobayashi (Japan, right), who munched six hotdogs in 3 minutes in Kashiwanohakoen Stadium just outside Tokyo on August 25, 2009 (*see p.140 for details*).

★ NEW RECORD
★ UPDATED RECORD

"Traveling to different shows around the world I get to meet truly talented people that inspire me and make my job fun!"
GWR's Marco Frigatti

GREECE

The second series of *Guinness World Records* in Greece saw an audience share of over 25% of the country's viewing public! The show, broadcast by MEGA, the country's largest broadcaster, stars Kostas Fragolias, Lorentzo Cariere, and Giorgos Lianos, pictured here celebrating with new record holder Daniele Seccarecci (Italy), the **heaviest competitive bodybuilder (male)** at 297 lb 9.9 oz (135 kg).

AUSTRALIA

Produced by Eyeworks and airing on the Seven Network, Australia's *Guinness World Records* takes record breaking to the masses, with locations shoots where attempts are performed live before an astounded public. Studio feats included Mon Tanner's record for **fire eating – most torches extinguished in one minute**, with 88. But like so many before him he lost his record just a few months later...

CHINA

This was our fifth year working with CCTV, China's state broadcaster, and record breaking has never been so popular – *Zheng Da Zong Yi - Guinness World Records Special* has a regular audience of more than 50 million! The show mixes highly competitive record-breaking spectaculars with popular acts and demonstrations of skill, such as an exhilarating performance by the Shaolin warrior monks, pictured center.

ZOO
THE LATEST ITALIAN SERIES WAS VERY "ANIMAL-FRIENDLY." IT FEATURED GIANT CENTIPEDES, TARANTULAS, KING COBRAS, RATTLE SNAKES, DOGS, AND A WHITE OX!

WHO
GWR COMMISSION PHOTOGRAPHERS TO ATTEND FILMING AT OUR TV SHOWS TO ENSURE WE HAVE THE BEST AND MOST UP-TO-DATE PICTURES OF OUR RECORD HOLDERS.

POLAND

Broadcast by Polsat, Poland's second biggest television channel, *Guinness World Records* is a localized Polish edition of our popular Italian *Lo Show dei Record* featuring many of the same record-breaking guests as the Italian program. Now in its second series, our Polish show is presented by the former TV sports news anchor Maciej Dowbor. He is pictured here, in a return to his sporting roots, talking to Federica Pellegrini (Italy), women's 200 m freestyle (long course and short course) and 400 m (long course) freestyle world record holder.

NEW ZEALAND

Hosted by Marc Ellis, former All Black player and a Guinness World Record holder, TV2's *NZ Smashes Guinness World Records* saw a slight twist to our format – Eyeworks, the production company behind the show, handpicked record attempts that had featured in other TV shows, and lined up ambitious Kiwis to try to claim the records as their own! The success of this format in New Zealand – it frequently got an audience twice as large as that of *The Simpsons* (see p.177) when shown in New Zealand – led to a similar production in Australia, whereby these famously competitive nations could go head-to-head to see who could break the most Guinness World Records. The picture to the left shows 121 New Zealanders attempting the record for the **largest human mattress dominoes**.

ITALY

Euro Produzione, our long-standing production partners in Europe, hit gold with *Lo Show dei Record* in Italy, with 143 fresh record attempts and a new hostess in the shapely form of former model Paola Perego. Paola's personal touch was key to getting all the people who are "unici al mondo" (unique in the world) to reveal the stories behind their attempts and achievements. Among the many successful record breakers were White Rope Skippers (all UK, pictured left) setting the record for the **most consecutive Double Dutch style skips by a team**, with 362.

FRANCE

Le Monde des Records is now in its 11th year in France and is as popular as ever. We broadcast more programs by volume in this country than any other territory, and have also featured on more TV channels here than anywhere else. Pictured is Bruno Wattier's attempt at the **most stripper trousers worn and removed in one minute**. He set this record with five on September 29, 2009, but lost it on March 18, 2010 when it was beaten on the set of *Lo Show dei Record* in Rome, Italy!

★HEAVIEST SHOES WALKED IN

Physical fitness fan Zhang Zhenghui (China) appeared on the set of *Lo Show dei Record* in Rome, Italy, on March 18, 2010, where he managed to walk 32 ft 9 in (10 m) while wearing cast-iron shoes weighing a hefty 270 lb 11.6 oz (122.8 kg).

INTERVIEW MEET MR MOLLOY...

Rob Molloy (pictured right with champion gurner Tommy Mattinson) is Director of Television at Guinness World Records.

He took time out from his busy schedule to tell us what it's like on the set of a Guinness World Records show...
Well, each show is different. Many of them reflect the cultures of the country they are based in, and that's always interesting to see. Sometimes filming can be stressful, but it's always entertaining.

What are your favorite records that have featured on GWR TV programs?
My personal favorite is the man who ran through 15 sheets of tempered glass on our New Zealand show. Or the record for the longest duration for three contortionists in a box. That was pretty crazy; they were filmed in countries all over Europe doing that!

And what exciting new projects can we expect in the next year?
As well as our studio-based shows we are planning on taking audiences behind the scenes and on the road with our adjudicators, allowing them to see world records as they happen!

BEHIND THE SCENES AT GWR TV

There were 11 cameras on set at all times during the making of *Lo Show dei Record* in Rome, Italy, which began filming on February 25 and wrapped on April 29, 2010.
It had a production team of 118 behind it (who ate 330.6 lb/150 kg of food between them while working), and it took 40 days to construct the set, which measured 131 ft 2 in x 131 ft 2 in (40 m x 40 m).

EXTRA!
FOR MORE RECORD-BREAKING TV, TURN TO PP.168–169.

GUINNESS WORLD RECORDS LIVE!

GUINNESS WORLD RECORDS LIVE! IS ALL
ABOUT TAKING RECORD BREAKING ON THE
ROAD. WE'VE INVITED PEOPLE FROM ALL
AROUND THE GLOBE TO COME TO OUR
CHALLENGE FAIRS - THE ONLY PLACES
IN THE WORLD WHERE YOU CAN WALK IN
A HUMBLE MORTAL AND WALK OUT A
GENUINE GWR RECORD HOLDER!

★ **NEW RECORD**
★ **UPDATED RECORD**

CROWD PLEASERS
REDCOATS MICHEALA LORMIER AND DAVE CLARK HOSTED GUINNESS WORLD RECORDS LIVE! AT THE BUTLINS RESORT IN BOGNOR REGIS, UK.

DALLAS, USA

★**MOST POINTS SCORED AS KOBE BRYANT PLAYING THE 2K SPORTS NBA 2K10 VIDEO GAME**

Chico Kora (USA, above) scored 29 points playing as Kobe Bryant on *NBA 2K10* at the NBA Jam in Dallas, Texas, USA, on February 13, 2010.

X GAMES
LA, CA & ASPEN, CO, USA

GWR Live! got involved once again in the Summer and Winter X Games. Various BMX records were attempted (above and below), and Phil Smage (USA, below right) successfully set the record for the ★ **highest ollie on a snowskate**, at 28.5 in (72.4 cm).

TRIVIA

DID YOU KNOW?

GWR LIVE! HAS WITNESSED OVER 250 RECORDS BEING BROKEN IN EIGHT COUNTRIES. THE MOST CULTURALLY DIVERSE CHALLENGE FAIR WAS AT GLOBAL VILLAGE IN DUBAI, UAE, WHICH WAS ATTENDED BY 34 DIFFERENT NATIONALITIES.

BED HEADS
A TEAM OF SIX (ALL UK) MADE UP A BUNK BED IN 1 MIN 11 SEC AT A GWR LIVE! EVENT AT BUTLINS, MINEHEAD, UK, ON MARCH 7, 2010.

BOGNOR REGIS, UK
★FASTEST TIME TO DRESS A BARBIE DOLL
This challenge proved endlessly fascinating for younger guests (above) at Butlins. The record to dress a Barbie doll in three items of clothing, shoes and an accessory is jointly held by Andrea Benjamin (UK) and Debbie Watson (UK), with a time of 36.99 sec on 15 April 2010.

OSAKA, JAPAN
★MOST BALLS CAUGHT, NO HANDS
The Guinness World Records Live! Challenge in the Park in Tokyo Midtown saw massive crowds trying their hand at rolling, spinning, throwing, sorting, folding, recycling and leap-frogging as they attempted to win a place in history. Pictured is 61-year-old Tsuyoshi Kitazawa from Akasaka, Tokyo, who set the record for the ★**most tennis balls caught with no hands in one minute**, with 15.

TURKEY
CAN STACKING
The GWR Live! Challenge Fair for Multi Corporation in Turkey started at Europe's largest shopping mall, the Forum Istanbul, and then toured Forum malls in cities across Turkey. Pictured is Deniz Özeskici (Turkey), who built a 20-can pyramid in just 6.49 sec on April 4, 2010.

BIG IN JAPAN
THE GWR LIVE! PARK CHALLENGE LAUNCHED IN TOKYO MIDTOWN, AKASAKA, TOKYO, ON 29 APRIL 2010. ON THE VERY FIRST DAY, EIGHT NEW GUINNESS WORLD RECORDS WERE SET.

SCREAM

DUBAI
LOUDEST SHOUT...
At Global Village in Dubai, UAE, members of the public broke 61 records over 110 days throughout early 2010. One of the most popular challenges was the **loudest shout** (pictured left), but no one was able to equal Annalisa Wray (UK), who achieved a shout of 121.7 dBA way back on April 16, 1994. It's still the record to beat...

DUNKIRK, FRANCE
The **greatest evacuation in military history** was carried out by 1,200 Allied naval and civil craft from Dunkerque (Dunkirk), France, between May 26, and June 4, 1940. A total of 338,226 British and French troops were rescued.

51°02'N 2°22'E

INTRODUCTION
HOW TO BE A
RECORD BREAKER

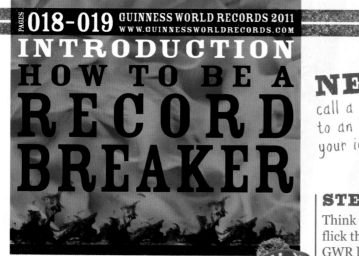

★ ★ ★ ★ ★ ★ ★ ★ ★ ★ ★ ★

SO, YOU FANCY YOURSELF AS A RECORD BREAKER? WANT TO GET YOUR NAME IN PRINT? HERE'S OUR IDIOT'S GUIDE TO TURNING YOUR IDEAS INTO ACTION. APPLYING IS FREE AND EASY, SO YOU'VE GOT NO EXCUSES...

EXTRA!
IF ANIMATION GETS YOU ANIMATED, TAKE A TRIP TO TOON WORLD ON P.176.

NEW CATEGORY:
This is what we call a record claim that we've never seen before (as opposed to an "existing category"). But you have to convince us that your idea is a good one before we open a new category!

STEP 1
Think of a record! Or better, flick through a copy of the GWR book and find a record you think you can break. Looking through the book will also give you an idea of the kinds of records we like.

STEP 2
Visit **www.guinnessworld records.com** and click on "APPLY NOW" – then tell us about your record idea. Give us as much notice as you can (about three months is ideal!).

STEP 6
Now you practice, practice, practice. This is Luke, by the way, and he wants to try the **longest time juggling three objects blindfolded**.

STEP 7
When you're ready, attempt your record as per the guidelines. Be sure to have at least two independent witnesses, and film the entire event. Invite the press, too!

STEP 8
Next, mail us your evidence, your video footage, your signed witness statements, and whatever else we've requested in the guidelines. Then there's more waiting to do...

SNAP!
IF YOU *REALLY* WANT TO SEE YOUR RECORD IN THE BOOK, BE SURE TO SUBMIT THE BEST POSSIBLE PHOTOS – WE LOVE RECORDS WITH EXCITING, DYNAMIC PHOTOGRAPHY!

36°42'N 3°13'E **ALGIERS, ALGERIA**
The world's **largest bowl of couscous** weighed 13,315 lb (6.04 tonnes) and was made by Semoulerie Industrielle de la Mitidja and displayed at the International Fair of Algiers, Algeria, on June 3, 2004.

STEP 3

The next bit's easy – you just have to wait while our Records Management Team (RMT) plow through their (enormous) inbox and get to your claim. This is why we need the time – also, we might need expert help assessing your idea.

STEP 4

If your record category already exists, we'll email you the guidelines that the last claimant followed. If it's a new category – and we like it – we'll create new guidelines and email them to you asap.

STEP 5

Congratulations, we like your idea and you've got the guidelines. Read and follow them carefully – if you ignore them, you're unlikely to succeed.

FAST TRACK
IF YOU'RE IN A RUSH, WHY NOT TRY OUR THREE-DAY FAST TRACK SERVICE? YOU PAY A FEE FOR A DEDICATED RECORDS MANAGER TO PROCESS YOUR CLAIM ASAP.

If you get a "no" from Marco's Records Management Team, don't despair – rethink your idea and then reapply. We reject about 85% of claims because they're too dangerous or too stupid... or just not impressive enough!

STEP 9

Back at GWR Towers, we'll watch your video, assess your witness statements, and consult with any necessary governing body or expert. Have you followed the guidelines? Have you beaten the record?

STEP 10

Congratulations – if you're a record breaker, we'll send you your official GWR certificate. You're now a member of an elite group, a special family of high achievers, a crack squad of record holders!

STEP 11

There's one last stage: if you're *really* lucky, your record will be selected for the annual GWR book. Not every record makes it – only the best of the best! Good luck, everyone!

GHENT, BELGIUM
Jos de Troyer (Belgium) created the **largest hanging basket** measuring 34 ft 5 in (10.5 m) in diameter and weighing 99,208 lb (45 tonnes) in Ghent, Belgium. It went on display in April 2000 above the Emile Braunplein Square.

51°03'N 3°44'E

INTRODUCTION
GWR DAY

★ NEW RECORD
★ UPDATED RECORD

★ ★ ★ ★ ★ ★ ★ ★ ★ ★ ★ ★ ★

GUINNESS WORLD RECORDS DAY IS OUR ANNUAL, GLOBAL CELEBRATION OF RECORD BREAKING, WHEN HUNDREDS OF THOUSANDS OF PEOPLE AROUND THE WORLD GET TOGETHER TO SET OR BREAK RECORDS. HERE IS JUST A SMALL SELECTION OF FEATS ATTEMPTED ON OR AROUND GWR DAY 2009!

GWR DAY 2009

RECORD	NAME	COUNTRY OF ORIGIN
Most push-ups with claps (73)	Stephen Buttler	UK
Tallest matchstick model (21 ft 5 in; 6 million matches)	Toufic Daher	Lebanon
Largest sports lesson (884)	multiple	Ireland
Fastest hot water bottle burst (18.81 seconds)	Shaun Jones	UK
Fastest time to peel and eat three lemons (28.5 seconds)	Jim Lyngvild	Denmark
Largest cup of hot chocolate (4 gallons; 4.5 liters)	Serendipity 3	USA
Largest paintbrush mosaic (32 ft 9 in x 8 ft 6 in; 10 x 2.6 m)	Saimir Strati	Albania
Highest wall climb on darts (16 ft 4 in; 5 m)	Maiko Kiesewetter	Germany

UK
★ FARTHEST DISTANCE TO PULL A BUS WITH THE HAIR

Manjit Singh (UK), the "Iron Man of Leicester", pulled an 8.8-ton (8-tonne) double-decker bus 69 ft 6 in (21.2 m) using just his hair as part of the GWR celebrations in London. He tried the same stunt in 2007 using his ears but failed to move the bus the required distance.

NORTHERN IRELAND
★ STORYBOOK CHARACTERS

The largest gathering of people dressed as storybook characters is 300, achieved by Carr's Glen Primary School in Belfast, Northern Ireland, UK.

ITALY
★ FASTEST TIME TO EAT PASTA

Ernesto Cesario (Italy) ate his way into the record books on GWR Day 2009 by eating a 5.2-oz (150-g) bowl of pasta in 1 min 30 sec in Milan.

USA
★ LARGEST CHEERLEADING DANCE

GWR Day is now so popular in America, it takes up the entire week! One of our favorite events from last year involved 297 participants from the University Cheerleaders Association (USA) performing the largest cheerleading dance at the University of Memphis in Tennessee. Each participant danced for a muscle-pounding 5 min 43 sec!

GERMANY
★ FARTHEST JOURNEY BY WATERSLIDE

To commemorate GWR Day in Germany, a team of 10 (all Germany) broke the 24-hour water-slide distance record, covering a fantastic 843.33 miles (1,357.22 km) at the Galaxy Erding indoor waterpark, the largest of its kind in Europe.

THE HAGUE, THE NETHERLANDS
52°04'N 4°18'E

The largest clog dance involved 475 participants at an event organized by Introdans Education and Dance and Child International at the Spuiplein in The Hague, the Netherlands, on July 8, 2006.

FINLAND
★ FASTEST 40 M BY HUMAN WHEELBARROW
The truly international team of Adrian Rodriguez (Mexico, standing) and Sergiy Vetrogonov (Ukraine) achieved the fastest 40 m (131 ft) by a human wheelbarrow, taking just 17 seconds in Helsinki, Finland. The dynamic duo averaged a speed of 0.951 ft/s (0.29 m/s).

NETHERLANDS
★ MOST BASKETBALL BOUNCES (1 MIN)
Congratulations to Kiran Harpal (Netherlands), who broke the one-minute basketball-bounce record at the Hiernasst Youth Center in Wijchen with 384 consecutive bounces in the allotted time!

TURKEY
★ MOST CONCRETE BLOCKS BROKEN (30 SEC)
Martial arts expert Ali Bahçetepe (Turkey) broke 655 blocks using just his hands in 30 seconds in Datça Cumhuriyet Meydani, Turkey, on November 11, 2009.

UK
★ MOST PEOPLE HUGGING (1 MIN)
To kick off GWR Day in the UK, a total of 112 morning commuters hugged one another at St Pancras station in London for one minute.

EXTRA! FOR MORE SHOWS OF STRENGTH, FLEX YOUR MUSCLES AND TURN TO PP. 90-91.

NORWAY
★ LARGEST GINGERBREAD MAN
Getting in on the action was IKEA Furuset in Oslo, Norway, where this ginormous gingerbread man weighing 1,435 lb 3 oz (651 kg) was baked and decorated.

ITALY
★ LONGEST PLATFORM-TO-PLATFORM BICYCLE JUMP
Bicycle daredevil Vittorio Brumotti (Italy) successfully cleared a jump of 13 ft 2 in (4.02 m) between the top of two trucks in Fiera Milano, Milan, Italy.

NEW ZEALAND
FARTHEST MALTESER BLOW
Over in NZ, we could rely on multiple record holder Alistair Galpin to lead the charge. First off was the **farthest distance to blow a Malteser** (a chocolate covered honeycomb malt ball) **using a straw** – 37 ft (11.29 m).
• Later the same day, Alistair achieved the ★ **farthest distance to spit a champagne cork** at 16 ft 3 in (5 m).
• He then rounded the day off with the ★ **farthest distance to blow a coin** – an epic 14 ft 4 in (37.6 cm).

SPACE

★ ★ ★ ★ ★ ★ ★ ★ ★ ★ ★

CONTENTS

LARGEST SPACE TELESCOPE

NASA's Hubble Space Telescope (HST, inset), named after the eminent American astronomer Edwin P Hubble, celebrated its 20th anniversary in April 2010. The telescope, which weighs 24,250 lb (11 tonnes) and is 43 ft (13.1 m) in overall length, with a 94.8-in (240-cm) reflector, was launched into space by the US space shuttle *Discovery* on April 24, 1990. It has been serviced five times while in orbit and is currently due to remain in use until at least 2014. During its operational lifespan, the HST has captured spectacular images of many deep-space objects, such as this image of R136, a young stellar grouping in the 30 Doradus Nebula.

52°01'N
4°22'E

DELFT, THE NETHERLANDS

The **largest flying paper aircraft**, with a wingspan of 45 ft 10 in (13.97 m), was constructed by a team of students from the Faculty of Aerospace Engineering at Delft University of Technology, the Netherlands, and flown on May 16, 1995.

SPACE
A SENSE OF SCALE

★ ★ ★ ★ ★ ★ ★ ★ ★ ★

TRIVIA

DID YOU KNOW?
THE EARTH HAS A DIAMETER OF 7,926 MILES (12,756 KM) AND A MASS OF 13,170,000,000,000,000,000,000,000 LB. IT'S 92.9 MILLION MILES (149 MILLION KM) FROM THE SUN, BUT HOW DOES IT COMPARE TO OTHER BODIES IN THE UNIVERSE?

★ NEW RECORD
★ UPDATED RECORD

LARGEST STRUCTURE IN THE UNIVERSE
A team of astronomers led by Richard Gott III and Mario Juric (both USA) of Princeton University, Princeton, New Jersey, USA, have discovered a huge wall of galaxies some 1.37 billion light-years long. They used data from the Sloan Digital Sky Survey, which is mapping the locations of one million galaxies in the universe. Their discovery was announced in October 2003.

LARGEST SPIRAL GALAXY
Discovered in 1986, from photographs taken by the Anglo-Australian astronomer David Malin, and later named after him, Malin 1 is a spiral galaxy some 1.1 billion light-years away. In terms of its diameter, it is the largest known spiral galaxy in the Universe, measuring around 650,000 light-years across – several times the size of our Milky Way, which has a diameter of around 100,000 light-years. Malin 1 contains some 50 billion suns'-worth of free-floating hydrogen.

LARGEST GLOBULAR CLUSTER
Omega Centauri, in the southern constellation of Centaurus, is the most massive of the roughly 140 globular clusters surrounding our galaxy. Consisting of several million stars with a combined mass equivalent to 5 million Suns, it is visible to the naked eye as a hazy star. However big this might seem, it would still take around a thousand Omega Centauris to equal just one spiral galaxy such as the galaxy in which we live, the Milky Way.

LARGEST STAR
Due to the physical difficulties in directly measuring the size of a distant star, not all astronomers agree on the largest star, but the most likely candidate is VY Canis Majoris, a red supergiant some 5,000 light-years away. Estimates of its size give it a diameter of between 1.55 and 1.86 billion miles (2.5–3 billion km). If placed at the center of the Solar System, its outer surface would reach beyond the orbit of Jupiter.

LARGEST GALAXY
The central galaxy of the Abell 2029 galaxy cluster, located 1,070 million light-years away from the Earth in the constellation Virgo has a major diameter of 5,600,000 light-years – 80 times the diameter of our own Milky Way galaxy – and a light output equivalent to 2,000,000,000,000 (two trillion) Suns. Scientists suspect Abell 2029 attained its massive size by pulling in nearby galaxies.

= 16,000 LIGHT

= 560,000 LIGHT-YEARS

= 100 MILLION LIGHT-YEARS

LARGEST STAR WITH A PLANET
In January 2003 astronomers announced their discovery of a planet orbiting the orange giant star HD 47536. This star is expanding at the end of its life and currently measures around 20.5 million miles (33 million km, or 23 times the size of the Sun) across. The planet is some 186 million miles (300 million km) from its star but will eventually be consumed in a few tens of

> *"Space is big. You just won't believe how vastly, hugely, mind-bogglingly big it is. I mean, you may think it's a long way down the road to the chemist's, but that's just peanuts to space."*
>
> **Douglas Adams,**
> *The Hitchhiker's Guide to the Galaxy*

= 12,000 MILES (20,000 KM)

= 0.5 BILLION MILES (0.8 BILLION KM)

EXTRA! FOR LARGE-SCALE MANMADE OBJECTS, TURN TO BIG STUFF ON P.204.

LARGEST PLANET IN THE SOLAR SYSTEM

Jupiter, with an equatorial diameter of 89,405 miles (143,884 km) and a polar diameter of 83,082 miles (133,708 km), is the largest of the eight major planets, with a mass 317 times that of the Earth. However, despite its large size, Jupiter has a very short period of rotation, resulting in a Jovian day of only 9 hr 55 min 29.69 sec –the ★**shortest planetary day in the Solar System**.

★LARGEST KNOWN PLAETARY SYSTEM

Of the 429 planets orbiting other stars discovered to date, none are yet known to exist within a planetary system as large as our own Solar System, which is thought to be 100,000 AU (9.3 billion miles; 15 billion km) across.

LARGEST NEBULA VISIBLE TO THE NAKED EYE

The Tarantula Nebula in the constellation of Doradus, in the southern sky, is large and bright enough to be visible to the naked eye, despite being at a distance of 170,000 light-years (10.7 billion AU). The huge cloud of glowing gas has a diameter of around 1,000 light-years (63 million AU) and is the only nebula outside our galaxy which is visible to the naked eye.

1,490 miles (2,400 km). Before the reclassification of Pluto as a dwarf planet, Eris was regarded by many as the tenth planet of the Solar System. Eris has a small moon, Dysnomia, around 217 miles (350 km) across.

LARGEST KUIPER BELT OBJECT

The Kuiper belt is the cloud of frozen gases and debris at the edges of our Solar System around 55 AU (5 billion miles; 8.1 billion km) from the Sun. The Kuiper Belt object 50000 Quaoar measures around 800 miles (1,300 km) across and was discovered by Chad Trujillo and Mike Brown (both USA) at Caltech, Pasadena, California, USA, on June 4, 2002. The object, originally dubbed 2002 LM60, is named after a creation god of the

Tongva tribe – the original inhabitants of the Los Angeles area. It orbits the Sun at a distance of around 4 billion miles (6 billion km) and has an orbital period of 288 years.

LARGEST ASTEROID IN THE ASTEROID BELT

Among all the objects in the asteroid belt between Mars and Jupiter, Ceres is the largest, with an average diameter of 584.7 miles (941 km). Discovered by Giuseppe Piazzi in Palermo, Sicily, on January 1, 1801, Ceres is large enough to have an almost spherical shape. It is classified as the **smallest dwarf planet** and is due to be visited by NASA's *Dawn* probe in 2015.

★LARGEST ASTEROID VISITED BY SPACECRAFT

First discovered in 1885, 253 Mathilde, like Ceres, is found in the Asteroid Belt. It measures 41 x 29 x 28 miles (66 x 48 x 46 km) and became the third and largest asteroid to be encountered by a spacecraft in June 1997, when NASA's *NEAR Shoemaker* spacecraft passed it.

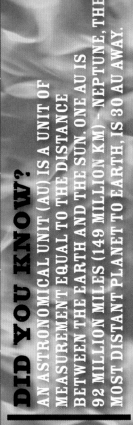

DID YOU KNOW? AN ASTRONOMICAL UNIT (AU) IS A UNIT OF MEASUREMENT EQUAL TO THE DISTANCE BETWEEN THE EARTH AND THE SUN. ONE AU IS 92 MILLION MILES (149 MILLION KM) – NEPTUNE, THE MOST DISTANT PLANET TO EARTH, IS 30 AU AWAY.

A light-year, the distance light travels in a year is equivalent to 5.8 trillion miles (9.4 trillion km).

TRIVIA

millions of years as the star continues to expand into a red giant.

★LARGEST EXTRASOLAR PLANET

Discovered in 2006, TrES-4 is an extrasolar planet some 1,400 light-years away, orbiting its parent star GSC 02620-006648 once every 3.5 days. It was discovered using the transit method, where the planet eclipses its star during its

short orbit as seen from Earth. With a diameter of around 150,00 miles (240,000 km), it is some 1.7 times the size of Jupiter.

LARGEST DWARF PLANET

The icy world Eris was discovered in January 2005. It has a highly elliptical orbit, with its distance from the Sun ranging from between 3.4 and 9.07 billion miles (5.6 and 14.6 billion km), and a diameter of around

SPACE
SATURN

★LARGEST PLANETARY RING

The Phoebe ring, discovered by NASA's Spitzer Infrared Telescope and announced on October 6, 2009, is a sparse disk of dust that extends to the orbit of the moon Phoebe, some 8,050,335 miles (12,955,759 km) from Saturn itself. It is believed to be formed by dust kicked off the surface of Phoebe by micrometeorite impacts.

LEAST ROUND PLANET

A combination of its low density (less than water) and rapid rotation (10.6 hours) gives Saturn the most oblate shape among the planets. Its equatorial diameter is 74,897.5 miles (120,536 km) while its polar diameter is just 67,560 miles (108,728 km).

★LONGEST-LASTING LIGHTNING STORM

A lightning storm in Saturn's upper atmosphere raged for more than eight months in 2009. Monitored by the *Cassini* spacecraft, the storm, with a diameter of several thousand miles, caused lightning flashes in Saturn's atmosphere around 10,000 times the intensity of their terrestrial counterparts.

★LARGEST ERUPTIVE ICE PLUMES

Active cryovolcanism on Enceladus, Saturn's sixth-largest moon, had been predicted by scientists ever since the encounters by the two *Voyager* spacecraft in the early 1980s had revealed the geologically young surface of this icy moon. In 2005, observations from the *Cassini* spacecraft showed immense plumes of water ice above the moon's south pole. They are formed by the eruption of pressurized water reservoirs beneath the ice, forced to the surface by volcanic activity. They are at least as tall as the moon's 313-mile (505-km) diameter.

★CLOSEST MOON TO SATURN

Discovered in July 2009 using observations from the *Cassini* spacecraft, S/2009 S 1 is a tiny moon just 985 ft (300 m) across that orbits Saturn at a distance of just 35,251 miles (56,732 km), less than the radius of the planet. It orbits within the outer B Ring and was discovered using the shadow it cast across the rings themselves.

★OUTERMOST DISCRETE RING

The most outwardly discrete ring, as opposed to a diffuse dust disk, is the contorted F Ring, with an orbital radius of 87,600 miles (141,000 km). It lies some 2,500 miles (4,000 km) beyond the edge of the main ring system and is probably the most dynamically active ring in the Solar System. Just a few hundred miles wide, the F Ring is thin and held in place by two shepherd moons, Pandora and Prometheus, whose gravitational interactions with the ring particles produce twisted knots within the ring that can change appearance in just a few hours.

★SMALLEST ROUND WORLD

Mimas, the 20th largest moon in the Solar System, is just 246.4 miles (396.6 km) across. It is the smallest known body in the Solar System whose shape has been rounded due to its own gravity. The largest crater on Mimas is Herschel, which is 80 miles (130 km) across. It has 3-mile-high (5-km) walls, and a 4-mile-high (6-km) central peak.

GREATEST RING SYSTEM

The intricate system of rings around Saturn have a combined mass of around 9×10^{19} lb (4×10^{19} kg) – equivalent to the mass of an icy moon around 250 miles (400 km) across, or 1,800 times less massive than our Moon. Gaps in the ring (such as the Colombo Gap) are caused by the gravitational influence of Saturn's moons. Rings G and E are more distant and not shown below.

EXTRA! TURN THE PAGE FOR EVERYTHING YOU NEED TO KNOW ABOUT THE SPACE SHUTTLE.

Colombo Gap

Maxwell Gap

D RING

C RING

LEAST DENSE PLANET

Saturn is composed mostly of hydrogen and helium, the two lightest elements in the universe. It has an average density of only 0.71 times that of water. As Saturn is actually less dense than water, it would float – if there were an area of water in the Solar System large enough to accommodate it!

HOT!
THE PASTEL AND YELLOW HUES ON THE PLANET REVEAL MANY CONTRASTING BRIGHT AND DARKER BANDS IN BOTH HEMISPHERES OF SATURN'S WEATHER SYSTEM.

SHOT!
THIS TRUE COLOR PHOTOGRAPH WAS ASSEMBLED FROM *VOYAGER 2* SATURN IMAGES OBTAINED ON AUGUST 4, 1998 FROM A DISTANCE OF 13 MILLION MILES (21 MILLION KM).

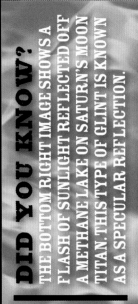

DID YOU KNOW?
THE BOTTOM RIGHT IMAGE SHOWS A FLASH OF SUNLIGHT REFLECTED OFF A METHANE LAKE ON SATURN'S MOON TITAN. THIS TYPE OF GLINT IS KNOWN AS A SPECULAR REFLECTION.

Cassini took the image of Kraken Mare on July 8, 2009 from 120,000 miles (200,000 km).

TRIVIA

TALLEST RIDGE IN THE SOLAR SYSTEM

Observations of Saturn's moon Iapetus by the NASA/ESA spacecraft *Cassini-Huygens* on December 31, 2004 revealed a ridge at least 800 miles (1,300 km) long, reaching an altitude of around 12 miles (20 km) above the surface. Iapetus is just 890 miles (1,400 km) across.

LARGEST CHAOTICALLY ROTATING OBJECT

Saturn's moon Hyperion measures 254 x 161 x 136 miles (410 x 260 x 220 km) and is the largest highly irregularly shaped body in the Solar System. It is one of only two bodies in the Solar System discovered to have completely chaotic rotation, tumbling in its orbit around Saturn. The other is asteroid 4179 Toutatis, measuring 2.7 x 1.5 x 1.1 miles (4.5 x 2.4 x 1.9 km).

CLOSEST MOONS TO EACH OTHER

Janus and Epimetheus share the same average orbit some 56,500 miles (91,000 km) above Saturn. As their orbital paths are only 31 miles (50 km) apart, one of the moons is always catching the other up. Every four years they come within 6,200 miles (10,000 km) of each other and swap orbits, before drifting apart again.

SATELLITE WITH THE THICKEST ATMOSPHERE

Saturn's large moon Titan has the thickest atmosphere of any moon in the Solar System, exerting a surface pressure of 1.44 bar. It consists mainly of nitrogen gas and is the most similar atmosphere to our own in the Solar System.

★ **NEW RECORD**
★ **UPDATED RECORD**

★ LARGEST METHANE SEA

Kraken Mare, on Titan, is a body of liquid methane 727 miles (1,170 km) across and with an area similar to that of the Caspian Sea on Earth (1,400,000 miles²; 3,626,000 km²). In July 2009, *Cassini* imaged the glint of reflected sunlight off Kraken Mare.

Huygens Gap

Encke Gap

Keeler Gap

B RING

A RING

F RING

LYON, FRANCE

An international team of eight surgeons carried out the **earliest hand transplant operation** when they stitched the hand of a dead man to the wrist of 48-year-old Clint Hallam (New Zealand) in 1998, after he had suffered a chainsaw accident nine years previously.

FEATURE
SPACE SHUTTLES

★ ★ ★ ★ ★ ★ ★ ★ ★ ★ ★ ★ ★ ★

THE SPACE SHUTTLE – or, more accurately, the Shuttle Transportation System (STS) – made its first test flights in 1981, and orbital missions began the following year. It is the world's first – and to date only – spacecraft to make multiple orbital flights and landings.

Now, nearly 30 years later, NASA has announced the retirement of the space shuttle program. With its end in sight, we take a look at the shuttle's record-breaking history and its major achievements.

★ MOST REUSED SPACECRAFT

NASA's space shuttle *Discovery* was last launched on April 5, 2010, beginning its 38th spaceflight, STS-131. *Discovery*, the third orbiter in the shuttle fleet, first flew in August 1984.

★ FIRST SPACECRAFT WITH A GLASS COCKPIT

Glass cockpits are characterized by electronic instrument displays, replacing older consoles that relied on mechanical gauges to display flight information. All three of NASA's operational shuttles have glass cockpits, the first to receive one being *Atlantis*, which flew with the new interface in 2000 during STS-101.

LARGEST SOLID ROCKET BOOSTER

The two boosters that assist the launch of the US space shuttle use solid rather than liquid fuel. They are the largest solid rocket boosters (SRBs) ever flown. Each booster is 149 ft (45.4 m) long and 12 ft (3.6 m) wide. Each contains more than 1,000,000 lb (450,000 kg) of propellant and provides a thrust of 3.3 million lb (1.49 million kg), or around 83% of liftoff power. Unlike the shuttle's external fuel tank, the SRBs are reusable.

LONGEST SHUTTLE FLIGHT

The lengthiest shuttle flight was by *Columbia* and its crew of five astronauts during the STS-80 mission. Launched on November 19, 1996, it had 17 days 15 hr 53 min 26 sec of mission elapsed time.

LARGEST SHUTTLE CREW

The shuttle mission with the largest crew to date was STS-61-A, which launched on October 30, 1985, carrying eight astronauts on board *Challenger*. This flight carried the West German *Spacelab* D-1 laboratory. The flight lasted 7 days 44 min 51 sec.

★ NEW RECORD
UPDATED RECORD

USA

FIRST! SPACE SHUTTLE *COLUMBIA* WAS THE FIRST SPACECRAFT TO LAND ON WHEELS. BEFORE THIS, SPACECRAFT USED PARACHUTES TO REACH EARTH.

LAST! AT THE TIME OF GOING TO PRESS, THE LAST SHUTTLE MISSION PLANNED BY NASA WAS STS-133, A *DISCOVERY* FLIGHT DUE TO LAUNCH ON SEPTEMBER 16, 2010.

United States

GUINNESS WORLD RECORDS 2011

LARGEST OBJECTS TRANSPORTED BY AIR

Although not the heaviest, the largest single objects to be transported by air are the 122-ft 2-in (37.23-m) space shuttles, which are "piggybacked" on top of modified Boeing 747 jets from alternative airstrips back to Cape Canaveral in Florida, USA. *Discovery*, *Atlantis* and *Endeavour* each weigh around 110 tons (100 tonnes) when transported.

SPACE TOILET:

The toilet on the space shuttle uses foot straps and thigh bars to hold the user in place. Solids are stored on board until landing and waste liquids are vented into space.

LARGEST DOOR

Each of the four doors in the NASA Vehicle Assembly Building near Cape Canaveral, Florida, USA, is 460 ft (140 m) high, as tall as a 35-story building. Their massive size was originally to allow fully assembled Saturn V rockets to pass through them.

★ MOST PEOPLE ON A SPACEWALK

The first flight of *Endeavour* on May 7, 1992 was to repair the failing *Intelsat VI* satellite. Retrieving the satellite proved problematic until Pierre Thuot, Richard Hieb, and Thomas Akers (all USA) performed a spacewalk and were able to capture *Intelsat VI* by hand. In the meantime, mission commander Daniel Brandenstein (USA) maneuvered *Endeavour* to within a few feet of the stricken satellite. This is the only occasion in history that three people have walked in space at the same time.

★ FIRST MANNED MAIDEN SPACEFLIGHT

The first ever shuttle launch was a test flight by astronauts John Young and Robert Crippen (both USA) on April 12, 1981. This was the first time a new spacecraft system had ever flown in space without a prior unmanned spaceflight.

★ HEAVIEST GLIDER

The heaviest shuttle landing was *Columbia* during the STS-83 mission, which touched down on April 8, 1997 with a mass of 213,060 lb (96,642 kg). To return to Earth, the shuttle fires its orbital maneuvering engines to slow down and decrease its altitude, and uses friction to reduce speed in the upper atmosphere. From then on, the landing sequence is unpowered, with the shuttle acting as a glider, performing a series of high-altitude turns to dissipate speed, and eventually approaching the runway and touching down with the rear wheels first.

★ HEAVIEST COMPONENT

At liftoff, the space shuttle consists of the orbiter itself, the external fuel tank that feeds its main engines, and two solid rocket boosters attached to the tank that provide additional thrust. The heaviest component at liftoff is the tank, weighing 1,680,000 lb (760,000 kg).

HEAVIEST PAYLOAD LAUNCHED

The *Chandra X-ray Observatory* was launched by *Columbia* on 23 July 1999. With a mass of 50,161 lb (22,753 kg), this was the heaviest satellite that has ever been launched by the space shuttle.

★ FIRST SHUTTLE DOCKING

On June 29, 1995, *Atlantis* docked with the Russian *Mir* space station, beginning the Shuttle-*Mir* Program. This was the 100th spaceflight by the USA. *Atlantis* brought cosmonauts Anatoly Solovyev and Nikolai Budarin to *Mir*, and returned Vladimir Dezhurov, Gennady Strekalov (both Russia), and Norm Thagard (USA) to Earth. This was the first time a shuttle crew had changed in orbit.

★ FIRST INFLIGHT REPAIR

On July 26, 2005, the shuttle *Discovery* launched on the STS-114 mission. During a spacewalk, Stephen Robinson (USA) was able to pull out manually two protruding "gap fillers" between the thermal tiles on *Discovery*'s underbelly. This photograph was taken by Robinson using a digital camera. It shows the thermal tiles on the underside of the shuttle, reflected in the visor of his helmet.

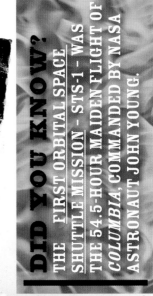

DID YOU KNOW? THE FIRST ORBITAL SPACE SHUTTLE MISSION – STS-1 – WAS THE 54.5-HOUR MAIDEN FLIGHT OF *COLUMBIA*, COMMANDED BY NASA ASTRONAUT JOHN YOUNG.

52°05'N 5°08'E

SPACE
THE SUN

★ ★ ★ ★ ★ ★ ★ ★ ★ ★ ★ ★ ★

★ FIRST FLYBY OF THE SUN'S POLES

The joint NASA/ESA *Ulysses* spacecraft was launched from the space shuttle *Discovery* in 1990. It headed out to Jupiter, where it used a gravitational slingshot to send it into a polar orbit around the Sun, from where it has directly observed both solar poles. The spacecraft ceased operations on June 30, 2009.

LARGEST SUNSPOT GROUP

On April 8, 1947, the largest sunspot group ever identified was found in the Sun's southern hemisphere. At its greatest length, it measured 187,000 miles (300,000 km), with a maximum width of 90,000 miles (145,000 km). It was roughly 36 times greater than the surface area of the Earth and was even visible to the naked eye, close to sunset.

LARGEST SOLAR FLARE

On November 4, 2003, a solar flare – seen at the lower right-hand side of this photograph – erupted from the surface of the Sun. It was rated as an X28 event by the Space Environment Center of the National Oceanic and Atmospheric Administration (NOAA), in Boulder, Colorado, USA.

SOL: The scientific term for the Sun. It is found in Latin, among other languages, as is the word for the Moon: "Luna".

★ LONGEST LASTING SUNSPOT GROUP

Between June and December 1943, a group of sunspots was observed to last for 200 days. The smallest sunspots, known as pores, and less than 1,553 miles (2,500 km) across, can last less than one hour.

★ LONGEST AND SHORTEST SOLAR CYCLES

The solar cycle is a periodic change in the number of sunspots on the surface of the Sun and relates directly to solar magnetic activity. It was first discovered in 1843 and, by examining older observations of sunspots, astronomers now have data on sunspot activity going back to the early 17th century. The cycle lasts an average of 11 years, with the longest so far ending in 1798 having lasted 13.7 years, and the shortest ending in 1775, having lasted just nine years.

★ BIGGEST OBJECT IN THE SOLAR SYSTEM

The Sun has a mass 332,900 times greater than that of Earth, and a diameter of 865,000 miles (1,392,000 km). It accounts for 99.86% of the mass of the whole Solar System.

CLOSEST APPROACH TO THE SUN BY A SPACECRAFT

The unmanned spacecraft *Helios 2* approached within 27 million miles (43.5 million km) of the Sun, carrying both US and West German instrumentation, on April 16, 1976.

Due for launch in 2015, NASA's *Solar Probe+* will attempt to study the Sun from as close as 3.9 million miles (6.2 million km), from within the Sun's outer atmosphere or corona. Traveling at a speed of 125 miles/sec (200 km/sec), the spacecraft will have to survive temperatures of up to 2,600°F (1,420°C).

HIGHEST-RESOLUTION SOLAR TELESCOPE

The Swedish 3-ft 2-in (1-m) Solar Telescope on La Palma in the Canary Islands uses a mirror in the path of the sunlight that minutely changes shape a thousand times per second to counter the effects of atmospheric turbulence. It can see details on the surface of the Sun (inset) as small as 43 miles (70 km) across.

EXTRA! TAKE A TRIP TO SATURN BY TURNING BACK TO PP.26-27.

CONVECTIVE ZONE

Energy from the core moves through this zone by convection, similar to the turbulent movement in boiling water.

HOT! THE SUN SHINES AT 383,000,000,000,000,000,000,000 WATTS.

HOTTEST PLACE IN THE SOLAR SYSTEM

The very center of the Sun is the hottest place in the Solar System. The latest estimates of the temperature put it at 28,080,000°F (15,600,000°C). The pressure in the core is also immense, around 250 billion times the pressure at sea level on Earth. These conditions allow nuclear fusion to take place, which is what makes the Sun shine.

★ **NEW RECORD**
★ **UPDATED RECORD**

RADIATIVE ZONE

Radiation produced in the core can "bounce around" among the matter in the radiative zone for millions of years.

GALACTIC
THE SUN ORBITS THE CENTER OF OUR MILKY WAY GALAXY AT AROUND 136 MILES/SEC (220 KM/SEC). IT TAKES 225-250 MILLION YEARS TO COMPLETE ONE ORBIT.

CORE

The Sun's core is approximately 28,080,000°F (15,600,000°C). Around 661 million tons of hydrogen are fused into around 657 million tons of helium every second by nuclear fusion.

PROMINENCE

Vast eruptions of plasma from the photosphere can extend into space for hundreds of thousands of miles.

PHOTOSPHERE

The visible surface of the Sun is where we see phenomena such as sunspots. Its average temperature is around 9,932°F (5,500°C). Sunspots are cooler, at around 5,432°F (3,000°C).

★ **NEAREST STAR**

The pioneering work of Father Angelo Secchi (Italy, 1818–78) in spectroscopy led to his classification scheme for stars, and to his conclusion that our own Sun was a star and not a phenomenon unique to the Solar System. At just 93,000,000 miles (149,000,000 km) from Earth, the Sun is astronomically close. The next nearest star, Proxima Centauri, is 4.2 light years away, or 24,000,000,000,000 miles (40,000,000,000,000 km).

★ LARGEST TORNADOES IN THE SOLAR SYSTEM

In April 1998, scientists announced the discovery of rotating tornado-like storms in the atmosphere of the Sun, using observations made by the *SOHO* satellite. Occurring mainly near to the poles of the Sun, these phenomena are around the size of Earth and the ionized gas within them moves at around 300,000 mph (500,000 km/h).

DID YOU KNOW?

THE MEAN DISTANCE BETWEEN THE SUN AND THE EARTH IS AROUND 93 MILLION MILES (149 MILLION KM). AT THIS DISTANCE, IT TAKES LIGHT 8 MIN 19 SEC TO REACH THE EARTH.

The Sun formed 4.57 billion years ago. In another 5 billion years it will start to run out of fuel and swell into a red giant.

TRIVIA

★ STRONGEST GEOMAGNETIC STORM

On September 1, 1859, at 11:18 a.m., British astronomer Richard Carrington observed two blinding explosions occurring on the surface of the Sun. The following dawn, all over the world the skies were ablaze with auroras caused by the charged particles from the eruptions interacting with Earth's magnetosphere, having taken just 18 hours to cross the space between the Sun and the Earth (the journey normally takes three or four days).

The study of ice cores suggest that events of this magnitude occur roughly every 500 years. The magnetic disruptions caused by the "Carrington Event" affected telegraph systems all over Europe and North America.

MOST DESTRUCTIVE GEOMAGNETIC STORM

The "Great Geomagnetic Storm" of March 13, 1989 was the most destructive geomagnetic storm ever recorded. The record-breaking event was classified G5 (the most severe rating) on the space weather scale. The result of an abnormally strong solar wind, it caused large-scale disruption to the power grid in Canada and the USA, and even changed the orbit of a satellite. The power outages – caused by failures at the Hydro-Québec systems in Canada – saw 6 million people losing electricity for nine hours.

EARTH

CONTENTS

★ NEW RECORD
★ UPDATED RECORD

LIGHT
PICTURED (AND INSET) IS ANTELOPE CANYON, NEAR PAGE IN ARIZONA, USA – THE MOST VISITED SLOT CANYON IN THE SOUTHWEST OF AMERICA.

DARK
THE MAIN PICTURE SHOWS A VIEW FROM THE BOTTOM OF THE UPPER ANTELOPE CANYON LOOKING UP THROUGH A CHANNEL TO THE OUTSIDE WORLD.

★LARGEST CONCENTRATION OF SLOT CANYONS

Slot canyons are deep, narrow, winding passages that have been carved into sedimentary rock by millions of years of erosion from sandstorms, rain, and fast-flowing waters. They are characterized by narrow openings and deep sides, often with cavernous interiors and beautifully colored striations.

According to SummitPost, the climbing and outdoor activity group, the Colorado Plateau in southwestern North America has a greater number of slots than anywhere on Earth, perhaps as many as 10,000.

EARTH
PEAKS & TROUGHS

★ ★ ★ ★ ★ ★ ★ ★ ★ ★ ★ ★ ★ ☆

HIGHS

TALLEST MOUNTAIN

Mauna Kea on the island of Hawaii, USA, is the world's tallest mountain. Measured from its submarine base in the Hawaiian Trough to its peak, the mountain has a height of 33,480 ft (10,205 m), of which 13,796 ft (4,205 m) is above sea level.

TALLEST UNCLIMBED MOUNTAIN

At 24,835 ft (7,570 m), Gangkar Punsum in Bhutan is ranked as the world's 40th highest peak, and the highest mountain yet to be climbed. Unsuccessful attempts were made to summit the peak in the 1980s, then in 1994, a partial ban of mountaineering in the country was declared. Since 2003, all climbing in Bhutan has been outlawed – for religious reasons – so it could remain unclimbed for many years to come.

TALLEST MOUNTAIN FACE

The Rupal face of Nanga Parbat, in the western Himalayas, Pakistan, is a single rise of some 15,000 ft (4,600 m) from the valley floor to the summit. The mountain itself, with a summit of 26,656 ft (8,125 m), is the world's ninth highest mountain.

★HIGHEST POLAR ICE CAP

Dome Argus is a vast ice plateau near the center of eastern Antarctica. Its highest point is 13,428 ft (4,093 m) above sea level. It is the highest ice feature on Antarctica and it overlies the 745-mile-long (1,200-km) Gamburtsev Mountain Range.

★HIGHEST HISTORICALLY ACTIVE VOLCANO

Llullaillaco, on the Argentina–Chile border, is a stratovolcano on a plateau within the Atacama Desert. Its last eruption was in 1877 and, at 22,109 ft (6,739 m) high, it is the highest recorded active volcano.

FASTEST-RISING MOUNTAIN

Nanga Parbet in Pakistan is growing taller at a rate of 0.27 in (7 mm) per year. Part of the Himalayan Plateau, it formed when India began colliding with the Eurasian continental plate between 30 and 50 million years ago.

LARGEST SUBGLACIAL MOUNTAIN RANGE

The Gamburtsev Mountains in eastern Antarctica extend for approximately 745 miles (1,200 km) across the continent. They reach up to 8,850 ft (2,700 m) high and are permanently buried under more than 1,968 ft (600 m) of ice. Discovered by a Soviet team in 1958, the mountains are believed to be around 500 million years old.

LONGEST SUBMARINE MOUNTAIN RANGE

The Mid-Ocean Ridge extends some 40,000 miles (65,000 km) from the Arctic Ocean to the Atlantic Ocean, around Africa, Asia, and Australia, and under the Pacific Ocean to the west coast of North America. It has a maximum height of 13,800 ft (4,200 m) above the base ocean depth.

LONGEST UNDERWATER CAVE SYSTEM

Sistema Ox Bel Ha (meaning "Three Paths of Water" in the Mayan language), in the state of Quintana Roo, Mexico, is a complex series of underwater passages accessible by exposed lakes called cenotes. As of May 2009, some 111.870 miles (180.038 km) of underwater passages had been explored and mapped by cave divers.

EXTRA!
EXPLORE FASCINATING FISH & SEALIFE BY TURNING TO PP.56-57.

★DEEPEST MINE

TauTona, which means "great lion" in the Setswana language, is a gold mine situated near Carletonville, South Africa, owned by AngloGold Ashanti. Originally built by the Anglo American Corporation, the 1.24-mile (2-km) original main shaft was sunk in 1957. The mine began operation in 1962 and, by 2008, had reached a depth of 2.4 miles (3.9 km). At this depth, the temperature of the rock faces can reach 140°F (60°C). The mine now has around 497 miles (800 km) of tunnels and employs 5,600 miners.

★HIGHEST ACTIVE CARBONATITE VOLCANO

Oldoinyo Llengai, Tanzania, is a rare type of volcano that erupts natrocarbonatite lava. At 9,718 ft (2,962 m) high, it is the only active volcano of this type on Earth. It erupts a bizarre runny lava that appears like molten chocolate at 930–1,110°F (500–600°C) and turns white upon cooling.

INSTANT EXPERT

✪ THE TIBETAN PLATEAU IS THE LARGEST AND HIGHEST ON EARTH, WITH AN AREA OF 715,000 MILES² (1,850,000 KM²) AND AN AVERAGE ALTITUDE OF 16,000 FT (4,900 M).

✪ IT CONTAINS THE HIMALAYA MOUNTAIN RANGE ON ITS SOUTHERN EDGE, WHICH CONTAINS EVEREST, THE WORLD'S HIGHEST MOUNTAIN, AT 29,029 FT (8,848 M).

✪ THE GREATER HIMALAYA CONTAINS 100 MOUNTAINS TALLER THAN 23,622 FT (7,200 M).

✪ THE EARTH'S CRUST IS THE THICKEST IN THE WORLD AT THE HIMALAYAS, WITH A THICKNESS OF AROUND 46 MILES (75 KM).

LOWS

DEEPEST CAVE

In September 2007, cavers from the Ukrainian Speleological Association reached a record depth of 7,188 ft 3 in (2,191 m) in the Krubera Cave (also known as the Voronya Cave) in the Arabika Massif, Georgia. More than 8,202 ft (2.5 km) of new cave passages were explored during this 29-day underground expedition.

DEEPEST PENETRATION INTO THE EARTH'S CRUST

A geological exploratory borehole near Zapolyarny on the Kola peninsula of Arctic Russia, which began on May 24, 1970, had reached a depth of 40,236 ft (12,261 m) by 1983, when funding stopped. The temperature of the rocks at the bottom of the hole is about 410°F (210°C).

LARGEST SEA CAVE

The Sea Lion Caves, close to Florence on the coast of Oregon, USA, have a chamber 310 ft (95 m) long, 165 ft (50 m) wide, and around 50 ft (15 m) high in a wave-cut passage measuring 1,315 ft (400 m) long.

DEEPEST VALLEY

The Yarlung Zangbo valley in Tibet has an average depth of 16,400 ft (5,000 m), but in 1994 explorers discovered that its deepest point was 17,657 ft (5,382 m). This deepest point is more than three times deeper than the Grand Canyon, which is the **largest land gorge** with a depth of 1 mile (1.6 km) and a width ranging of 0.25–8 miles (0.5–29 km).

The peaks on either side of the Yarlung Zangbo valley are Namche Barwa (25,436 ft; 7,753 m) and Jala Peri (23,891 ft; 7,282 m). They are just 13 miles (21 km) apart, with the Yarlung Zangbo River flowing between them at an elevation of 8,000 ft (2,440 m).

LARGEST CAVE OPENING

The entrance to Cathedral Caverns in Grant, Alabama, USA, is the world's largest cave opening. At 126 ft (38.4 m) wide and 25 ft (7.6 m) high, Cathedral Caverns was originally known as the Bat Cave until it was developed into a tourist attraction in 1955.

DEEPEST LAVA CAVE

Kazumura Cave in Hawaii, USA, is both the deepest and also the longest lava cave – an open tube down the inside of a lava flow. It is 36.9 miles (59.3 km) long and descends 3,605 ft (1,099 m) down the eastern flank of Kilauea volcano.

★GREATEST VERTICAL DROP

Mount Thor on Baffin Island, Nunavut, Canada, is a granite peak whose west face consists of a vertical drop of 4,101 ft (1,250 m). It is technically an overhang, with the average angle of repose of the cliff being at 105° – 15° beyond the vertical. The mountain was first climbed in 1953 by a team from the Arctic Institute of North America (AINA).

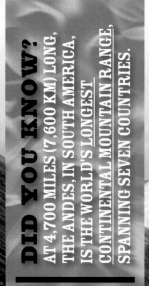

DID YOU KNOW?

AT 4,700 MILES (7,600 KM) LONG, THE ANDES, IN SOUTH AMERICA, IS THE WORLD'S LONGEST CONTINENTAL MOUNTAIN RANGE, SPANNING SEVEN COUNTRIES.

Some fifty Andes peaks exceed 20,000 ft (6,000 m) – 18.5 times higher than the Eiffel Tower.

TRIVIA

UP! MOUNT THOR HAS AN AVERAGE ANGLE OF 105°, WHICH MAKES IT VERY POPULAR WITH CLIMBERS. IT WAS FIRST SCALED IN 1953 (SEE RIGHT).

DOWN! MOUNT THOR IS MADE OF GRANITE AND IS PART OF THE BAFFIN MOUNTAINS. THESE, IN TURN, FORM PART OF THE ARCTIC CORDILLERA MOUNTAIN RANGE.

★ NEW RECORD
UPDATED RECORD

GENEVA, SWITZERLAND

The **most expensive cell phone** was designed by GoldVish of Geneva, Switzerland, and was sold for €1,000,000 ($1,287,200) at the Millionaire Fair in Cannes, France, on September 2, 2006.

46°12'N
6°09'E

EARTH
RIVERS & LAKES

★ ★ ★ ★ ★ ★ ★ ★ ★ ★ ★ ★ ★ ★

HIGHEST LEVEL OF ALKALINITY IN A LAKE SYSTEM

The Magadi–Natron basin in the Great Rift Valley of Kenya–Tanzania contains saline (salt) bodies of water with temperatures as high as 120°F (50°C) and alkalinity that reaches levels as high as pH 10–12 – strong enough to burn the skin. The corrosiveness of these lakes – notably Natron, Magadi, and Nakuru – is caused by high concentrations of minerals from hot springs, along with a high evaporation rate. Lake Natron's characteristic deep-red color is the result of pigments produced by algae that live in the hypersaline environment.

★ LARGEST RAPIDS BY FLOW RATE

Inga Falls, on the Congo river in the Democratic Republic of Congo, drops in height by 315 ft (96 m) over a length of around 9 miles (15 km). The average flow rate has been measured at around 1,500,000 ft³/sec (42,400 m³/sec), enough to fill London's Albert Hall in around two seconds. Inga Falls has a maximum flow rate of around 2,500,000 ft³/sec (70,800 m³/sec).

★ LARGEST INLAND DELTA

The Okavango Delta in Botswana is formed by the Okavango river as it enters an endorheic basin in the Kalahari Desert. (The term "endorheic" means it has no outlets other than evaporation for its water.) Millions of years ago it emptied into an inland sea until tectonic activity interrupted the river and formed the delta. The size of the delta varies seasonally from around 6,100 miles² (16,000 km²) to around 3,400 miles² (9,000 km²).

★ LARGEST CRATER LAKE

Lake Toba, on the Indonesian island of Sumatra, is the site of a supervolcanic eruption around 75,000 years ago that was probably the largest anywhere on Earth during the last 25 million years. The crater formed by the eruption is now filled with water that makes Lake Toba, which is around 60 miles (100 km) by 18 miles (30 km) in extent, and 1,656 ft (505 m) deep at its deepest point.

★ LARGEST TIDAL BORE

Tidal bores are formed when the front of the incoming tide forms a wave or series of waves that travels up a river against its direction of flow. This phenomenon occurs in several dozen locations around the world, but by far the largest and most spectacular happens in the Qiantang river, China, where it can form a massive wave of water up to 30 ft (9 m) high, traveling upstream at up to 25 mph (40 km/h). The bore is so dangerous that it is thought only a handful of people have been able to surf it.

★ LARGEST DESERT LAKE

Lake Turkana in the Great Rift Valley, Kenya, has a surface area of 2,472 miles² (6,405 km²) and an average depth of 99 ft (30.2 m). It is the fourth largest salt lake in the world and is fed by the Omo, Turkwel, and Kerio rivers. There is no outflow from Lake Turkana and the only method of water loss is by evaporation.

LARGEST TROPICAL LAKE

With a surface area of around 26,563 miles² (68,800 km²), Lake Victoria is the biggest lake in the world that lies within the tropics. Containing some 659 miles³ (2,750 km³) of water, it is ranked as the seventh largest freshwater lake in the world. It is the main source of the Nile river, the world's **longest river**.

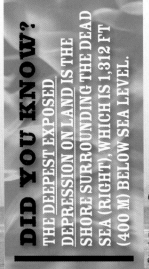

The deepest point on the bed of the Dead Sea is located 2,624 ft (800 m) below sea level.

★ DEEPEST HYPERSALINE LAKE

The Dead Sea on the Israel–Jordan border is the deepest hypersaline (very salty) lake in the world, with a maximum depth of 1,240 ft (378 m). The Dead Sea has an average salinity of more than 8.5 times that of seawater. Dead Sea mud is believed by many people to have healing properties when rubbed on to the skin (right).

SALTIEST LAKE

Don Juan Pond in Wright Valley, Antarctica, has such a high salt content that it remains a liquid even at temperatures as low as -63.4°F (-53°C). At its saltiest, the lake's percentage of salt by weight is 40.2%, compared with 23.1% in the Dead Sea and an average of 3.38% in the world's oceans as a whole.

GREATEST RIVER FLOW

The Amazon river in South America has the greatest flow of any river, discharging an average of 7,100,000 ft³/sec (200,000 m³/sec) into the Atlantic Ocean, which increases to more than 12,000,000 ft³/sec (340,000 m³/sec) in full flood. The lower 900 miles (1,450 km) averages 55 ft (17 m) in depth, but the river has a maximum depth of 407 ft (124 m).

The Amazon is fed by more than 1,000 tributaries and its flow is 60 times greater than that of the Nile. The river accounts for about 20% of the freshwater that drains into the world's oceans.

★ LARGEST WATERFALL (VERTICAL AREA)

Victoria Falls, on the Zambezi river between Zimbabwe and Zambia, is neither the tallest nor the widest in the world, but it is the largest by vertical area. Being 5,604 ft (1,708 m) wide and 354 ft (108 m) high, it creates a sheet of falling water with an area of around 1,984,000 ft² (184,400 m²).

★ LARGEST EPHEMERAL LAKE

Like Lake Turkana (see p.36), Lake Eyre – which is located at the lowest point in Australia – is an example of an endorheic system. It usually contains little or no water but occasionally floods due to heavy monsoon rains. In 1974, the greatest flooding of this salt flat basin created a temporary inland sea with an area of around 3,600 miles² (9,500 km²).

FAST!
VICTORIA FALLS IS ALSO KNOWN AS MOSI-OA-TUNYA – "THE MIST THAT THUNDERS". IT HAS AN AVERAGE ANNUAL FLOW RATE OF 38,422 FT³/SEC (1,088 M³/SEC).

FLUSH!
THE INCREDIBLE VOLUME OF WATER GOING OVER THE FALLS EACH SECOND IS ENOUGH TO FLUSH 83,692 TOILETS, OR 7,230,988,800 TOILETS EVERY DAY!

EARTH
OCEANS & SEAS

★ ★ ★ ★ ★ ★ ★ ★ ★ ★ ★ ★ ☆

SMALLEST COASTLINES

	STATE/NATION	DISTANCE (IMPERIAL)	DISTANCE (METRIC)
1	Monaco (below left)	3.5 miles	5.6 km
2	Nauru (below right)	12 miles	19 km
3	Bosnia	13 miles	20 km
4	Jordan	16 miles	25 km
5	Slovenia	19 miles	30 km

★ NEW RECORD ★ UPDATED RECORD

★ FIRST PROVEN ROGUE WAVE

Rogue waves are waves with abnormal height compared to others, and were long believed to be legendary. On January 1, 1995, the first confirmed measurement of this phenomenon occurred as a wave with a height of 84 ft (25.6 m) struck the Draupner platform in the North Sea.

★ LARGEST DEAD ZONE

Regions of coastal waters where seawater is depleted of oxygen are called "dead zones." More than 400 have been mapped around the world, but the Baltic Sea, with an area of around 145,000 miles^2 (377,000 km^2), is the largest. The bottom of the Baltic lacks oxygen year-round.

★ OLDEST SEAWATER

The seawater at the bottom of the 12,400-ft-deep (3,800-m) Canada Basin has remained unstirred for several thousand years. The Basin, which is north of Canada and Alaska, USA, is connected to the Pacific Ocean only by the 230-ft-deep (70-m) Bering Strait and is protected from the power of the Atlantic Ocean by tall submarine ridges.

WIDEST CONTINENTAL SHELF

The Siberian continental shelf extends 750 miles (1,210 km) off the coast of Siberia, Russia, into the Arctic Ocean. Huge concentrations of methane exist beneath this shelf. In 2008, scientists found evidence that global warming is starting to allow this trapped methane to enter the atmosphere.

★ YOUNGEST OCEAN

Of the major oceans of the world, the Southern Ocean (also known as the Antarctic Ocean and the South Polar Ocean) is the youngest. It formed when Antarctica split away from Australia and South America around 30 million years ago, also forming the Drake Passage in the process.

★ LARGEST VOLCANIC ZONE

The Pacific Ring of Fire is a huge horseshoe-shaped arc of concentrated earthquake and volcanic activity around 24,800 miles (40,000 km) long, located in the Pacific Ocean. It comprises some 452 volcanoes and more than 75% of the world's active and dormant volcanoes.

DID YOU KNOW?

ONLY A FEW SUBSTANCES KNOWN TO SCIENCE, INCLUDING ANTIMONY AND BISMUTH, EXPAND WHEN THEY FREEZE. WATER IS THE BEST KNOWN OF ALL THESE SUBSTANCES.

At 35,797 ft (10,911 m), the Marianas Trench in the Pacific is the **deepest point in any ocean**.

TRIVIA

250 km

★ LARGEST AREA OF GLOWING SEA

In 1995, scientists at the US Naval Research Laboratory discovered an area of luminous sea in the Indian Ocean off the coast of Somalia using satellite images. The patch of water (pictured) was more than 155 miles (250 km) long, with an area of around 5,400 miles² (14,000 km²). Bioluminescent bacteria are thought to have been responsible for the water's appearance.

★ WARMEST OCEAN

The Indian Ocean has the warmest surface temperature of all the world's oceans, as most of it is found in the tropics. Its minimum surface temperature is around 72°F (22°C), but can be as high as 82°F (28°C) toward the east; temperatures in the south can be considerably lower. At 28,400,000 miles² (73,556,000 km²) the Indian Ocean is the third largest of the Earth's oceanic divisions, covering approximately 20% of the Earth's surface.

★ DEEPEST OBSERVED VOLCANIC ERUPTION

On December 18, 2009, US scientists announced the discovery of a volcanic eruption around 3,900 ft (1,200 m) deep in the Pacific Ocean. The footage, captured in May 2009 by a robotic submersible, shows molten lava erupting from the West Mata volcano, which is 125 miles (200 km) southwest of the Samoas and is one of the most active submarine volcanoes in the world.

★ NEWEST FORMING OCEAN

In 2005, a rift some 35 miles (56 km) long opened up in the Afar Depression (also known as the Danakil Depression, the lowest point in Africa) in Ethiopia. In November 2009, scientists announced that results of their analysis showed that this rift is the beginning of the formation of a new ocean. The tectonic processes occurring under Afar are the same as those on the ocean floor at the ridges where new crust is formed and existing crust is pushed apart.

It is expected that, around a million years from now, seawater from the Red Sea will pour into the Afar Depression as it stretches and thins, and the resulting body of sea will gradually grow, possibly to become as large as the Atlantic or Pacific Oceans.

LARGEST SUBMARINE TAR FLOW

In 2003, a team of scientists led by Texas A&M University, USA, discovered the world's first asphalt-erupting volcano 9,842 ft (3,000 m) deep on the seafloor of the Gulf of Mexico. Using a remotely operated camera, the team found tar flows from the volcano, named Chapopote, covering at least 0.4 miles² (1 km²). Their results were published in the journal *Science* in May 2004.

★ SHALLOWEST OCEAN

The Arctic Ocean is the shallowest (and smallest) of the five main oceans. At 5,426,000 miles² (14,056,000 km²) it is roughly the size of Russia and covers 2.8% of the Earth's surface, but has an average depth of 3,450 ft (1,050 m).

★ HIGHEST OCEAN TEMPERATURE

In August 2008, an international team of scientists announced they had recorded water at a temperature of 867°F (464°C) spewing from a hydrothermal vent on the ocean floor, 9,842 ft (3,000 m) deep at the Mid-Atlantic Ridge. Above 764°F (407°C) at this depth, water becomes "supercritical" and lighter than normal water. The water at the "black smoker" was measured using sensors on a remote-controlled robot.

★ FASTEST SEAFLOOR SPREADING CENTER

The East Pacific Rise is a tectonic plate boundary that runs from Antarctica to the west coast of the USA. At this boundary, a new crust is being created and the continental plates are moving apart. A portion of the East Pacific Rise – the Pacific-Nazca boundary – is pushing continental plates apart at a rate of around 93 miles/million years (150 km/million years).

KRAKA- PICTURED IS ISLAND-VOLCANO KRAKATOA ERUPTING IN MAY 2009. AN ERUPTION ON AUGUST 27, 1883 WAS THE LOUDEST NOISE EVER...

...TOA! ...THE EXPLOSION WAS HEARD FROM MORE THAN 3,100 MILES (5,000 KM) AWAY. THAT'S 8% OF THE EARTH'S SURFACE!

EARTH
ISLANDS & REEFS

★ ★ ★ ★ ★ ★ ★ ★ ★ ★ ★ ★ ★ ★ ★

LARGEST ISLAND
Greenland, the largest island, is about 840,000 miles² (2,175,600 km²) in size – just over three times larger than the US state of Texas.

At around 39,768 miles² (103,000 km²), the **largest volcanic island** is Iceland, formed from eruptions from the Mid-Atlantic Ridge, on which it sits. Iceland is essentially seafloor exposed above the ocean.

★LARGEST RIVER ISLAND
Majuli, in the Brahmaputra River in northeast India, covers around 340 miles² (880 km²) – twice the size of Barbados. Many years ago, the island was a long, thin strip of land called Majoli ("land between two parallel rivers") until earthquakes and floods in the 17th and 18th centuries changed the rivers' flow.

★LONGEST BARRIER ISLAND
Barrier islands are narrow, run parallel to mainland coasts, and are formed by the action of waves and currents.

LONGEST REEF
The Great Barrier Reef off Queensland, northeastern Australia, is 1,260 miles (2,027 km) in length. This mammoth feature is not actually a single structure, but consists of thousands of separate reefs. The reef is the **largest marine structure built by living creatures**, because it consists of countless billions of dead and living stony corals (order Madreporaria and Scleractinia).

★LARGEST ISLAND IN A LAKE ON AN ISLAND IN A LAKE ON AN ISLAND
The island of Luzon in the Philippines is home to Lake Taal, and within the lake lies the Taal volcano; the central volcanic crater of Taal is now a lake, named Crater Lake, and Vulcan Point is an island, approximately 130 ft (40 m) across, situated within Crater Lake.

Padre Island in the Gulf of Mexico, off the Texas coast, formed just a few thousand years ago and is around 130 miles (210 km) long.

★ARCHIPELAGO WITH THE MOST ISLANDS
The Archipelago Sea lies within Finnish waters in the Baltic Sea and contains around 40,000 islands. The whole archipelago – or chain or group of islands – is slowly rising as the land is still "rebounding" since the weight of ice from the last Ice Age was removed.

★LARGEST ATOLL
An atoll is a marine structure that comprises a body of water (lagoon) enclosed by a ring (or partial ring) of coral. The Great Chagos Bank in the Indian Ocean is an atoll covering 4,881 miles² (12,642 km²) – yet the seven named islands that form its rim have an area of just 1.7 miles² (4.5 km²).

★MOST ISLANDS WITHIN AN ATOLL
Huvadhu Atoll in the Indian Ocean comprises around 255 islands and covers an area of 1,120 miles² (2,900 km²).

LIFE
THE CROWN-OF-THORNS STARFISH FEEDS ON THE CORAL POLYPS THAT MAKE UP THE GREAT BARRIER REEF. IN 2000, AN OUTBREAK KILLED 66% OF LIVE CORAL COVER.

SUPPORT
THE GREAT BARRIER REEF SUPPORTS AN EXTRAORDINARY DIVERSITY OF LIFE, INCLUDING 1,500 SPECIES OF FISH AND MORE THAN 125 SPECIES OF SHARKS.

★YOUNGEST ISLAND

The island of Surtsey, off the south coast of Iceland, formed on November 14, 1963 when the new land being created by an undersea volcano finally breached the surface of the ocean. The volcanic activity, which had begun 426 ft (130 m) below the surface, lasted until June 5, 1967. By this time, Surtsey had grown to around 1 mile² (2.7 km²). Since then, the island has been gradually shrinking because of erosion.

★LARGEST SUBMERGED BANK

The reef Saya de Malha Bank in the Indian Ocean covers 15,756 miles² (40,808 km²). It rises to within 22 ft (7 m) of the surface and would be the world's largest atoll – three times the size of the Great Chagos Bank – if it were above sea level.

★OLDEST CORAL REEF

The Chazy Reef Formation is a fossilized coral reef that extends from the US state of Tennessee to Newfoundland in Canada. Its most significant outcrop occurs at Isle La Motte in Vermont, USA. It originally formed c. 450 million years ago in what was then the Iapetus Ocean. It is the oldest known example of structures built by coral.

★LARGEST FRINGING REEF

Fringing reefs occur right off the shoreline of a landmass – unlike a barrier reef, which occurs farther out into the ocean and often forms a lagoon. Ningaloo Reef, on the shore of Western Australia, extends for around 180 miles (300 km) in length and is just 330 ft (100 m) from the shore at its closest point.

REEFS:

USS Oriskany, the largest artificial reef, is affectionately known as the "Great Carrier Reef." Why? See below...

LARGEST ARTIFICIAL REEF

The US Navy's attack aircraft carrier USS *Oriskany* (aka the "Mighty O," laid 1944) was decommissioned in 1976 after a long service, and was scheduled for scrapping until the decision was made to sink it as an artificial reef in the Gulf of Mexico, 24 miles (38 km) off Pensacola, Florida, USA. It was sunk on May 17, 2006, using 500 lb (226 kg) of C4 explosives, and took 37 minutes to reach the seabed.

It is around 150 ft (45 m) tall and 888 ft (270 m) long, and attracts an abundance of marine life rarely seen in the northern Gulf of Mexico.

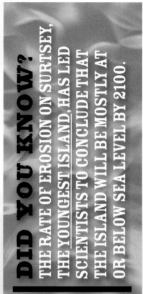
TRIVIA

★ **NEW RECORD**
★ **UPDATED RECORD**

★OLDEST ISLAND

Madagascar, in the Indian Ocean off the southeastern coast of Africa, became an island around 80–100 million years ago, when it split off from the Indian subcontinent. With an area of 226,657 miles² (587,041 km²), it ranks as the fourth largest island in the world and is home to 5% of the world's plant and animal species.

EXTRA! FOR A REVIEW OF THE WORLD'S WORST NATURAL DISASTERS, GO TO PP. 44–45.

EARTH
WEATHER & CLIMATE

★ ★ ★ ★ ★ ★ ★ ★ ★ ★ ★ ★ ★

★ HIGHEST STORM PHENOMENA

Elves are ethereal reddish phenomena that occur above thunderstorms. They were discovered in 1992 using a low-level camera on board the space shuttle. Lasting less than a millisecond, they appear as disk-shaped luminous regions up to 300 miles (480 km) across and occur at altitudes of around 60 miles (97 km).

GREATEST SNOWFALL (DEPTH)

The deepest snowfall recorded to date measured 37 ft 7 in (11.46 m) at Tamarac, California, USA, in March 1911. The **greatest snowfall in 12 months** fell between 1971 and 1972, when a total of 1,224 in (31,102 mm) was recorded at Paradise, Mount Rainier, Washington, USA.

MOST TREES DESTROYED BY STORMS

A record 270 million trees were felled or split by storms that hit France on December 26–27, 1999.

FASTEST WIND SPEED

On April 10, 1996, a wind speed of 253 mph (408 km/h) was recorded at Barrow Island, Australia, during Tropical Cyclone Olivia. This is the fastest wind speed ever recorded on Earth not associated with a tornado.

HOTTEST PLACE ON EARTH

For a fraction of a second, the air around a lightning strike is heated to around 54,000°F (30,000°C), or roughly five times hotter than the visible surface of the Sun.

EXTRA! WHAT HAPPENS WHEN THE NATURAL WORLD TURNS VIOLENT? TO FIND OUT, TURN THE PAGE...

MOST VIOLENT PLACE IN A TROPICAL CYCLONE

Just beyond the calm eye of a hurricane or typhoon is the eye wall. This is a complete circle of storm clouds, often in a towering vertical structure, whirling around the eye. It is here that the highest winds and strongest rainfall occur. In cyclones with very high wind speeds of above 110 mph (177 km/h), a second eye wall will often form around the first.

WORST DAMAGE TOLL FROM AN ICE STORM

The most damaging ice storm on record occurred in the first week of January 1998 in eastern Canada and adjoining parts of the USA. The storm, which began on January 6, shut down airports and railway stations, blocked highways, and cut off power to 3 million people – almost 40% of the population of Québec. Over five days, freezing rain coated power lines with 4 in (10 cm) of ice, more weight than they could carry, and tens of thousands of poles were toppled. The bill was estimated at a massive CAN$1 billion ($650 million).

★ FIRST CLOUD SEEDING EXPERIMENT ON A TROPICAL CYCLONE

On October 13, 1947, the US military dumped 80 lb (36 kg) of dry ice into an Atlantic hurricane. "Pronounced modification of the cloud deck seeded" was recorded by the crew before the hurricane changed direction and hit the coast of Georgia. The damage caused by the cyclone was blamed on the experiment and the program, Project Cirrus, was canceled.

★ MOST RECENTLY CLASSIFIED CLOUD FORMATION

The last cloud type to be recognized as distinct was cirrus intortus in 1951. In 2009, a new type, undulatus asperatus, was proposed by experts as a new type of cloud formation. Its characteristic appearance (pictured) resembles ocean waves, although it is rare. Undulatus asperatus clouds tend to dissipate without forming storms.

DID YOU KNOW?

LIGHTNING IS A DISCHARGE OF ELECTRICAL CURRENT IN THE ATMOSPHERE. ALTHOUGH SEVERAL THEORIES EXIST, SCIENTISTS ARE NOT SURE OF ITS PRECISE CAUSE.

Up to 16 million lightning storms occur each year. Some lightning forks may be 5 miles (8 km) long.

TRIVIA

POW!
POSITIVE LIGHTNING STRIKES ARE KNOWN AS "BOLTS FROM THE BLUE," AS THEY OFTEN BREAK FORTH OUT OF CLEAR OR ONLY SLIGHTLY CLOUDY SKIES.

ZAP!
AS WELL AS THUNDER STORMS, LIGHTNING CAN BE CAUSED BY VOLCANO ERUPTIONS AND FOREST FIRES, WHICH CAN CREATE ENOUGH DUST IN THE ATMOSPHERE TO GENERATE A STATIC CHARGE.

★ MOST POWERFUL LIGHTNING

No one knows exactly how lightning is created, but ice in clouds may be a factor, perhaps helping to divide electrical current into positive and negative charges. Less than 5% of all lightning strikes involve positive lightning – in which the net transfer of charge from the cloud to the ground is positive. Positive lightning outlasts normal (negative) lightning strikes and causes a stronger electrical field, giving rise to strikes of up to a billion volts and an electrical current that may reach 300,000 amperes.

★ GREATEST CLOUD COVER DUE TO HUMAN ACTIVITY

Contrails are condensation trails in the atmosphere left by aircraft. Depending upon local atmospheric conditions, they can last between seconds and hours. In the busiest air corridors, the combined effect of aircraft contrails can increase the cloud cover by up to 20%.

★ NEW RECORD
★ UPDATED RECORD

★ STRONGEST HURRICANE

The category-5 Hurricane Wilma, which occurred during October 2005 and caused damage to the Yucatán Peninsula, Mexico, was the strongest hurricane since records began in 1851. A hurricane hunter plane measured a barometric pressure in the eye of just 882 millibars – the lowest ever recorded for a hurricane. Wind speeds in Wilma's eye wall reached 165 mph (270 km/h).

★ LARGEST BLUE JET

Blue jets are electrical phenomena that project upward in a cone from the tops of cumulonimbus clouds during thunderstorms. They were discovered in 1989.
On September 14, 2001, scientists in Puerto Rico recorded a blue jet that reached around 49 miles (80 km) above a storm, and lasted less than a second.

★ FIRST IDENTICAL SNOW CRYSTALS

One often heard statement about snow is that no two snowflakes are ever alike. However, in 1988, Nancy Knight (USA), a scientist at the National Center for Atmosphere Research in Boulder, Colorado, USA, found two identical examples while using a microscope to study snow crystals from a storm in Wisconsin, USA.

CLOUDS WITH THE GREATEST VERTICAL RANGE

Cumulonimbus clouds have been observed to reach a vertical height of almost 65,600 ft (20,000 m – or nearly three times the height of Mount Everest) in the tropics.

MOST COWS KILLED BY LIGHTNING

A single bolt of lightning killed 68 Jersey cows that were sheltering under a tree at Warwick Marks' farm near Dorrigo, NSW, Australia, on October 31, 2005. So, don't shelter under trees in a storm!

EARTH
NATURAL DISASTERS

★ FASTEST VOLCANIC HAZARD

Pyroclastic flows are the most dangerous of volcanic hazards. They are a mixture of gas and rock that travel down and away from a volcano at temperatures of up to 1,830°F (1,000°C) and speeds of up to 450 mph (720 km/h). In 1902, a pyroclastic flow at Mount Pelée on Martinique overwhelmed the city of Saint-Pierre, killing 30,000 people.

★ HIGHEST DEATH TOLL FROM A BLIZZARD

A week-long blizzard from February 3 to 9, 1972 dumped more than 10 ft (3 m) of snow across parts of rural Iran, ending a four-year drought. Approximately 4,000 people are estimated to have died as a result of the blizzard.

★ HIGHEST DEATH TOLL FROM A WILDFIRE

On October 8, 1871, forest fires burned through northeast Wisconsin and upper Michigan, USA, killing an estimated 1,200 to 2,500 people. More than 1,500 miles² (3,800 km²) of forest and farmland was destroyed. The event is known as the "Peshtigo tragedy," after a village that lost half its population in the fire.

MOST DAMAGE CAUSED BY A CYCLONE

Hurricane Katrina, which devastated the coast of Louisiana, USA, and surrounding states on August 29, 2005, caused damage estimated to be as high as $156 billion. At least 1,836 people lost their lives in the hurricane and subsequent floods. Katrina was the first category-5 hurricane of the 2005 season, the sixth strongest Atlantic hurricane ever recorded, and represents the **costliest natural disaster**.

★ CLOSEST POINT TO HUMAN EXTINCTION

The eruption of the Toba supervolcano around 75,000 years ago threw some 191 miles³ (800 km³) of ash into the atmosphere, creating Earth's largest volcanic crater. The resulting tsunamis and volcanic winter are thought to have reduced the human population to 10,000.

COSTLIEST YEAR FOR NATURAL DISASTERS

According to reinsurers Swiss Re, the Asian tsunami, an unusually active hurricane season, and disasters such as floods pushed the total economic loss for 2005 to $225 billion.

DID YOU KNOW?

A PYROCLASTIC FLOW IS LIKE A FAST-MOVING LIQUID, WITH ROCKS AND DEBRIS SUSPENDED IN IT BY HOT, EXPANDING GASES AND ITS FORWARD MOMENTUM. IT FLOWS LIKE A SNOW AVALANCHE.

More people have been killed by pyroclastic flow than any other type of volcanic hazard.

TRIVIA

HIGHEST DEATH TOLL FROM A TSUNAMI

On December 26, 2004, an earthquake with a magnitude of 9 occurred under the Indian Ocean, off the coast of Indonesia. The resulting tsunami wave inundated the coastlines of nine different countries around the Indian Ocean. The total death toll will never be known but, as of January 20, 2005, at least 226,000 people are known to have perished.

EXTRA! TURN BACK TO PP. 30–31 TO READ ABOUT THE AWESOME POWER OF THE SUN.

★HIGHEST DEATH TOLL FROM A HEAT WAVE

The hottest August on record for the northern hemisphere was in 2003. At least 35,000 fatalities are thought to have resulted from the extreme heat, with some estimates as high as 52,000. France suffered worst, with 14,802 deaths, mainly among the elderly; the temperature reached 104°F (40°C) on seven consecutive days there.

★HIGHEST DEATH TOLL FROM A FIRE WHIRL

Under the right circumstances, tornado-like phenomena can occur within fires. The deadliest example on record happened as a result of the Great Kanto Earthquake of September 1, 1923, which devastated the Kanto region of Honshu, Japan. Around 38,000 people were incinerated by a fire whirl while packed into the Former Army Clothing Depot in Tokyo.

WORST AVALANCHE DISASTER – MOST PEOPLE TRAPPED

At least 265 people died and more than 45,000 were trapped on January 20, 1951 during the "Winter of Terror," when a series of 649 reported avalanches, caused by a combination of hurricane-force winds and wet snow overlaying powder snow, thundered through the Swiss, Austrian, and Italian Alps.

MOST EXTENSIVE FLOOD DAMAGE

Flooding from the Hwai and Yangtze Rivers in China in August 1950 destroyed 890,000 homes and left 490 people dead and 10 million homeless. Around 5 million acres (2 million ha) of land was left under water, rendering 3.5 million acres (1.4 million ha) unfit for the planting season.

MOST POWERFUL EARTHQUAKE

The Valdivia earthquake or Great Chilean Earthquake of May 22, 1960 had a magnitude of 9.5 on the moment magnitude scale. (Like the Richter scale, this records the energy released in an earthquake.) It is estimated to have killed between 2,231 and 5,700 people and left 2 million homeless.

★HIGHEST MUDSLIDE DEATH TOLL

In December 1999, a torrential storm dumped 35 in (911 mm) of rain on Vargas state, Venezuela, in just a few days. The resulting mudslides from the mountainous areas close to the coast caused massive loss of life and infrastructure damage. Estimates of the death toll range from 10,000 to as high as 30,000, though – as with all natural disasters – exact figures are practically impossible to determine.

BRICKS TOWNS THAT WERE COMPLETELY DESTROYED BY THE MUDSLIDE WERE NOT REBUILT. INSTEAD, THEY WERE TURNED INTO PARKS AND COMMUNITY FACILITIES.

MORTAR THE MUDSLIDE DAMAGED AROUND 60% OF THE REGION'S INFRASTRUCTURE - ROADS, BRIDGES, AND UTILITY SERVICES, ETC. - AT AN ESTIMATED COST OF $3.2 BILLION.

NEW RECORD
UPDATED RECORD

HEIDELBERG, GERMANY
The **largest wooden wine cask** is the Heidelberg Tun, which lies in the cellar of the Friedrichsbau in Heidelberg Castle, Heidelberg, Germany. Installed in 1751, it is 23 ft (7 m) tall and 28 ft (8.5 m) across, with a capacity of 48,773 gallons (221,726 liters).

49°24'N 8°42'E

LIVING PLANET

LARGEST NOCTURNAL PRIMATE

The aye-aye (*Daubentonia madagascariensis*) of Madagascar has a body length of 16 in (40 cm), a tail length of 20 in (50.5 cm), and weighs approximately 6 lb (2.76 kg). These solitary animals spend up to 80% of the night foraging for food in the tree canopies and most of the daytime sleeping in tree nests.

Aye-ayes are also known for their skeletal, dexterous middle finger, which is used to tap tree bark to listen for evidence of edible insect larvae inside. They then make a hole in the tree trunk and use the middle finger to hook out the larvae – the primate equivalent of the woodpecker!

AYE!
AYE-AYES ARE THOUGHT TO USE ECHOLOCATION TO SEEK OUT PREY – LIKE BATS. THEY ARE THE ONLY PRIMATES TO DO SO.

AYE!
THESE NOCTURNAL LEMURS HAVE SQUIRREL-LIKE FRONT INCISOR TEETH THAT CONTINUE TO GROW AND NEVER WEAR DOWN.

BREMEN, GERMANY

53°04'N 8°47'E

Visible to the eye, *Thiomargarita namibiensis* is the **largest bacterium**. Heide Schulz, from Bremen's Max Planck Institute for Marine Microbiology, found samples up to 0.029 in (0.75 mm) wide off the Namibian coast.

QUIZ!
NO TALL TALES –
HOW LONG IS THE
AYE AYE'S TAIL?

SEE p.278 FOR THE ANSWER.

CONTENTS

★ **NEW RECORD**
★ **UPDATED RECORD**

LIVING PLANET
DINOSAURS

BIG
ANOTHER TITANOSAURID, *ANTARCTOSAURUS GIGANTEUS* (GIANT ANTARCTIC LIZARD), FOUND IN ARGENTINA AND INDIA, IS ESTIMATED TO HAVE WEIGHED BETWEEN 40 AND 80 TONNES (44 AND 88 TONS).

SMALL
THE ★SMALLEST SPECIES OF DINOSAUR IS THE FEATHERED MICRORAPTOR *ZHAOIANUS*. IT HAS A TOTAL LENGTH OF 15.3 IN (39 CM), OF WHICH 9.4 IN (24 CM) IS ACCOUNTED FOR BY ITS TAIL.

★ **NEW RECORD**
★ **UPDATED RECORD**

HEAVIEST DINOSAUR

In 1994, dinosaur researcher Gregory Paul used the fossil remains of a titanosaurid from Argentina called *Argentinosaurus* (above) to calculate that it had originally weighed up to 110 tons (100 tonnes), making it the heaviest dinosaur to have walked the Earth. Paul based his calculations on the creature's vertebrae.

★ **LARGEST AMMONITE**
An incomplete fossil shell of the ammonite *Parapuzosia*

seppenradensis discovered in Germany in 1895 measured 6 ft 3 in (1.95 m) across, but the complete shell is thought to have been around 8 ft 4 in (2.55 m). Ammonites were related to squids and octopuses but lived inside coiled shells, and this particular species was alive during the late Cretaceous Period (99.6 million to 65.5 million years ago).

LARGEST DINOSAUR FOOTPRINT

In 1932, the gigantic footprints of a large bipedal hadrosaurid ("duckbill") measuring 53.5 in (136 cm) in length and 32 in (81 cm) wide were discovered in Salt Lake City, Utah, USA.

LARGEST LAND-BASED CARNIVORES

The therapods (beast-footed) are the group of dinosaurs that many scientists believe evolved into birds. They included the fearsome *Tyrannosaurus rex*, *Allosaurus*, and the even bigger *Giganotosaurus* (left), which lived 93–89 million years ago and could grow to an estimated 43 ft (13 m) long with a weight of 13,230 lb (6 tonnes).

LONG
THE ★LONGEST DINOSAUR TAIL WAS THAT OF THE NORTH AMERICAN SAUROPOD *DIPLODOCUS*. IT MEASURED UP TO 42 FT 7 IN (13 M) LONG.

PERIOD   ERA   AEON

PHANEROZOIC (543–0 MILLION YEARS AGO [MYA])

MESOZOIC (251–65 MYA)

TRIASSIC (251–206 MYA)

JURASSIC (206–144 MYA)

245 MYA Globe is dominated by the "supercontinent" Pangea, the **largest ever continent**

230 MYA First dinosaurs – in the form of small, bipedal predators – emerge

225 MYA The shrewlike *Adelobasileus cromptoni* is the **first known mammal**

225 MYA Pterosaurs take to the skies; giant reptiles such as the ichthyosaur *Cymbospondylus* dominate seas

200 MYA Extinction event, but dinosaurs flourish and dominate life

210 MYA Longest dinosaur, *Amphicoelias*, estimated at around 197 ft (60 m)

180 MYA Archosaurs (dinosaurs, pterosaurs, crocodilians) dominant on land; marine reptiles continue to rule the waves

*Source: International Commission on Stratigraphy; *informal, not ratified by the ICS; colors defined by the Commission for the Geological Map of the World*

★ LARGEST SINOSAUROPTERYX FOSSIL

A complete *Sinosauropteryx* fossil measuring 12 ft 5 in (3.8 m) long is housed at the Shandong Tianyu Natural History Museum in Shandong province, China. The *Sinosauropteryx* is the first dinosaur found that displayed evidence of having had feathers.

LARGEST AND MOST COMPLETE TYRANNOSAURUS REX SKELETON

The largest, most complete, and best-preserved *Tyrannosaurus rex* skeleton ever found is "Sue," measuring 13 ft (4 m) tall and 41 ft (12.5 m) long and approximately 90% complete. It was found in South Dakota, USA, on August 12, 1990 by explorer Sue Hendrickson (USA), after whom the skeleton has been named.

★ LARGEST PREHISTORIC CARNIVOROUS BIRD

Brontornis burmeisteri, which lived in Patagonia, South America, during the Miocene Epoch, is recognized as the largest carnivorous bird ever. Standing approximately 9 ft 3 in (2.8 m) tall, this huge flightless bird weighed 770–880 lb (350–400 kg), more than twice the weight of today's largest bird, the ostrich (*Struthio camelus*).

LONGEST DINOSAUR GENUS NAME

Micropachycephalosaurus, meaning "small thick-headed lizard," is the longest generic name for a dinosaur, with an impressive 23 letters and nine syllables. Named in 1978 by Chinese paleontologists, this very small dinosaur, 6–12 in only (50–100 cm) long, is a thick-skulled plant-eater that lived in China around 83–73 million years ago, in the Cretaceous Period.

★ LARGEST MOSASAUR

Mosasaurs were prehistoric sea lizards, related to modern-day varanids or monitor lizards. The largest mosasaur known to science is *Hainosaurus*, which had a total length of up to 49 ft 2.5 in (15 m).

★ LONGEST DINOSAUR HORNS

The longest horns of any dinosaur were the paired horns borne above the eyes by the North American ceratopsian dinosaur *Triceratops*. Each horn measured up to 39 in (1 m) long and may have been used in courtship jousting bouts.

EXTRA! CAN'T GET ENOUGH OF OLD-TIMERS? CHECK OUT GOLDEN OLDIES ON PP. 82-83.

★ SMALLEST-BRAINED DINOSAUR

The *Stegosaurus* ("plated lizard") – which, about 150 million years ago, roamed the lands that comprise the present-day US states of Colorado, Oklahoma, Utah, and Wyoming – measured up to 30 ft (9 m) in length but had a walnut-sized brain weighing only 2.5 oz (70 g). This represented 0.002% of its computed body weight of 7,275 lb (3,300 kg) – compared to 0.06% for an elephant, or 1.88% for a human.

LARGEST CROCODILE EVER

Sarcosuchus imperator was a prehistoric species of crocodile that lived approximately 110 million years ago. Recent fossilized remains found in the Sahara Desert, Africa, suggest that this creature took 50–60 years to grow to its full length of around 37–40 ft (11–12 m) and its maximum weight of approximately 17,636 lb (8 tonnes).

from the Greek for "make life appear"; our current aeon, defined by abundant animal life

from the Greek for "middle life"

CRETACEOUS (144–65 MYA)

160 MYA Global warming leads to humid climates and lush jungles; large trees (conifers) and cycads common

155 MYA *Allosaurus* among the largest land predators of the Jurassic Period

150 MYA Emergence of *Archaeopteryx* marks the start of the evolution of the **first birds** from therapod dinosaurs

130 MYA Earth is now the land of the giants, with the appearance of *Giganotosaurus* and *Argentinosaurus*, the **largest-ever land animals**

115 MYA Mammals remain small in size but increasingly large in number; their size, shape, and diversity is restricted by the dominance of the dinosaurs

100 MYA Dinosaurs, the most dominant land vertebrates since the Jurassic Period, are at their most diverse

90 MYA Flowering plants diversify thanks to the emergence of pollinating insects

65 MYA Mass extinction event at the end of the Cretaceous Period removes 40% of animal families, including dinosaurs; the Age of the Reptile is over

LIVING PLANET
BEASTS

★ LARGEST BEAR

The giant short-faced bear (*Arctodus simus*) was the largest bear of all time. This prehistoric species, also known as the bulldog bear, had an estimated weight of 1,322–1,763 lb (600–800 kg). Males were bigger than females, and when on all fours would have stood around 5 ft 3 in (1.6 m) at the shoulder.

★ SMALLEST HOMINID

Discovered by Indonesian and Australian scientists in a cave on the island of Flores, Indonesia, in 2003, *Homo floresiensis* stood just 3 ft 3 in (1 m) tall. A species of great ape, *Homo floresiensis* lived on Flores as recently as 13,000 years ago.

★ LONGEST MASTODON TUSK

A mastodon tusk measuring 16 ft 6 in (5.02 m) was excavated between July 17 and 28, 2007 at a dig in Milia, Grevena, Greece, supervised by Evangelia Tsoukala, Dick Mol, and a paleontological team from the Aristotle University of Thessaloniki and the School of Geology.

NEW RECORD
UPDATED RECORD

★ MOST COMPLETE FOSSIL PRIMATE

On May 19, 2009, an international team of scientists unveiled the fossilized remains of a primate dating back 47 million years – the most complete fossil of an early primate found to date. The 3-ft-long (1-m) female specimen, closely resembling a modern-day lemur and named *Darwinius masillae*, had been found in Germany in 1993. The lengthy delay between discovery and announcement was the consequence of many years spent authenticating and preparing the specimen for sale. Time will tell how significant this fossil find proves to be.

FOSSIL
THE JARKOV MAMMOTH – NAMED AFTER GUENADI JARKOV, THE NINE-YEAR-OLD REINDEER HERDER WHO FOUND IT – IS THE OLDEST INTACT MAMMOTH. IT IS AN ESTIMATED 23,000 YEARS OLD.

FAMILY
ELEPHANTS AND MAMMOTHS ARE CLASSIFIED AS PART OF THE FAMILY ELEPHANTIDAE. THE ASIAN ELEPHANT IS A CLOSER RELATIVE TO THE MAMMOTH THAN THE AFRICAN ELEPHANT.

LARGEST ELEPHANT EVER

The Steppe mammoth *Mamuthus trogontherii* roamed over what is now central Europe a million years ago. A fragmentary skeleton of this species found in Mosbach, Germany, indicates a shoulder height of 14 ft 9 in (4.5 m) – this compares to the largest African elephant recorded, which had a shoulder height of 12 ft (3.6 m) and weighed more than 9 tons (8.1 tonnes).

PERIOD	ERA	AEON				

PHANEROZOIC (543–0 MILLION YEARS AGO [MYA])
CENOZOIC (65–0 MYA)

PALEOGENE (65–23 MYA)

64 MYA
Continents continue to drift toward their present position; supercontinent Laurasia not yet divided

60 MYA
Following mass extinction, only animals smaller than a crocodile remain alive; birds are the largest creatures and biggest predators

55 MYA
Explosion in (often giant) mammalian life as environment niches filled; elephants, rodents, primates, and whales appear

36 MYA
Antarctica begins to freeze over, cooling the oceans' climate; 25% of life on Earth perishes

30 MYA
New mammal species (ancestors of modern horses, pigs, and camels) emerge, many dinosaur-sized, such as the **largest-ever land mammal**, *Indricotherium*

23 MYA
First true carnivores appear; grassland becomes a dominant part of the landscape, covering one-fifth of the planet

EXTRA! ALL THESE BEASTS ARE LONG EXTINCT. FOR MUCH MORE ON MODERN MAMMALS LOOK LIVELY AND TURN TO PP. 64–65.

★LARGEST SLOTH

Megatherium, a giant ground sloth, lived in what is now South America during the Pliocene and Pleistocene epochs for around 5.3 million years. It stood 16 ft 8 in (5.1 m) high on its hind legs, and had an estimated average weight of 4.9 tons (4.5 tonnes).

LARGEST PREHISTORIC MAMMAL

Indricotherium, of the family Hyrachyidae, was a long-necked, hornless rhinocerotid that lived in western Asia and Europe about 35 million years ago. It measured 17 ft 9 in (5.41 m) to the top of the shoulder hump and was 37 ft (11.27 m) long.

★LARGEST THUNDER BEAST

Also known as *brontotheres* or *titanotheres*, thunder beasts were huge prehistoric odd-toed ungulates (mammals that, like horses, walk on their toenails) that resembled rhinoceroses. The largest thunder beast was *Brontotherium*, which lived in North America around 55.8–33.9 million years ago. Characterized by a very large Y-shaped, horn-like structure of bone on its nose, this mighty herbivorous mammal stood around 8 ft 2 in (2.5 m) high at the shoulder, and may have weighed up to 2,200 lb (1,000 kg). When native American Indians first found the huge fossilized bones of this mammal, they mistook them for those of a legendary beast called the thunder horse that jumped down from the sky to Earth and made loud noises during thunderstorms. Based on this folklore, scientists named the animal *Brontotherium* ("thunder beast").

★LARGEST EGG-LAYING MAMMAL

Hackett's long-beaked echidna (*Zaglossus hacketti*), known from fossil remains in Western Australia, weighed up to 220 lb (100 kg) and was the size of a sheep. A massive relative of modern echidna, or spiny anteaters, it lived around 2.6 million to 12,000 years ago.

★LARGEST SABER-TOOTHED CAT

Smilodon populator lived in what is now South America from around 1 million years ago to around 10,000 years ago and stood 5 ft 5 in (1.56 m) at the shoulder. Each of its two serrated saber-like canine teeth were up to 12 in (30 cm) long.

DID YOU KNOW?

KNOWN AS THE WEST RUNTON ELEPHANT, THE LARGEST COMPLETE MAMMOTH SKELETON WAS DISCOVERED IN CROMER, NORFOLK, UK, IN 1990. IT STANDS 13 FT (4 M) AT THE SHOULDER.

The *Megaloceros giganteus* had 14-ft-wide (4.3-m) antlers – similar in size to the length of an adult American alligator.

TRIVIA

from the Greek for "make life appear"; our current aeon, defined by abundant animal life

from the Greek for "new life"

NEOGENE (23–5 MYA)

QUARTERNARY (5–0 MYA)

20 MYA
Herbivores evolve new teeth and digestive systems to deal with the abundance of grass; they also herd and migrate with the seasons

15 MYA
Golden era for *Deinotherium* – the second largest land mammal ever – a proboscidian related to the modern-day elephant

10 MYA
The ★**largest ever predatory shark** is *Carcharodon megalodon*, around 53 ft (16 m) long, with a mouth perhaps 6 ft (2 m) wide

4 MYA
Our ancestors are prey to the saber-toothed *Dinofelis*, a successful carnivore mammal of the felid (cat) family

2.5 MYA
The tool-using *Homo habilis*, the ★**first recognizable human**, evolves from a hominid such as *Australopithecus aferensis*

2 MYA
The elephantine woolly mammoth *Mammuthus* appears; its shaggy coat and thick skin is perfect for surviving harsh winters during the last Ice Age

190,000 YA
Homo sapiens – yes, that's us – evolves in eastern Africa; within 40,000 years, we have spread across Asia, Europe, and the Far East

LIVING PLANET
INSECTS & ARACHNIDS

BEETLE: Beware – beetles can bite! Their name comes from the German for "little biter."

ACTUAL SIZE

★HARDIEST BEETLE

The world's most indestructible beetle is a small species known as *Niptus hololeucus*. Researcher Malcolm Burr revealed that 1,547 specimens were discovered alive and thriving inside a bottle of casein (a chemical present in milk) that had been stoppered for 12 years. Burr also discovered another collection found living for 15 years inside a can of leaves from the powerful poison plant *Datura stramontium*.

ACTUAL SIZE

STRANGEST DEFENSE MECHANISM

The bombardier beetle (genus *Brachinus*) stores two harmless chemicals in a special chamber in its abdomen. When it feels threatened, the liquids are released into a second chamber and mix with an enzyme, resulting in a violent chemical reaction and the release of considerable heat (up to 212°F, or 100°C) from the anus.

★LONGEST ANT MEMORY

Worker ants of two different species – *Formica selysi* and *Manica rubida* – that had been reared together for three months and then separated could still recognize one another after 18 months – the most tenacious ant memory demonstrated.

DEADLIEST ANT

The bulldog ant (*Myrmecia pyriformis*), found in coastal regions of Australia, uses its sting and jaws simultaneously. It has caused at least three human fatalities since 1936.

LARGEST BEETLE

The largest beetle in terms of weight, and indeed the **heaviest insect**, is Africa's goliath beetle (*Goliathus goliathus*), which can obtain larval weights (that is, its weight during its juvenile stage) up to 3.5 oz (100 g).

★LARGEST CRANE FLY

The world's largest species of crane fly or daddy longlegs is *Holorusia brobdignagius*. This species of crane fly can grow up to 9 in (23 cm) long, but is exceedingly slender and fragile.

★LONGEST SNOUT ON A BEETLE

South Africa's long-snouted cycad weevil (*Antliarhinus zamiae*) has the longest snout of any beetle. The 0.79-in-long (2-cm) snout is used for drilling holes in cycad seeds, inside which the 3-cm-long (1.18-in) weevil can then lay its eggs.

ACTUAL SIZE

★LONGEST ANIMAL NAME

The longest scientific binomial (two-part) name given to any animal is *Parastratiosphecomyia stratiosphecomyioides* (containing 42 letters), aka the soldier fly, which is a species of stratiomyid fly with a metallic-green thorax and abdomen.

★LARGEST ANIMAL FAMILY

The largest taxonomic family of animals is the weevil or snout beetle family, Curculionidae, which contains more than 60,000 species currently known to science.

LARGEST MILLIPEDE

A fully grown African giant black millipede (*Archispirostreptus gigas*) owned by Jim Klinger of Coppell, Texas, USA, measures 15.2 in (38.7 cm) in length, 2.6 in (6.7 cm) in circumference, and has 256 legs.

ACTUAL SIZE

100s DESPITE THEIR NAMES, CENTIPEDES (MEANING "100 FEET") DON'T HAVE 100 LEGS, AND MILLIPEDES ("1,000 FEET") DON'T HAVE 1,000 LEGS!

1,000s THE RECORD FOR THE ANIMAL WITH MOST LEGS GOES TO A SPECIMEN OF *ILLACME PLENIPES* - A MILLIPEDE FROM CALIFORNIA, USA, WHICH HAD 750 LEGS.

ACTUAL SIZE

"Pedipalps" (pincers) are used to catch prey and dig burrows, as well as playing a role in mating and defense.

LARGEST SCORPION

A specimen of *Heterometrus swannerdami* found during World War II in Krishnarajapuram, India, measured 11.5 in (29.2 cm) in overall length, from its stinger to its "pincer."

★ LARGEST ORB-WEAVER SPIDER

In 2000, an enormous female specimen of orb-weaver spider was discovered by Slovenian biologist Dr Matjaz Kuntner in a collection of specimens owned by the Plant Protection Institute in Pretoria, South Africa. Not only did it prove to belong to a hitherto unknown species – which Dr Kuntner later named *Nephila komaci* – but it was also found to constitute the world's largest orb-weaver spider species. Further specimens have since been obtained, some from Madagascar, revealing that females have a leg span of up to 4.7 in (12 cm), and can spin webs up to 3 ft 3.3 in (1 m) wide.

LARGEST SPIDER

A male goliath bird-eating spider (*Theraphosa blondi*) collected at Rio Cavro, Venezuela, in April 1965 had a record leg span of 11 in (28 cm) – long enough to cover a dinner plate.

STRONGEST SPIDERWEBS

The extremely tough webs spun by spiders of the genus *Nephila* can catch small birds and frogs (pictured), and are even capable of slowing down the passage of mammals up to the size of humans.

Spiders of the tropical African species *N. senegalensis* have a special garbage line in their web, in which the sucked-out remains of small birds have been found.

EXTRA! CHECK OUT SOME CREEPY CRUSTACEANS ON PP. 54–55 AND AMAZING MAMMALS ON PP. 64–65.

"*Dear GWR, my giant millipede is 15¼ inches – is this a world record?*" Jim Klinger, Jungle Jim's Bugs of the World. Erm, yes!

★ NEW RECORD
★ UPDATED RECORD

PADUA, ITALY

The world's **oldest botanical garden** to remain on its original site, is the Orto Botanico in Padua, Italy, which was created in 1545. The original design of a circular central plot (symbolizing the world), surrounded by a ring of water, is still in place.

45°25'N
11°52'E

LIVING PLANET
CRUSTACEANS & MOLLUSKS

★ SHARPEST NIGHT VISION

Gigantocypris is a marine crustacean (pictured) that lives at depths of more than 3,300 ft (1,000 m), where there is virtually no sunlight. Luckily, this genus of ostracod has the best night vision of any animal, boasting eyes with an f-number (a measure of light sensitivity) of 0.25 (humans measure around f-2.55). Each eye possesses a pair of high-powered parabolic reflectors that direct the very dim available light onto the retina at their center.

ACTUAL SIZE

★ LARGEST COPEPOD

Copepods are small marine crustaceans, typically 0.04–0.07 in (1–2 mm) in length, that constitute the biggest biomass in the oceans. The largest species of copepod is *Pennella balaeonpterae*, which lives exclusively as a parasite upon the backs of fin whales (*Balaenoptera physalus*). It can attain a maximum length of 12.5 in (32 cm).

LARGEST LAND CRUSTACEAN

The coconut or rubber crab (*Birgus latro*), which lives on tropical islands and atolls in the Indo-Pacific, is the largest land-living crustacean. Weights of up to 9 lb (4.1 kg) and leg spans of up to 39 in (1 m) have been recorded. The **largest crustacean** is the Japanese spider crab (*Macrocheira kaempferi*), with a claw span of up to 12 ft 1.6 in (3.7 m).

★ MOST RECENTLY DESCRIBED CLASS OF CRUSTACEANS

In 1979, while diving in Lucayan Cavern beneath the island of Grand Bahama, biologist Dr Jill Yager (USA) encountered tiny wormlike crustaceans that proved to be a new species, dubbed *Speleonectes lucayensis*. So different was *S. lucayensis* from all crustaceans that, in 1981, an entirely new taxonomic class -- Remipedia -- was created in order to accommodate it. Several additional, related species have since been discovered, all of which are blind and characterized by their oarlike limbs, hence these crustaceans are termed remipedes ("oar-footed").

★ MOST MATERNAL CRAB

The Jamaican bromeliad crab (*Metopaulias depressus*), which actually lives on land in mountainous forests, is the world's most maternal crab. The female lays her eggs in puddles of rainwater that collect in the large leaves of bromeliad plants, and three months after the eggs hatch she feeds her offspring with small insects and also chases away would-be predators such as lizards and large spiders.

★ LARGEST CHITON

Chitons (from the Greek for "tunic") are primitive marine mollusks. The largest is the gumboot or giant Pacific chiton (*Cryptochiton stelleri*), found off the Pacific coasts of North America and Japan, which grows up to 1 ft (33 cm) long and 0.43 in (13 cm) wide. Its red, leathery mantle (or "girdle") wraps around its body (like a tunic, hence its name), covering a series of armored plates that run down the chiton's back.

LARGEST CLAM

The largest of all existing bivalve shells is that of the marine giant clam (*Tridacna gigas*), found on the Indo-Pacific coral reefs. One specimen measuring 3 ft 9.25 in (1.15 m) in length and weighing 734 lb (333 kg) was collected off Ishigaki Island, Okinawa, Japan, in 1956; it probably weighed a little more than 750 lb (340 kg) when it was alive.

DID YOU KNOW?

"CRUSTACEAN" MEANS "HARD SHELLED," REFERRING TO THE ANIMALS' TOUGH EXOSKELETON. "MOLLUSK" IS DERIVED FROM "THIN SHELLED" AND "SOFT THING," SO EXPECT A SQUISHY BODY INSIDE A SHELL.

Slugs like beer! Research at Colorado University in the USA in 1987 identified Kingsbury Malt Beverage to be the slug's top tipple.

TRIVIA

CHOMP! SOME SLUGS POSSESS TENS OF THOUSANDS OF TINY, RAZOR-SHARP TEETH THAT ARE CONTINUALLY BEING REPLACED.

★ LARGEST BARNACLE

Barnacles are marine crustaceans that "encrust" themselves to surfaces. The largest is the giant acorn barnacle, *Balanus nubilis*, standing up to 5 in (12.7 cm) high.

★ LARGEST MOLLUSK

An adult male colossal squid (*Mesonychoteuthis hamiltoni*) weighing around 990 lb (450 kg) and measuring 33 ft (10 m) long was caught by fishermen in the Ross Sea of Antarctica. It was taken to New Zealand, and the catch was announced on February 22, 2007. Colossal squid are usually shorter than giant squid, but much heavier.

MOST VENOMOUS MOLLUSK

The two closely related species of blue-ringed octopus, *Hapalochlaena maculosa* and *H. lunulata*, are found around the coasts of Australia and parts of Southeast Asia. They carry a neurotoxic venom so potent that their relatively painless bite can kill in a matter of minutes. It has been estimated that each individual carries sufficient venom to cause the paralysis (or even death) of 10 adult people. Fortunately, blue-ringed octopuses are not considered aggressive and normally bite only when they are taken out of the water and provoked. These mollusks have a radial spread of just 4–8 in (100–200 mm).

LARGEST EYE-TO-BODY RATIO

The vampire squid (*Vampyroteuthis infernalis*) has the largest eye-to-body ratio of any animal. Its body can reach 11 in (28 cm) in length, while its eyes may have a diameter of 0.9 in (2.5 cm).

OLDEST MOLLUSK

In 2006, a quahog clam (*Arctica islandica*) that had been living on the seabed off the north coast of Iceland was dredged by a team from Bangor University's School of Ocean Sciences, Wales, UK. On October 28, 2007, researchers revealed that it was between 405 and 410 years old. The clam was nicknamed "Ming," after the Chinese dynasty in power when it was born!

GASTROPOD: From the Greek for "stomach foot," on the misunderstanding that slugs glide around on their bellies.

ACTUAL SIZE

★ LARGEST SLUG

The world's largest species of terrestrial slug is the ash-black slug, *Limax cinereoniger*. Found in ancient woodlands throughout all but the most northerly regions of Europe, this gastropod mollusk can grow to a length of up to 12 in (30 cm), and eats fungi.

LIVING PLANET
FISH & SEALIFE

★HOTTEST FISH EYES

Swordfish (*Xiphias gladius*) have special organs that heat up their eyes to as much as 82°F (28°C), improving their efficiency in cold water and enabling them to swiftly spot prey.

QUIZ!
OF ALL THE FISH IN THE SEA, WHICH IS THE LARGEST?
SEE P.278 FOR THE ANSWER.

★LARGEST SEA LILY

Despite looking like flowers, sea lilies are not plants. The largest sea lilies inhabit the Pacific Ocean and belong to the genus *Metacrinus*. They have a maximum stalk height of 2 ft (61 cm), with a 5.98-in (15.2-cm) arm length.

★LARGEST BARRACUDA

A barracuda specimen weighing 85 lb 1 oz (38.6 kg) was caught on April 11, 2002 off Christmas Island, Kiribati, in the Pacific Ocean.

LARGEST FISH EGG

The crew of a shrimp trawler in the Gulf of Mexico found a whale shark egg (*Rhincodon typus*) measuring 12 x 5.5 x 3.5 in (30.5 x 14 x 8.9 cm) on June 29, 1953.

★SMALLEST SEA URCHIN

The *Echinocyamus scaber* species of sea urchin, which is native to the seas off New South Wales, Australia, has a test (shell) diameter of just 0.22 in (5.5 mm).

★LARGEST FAMILY OF FISH

Family Cyprinidae, the carp family of freshwater fish, contains more than 2,400 species, housed in approximately 220 genera. Among its most familiar members are the carps (including goldfish), tench, barbs, and minnows.

LONGEST FISH FIN

All three species of thresher shark (family Alopiidae) have huge scythe-shaped caudal (tail) fins that are roughly as long as their entire bodies. The largest of the three species is the common thresher shark (*Alopias vulpinus*), which is found worldwide in temperate and tropical seas. Common threshers may grow to a length of 19 ft 8 in (6 m), of which almost 9 ft 10 in (3 m) consists of its greatly elongated upper tail fin; the fish's body itself is sleek and slender.

★LONGEST PREGNANCY

The common frilled shark (*Chlamydoselachus anguineus*), a primitive species native to all oceans, has a longer gestation period (pregnancy) than any other animal: an average of 3.5 years.

FASTEST FISH

In short-distance speed trials carried out at the Long Key Fishing Camp, Florida, USA, a cosmopolitan sailfish (*Istiophorus platypterus*) took out 300 ft (91 m) of line in 3 seconds, equivalent to a velocity of 68 mph (109 km/h). By comparison, cheetahs run at 62 mph (100 km/h). Sailfish achieve their incredible bursts of speed thanks to their highly oxygenated red muscles.

MOST VENOMOUS JELLYFISH

The box jellyfish (*Chironex fleckeri*, aka Flecker's sea wasp), found off the north coast of Australia, typically contains enough venom to kill 60 humans and is responsible for one death per year, on average.

★LARGEST FAMILY OF MARINE FISH

Family Gobiidae, the goby family, contains more than 2,000 species (including the whip coral goby *Bryaninops yongei*, below). Gobies range in length from less than 0.2 in to 12 in (1–30 cm), their most distinctive feature being their disk-shaped sucker derived from their fused pelvic fins.

LEIPZIG, GERMANY
51°18'N 12°22'E
The **largest bicycle bell ensemble** was organized by Professor Jörg Kärger and consisted of 503 participants playing German folk songs and hymns at the University of Leipzig, Germany, on November 23, 2003.

★ HEAVIEST STARFISH

On September 14, 1969, a specimen of *Thromidia catalai*, a hefty five-armed species of starfish native to the western Pacific, was caught off Ilot Amédée, New Caledonia. The starfish, which weighed an estimated 13 lb 3 oz (6 kg), was later deposited at New Caledonia's Nouméa Aquarium.

URCHIN: An old-fashioned word for the spiny hedgehogs that sea urchins resemble!

★ HEAVIEST FISH

A scientifically recorded specimen of whale shark (*Rhincodon typus*) captured off Baba Island, near Karachi, Pakistan, on November 11, 1949 measured 41 ft 6 in (12.65 m) long, making it the **largest fish**, but it also weighed an estimated 33,000–46,200 lb (15–21 tonnes), giving it the record for heaviest fish too. Sharks and rays are cartilaginous fish – their skeletons are composed of cartilage instead of the hard bone of many other fish species. The **heaviest bony fish** is the ocean sunfish (*Mola mola*), which has been recorded as weighing 4,400 lb (2 tonnes) and measuring 10 ft (3 m) from fin tip to fin tip.

LONGEST SURVIVAL OUT OF WATER FOR A FISH

Six species of lungfish live in freshwater swamps that dry out for months or even years at a time. Two of the four species found in Africa (*Protopterus annectens*, *P. aethiopicus*, *P. dolloi*, and *P. amphibius*) are considered to be real survival experts. As their swamp water recedes, they burrow deep into the ground and secrete mucus to form a moisture-saving cocoon around their bodies. They then build a porous mud plug at the entrance of the burrow – and wait. Abandoning gill breathing in favor of their air-breathing lungs, they can live for up to four years in this dormant position.

LONGEST FISH MIGRATION

A bluefin tuna (*Thunnus thynnus*) was tagged off Baja California, Mexico, in 1958 and was caught again 300 miles (483 km) south of Tokyo, Japan, in April 1963, by which time it had traveled a straight-line distance of at least 5,800 miles (9,335 km). Its weight also increased from 35 lb (16 kg) to 267 lb (121 kg) between catches.

★ LARGEST BRAIN CORAL COLONY

As large as a truck, a brain coral approximately 9 ft 10 in (3 m) high and 16 ft 4 in (5 m) across can be found on a dive site called Kelleston Drain, south of the island of Little Tobago, Trinidad and Tobago. Like all colonial corals, brain corals are not a single organism but composed of millions of individual coral polyps living together.

LARGEST JELLYFISH

Most jellyfish have a body diameter, or bell, ranging from 0.8 in to 15.8 in (2–40 cm), but some species grow considerably larger. The largest recorded specimen was an Arctic giant jellyfish (*Cyanea capillata arctica*) that washed up in Massachusetts Bay, USA, in 1870; it had a bell diameter of 7 ft 6 in (2.28 m) and tentacles stretching 120 ft (36.5 m).

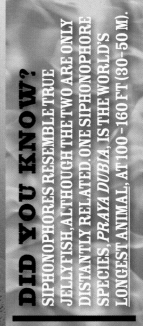

DID YOU KNOW? SIPHONOPHORES RESEMBLE TRUE JELLYFISH, ALTHOUGH THE TWO ARE ONLY DISTANTLY RELATED. ONE SIPHONOPHORE SPECIES, *PRAYA DUBIA*, IS THE WORLD'S LONGEST ANIMAL, AT 100–160 FT (30–50 M).

By way of comparison to *Praya dubia*, the blue whale, the world's **largest animal**, is 82–88 ft 6 in (25–27 m) long.

TRIVIA

UP
THE HIGHEST-LIVING FISH IS THE TIBETAN LOACH (FAMILY COBITIDAE), FOUND AT AN ALTITUDE OF 17,060 FT (5,200 M) IN THE HIMALAYAS!

DOWN
THE DEEPEST-LIVING FISH IS THE ABYSSOBROTULA GALATHEAE SPECIES OF CUSK EEL, WHICH LIVES AT A DEPTH

LIVING PLANET
AMPHI-BIANS

★LARGEST AMPHIUMA

Amphiumas are three highly distinctive species of aquatic North American salamander with elongated, superficially eel-like bodies, minute legs, and no tongue. The largest of these very unusual amphibians is the three-toed amphiuma (*Amphiuma tridactylum*), pictured. It can grow to 3 ft 3 in (1 m) long, possesses gill slits but lacks eyelids, and lives in marshes and lakes within the southeastern USA.

ACTUAL SIZE

★MOST TRANSPARENT AMPHIBIAN

Some so-called glass frogs (of the family Centrolenidae), native to the rainforests of Central and South America, have partially transparent abdominal skin that resembles frosted glass. Their heart, liver, and gut can be readily seen through it when viewed from underneath. The remainder of their skin is usually lime green.

LARGEST FROG

A specimen of the African goliath frog (*Conraua goliath*), captured in April 1899 on the Sanaga River, Cameroon, had a snout-to-vent length of 14.5 in (36.83 cm) and an overall length of 34.5 in (87.63 cm) with its legs extended, about the size of a house rabbit.

The world's **smallest frog**, and the **smallest known amphibian**, is *Eleutherodactylus limbatus* of Cuba, which is 0.33–0.47 in (8.5–12 mm) long from snout to vent.

★RAREST AMPHIBIANS

The Red List of Threatened Species lists two toads as "Extinct in the Wild":
• The Wyoming toad (*Bufo baxteri*) exists only within the Mortenson Lake National Wildlife Refuge in Wyoming, USA; believed extinct in 1980, it was rediscovered in 1987 but no known mating in the wild has occurred since 1991.
• The hundreds of remaining Kihansi spray toads (*Nectophrynoides asperginis*), a dwarf toad native to Tanzania, live at the Bronx Zoo, New York City, USA.

★LEAST FECUND AMPHIBIAN

Fecundity is the capacity for producing offspring. The world's least fecund frog is the Cuban frog (*Sminthillus limbatus*), a tiny species of poison-arrow frog whose female lays only a single egg.

In stark contrast, a single female of the world's **most fecund amphibian**, the cane toad (*Bufo marinus*), will lay as many as 30,000–35,000 eggs per spawning.

MOST POISONOUS...

Frog: The golden poison frog (*Phyllobates terribilis*) of South and Central America may measure only 1.6–2 in (4–5 cm) long, but it secretes enough toxin to provide a lethal dose to 10 adult humans or 20,000 lab mice.

QUIZ!
WHICH CLASSIC ARCADE VIDEO GAME FEATURES AN AMPHIBIAN ATTEMPTING TO CROSS A BUSY ROAD AND A FAST-FLOWING RIVER?
SEE P.278 FOR THE ANSWER.

★LARGEST GENUS OF FROG

The *Pristimantis* genus of frog comprises more than 400 species, with new ones being discovered each year. These small frogs are native to southern Central and northern South America, and are notable for laying their eggs on land. These hatch directly as froglets, thus bypassing the tadpole stage.

★ **NEW RECORD**
● **UPDATED RECORD**

LAND
THE WORD AMPHIBIAN COMES FROM THE GREEK "AMPHI-," MEANING "BOTH KINDS," AND "BIOS," MEANING "LIFE" – BOTH KINDS OF LIFE...

WATER
... "BOTH KINDS OF LIFE" REFERS TO THE AMPHIBIANS' ABILITY TO EXIST ON LAND AND IN THE WATER – A CLASS BETWEEN FISH AND REPTILES.

★ LARGEST CAECILIAN

Extant (living) amphibians can be divided into Anura (frogs and toads), Caudata (newts and salamanders), and Gymnophiona (caecilians). This last order are limbless tropical amphibians that generally resemble earthworms, and have eyes hidden beneath a layer of skin. The world's largest is Thompson's caecilian (*Caecilia thompsoni*), a Colombian species that can attain a length of 4 ft 11 in (1.51 m). It is native to moist tropical and subtropical lowland forests as well as plantations and even rural gardens.

LARGEST AMPHIBIAN

The giant salamanders (family Cryptobranchidae) are the greatest of the amphibians. The record-holder is the Chinese giant salamander (*Andrias davidianus*, pictured), which lives in mountain streams in northeastern, central, and southern China. One record-breaking specimen collected in Hunan Province measured 5 ft 11 in (1.8 m) in length and weighed 143 lb (65 kg).

Newt: One drop of blood from the California newt (*Taricha torosa*), which contains the toxic and powerful nerve poison tetrodotoxin, could kill several thousand mice.

LARGEST NEWT

The Spanish ribbed newt (*Pleurodeles waltl*), found in central and southern Iberia and Morocco, is 6–12 in (15–30 cm) long.

The world's **smallest newt** or **salamander** is the Mexican lungless salamander (*Bolitoglossa mexicana*), which attains a maximum length of approximately 1 in (2.54 cm).

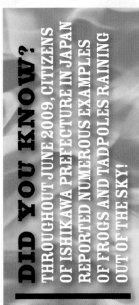

Frogs feature prominently in the classic 1980s videogame *Frogger*, in which players guide frogs to safety.

TRIVIA

★ HIGHEST FROG CROAK

The concave-eared torrent frog (*Odorrana tormota*) of eastern China emits a croak of 128 kHz – well beyond the range of human hearing, which cannot detect sound frequencies above 20 kHz.

ACTUAL SIZE

EXTRA!
DISCOVER MORE ABOUT HUMANITY'S RELATIONSHIP WITH ANIMALS IN OUR ANIMAL MAGIC CHAPTER, FROM P.150.

LIVING PLANET
REPTILES

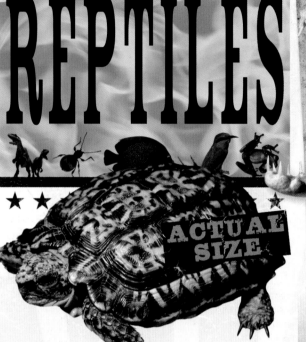

ACTUAL SIZE

★ FASTEST CROCODILE ON LAND

The freshwater crocodile (*Crocodylus johnstoni*) can attain speeds reaching 10.56 mph (17 km/h) when in full gallop – a mode of terrestrial locomotion that only a few species of crocodile can accomplish. Native to Australia, this crocodile rarely grows larger than 8–10 ft (2.5–3 m).

★ SMALLEST CHELONIAN

Of all the chelonians – turtles, tortoises, and terrapins – the smallest is the speckled cape tortoise or speckled padloper (*Homopus signatus*). It has a shell length of 2.3–3.7 in (6–9.6 cm) – so small that the tortoise can hide in tiny gaps between rocks.

★ LARGEST GECKO

Delcourt's giant gecko (*Hoplodactylus delcourti*) is known from only a single mounted and stuffed specimen measuring 2 ft (61 cm) long. It had been on display at the Marseille Natural History Museum in France for more than a century before, in 1979, it was recognized by curator Alain Delcourt as representing a species unknown to science. The gecko was formally named and described in 1986.

FASTEST LIZARD

In a series of experiments conducted by Professor Raymond Huey from the University of Washington, USA, and colleagues at the University of California at Berkeley, USA, the highest burst speed recorded for any reptile on land was 21.7 mph (34.9 km/h), achieved by *Ctenosaura*, a spiny-tailed iguana from Central America.

★ LONGEST REPTILIAN INCUBATION PERIOD

Of all the egg-laying reptiles the tuataras (see *Instant Expert*, p.61) have to keep their eggs warm the longest before they are ready to hatch. Scientists have recorded tuataras incubating eggs for as long as 13 to 15 months before their offspring emerge from their shells.

★ LARGEST CROCODILE EGGS

The false gharial (*Tomiostoma schlegelii*), a crocodilian with long, narrow jaws and a slender snout native to southeast Asia, lays eggs that typically measure 3.94 x 2.76 in (10 x 7 cm). Despite its name, recent studies have shown that the false gharial is more closely related to other gharials than crocodiles and alligators.

★ LARGEST VENOMOUS LIZARD

Measuring up to 10 ft 3 in (3.13 m) and weighing around 154 lb 5 oz (70 kg), the Komodo dragon (*Varanus komodoensis*) is the **largest lizard**. In 2009, researchers at Melbourne University, Australia, discovered that the reptile also possesses a pair of venom glands in its lower jaw that secretes a venom containing several different toxic proteins.

HORNS

HORNED LIZARDS OF THE GENUS *PHRYNOSOMA* CAN SQUIRT BLOOD OUT OF THEIR EYES TO FRIGHTEN POTENTIAL PREDATORS.

THORNS

AS ITS NAME MIGHT SUGGEST, THE THORNY DEVIL (*MOLOCH HORRIDUS*) IS COVERED IN SHARP SPINES THAT MAKE IT HARD FOR PREDATORS TO SWALLOW.

DID YOU KNOW?

LIKE THE KOMODO DRAGON, THE GILA MONSTER (*HELODERMA SUSPECTUM*) AND THE MEXICAN BEADED LIZARD (*HELODERMA HORRIDUM*) ARE ALSO VENOMOUS.

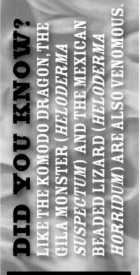

Of all the reptile groups, the crocodilians – crocodiles, alligators, and gharials – are the closest living relatives to birds.

TRIVIA

LARGEST TORTOISE

The giant tortoises (*Chelonoidis nigra*) of the Galápagos Islands are the largest tortoise species. A specimen named Goliath, who resided at the Life Fellowship Bird Sanctuary in Seffner, Florida, USA, from 1960 until his death in November 2002, was 4 ft 5.5 in (1.35 m) long, 3 ft 3.6 in (1.02 m) wide, and 2 ft 3 in (68.5 cm) tall, and weighed 920 lb (417 kg).

★MOST ACUTE NOCTURNAL COLOR VISION

Unlike most other animals with nocturnal vision, the helmeted gecko (*Tarentola chazaliae*) can perceive colors at night. This is thought to be due to the higher density of color-sensitive large cone cells in the lizard's retinas.

ACTUAL SIZE

★COUNTRY WITH MOST VENOMOUS SNAKE SPECIES

Australia not only has more species of venomous snake than any other country on Earth, but also includes among those snakes no less than nine of the world's top 10 most venomous snake species. These include such (in)famous serpents as the inland taipan (*Oxyuranus microlepidotus*) – perhaps the world's most venomous snake -- the eastern brown snake (*Pseudonaja textilis*) at the number two spot, the coastal taipan (*Oxyuranus scutellatus*) third, and the tiger snake (*Notechis scutatus*) fourth.

OLDEST SNAKE

The greatest reliable age recorded for a snake in captivity is 40 years 3 months 14 days for a male common boa (*Boa constrictor*) named Popeye, who died at Philadelphia Zoo, Pennsylvania, USA, on April 15, 1977.

LARGEST CROCODILIAN

The estuarine, or saltwater, crocodile (*Crocodylus porosus*) is found throughout the tropical regions of Asia and the Pacific. The Bhitarkanika Wildlife Sanctuary in Orissa State, India, houses four measuring more than 19 ft 8 in (6 m) in length, the largest being more than 23 ft (7 m) long. There are several unauthenticated reports of specimens up to 33 ft (10 m) in length. Adult males average 14–16 ft (4.2–4.8 m) in length and weigh about 900–1,150 lb (408–520 kg).

SMALLEST CROCODILIAN

The dwarf caiman (*Paleosuchus palpebrosus*) of northern South America is the smallest crocodilian in the world today. Females rarely exceed a length of 4 ft (1.2 m) and males seldom grow to more than 4 ft 11 in (1.5 m).

★ NEW RECORD / UPDATED RECORD

RAREST LIZARD

Until it was rediscovered in 1990, the Jamaican iguana (*Cyclura collei*) was thought to be extinct. With no more than 100 adult specimens located since 1990, the species is considered critically endangered and it is clinging to survival in southern Jamaica's remote Hellshire Hills -- the only sizeable area of dry forest remaining on the island.

LONGEST VENOMOUS SNAKE

The venom of a single bite from the king cobra (*Ophiophagus hannah*), found in southeast Asia and India, is enough to kill an elephant, or 20 people. What's more, it can grow to 12–15 ft (3.65–4.5 m) in length and can stand tall enough to look an adult human in the eye.

INSTANT EXPERT

⊙ TUATARAS MIGHT LOOK LIKE LIZARDS, BUT THEY ARE ACTUALLY THE ONLY LIVING REPRESENTATIVES OF AN OTHERWISE EXTINCT GROUP OF REPTILES NAMED THE SPHENODONTIDS, A GROUP THAT THRIVED AT THE TIME OF THE DINOSAURS.

★ NOT ALL REPTILES LIVE ON DRY LAND. THE MARINE IGUANA (*AMBLYRHYNCHUS CRISTATUS*) AND VARIOUS SPECIES OF SEA SNAKE LIVE IN SALT WATER.

★ THE COMMON BASILISK (*BASILISCUS BASILISCUS*) IS KNOWN AS THE "JESUS LIZARD" FOR ITS ABILITY TO RUN ON WATER!

RAREST CROCODILIAN

There were fewer than 200 Chinese alligators (*Alligator sinensis*) living in the wild in 2002. Found in the lower parts of the Yangtze River in wetlands, the species can grow to 6 ft 6 in (2 m) and weigh 88 lb (40 kg). Their numbers have dwindled over time due to habitat destruction and killing by local farmers.

EXTRA!
FOR MORE COLD-BLOODED CREATURES, PLOD ALONG TO PP. 48-49 TO EXPLORE THE LAND OF THE DINOSAURS.

★LARGEST TUATARA

There are only two species of tuatara, both of which are found exclusively in the islands off the main coast of New Zealand. Of the two, the greatly endangered Brothers Island tuatara (*Sphenodon guntheri*) is the largest. It can grow up to 2 ft 6 in (76 cm) long and have a maximum weight of 3 lb 1 oz (1.4 kg).

PALERMO, ITALY
The **largest Mafia trial** took place in Palermo, Sicily, Italy, on February 10, 1986. A total of 426 people were found guilty and 19 were sentenced to detention in perpetuity.

38°07'N 13°22'E

LIVING PLANET
BIRDS

★ ★ ★ ★ ★ ★ ★ ★ ★ ★

FASTEST BIRDS

• **In level flight**: The mean estimated speed recorded for a satellite-tagged gray-headed albatross (*Thalassarche chrysostoma*) is 78.9 mph (127 km/h) sustained for more than eight hours.

• **In a dive**: A peregrine falcon (*Falco peregrinus*) was recorded at a velocity of 168 mph (270 km/h) at a 30° angle of stoop, rising to a maximum of 217 mph (350 km/h) at 45°.

• **On land**: The **fastest (flightless) bird on land** is the ostrich (*Struthio camelus*), which can reach 45 mph (72 km/h) when running.

★ HUNGRIEST BIRDS

The world's hungriest birds are the hummingbirds (family Trochilidae), which have such high metabolic rates that they need to consume at least half of their total body weight in food every day in order to survive. Their food consists mostly of tiny insects and nectar.

• **In water**: The fastest bird swimmer is the gentoo penguin (*Pygoscelis papua*), which has a burst of speed of about 17 mph (27 km/h).

STRONGEST BIRD OF PREY

The female harpy eagle (*Harpia harpyja*) regularly kills and carries away animals equal or superior to its 20 lb (9 kg) weight.

SMALLEST BIRDS

Male bee hummingbirds (*Mellisuga helenae*) of Cuba and the Isle of Youth measure 2.24 in (57 mm) in total length, half of which is taken up by the bill and tail, and weigh just 0.056 oz (1.6 g). Females of the species are slightly larger.

Hummingbirds also have the **fastest wing beat**. The ruby-throated hummingbird (*Archilochus colubris*) can produce a wing-beat rate of 200 beats per second.

EXTRA! SEE HOW WELL WE HUMANS DO WHEN WE TAKE TO THE SKIES BY VISITING PP.116-117.

DID YOU KNOW?

NORTH AMERICAN PASSENGER PIGEONS ONCE FLOCKED IN THEIR TENS OF MILLIONS – BUT IN FEWER THAN 100 YEARS, THEY WERE HUNTED BY MAN TO EXTINCTION.

There is a bird known as the vampire finch (*Geospiza difficilis septentrionalis*) – and yes, its favorite food is blood!

TRIVIA

KEENEST SMELL FOR A BIRD

Few birds have a developed sense of smell, but the black-footed albatross (*Diomedea nigripes*) can smell bacon fat poured into the ocean from at least 18 miles (30 km) away.

HEAVIEST BIRDS

The **heaviest bird of prey** is the Andean condor (*Vultur gryphus*, pictured), males of which average 20–27 lb (9–12 kg) and have a wingspan of 10 ft (3 m). The **heaviest flying bird** is the kori bustard (*Ardeotis kori*) of south and east Africa; males can reach 40 lb (18.2 kg). The **heaviest (and largest) of all birds** is the ratite male ostrich (*Struthio camelus camelus*). It can grow 9 ft (2.75 m) tall and may weigh 345 lb (156.5 kg).

NEW RECORD
★ **UPDATED RECORD**

LAZY! KORI BUSTARDS – THE HEAVIEST FLYING BIRDS – ARE RARELY SEEN IN THE AIR: THEY ARE SO HEAVY, THEY PREFER TO WALK EVERYWHERE!

BONES! ANDEAN NATIVES COLLECT THE BONES OF THE ANDEAN CONDOR – THE HEAVIEST BIRD OF PREY – BELIEVING THAT THEY HAVE HEALING POWERS.

RATITE: "Flightless." The name is from the Latin for "raft": just as a raft has no keel, these birds have no lengthwise ridge in their breast bone.

52°31'N 18°25'E

BERLIN, GERMANY

The **largest single rock concert**, in terms of participants and organization, was Roger Waters's production of Pink Floyd's *The Wall*, staged on July 21, 1990 in Potsdamer Platz, straddling East and West Berlin, Germany, when 600 people performed on stage.

★HIGHEST YOLK CONTENT

The bird eggs with the highest yolk content to egg volume are those of New Zealand's kiwis (order Apterygiformes). Some 60% of a kiwi egg's volume is taken up by yolk (compared with 31% of a hen's egg), and contains so much nutrient that the kiwi chick does not have to eat for several days after hatching.

SMALLEST NEST

The nest of the vervain hummingbird (*Mellisuga minima*) is about half the size of a walnut shell, while the deeper but narrower one of the bee hummingbird (*M. helenae*) is thimble sized.

LARGEST COMMUNAL NEST

The sociable weaver (*Philetairus socius*) of southwestern Africa builds a nest that can be up to 26 ft (8 m) long and 6 ft 6 in (2 m) high. Resembling a giant haystack that hangs from a tree or telegraph pole, it contains up to 300 individual nests. Not surprisingly, these enormous communal nests can get so heavy that the tree on which they are built sometimes collapses.

★LOWEST NESTING ALTITUDE

The little green bee-eater (*Merops orientalis*) nests at 1,312 ft (400 m) below sea level in the Dead Sea area of the Middle East. This is the lowest nesting altitude recorded for any species of bird.

★HIGHEST NESTS

The highest tree nest constructed by any bird is that of the marbled murrelet (*Brachyramphus marmoratus*), a small North Pacific member of the auk family of seabirds. Its nests have been discovered as high as 147 ft (45 m), usually on moss-covered branches of old conifer trees.

This may explain why the first formally identified nest from this species was not recorded by science until as recently as 1961, in Asia; the first North American example was not found until 1974.

★MOST BIRDSONGS RECORDED

The red-eyed vireo (*Vireo olivaceus*), a small New World species of songbird, has been recorded singing 22,197 songs in a 10-hour period, an average of over 2,000 songs per hour!

★SMALLEST EGGS

Surprisingly, bearing in mind that it lays the **largest eggs** of any bird, the bird that lays the smallest eggs relative to body weight is the ostrich (*Struthio camelus*). This is because the egg's weight is only 1.4–1.5% of the ostrich's total weight. A comparable percentage has also been recorded for the emperor penguin (*Aptenodytes forsteri*).

★SHORTEST MIGRATION

In stark contrast to the thousands of miles flown by certain migrating birds, North America's blue grouse (*Dendragapus obscurus*) descends a mere 984 ft (300 m) from its winter home in the mountainous pine forests to deciduous woodlands in order to feed upon the early crop of seeds and fresh leaves.

JINX!
BECAUSE A WRYNECK CAN TWIST ITS HEAD AND NECK THROUGH NEARLY 180°, SOME PEOPLE BELIEVED THAT WITCHES USED THE BIRD TO MAKE CURSES. THE WORD "JINX" DERIVES FROM THEIR LATIN GENUS NAME: JYNX!

★LONGEST BIRD TONGUE

Relative to body size, the longest tongue of any bird is that of the wryneck (*Jynx torquilla*), a European relative of woodpeckers. Its tongue is two-thirds of its 6.4-in (16.5-cm) body length. On a human scale, this would mean you could lick your knees without bending over!

LIVING PLANET
MAMMALS

★STRONGEST MAMMAL BITE

In tests, the Tasmanian devil (*Sarcophilus harrisii*) produced a bite force quotient (the scientific measure of the power of an animal's bite relative to its size) of 181. By comparison, the tiger's bite force quotient is 127 and the lion's a mere 112.

EXTRA!
FOR MORE ON MAMMALS, DON'T FORGET TO CHECK OUT LIFE DOWN ON THE FARM ON PP. 158-159.

★LARGEST MAMMAL FAMILY

Family Muridae, a group containing many rodents, is the largest of all mammal families. The group contains more than 600 species, including the true mice and rats, as well as the gerbils and jirds. Rodents were already widely distributed globally, but have since been introduced by man to many islands that were previously rodent-free.

TALLEST MAMMAL

Native to the dry savannah and open woodland areas of sub-Saharan Africa, a typical adult male giraffe (*Giraffa camelopardalis*) measures between 15 ft and 18 ft (4.6–5.5 m) tall. The tallest recorded giraffe was a 19-ft (5.8-m) Masai bull (*G. c. tippelskirchi*) named George, received by Chester Zoo, UK, on January 8, 1959.

SLOWEST MAMMAL

Despite its undeserved reputation, the three-toed sloth (*Bradypus tridactylus*) of tropical South America is not really a lazy creature – it is just very slow. On the ground its average speed is 6–8 ft (1.8–2.4 m) per minute (0.07–0.1 mph; 0.1–0.16 km/h), but in the trees it can accelerate to 15 ft (4.6 m) per minute (0.17 mph; 0.27 km/h)!

★SMALLEST HYRAX

Africa's hyraxes are small mammals that superficially resemble rodents but are most closely related to the African elephant (*Loxodonta africana*) – the **largest land mammal** at 8,800–15,400 lb (4–7 tonnes). Despite links to the biggest of land beasts, the yellow-spotted rock hyrax (*Heterohyrax brucei*) is no bigger than 18.5 in (47 cm) in total length – adult specimens can be as short as 12.7 in (32.5 cm) – and weighs a mere 5.29 lb (2.4 kg), at most.

By comparison, the **smallest land-dwelling mammal** is Savi's pygmy shrew (*Suncus etruscus*), an insect-eating mammal that inhabits the Mediterranean and southern Asia regions. The shrew is about the size of a human thumb, with an average body length of 1.4–2 in (36–53 mm), a tail length of 0.9–1 in (24–29 mm), and weighs just 0.05–0.09 oz (1.5–2.6 g).

★LIGHTEST EGG-LAYING MAMMAL

Of the five species of monotreme (see *Did You Know?*), the platypus (*Ornithorhynchus anatinus*) of mainland Australia and Tasmania is the lightest. Male platypuses typically weigh 2.2–5.2 lb (1.0–2.4 kg) while females weigh just 1.5–3.5 lb (0.7–1.6 kg).

★FASTEST-PANTING WILD DOG

The big-eared fennec fox (*Fennecus zerda*) has a novel way of cooling down in its Saharan home. When the temperature reaches 100°F (38°C), it loses heat by panting at a rapid rate of 690 breaths per minute!

★HUNGRIEST BEAR

The giant panda (*Ailuropoda melanoleuca*) can only digest around 21% of all the bamboo that it consumes. Consequently, it must eat up to 38% of its own weight in bamboo shoots each day.

★ NEW RECORD
★ UPDATED RECORD

DID YOU KNOW?

MOST MAMMALS GIVE BIRTH TO LIVE YOUNG – EXCEPT FOR THE EGG-LAYING MONOTREMES: THE DUCK-BILLED PLATYPUS AND THE LONG- AND SHORT-NOSED ECHIDNAS.

Giant pandas do not hibernate and have to eat all year round because of their inefficient diet.

TRIVIA

★ LONGEST-LIVED RODENT

The naked mole rat (*Heterocephalus glaber*) is a bizarre-looking mammal that spends its life in underground burrow systems beneath East Africa's drier tropical grasslands. An extremely social creature, mole rats reside in colonies and can live for up to 28 years.

However, Sarah's speed has no staying power compared with that of a pronghorn (*Antilocapra americana*). Native to western North America, pronghorns have been recorded traveling continuously at 35 mph (56 km/h) for as far as 4 miles (6 km), giving them the title of the **fastest land mammal over long distances**.

Finally, the **fastest marine mammal** is the bull killer whale (*Orcinus orca*). On October 12, 1958, one specimen was recorded traveling at 34.5 mph (55.5 km/h) in the northeastern Pacific.

★ LARGEST MAMMAL GENOME

An animal's genome is the map of all of its genetic information and is found in the nucleus of every cell in its body. The red vizcacha rat (*Tympanoctomys barrerae*) has a genome containing 16.8 picograms (1 picogram = 1 trillionth of a gram) of DNA. Most other mammals have a genome containing only 6–8 picograms. The red vizcacha also has the ★**most chromosomes of any mammal** with a total of 102 chromosomes, split into 51 pairs. By comparison, humans have only 46 chromosomes, divided into 23 pairs.

FASTEST

When measured over a short distance, the cheetah (*Acinonyx jubatus*) can maintain a steady maximum speed of approximately 62 mph (100 km/h) on level ground, making it the **fastest land mammal over short distances**.

A prime example of a speedy cheetah is Sarah, an eight-year-old that ran 328 ft (100 m) in 6.13 seconds at Cincinnati Zoo, Ohio, USA, on September 10, 2009, giving her the record for the ★**fastest 100 m by a land mammal**, trouncing Usain Bolt's (Jamaica) 100 m time of 9.59 seconds (see p.268).

★ BONIEST MAMMAL TAIL

The long-tailed pangolin (*Manis tetradactylus*) has up to 47 vertebrae in its tail – more than any other mammal. All eight species of pangolin, or scaly anteater, have impressive spines and claws that are composed of keratin, the same substance as human fingernails.

★ LONGEST WHALE TOOTH

The ivory tusk of the male narwhal (*Monodon monoceros*) grows to an average length of roughly 6 ft 6 in (2 m) but can exceed 9 ft 10 in (3 m) and weigh up to 22 lb (10 kg). In past centuries, the single (or, very rarely, paired) spiraled tusks were sometimes thought to be unicorn horns when found washed up on the beach.

BIG!
THE LARGEST MAMMAL IS THE BLUE WHALE (*BALAENOPTERA MUSCULUS*), WITH AN AVERAGE LENGTH OF 80 FT (24 M)!

SMALL!
THE SMALLEST MAMMAL IS THE BUMBLEBEE BAT (*CRASEONYCTERIS THONGLONGYAI*), WITH A HEAD-BODY LENGTH OF ONLY 1.14–1.29 IN (29–33 MM).

LIVING PLANET
PLANT LIFE

★ ★ ★ ★ ★ ★ ★ ★ ★ ★ ★ ★ ★ ★

"[The corpse flower] smells like a dead person... I happen to be a nurse and that is exactly what it smells like."

A visitor to Huntington Botanical Gardens, San Marino, California, USA, tells it like it is

EXTRA! FOR THE FASTEST TIME TO EAT VARIOUS FRUIT, VEGETABLES AND OTHER FOODSTUFFS, CHECK OUT THE CHOMP-IONS ON P.140.

★ RAREST FLAX PLANT

Flax is a fibrous plant that has long been used to make fabric. The rarest species of flax plant is the Floreana flax (*Linum cratericola*), native to the Galápagos Islands. Only discovered by science in the 1960s, then feared extinct from 1981 until rediscovered in 1997, this small subshrub is presently limited to three small groups on Floreana Island. Here it is threatened with extinction by feral goats, invasive plants, and periods of dry weather.

SMALLEST PLANT KINGDOM

Of the six biogeographical plant zones – Boreal, Neotropical, Paleotropical, South African, Australian, and Antarctic – the South African is the smallest.

★ MOST CHROMOSOMES IN A PLANT

All living organisms contain chromosomes -- the part of a cell that contains all the genetic information that determines what characteristics the organism will possess. While humans have 46 chromosomes in 23 pairs, many other organisms have far more. The adder's tongue fern (*Ophioglossum reticulatum*) is reported to have 1,440 chromosomes arranged into 720 pairs, making it the record holder for both the greatest number of chromosomes in a plant and the ★ **most chromosomes in an organism**.

MOST SELECTIVE CARNIVOROUS PLANT

Nepenthes albomarginata is a carnivorous plant that grows in Malaysia and Indonesia and feeds only on *Hospitalitermes bicolor* termites. The termites are attracted to edible hairs, called trichomes, on the plant, but sometimes slip down the plant's "throat" and are digested by liquids at the bottom of the flower.

HIGHEST CONCENTRATION OF ENDANGERED PLANT SPECIES

South Africa's Cape Flats hosts 15 species per square kilometre that are threatened by extinction.

★ RAREST WILLOW

Deciduous willows are a common tree throughout the northern hemisphere. However, one species, the Tarragonès willow (*Salix tarraconensis*) is considered critically endangered and is known only from a few dispersed populations of 10–40 specimens located between Castellón and Tarragona in Spain.

★ OLDEST YEW

The world's oldest yew tree is a specimen of common yew (*Taxus baccata*) that grows in the churchyard of St Digain's parish church, in Llangernyw, North Wales, UK. It is estimated to be 4,000 years old.

HIGHEST CONCENTRATION OF HEATHERS

The fynbos (Afrikaans for "fine bush") plant ecosystem, exclusive to South Africa's Cape floristic region, contains more than 600 species of heather (genus *Erica*). Only 26 species of heather occur in the rest of the world.

★ RAREST ONION

The rarest member of the onion genus *Allium* is *Allium rouyi*, a Spanish species with fewer than 300 known specimens fragmented among five subpopulations confined within a very small area of Bética province in Andalusia, Spain.

MOST TOXIC PLANT

Based on the amount it takes to kill a human, the most toxic common plant in the world is the castor bean (*Ricinus communis*). The toxin – ricin – causes the clumping and breakdown of red blood cells and internal bleeding. It is 6,000 times more toxic than cyanide and 12,000 times more toxic than rattlesnake venom.

SMELLIEST PLANT

Native to the Sumatran rainforests, the "corpse flower," or titan arum, *Amorphophallus titanum*, is believed to be the smelliest plant on Earth. When it blooms, it releases a foul odor similar to that of rotting flesh to attract flies to aid in its pollination. The stench can be smelled up to half a mile (0.8 km) away.

ONION:
Comes from the Latin *unionem*, which literally means "unity," and describes the many layers of an onion's skin.

In 1978, Bulgarian Georgi Markov was assassinated in London, UK, by a ricin-coated umbrella tip that was jabbed into his leg.

★ RAREST CLUB MOSS
Club mosses are a primitive form of plant endemic to wet forests and cliffside shrublands. The wawae'iole (*Huperzia nutans*) is the rarest variety and grows only on Koolau Mountain on Oahu in Hawaii, USA.

★ OLDEST CYPRESS
A cypress tree (*Cupressus sempervirens*) known as Sarv-e-Abarkooh, or Zoroastrian Sarv, is a tourist attraction in Abarkooh, Yazd, Iran. It is estimated to be more than 4,000 years old and is a national monument.

FASTEST ENTRAPMENT BY A PLANT
Carnivorous plants trap their prey in movements considered to be among the fastest in the entire plant kingdom. On land, the clamshell-like leaves of the Venus flytrap (*Dionaea muscipula*) shut in one-tenth of a second (100 milliseconds) from the moment they are stimulated. Underwater, the hinged trapdoor of the bladderwort (*Utricularia vulgaris*) captures its victim in 1/15,000th of a second.

★ LARGEST SEED COLLECTION
The Millennium Seed Bank Project, housed at the Wellcome Trust Millennium Building, Wakehurst Place, West Sussex, UK, had 24,200 species collected as of March 20, 2010.

SMALLEST ORCHID
The platystele (*Platystele jungermannioides*) found in the lower cloud forest of Mexico, Guatemala, Costa Rica, and Panama at an elevation of 656–3,280 ft (200–1,000 m) grows around 0.25 in (6.3 mm) high and 0.78 in (20 mm) wide. This smallest of orchid species blooms in the spring with just two or three tiny flowers that are a mere 0.09 in (2.5 mm) wide. With roughly 25,000 species, the orchid family is also the second largest flowering plant family behind the Compositae family of daisies, the ★ **largest family of flowering plants**, with more than 26,000 species.

MOST VISITED GARDEN (PAYING VISITORS)
The Royal Botanic Gardens, Kew, Surrey, UK, has an average of 1 million paying visitors per year. The 326-acre (132-ha) site has 40 historically important buildings and collections of more than 40,000 species of plants. Kew Gardens became a United Nations World Heritage site on July 3, 2003.

★ TALLEST HARDWOOD TREE
A specimen of Australian swamp gum tree (*Eucalyptus regnans*) known as "Centurion" stands 331.36 ft (101 m) tall and has a diameter of 13.12 ft (4 m). It is located just 49 miles (80 km) from Tasmania's capital, Hobart.

★ NEW RECORD
★ UPDATED RECORD

FAST!
SOME SPECIES OF BAMBOO GROW AT A RATE OF UP TO 35 IN (91 CM) PER DAY, OR 0.00002 MPH (0.00003 KM/H). THIS MAKES THEM THE FASTEST-GROWING PLANTS.

SLOW!
THE SLOWEST-GROWING TREE IS THE WHITE CEDAR (*THUJA OCCIDENTALIS*). IT TOOK 155 YEARS FOR ONE TREE TO REACH A HEIGHT OF JUST 4 IN

LIVING PLANET
AMERICAN WILDLIFE

FASTEST-RUNNING FLYING BIRD

Native to the southwestern USA, the North American roadrunner (*Geococcyx californianus*) has been clocked at 26 mph (42 km/h) when pursued by an automobile.

LARGEST STRUCTURE BUILT BY A LAND ANIMAL

Found throughout the USA and Canada, the North American beaver (*Castor canadensis*) uses mud, wood, and stones to dam up streams, ensuring a plentiful supply of fish, and then builds a lodge within its dam for winter refuge. The largest lodge ever recorded was 40 ft (12.1 m) across and 16 ft (4.8 m) high.

SMELLIEST ANIMAL

The striped skunk (*Mephitis mephitis*), a member of the mustelid family found throughout the USA, ejects a truly foul smelling liquid from its anal glands if threatened. This defensive secretion contains seven major volatile and stench-filled components. Two of these substances, both sulfur-containing thiols, are responsible for the secretion's strongly repellent odor, and are known respectively as (E)-2-butene-1-thiol and 3-methyl-1-butanethiol. They are so potent that they can be detected by humans at a concentration of 10 parts per billion – a low dilution that is equivalent to a teaspoonful in an Olympic-sized swimming pool of water!

FASTEST EATER

According to research published in February 2005 by Dr Kenneth Catania at Vanderbilt University, Tennessee, USA, the star-nosed mole (*Condylura cristata*) handles its food for an average of 230 milliseconds before eating it. The fastest recorded handling time in the study was 120 milliseconds.

MOST RESTRICTED AMPHIBIAN DISTRIBUTION

The Peaks of Otter salamander (*Plethodon hubrichti*) is confined to an 11.8-mile-long (19-km) expanse in the Blue Mountains of Virginia, USA – the most limited range for any species of amphibian.

LARGEST MAMMAL COLONY

A black-tailed prairie dog (*Cynomys ludovicianus*) colony found in 1901 contained 400 million individuals and covered an estimated 23,705 miles² (61,400 km²).

LEWIS
MERIWETHER LEWIS AND WILLIAM CLARK'S TRANSCONTINENTAL EXPEDITION ACROSS NORTH AMERICA IS REPORTED TO HAVE DESCRIBED OVER 100 SPECIES.

CLARK
THE EXPEDITION ALSO DISCOVERED THE BLACK-TAILED PRAIRIE DOG AND SHIPPED A LIVE SPECIMEN FROM NORTH DAKOTA TO WASHINGTON, DC, TO PRESIDENT JEFFERSON.

MAMMAL WITH THE MOST NAMES

With a range that extends from the Yukon in Canada to the southern Andes of South America and includes the entire continental USA, the puma (*Puma concolor*) has more than 40 common names in English, including "cougar," "mountain lion," "catamount," and "Florida panther."

EXTRA! FOR MORE GREAT AMERICAN RECORDS GO GET YOUR KICKS ON ROUTE 66 (PP.148–149).

LONGEST TERRESTRIAL MIGRATION

Grant's caribou (*Rangifer tarandus granti*), aka the porcupine caribou, lives in western Alaska and the Yukon Territory of Canada and travels up to 2,982 miles (4,800 km) during its regular migration to more sheltered wintering grounds.

COUGAR: A term thought to come ultimately from "susuarana" ("false deer") from the Tupi people of Brazil.

SMALLEST BEE

A bee that nests in the sandy soil of southwestern USA, *Perdita minima* is just under 0.07 in (2 mm) long and weighs just 0.333 mg.

ANIMAL MOST LIKELY TO PROCREATE QUADRUPLETS

Native to the southeastern states from Arizona to Florida, USA, the nine-banded armadillo (*Dasypus novemcinctus*) is a close relative of the anteater and is the only mammal known to bear identical quadruplets regularly. All four, all of the same sex, develop from the same egg and share one placenta in the womb.

★LARGEST PIECE OF NATURAL SPIDER SILK

On September 25, 2009, an 11 x 4 ft (3.3 x 1.2 m) piece of cloth made from natural spider silk was put on display at the American Museum of Natural History in New York, USA. A team of 70 people spent four years collecting golden orb spiders from telephone poles in Madagascar (although their natural range includes the southeastern USA, from North Carolina to Texas). A second team of 12 removed up to 80 ft (24 m) of silk filament from each spider. To create 1 oz (28 g) of silk, 14,000 spiders must be "milked" – the equivalent of 50,000 spiders for 2.2 lb (1 kg) of silk.

MOST DANGEROUS AMERICAN LIZARD

The Gila monster (*Heloderma suspectum*) is a large lizard that can measure up to 2 ft (60 cm) and inhabits Mexico and the southwestern USA from California to Arizona. Its main claim to fame are the venom glands in its jaw that carry enough venom to kill two adult humans. The venom is not injected, but seeps into the wound the reptile causes when it bites and chews its victims with its sharp fragile teeth. In a study of 34 people bitten by these animals, there were eight recorded fatalities. Fortunately, the lizard, like the similarly venomous Mexican beaded lizard (*Heloderma horridum*) and the Komodo dragon (*Varanus komodoensis*, see p.60) only attacks when provoked.

LARGEST FLEA

The largest known flea species is *Hystrichopsylla schefferi*, which was described from a single specimen taken from the nest of a mountain beaver (*Aplodontia rufa*) at Puyallup, Washington, USA, in 1913. Females measure up to 0.3 in (8 mm) long – roughly the diameter of a pencil.

★ **NEW RECORD**
★ **UPDATED RECORD**

TRIVIA

LARGEST DEER

When it comes to deer, the biggest beast is the Alaskan moose (*Alces alces gigas*). A bull standing 7 ft 8 in (2.34 m) and weighing an estimated 1,800 lb (816 kg) was shot in the Yukon Territory, Canada, in September 1897.

MOOSE
THE AMERICAN MOOSE IS A SUBSPECIES OF THE EURASIAN ELK (*ALCES ALCES*). CONFUSINGLY, THE WORD "ELK" IS ALSO USED TO REFER TO THE (*CERVUS CANADENSIS*) DEER SPECIES.

HUMAN BEINGS

★ ★ ★ ★ ★ ★ ★ ★ ★ ★ ★ ★ ★ ★

LABRET: A piercing or adornment of the lip, and in particular the lower lip. Ornaments range from simple studs to enormous clay plates.

HOOK!
BEFORE BECOMING THE MOST PIERCED MAN, JOHN LYNCH WAS A BANK MANAGER. AFTER QUITTING HIS JOB, HE BECAME HOOKED ON PIERCINGS AND TATTOOS.

COOK!
ELAINE DAVIDSON RAN A BRAZIL-THEMED CAFE/RESTAURANT IN EDINBURGH, SCOTLAND, UK, BEFORE BECOMING A FULL-TIME HUMAN PINBOARD!

{ *"People often just want to look at me or touch me. Some even want to kiss me."*
**Elaine Davidson,
most pierced woman** }

MOST PIERCED PEOPLE

Since having her first piercing in January 1997, Elaine Davidson (UK) has had 4,225 pieces of metal attached to, and inside, her body. Elaine is the world's **most pierced person**. Her male equivalent is John Lynch (UK, aka Prince Albert), who had, at the last count, 241 piercings, including 151 in his head and neck.

CONTENTS

CAPE TOWN, SOUTH AFRICA

33°55'S
18°25'E

The **first heart transplant operation** was performed on Louis Washkansky (South Africa) at the Groote Schuur Hospital, Cape Town, South Africa, on December 3, 1967, by a team of 30 headed by Prof. Christiaan Neethling Barnard (South Africa).

FEATURE
TALLEST MAN

EXTRA!
FOR MORE TALL TALES AND SHORT STORIES, TURN TO P.76.

SULTAN AND THE METS

Of all the places Sultan Kösen (Turkey) visited, nowhere made as big an impression on him as New York City. It was the size of the buildings that impressed him the most – he had never seen so many skyscrapers before!

MADRID

LONDON

TALL TOUR 2009

Sultan once lived a quiet life on a farm in the Mardin region of Turkey. Now, he's an international jet-setter! Here he is making a big impression in London, UK (right), Madrid, Spain (above right), and Milan, Italy (left). He also traveled to Reykjavik, Iceland, where he enjoyed a spa bath, and Vienna, Austria, where he became a media star!

MILAN

HIGH HOPES

So what are the newly famous gentle giant's dreams for the future? "I want what everyone else wants," says Sultan. "A wife, a family, a nice home. I'd also like the chance to find some decent clothes that fit! I've already had a suit made for me, and at least one dream has come true: I now own a pair of jeans made specially for me!"

TALLEST LIVING MAN

At 8 ft 1 in (246.5 cm), Sultan is the world's **tallest living man** and **tallest living human being**. Indeed, he is the tallest person in history to be officially ratified as over 8 ft by Guinness World Records.

Sultan was first measured by GWR's Editor-in-Chief, Craig Glenday, in Ankara, Turkey, on February 11, 2009. "To avoid any controversy, I had to measure him myself," said Craig. "It's the only way to be totally sure of a claimant's height. There is too much at stake to leave it to anyone other than a GWR representative."

One of the most difficult aspects of being so tall, says Sultan, is finding clothes and shoes to fit. His 1-ft 2-in-long (36.5-cm) feet – the **largest feet on a living person** – require extra-large shoes (inset, compared with a US size-9.5 sneaker), which are expensive to make.

Sultan also holds the record for the ★ **largest hands on a living person**, measuring 10.83 in (27.5 cm) from the wrist to the tip of the middle finger.

TALL
SULTAN IS PICTURED HERE WITH NYC COP THE TURKISH TITAN TOWERS ONE-THIRD TALLER THAN THE AVERAGE HUMAN MALE!

TALES
SULTAN DIDN'T START HIS INCREDIBLE GROWTH SPURT UNTIL HE WAS 10 YEARS OLD. HE ONLY STOPPED GROWING IN 2007, AGED 24!

HUMAN BEINGS
BODY PARTS

★ WIDEST TONGUE

Here's a record that will take some lickin'! The tongue of Jay Sloot (Australia) was measured to be 3.1 in (7.9 cm) at its widest point on the set of *Lo Show dei Record* in Rome, Italy, on March 18, 2010.

ACTUAL SIZE

LONGEST TONGUE

Jay might have the edge in width, but when it comes to length, Stephen Taylor (UK) is the tongue champ. Stephen's tongue was 3.86 in (9.8 cm) from its tip to the middle of his closed top lip when it was measured at the Westwood Medical Centre, Coventry, UK, on February 11, 2009.

★ LONGEST TOOTH REMOVED

Loo Hui Jing (Singapore) had a tooth measuring 1.26 in (3.2 cm) extracted by Dr Ng Lay Choo at the Eli Dental Surgery, Singapore, on April 6, 2009.

ACTUAL SIZE

★ MOST ELASTIC MOUTH

The lips (oral labia) and cheeks (buccal cavity) of Francisco Domingo Joaquim "Chiquinho" (Angola), at full stretch, measured 6.69 in (17 cm) wide on March 18, 2010. Incredibly, he does not have the widest gape (see p.75). Chiquinho suffers from a connective tissues disorder.

★ MOST TEETH IN THE MOUTH

The record for the most teeth in the mouth belongs to Kanchan Rajawat (India) and Luca Meriano (Italy), both of whom had 35 adult teeth as of October 17, 2008.

★ SMALLEST TOOTH EXTRACTED

A primary tooth extracted from Colton Laub (USA) on October 30, 2002 by Dr Scott Harden at Fountain View Family Dentistry, Acworth, Georgia, USA, measured 0.1 in (3 mm).

LONGEST MILK TOOTH

Ahmed Afrah Ismail (Maldives) had a milk tooth measuring 0.9 in (2.3 cm). The tooth was measured in Male, Republic of Maldives, on December 28, 2000.

LONGEST TOENAILS

Since 1982, Louise Hollis (USA) has been growing her toenails to exceedingly great lengths. When measured at their longest in 1991, the combined length of all 10 toenails was 87 in (221 cm).

AHH! LOUISE WAS INSPIRED TO GROW HER TOENAILS IN 1982, AFTER SEEING A TV PROGRAM FEATURING THE LONGEST FINGERNAILS.

AHH! CHIQUINHO'S MALLEABLE MOUTH IS SO BIG THAT IT CAN COMFORTABLY ACCOMMODATE A WHOLE DRINKS CAN!

"I'd seen a video of him on the internet, but nothing compares to the experience of measuring him in real life."
Vice President of Records Marco Frigatti on meeting Chiquinho

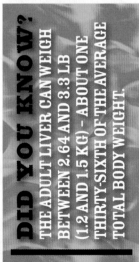

★ LONGEST FINGERNAILS

We were saddened in December 2009 to learn of the passing of Melvin Boothe (USA). Melvin first contacted us about his fantastic fingernails in 2006, and when last measured on May 30, 2009 at his home in Troy, Michigan, USA, they had a combined length of 32 ft 3.8 in (9.85 m).

EXTRA! FOR MORE MEDICAL RECORDS, GO TO PP.84–85.

NARROWEST WAIST

Cathie Jung (USA) is 5 ft 8 in (1.73 m) tall but her waist is much smaller than you might expect – just 21 in (53.34 cm). And that figure narrows to just 15 in (38.1 cm) when she is wearing a corset, which pulls in the lower ribs. Cathie developed her tiny waist as part of her enthusiasm for Victorian clothing. Look at pictures of ladies in the Victorian era, when corsets were normal attire, and see how narrow their waists and ribcages were!

★ NEW RECORD
★ UPDATED RECORD

LONGEST LEGS (FEMALE)

Svetlana Pankratova's (Russia) legs measured 51.9 in (132 cm) long in Torremolinos, Spain, on July 8, 2003. Her unique gift presents certain challenges -- she has to have some clothes specially made, she ducks through doorways, and needs lots of legroom when traveling in automobiles and planes.

LARGEST FEET EVER

Robert Wadlow (USA) wore US size 37 AA shoes (UK 36; approx. European 75), equivalent to 18.5 in (47 cm) long. To say thanks to the International Shoe Company (USA), who provided his $100 shoes for free, Wadlow visited an estimated 800 US cities on a goodwill promotional tour.

LARGEST HANDS

Robert Wadlow (USA), the **tallest man ever** (see pp.76--77 to discover the heights he reached), had hands that measured 12.75 in (32.3 cm) from the wrist to the tip of his middle finger. He wore a size 25 ring.

LONGEST FINGERNAILS ON A SINGLE HAND

The aggregate measurement of the five nails on the left hand of Shridhar Chillal (India, b. August 18, 1937) was 23 ft 1.5 in (705 cm) on February 4, 2004. His thumb measured 62.2 in (158 cm), his index finger 51.5 in (131 cm), his middle finger 54.3 in (138 cm), his ring finger 55.1 in (140 cm), and his little finger 54.3 in (138 cm). Chillal last cut his fingernails in 1952.

LONGEST FINGERNAILS EVER (FEMALE)

Lee Redmond (USA) started to grow her fingernails in 1979 and, over the years, she carefully manicured them to reach a total length of 28 ft 4.5 in (8.65 m), as measured on the set of *Lo Show dei Record* in Madrid, Spain, on February 23, 2008. Sadly, Lee lost her nails in a motor vehicle accident in early 2009, but since that time no one has beaten her all-time record.

FEWEST TOES

The two-toed ("ostrich-foot") syndrome exhibited by some members of the Wadomo tribe of the Zambezi Valley in Zimbabwe, and the Kalanga tribe of the eastern Kalahari Desert in Botswana, is hereditary via a single mutated gene.

LARGEST GAPE

J J Bittner (USA) is able to open his mouth to a gap of 3.4 in (8.4 cm). His gape was measured from the incisal edge of his maxillary central incisors to the incisal edge of his mandibular central incisors – that is, between the tips of the front teeth in his upper and lower jaws.

DID YOU KNOW?

THE ADULT LIVER CAN WEIGH BETWEEN 2.64 AND 3.3 LB (1.2 AND 1.5 KG) – ABOUT ONE THIRTY-SIXTH OF THE AVERAGE TOTAL BODY WEIGHT.

The liver is the **largest gland**, and the **largest solid organ**, in the body.

TRIVIA

LONGEST NOSE ON A LIVING PERSON

The nose of Mehmet Ozyurek (Turkey) was measured at 3.46 in (8.8 cm) long from bridge to tip on the set of *Lo Show dei Record* in Rome, Italy, on March 18, 2010.

CHOO! IT IS CLAIMED THAT THOMAS WEDDERS, WHO LIVED IN ENGLAND IN THE 1770s, HAD A RECORD-BREAKING NOSE THAT WAS 7.5 IN (19 CM) LONG.

HUMAN BEINGS
SIZE

★ SHORTEST TEENAGERS

Jyoti Amge (India, b. December 16, 1993) measured 2 ft (61.95 cm) on September 6, 2009 in Tokyo, Japan. The **shortest male teenager** is Khagendra Thapa Magar (Nepal, b. October 14, 1992), who measured 2 ft 1.8 in (65.58 cm) on February 25, 2010, when measured by doctors.

SHORTEST MAN

Ever: The shortest mature human of whom there is independent evidence was Gul Mohammed (India, 1957–97). On July 19, 1990, he was examined at Ram Manohar Hospital, New Delhi, India, and found to have grown to a height of 22.5 in (57 cm).

Living: Lin Yih-Chih (Taiwan), who is wheelchair-bound owing to the condition osteogenesis imperfecta, measures 27 in (67.5 cm).

Living (mobile): *See p.77.*

SHORTEST WOMAN

Ever: Pauline Musters (Netherlands, 1876–95) measured 12 in (30 cm) at birth and 21.5 in (55 cm) tall at the age of nine. When she died of pneumonia with meningitis in New York City, USA, on March 1, 1895 at the age of 19, she had reached a height of 2 ft (61 cm).

Living: Madge Bester (South Africa) measures 2 ft 1.5 in (65 cm) tall. A sufferer of the skeletal disorder type III osteogenesis imperfecta, she has extremely brittle bones and is confined to a wheelchair in a home in Bloemfontein, South Africa. Her mother, Winnie (d. 2001), also a sufferer, measured 2 ft 3.5 in (70 cm).

Living (mobile): This category remains unfilled as of May 10, 2010.

★ HEAVIEST LIVING MAN

At his last weigh-in (December 2009), Mexico's Manuel Uribe registered 918 lb (416.5 kg; 65.5 st) – a reversal of fortune for the dieting 43-year-old, who had been experiencing regular weight loss since peaking at 1,235 lb (560 kg; 88 st) in 2006. Despite being bed-bound, Uribe married his second wife Claudia Solis (above right) in 2008.

LIGHTEST PERSON

Lucia Xarate (Mexico, 1863–89) of San Carlos, Mexico, an emaciated ateleiotic dwarf of 26.8 in (67 cm), weighed 2.8 lb (1.1 kg) at birth and only 4 lb 11 oz (2.13 kg) at the age of 17. She fattened up to 13 lb (5.9 kg) by her 20th birthday.

CERTIFICATE

A Guinness World Record was achieved on the set of *Lo Show Dei Record* in Rome, Italy in 2010

GUINNESS WORLD RECORDS LTD

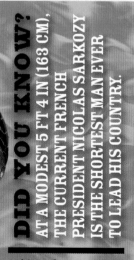

DID YOU KNOW? AT A MODEST 5 FT 4 IN (163 CM), THE CURRENT FRENCH PRESIDENT NICOLAS SARKOZY IS THE SHORTEST MAN EVER TO LEAD HIS COUNTRY.

At his peak, Tonga's King Taufa'ahau Tupou IV was the world's heaviest ruler, at 462 lb (209.5 kg).

TRIVIA

★SHORTEST LIVING MOTHER

Stacey Herald (USA), who stands 2 ft 4.5 in (72.39 cm) tall, gave birth to her first child, Kateri, in Dry Ridge, Kentucky, USA, on October 21, 2006. Her second baby girl, Makaya, was born on January 1, 2008. Stacey is pictured here with her husband, Will, and their two girls. Her third child, a boy named Malachi, was born in November 2009.

★HEAVIEST LIVING WOMAN TO GIVE BIRTH

Donna Simpson of New Jersey, USA, weighed 532 lb (241 kg; 38 st) when she delivered daughter Jacqueline in February 2007. It took a team of up to 30 medics to help perform the high-risk cesarean birth. "I want this record made public to remind women of size that they too may be able to bear a child," said Donna.

TALLEST MAN

Ever: When Robert Pershing Wadlow (USA, 1918–40) was last measured – on June 27, 1940 – he was 8 ft 11.1 in (2.72 m) tall, the tallest height ever authenticated in medical history.
Living: *See pp.72–73.*

TALLEST WOMAN

Ever: Zeng Jinlian (China, 1964–82) of the Bright Moon Commune, Hunan province, China, measured 8 ft 1.75 in (2.48 m) on her deathbed.
Living: ★Yao Defen (China) recorded an average height of 7 ft 7 in (233.3 cm) when last documented. Evidence suggests that Defen may still be growing as a portion of tumor remains on her pituitary gland, the organ that regulates the production of growth hormone. She is too ill to be remeasured at present.

HEAVIEST TWINS

Billy Leon (1946–79) and Benny Loyd (1946–2001) McCrary, alias McGuire (both USA), were of average size until the age of six. By November 1978, however, Billy and Benny weighed 743 lb (53 st 1 lb; 337 kg) and 723 lb (51 st 9 lb; 328 kg) respectively, and each had waists measuring 84 in (2.13 m).

MOST VARIABLE STATURE

Adam Rainer (Austria, 1899–1950) measured just 3 ft 10.5 in (1.18 m) at the age of 21 but then started growing at a rapid rate. By 1931, he had nearly doubled to 7 ft 1.75 in (2.18 m), but became so weak that he was bedridden for the rest of his life. At the time of his death, he measured 7 ft 8 in (2.34 m) – twice his height at 21. He remains the only person in history to have been both a dwarf and a giant.

SHORTEST MAN

Following the death of He Pingping (China) in 2010, the title of shortest mobile man passed to Edward Niño Hernandez (Colombia, b. May 10, 1986), who measures 2 ft 3.46 in (70.21 cm) tall.

Edward's reign as holder of this famous category may be one of the briefest in GWR history, however. It is expected that Khagendra Thapa Magar (*see Shortest teenagers, p.76*) will assume the title of the world's shortest man in October 2010, upon turning 18.

WEIGH!
ROSALIE BRADFORD (USA, 1943–2006) – THE HEAVIEST WOMAN EVER – PEAKED AT 1,200 LB (85 ST; 544 KG) IN JANUARY 1987.

NO WEIGH!
DOCTORS UNABLE TO WEIGH THE HEAVIEST MAN EVER – JON BROWER MINNOCH (USA, 1941–83) – ESTIMATED HIM TO BE 1,400 LB (100 ST; 635 KG) AT HIS PEAK.

HUMAN BEINGS

SKIN DEEP

EXTRA!
IF YOU'RE A SUCKER FOR SIDESHOW ARTS, DON'T HANG AROUND – TURN TO P.96.

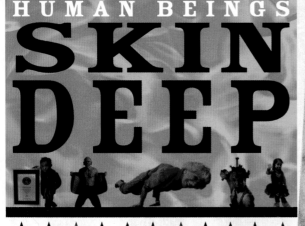

★ ★ ★ ★ ★ ★ ★ ★ ★ ★ ★ ★ ★ ★

★MOST NEEDLES IN THE HEAD

Wei Shengchu (China) had 2,009 needles inserted into his head on the set of *Lo Show dei Record* in Milan, Italy, on April 11, 2009.

LARGEST ORGAN

An organ is defined loosely as any part of an animal or plant that is adapted for a particular function – for example, respiration, digestion or excretion. When it comes to the human body, the skin is the largest organ. It provides a protective covering for the body, insulates us from the cold, regulates our temperature, and protects us from infection.

★FARTHEST DISTANCE TO PULL A VEHICLE USING MEAT HOOKS

Hannibal Helmurto (Germany) pulled an 8,818-lb (4-tonne) van a total of 351 ft (107 m) using two meat hooks inserted through the skin in the small of his back in Edinburgh, UK, on August 13, 2007.

MOST BODY PIERCINGS IN ONE SESSION

Josh Brown and Yuri Dubon (both USA) carried out 1,200 piercings in one session lasting 2 hr 53 min at the Sign of the Times, Norco, California, USA, on August 16, 2009.

MOST TATTOOED SENIOR CITIZENS

The **most tattooed female senior citizen** is 73-year-old grandmother Isobel Varley (UK). Isobel had her first tattoo – a small bird on her right shoulderblade – on August 14, 1986 after a visit to a tattoo convention in Hammersmith, London, UK. As of April 2010, she had a 93% body coverage.

The ★**most tattooed male senior citizen** is Tom Leppard (UK) – see opposite.

★MOST PEOPLE TATTOOED SIMULTANEOUSLY

A total of 178 people were tattooed at the same time at the 5th annual London Tattoo Convention 2009, held at the Tobacco Dock in London, UK, on September 24, 2009.

★MOST TATTOOED WOMAN

Julia Gnuse (USA, below) has had approximately 95% of her body decorated with tattoos; her first tattoo was in 1991. She shares her ink-redible record with Krystyne Kolorful (Canada), who has taken 10 years to achieve 95% coverage.

★ MOST TATTOOED SENIOR CITIZEN

Former **most tattooed man** Tom Leppard (aka Tom Woodbridge, UK), has 99.9% of his body covered in a saffron-yellow and black leopard-print tattoo. The 73-year-old ex-soldier lived for 20 years in the wilds of the island of Skye in the Scottish Hebrides before finally changing his spots and moving into an assisted living facility in the Skye village of Broadford in 2008.

The skin (the **largest organ**) protects us against infection, and helps us to retain moisture and regulate body temperature.

TRIVIA

★ LONGEST TATTOO SESSION

Andy Kynes (UK) underwent a grueling 48-hr 11-min tattoo session under the needle of Lady Kaz Wilson (UK) at the Diamond Tattoo Studio in Wigan, Lancashire, UK, on November 18–21, 2009. The event was organized to raise money for UK charity Children in Need.

★ MOST TATTOOS BY A SINGLE ARTIST (24 HOURS)

Hollis Cantrell (USA) created 801 tattoos in 24 hours at Artistic Tattoo in Phoenix, Arizona, USA, on November 16, 2008.

STRETCHIEST SKIN

Garry Turner (UK) is able to stretch the skin of his stomach to a length of 6.25 in (15.8 cm) thanks to a rare medical condition named Ehlers-Danlos Syndrome, a disorder of the connective tissues affecting the skin, ligaments, and internal organs. With this condition, the collagen that strengthens the skin and determines its elasticity becomes defective, resulting in, among other things, a loosening of the skin, and "hypermobility" of the joints. In more serious cases, it can cause the rupturing of blood vessels.

ATHLETE'S FOOT:

AKA Tinea pedis — a contagious fungal infection of the skin that afflicts most men between the ages of 20 and 40.

METAL TEETH

Gone are Lucky's original teeth and in their place are silver fangs.

WHITE INK

Lucky has started inking white tattoos on top of the black.

OUCH! LUCKY IS TATTOOED ON THE EYELIDS, THE DELICATE SKIN BETWEEN THE TOES, AND DOWN INTO THE EARS. HE EVEN HAS HIS GUMS TATTOOED!

COLORED INK

Inked in red across his face and scalp is the Tibetan mantra "Om Mani Padme Hum," usually translated as "Praise to the Jewel in the Lotus."

SCALP

Lucky has gouged out three strips of skin from his scalp, revealing the skull beneath!

STRETCHED EARLOBES

Lucky's ears are not just pierced, they're stretched and fitted with a spacer or "flesh tunnel."

BLACK INK

An all-over "body suit" of black ink.

CHEST IMPLANTS

Through his pectoral muscles, Lucky has placed two titanium rods; these will eventually be removed, creating a hollow through which he can attach weights and hooks.

FIRST PLASTIC SURGERY

Walter Ernest O'Neil Yeo (UK, 1890–1960) was the first person in the world to have plastic surgery. In 1917, skin grafts were transferred from his shoulder to his face in order to replace his upper and lower eyelids. The gunnery warrant officer had lost them while manning the guns aboard HMS *Warspite* in 1916, in the Battle of Jutland, during World War I. The pioneering surgery was performed by Sir Harold Gillies (UK), regarded as the father of plastic surgery.

MOST COMMON SKIN INFECTION

Tinea pedis, usually called "athlete's foot", is the most common skin infection in humans. The fungus afflicts up to 70% of the worldwide population and almost everyone will get it at least once in our lifetime. The infection manifests when the skin between the toes becomes soft and peels away and it may even crack, ooze, and bleed.

MOST TATTOOED PERSON

Lucky Diamond Rich (Australia, b. NZ) has spent over 1,000 hours having an entire "body-suit" of tattoos (plus a layer of solid black) applied – coverage in excess of 200%.

RIGA, LATVIA

The **most Mentos and soda fountains** created in the same place is 1,911 and was achieved by the people of Latvia and students of TURIBA in Riga, Latvia, on June 19, 2008.

56°56'N 24°06'E

HUMAN BEINGS
HAIR

★★★★★★★★★★★★

★ LARGEST BALL OF HUMAN HAIR

Over the past 50 years, Henry Coffer (USA) has been collecting human hair and amassing a giant hairball that, as of December 8, 2008, weighs 167 lb (75.7 kg) and measures 14 ft (4.26 m) in circumference. Coffer, a 77-year-old barber from Charleston, Missouri, began saving hair at the request of a customer. Over the years he has been collecting, he has found many uses for his hair clippings, including patching potholes, gardening, and fertilizing soil.

LARGEST HUMAN HAIRBALL

"Trichobezoar" is the medical name for a hairball, which occurs as a result of Rapunzel Syndrome or "trichophagia" – the eating of one's own hair (from the Greek for "hair eating"). The largest trichobezoar surgically removed from a human was a hairball weighing 10 lb (4.5 kg) found in the stomach of an unnamed 18-year-old woman treated at Rush University Medical Center in Chicago, Illinois, USA, in November 2007.

DID YOU KNOW?

THE SIKH FAITH OPPOSES THE CUTTING OF FACIAL HAIR, SO SARWAN SINGH HAS NEVER SHAVED IN HIS LIFE. "MY BEARD IS MY FAVORITE BODY PART."

In 2001, Ismael Rivas Falcon (Spain) pulled a train weighing 6,069 lb (2,753.1 kg) with his beard.

TRIVIA

TRIM
CHUY - PRONOUNCED "CHEWIE" - IS SHOWN HERE RECEIVING A TRIM AT THE I GRI.SIANI HAIR SALON IN ROME BEFORE HIS FIRST APPEARANCE ON ITALIAN TV.

HAIRIEST FAMILY

Pictured is "Chuy" Jesus Fajardo Aceves, one of a family of 19 – covering five generations – from Mexico that suffers from hypertrichosis, aka "werewolf syndrome." The women are covered with a light to medium coat of hair, while the men of the family have thick hair on every inch of their body, apart from their hands and feet.

★ MOST HAIRSTYLES APPLIED (8 HOURS)

Rachel Brown (USA) of Salon Mimosa in Lake Park, Florida, USA, styled the hair of 32 customers in eight hours on February 16, 2009. Each client had to have his/her hair washed and rinsed, and then cut, completely dried, and styled before Rachel moved on to the next client.

★ MOST HAIRCUTS BY A TEAM (24 HOURS)

Ten hairdressers from Supercuts in Houston, Texas, USA, cut 349 heads of hair on October 10, 2009.

★ LONGEST BEARD

On March 4, 2010, Sarwan Singh's (Canada) beard was measured at 7 ft 9 in (2.37 m) on the set of *Lo Show dei Record* in Rome, Italy, the longest beard on a living person. The iconic Sikh -- head Giani (priest) at Guru Nanak Sikh Temple in Surrey, Canada – said, "It's not a talent, like playing music... It's a gift from God."

QUIZ!
WHICH OF THESE MEASURES THE MOST: THE LONGEST BEARD, LONGEST MUSTACHE OR HIGHEST HAIRSTYLE?
SEE P.278 FOR THE ANSWER.

EXTRA!
THE HUMAN BODY IS MORE AMAZING THAN YOU CAN IMAGINE. FIND OUT MORE ON PP. 74-75.

TALLINN, ESTONIA
59°26′N 24°44′E
Intan Pragi (Estonia) spun a roulette wheel more than 1,650 times over 48 hours during the **longest croupier marathon** at the Olympic Casino in Tallinn, Estonia, on February 18–20, 2005.

★ HAIRIEST TEENAGE GIRL

The most hirsute female teen – according to the Ferriman-Gallwey method – is Supatra "Nat" Sasuphan (Thailand). She was assessed on the set of *Lo Show dei Record* in Rome, Italy, on March 4, 2010. The Ferriman-Gallwey score is a method of quantifying hirsutism (hairiness) in women.

★ TALLEST MOHICAN

The tallest mohawk measures 31.5 in (80 cm) and belongs to Stefan Srocka (Germany). The length was verified at Hairgallery Daniela Schorn in Marktrodach, Germany, on June 2, 2009.

★ LONGEST MUSTACHE

Ram Singh Chauhan (India) has a mustache that measured 14 ft (4.29 m) on the set of *Lo Show dei Record* in Rome, Italy, on March 4, 2010.

HAIR

WITH THE FERRIMAN-GALLWEY METHOD, FEMALE HAIR GROWTH IS RATED FROM 0 (NO GROWTH) TO 4 (HEAVY COVERAGE) IN NINE LOCATIONS.

WHERE

THE NINE LOCATIONS ARE THE UPPER LIP, CHIN, CHEST, UPPER BACK, LOWER BACK, UPPER ABDOMEN, LOWER ABDOMEN, UPPER ARMS, AND THIGHS.

★ HIGHEST HAIRSTYLE

A hairdo measuring 8 ft 8 in (2.66 m) high was created by several hairdressers in an event organized by KLIPP unser Frisör in Wels, Austria, on June 21, 2009.

★ TALLEST WIG

An enormous wig of human hair was made by Emilio Minnicelli (Italy) and modeled in the main square of the Bologna Piazza Maggiore in Italy on May 15, 2004. It measured 46 ft 11 in (14.3 m) tall and weighed 57 lb (26 kg).

★ LONGEST FEMALE DREAD-LOCKS

The dreadlocks of Asha Mandela (USA) reached a record 19 ft 6.5 in (5.96 m) when professionally unknotted and measured on CBS's *The Early Show* in New York City, USA, on November 11, 2009 for GWR Day.

★ LONGEST EXTENSIONS

A hair extension piece of 53 ft 10 in (16.25 m) in length was applied by Kay Meinecke (Germany) to the hair of a model at a shopping mall in Hamburg, Germany, on November 10, 2007.

LONGEST HAIRS

Arm: 5.75 in (14.61 cm), Justin Shaw (USA), October 7, 2009.
Chest: 9 in (22.8 cm), Richard Condo (USA), April 29, 2007.
Ear: 7.12 in (18.1 cm), Anthony Victor (India), September 17, 2007.
Eyebrow: 7.01 in (17.8 cm), Toshie Kawakami (Japan), July 22, 2008.
Eyelash: 2.75 in (6.99 cm), Stuart Muller (USA), December 7, 2007.
Leg: 6.5 in (16.51 cm), Wesley Pemberton (USA), February 9, 2008.
Nipple: 5.07 in (12.9 cm), Douglas Williams (USA), May 26, 2007.

MOST EXPENSIVE HAIRCUT

An Italian customer of the Stuart Phillips Salon in Covent Garden, London, UK, paid £8,000 ($16,420) on October 29, 2007 for a luxury haircut.

★ MOST HAIR DYED (24 HOURS)

Ten hairdressers and their assistants from Schwarzkopf & Sergio & Margarida Hair Salon in Lisbon, Portugal, dyed 380 heads of hair in 24 hours on October 21, 2009.

LONGEST BEARD (FEMALE)

Melinda Maxie – the stage name of Vivian Elaine Wheeler (USA) – has a beard that, when last measured in 2000, had a maximum length of 11 in (27.9 cm). "A sideshow wouldn't be a sideshow without the bearded lady," said Melinda, who has been in and out of circuses since the age of 8.

LONGEST HAIR

The world's longest documented hair belongs to Xie Qiuping (China), at 18 ft 5.54 in (5.627 m) when measured on May 8, 2004. She has been growing her hair since 1973, from the age of 13. "It's no trouble at all. I'm used to it," she said. "But you need patience and you need to hold yourself straight when you have hair like this."

★ NEW RECORD
UPDATED RECORD

HUMAN BEINGS
GOLDEN OLDIES

★ ★ ★ ★ ★ ★ ★ ★ ★ ★ ★

OLDEST LIVING

	NAME	AGE	DATE OF BIRTH
1	Eugénie Blanchard (St Barts/France)	114	Feb 16, 1896
2	Eunice Sanborn (USA)	113	Jul 20, 1896
3	Besse Cooper (USA)	113	Aug 26, 1896
4	Walter Breuning (USA) **m**	113	Sep 21, 1896
5	Chiyono Hasegawa (Japan)	113	Nov 20, 1896
6	Venere Pizzinato-Papo (Italy)	113	Nov 23, 1896
7	Shige Hirooka (Japan)	113	Jan 16, 1897
8	Mississippi Winn (USA)	113	Mar 31, 1897
9	Dina Manfredini (USA)	113	Apr 4, 1897
10	Mineno Yamamoto (Japan)	113	Apr 8, 1897

Source: Gerontology Research Group, extracted May 11, 2010   **m** = male

OLDEST LIVING...
★**Person** (and ★**woman**): Eugénie Blanchard, who lives on the French-owned island of St Barthélemy in the Caribbean, was born on February 16, 1896 and became the world's oldest human at the age of 114 years old 75 days; *see table left for the top 10 oldest living people as of May 11, 2010.* ★**Man**: Walter Breuning (USA). *See opposite page.* ★**Twin**: The oldest living single twin is 110-year-old

★OLDEST SIBLINGS
With a combined age of 325 years 289 days, the Thornton sisters of Shreveport, Louisiana, USA, are the oldest ever siblings. All three passed away within a few weeks of each other: Rosie Thornton Warren (left) on December 18, 2009; Carrie Thornton Miller (right) on January 5, 2010; and Maggie Lee Thornton Renfro (pictured middle) on January 22, 2010.

Ruth Peter Anderson (USA, b. July 24, 1899). Her fraternal twin, Abel, died in 1900 at the age of one year. *To our knowledge, no pair of twins has ever reached super-centenarian status (over 110).* **Twins**: As we go to press, Guinness World Records is attempting to identify the holders of the record for the **oldest identical twins**. Widespread media coverage has been devoted to the

claim of Cao Daqiao and Cao Xiaoqiao (China, b. October 3, 1905), said to be 104 years old, though GWR is still to secure documentary evidence confirming this age. The twins live in Weifang in east China's Shandong province.

★LONGEST WORKING ICE-CREAM SELLER
Charlie D'Angelo (b. September 26, 1919) of Clifton, New Jersey, USA, has been working as an ice-cream man nonstop for 30 years, delivering confections from his Iggy's Igloo ice-cream truck since 1979. He has worked in the ice-cream trade intermittently since the age of 12!

EXTRA! NOT OLD ENOUGH FOR YOU? SHUFFLE ON OVER TO DINOSAURS ON PP. 48-49.

CAUTION: CHILDREN

DID YOU KNOW?
ON FEBRUARY 20, 2010, THERE WERE 76 PEOPLE CONFIRMED AND AUTHENTICATED AS BEING OVER THE AGE OF 110. OF THESE, ONLY THREE WERE MEN!

The chance of you living to 128 years old is about 1 in 2,560,000,000,000 (that's 1 in 2.56 trillion)!

TRIVIA

The title of oldest man ever, then, passes to Thomas Peter Thorvald Kristian Ferdinand "Christian" Mortensen (Denmark/USA, August 16, 1882–April 25, 1998), who died aged 115 years 252 days – the only Nordic person to live beyond the age of 113.

★OLDEST MICHELIN THREE-STAR CHEF

Jiro Ono (Japan, b. October 27, 1925), owner of the Sukiyabashi Jiro sushi restaurant in Tokyo, Japan, was first acknowledged as a three-star chef in the *Michelin Guide Tokyo 2008* when he was 82.

★OLDEST SALSA DANCER

In December 2009, salsa dancer Sarah Paddy Jones (UK, born July 1, 1935) and her partner, Nicko, took first prize on the Spanish TV talent show *Tu Si Que Vales.*

DAME
THE OLDEST PERSON – AND OLDEST WOMAN – WHOSE AGE HAS BEEN AUTHENTICATED WAS JEANNE CALMENT (FRANCE), WHO DIED AGED 122 YEARS.

OLDEST LIVING MAN

On the death of Henry Allingham (UK, 1896–2009), the title of oldest living man passed to 113-year-old Walter Breuning (b. September 21, 1896, above) of Great Falls, Montana, USA. At his last birthday, he became only the 12th man in history verified to reach 113 or older.

Conjoined twins: Ronnie and Donnie Galyon (USA, b. October 25, 1951) are the oldest living conjoined twins. For 36 years, they traveled in circuses, but retired in 1991. They share a passport but can cast two votes.

Married couple (aggregate age): Karl Dølven (Norway, b. August 31, 1897) married Gudrun Haug (Norway, b. October 14, 1900) on June 4, 1927. They were married until Gudrun's death on April 24, 2004, when she was 103 years 193 days and

Karl was 106 years 237 days – an aggregate age of 210 years 65 days.

The ★**longest marriage** is currently 86 years for Herbert and Zelmyra Fisher. For more on this record-breaking couple, see p.122.

★OLDEST MAN EVER

New evidence has come to light that casts doubt on the long-standing longevity record held by Shigechiyo Izumi (Japan). The birth certificate submitted as evidence might actually belong to his older brother, who died at a young age; if the family used Izumi as a "necronym" – that is, gave him his dead brother's name, as the new research suggests – this means his final age was 105 years old, not 120.

★OLDEST FEMALE TRACK AND FIELD RECORD HOLDER

On October 11, 2009, 100-year-old Ruth Frith (Australia) threw a record 13-ft 4-in (4.07-m) shot put in the over-100s category at the World Masters Games in Sydney, Australia. The Games are open to athletes of all abilities.

GAMES
THE WORLD MASTERS GAMES ARE THE ★LARGEST PARTICIPATORY MULTI-SPORT EVENT ON THE PLANET. THE 2002 GAMES ATTRACTED A RECORD 24,886 ATHLETES.

★OLDEST FEMALE YOGA TEACHER

At 83 years old, Australia's Bette Calman is the oldest woman to teach the Indian mental and physical discipline of yoga.

YOGA
GRANDMOTHER BETTE HAS TAUGHT YOGA FOR 40 YEARS. HERE SHE IS PICTURED IN THE (DEMANDING) PEACOCK POSITION!

★ **NEW RECORD**
UPDATED RECORD

HUMAN BEINGS
MEDICAL RECORDS

★★★★★★★★★★★★

> *"We chose him because he is tenacious, motivated and persistent."*
>
> **Arm transplant surgeon Dr Jean-Michel Dubernard on his patient, Denis Chatelier (see below)**

★ FIRST DOUBLE ARM TRANSPLANT

In January 2000, an international team of 18 surgeons and 32 support staff led by Professor Jean-Michel Dubernard (France) made history by performing the first double arm transplant. The recipient – Denis Chatelier, a 33-year-old French explosives worker (pictured) who had lost his arms in an accident four years previously – received the forearms of an 18-year-old cadaveric donor.

The procedure took 17 hours to complete and was performed at the Edouard-Herriot Hospital in Lyon, France. Dubernard had previously performed the **first arm transplant** back in 1998.

MOST FINGERS AND TOES

On March 19, 2010, an anonymous six-year-old boy was admitted to a hospital in Shenyang, Liaoning province, China, with 31 fingers and toes (15 fingers and 16 toes). Three fingers on each hand are fused; however, x-rays show each finger had full skeletal development.

★ MOST EYE TESTS CARRIED OUT IN AN HOUR

Volunteers from Specsavers International BV conducted a total of 648 eye tests in 92 locations throughout the Netherlands on May 15, 2009.

LARGEST TUMMY TUCK OPERATION PERFORMED ON A WOMAN

Plastic surgeons at the Hospital de Cruces in Barakaldo, Spain, removed an "apron" of fat weighing 132 lb (60 kg) from a morbidly obese woman in March 2006. During the nine-hour operation, surgeons needed small cranes to help support the fat and skin removed from her stomach. The weight removed is similar to that of an average 17-year-old girl, and had an energy content of 462,000 calories.

AHH!
BALAMURALI AMBATI (USA, B. JULY 29, 1977) BECAME THE WORLD'S **YOUNGEST PHYSICIAN** ON MAY 19, 1995 AT THE AGE OF 17 YEARS 294 DAYS.

ARGH!
STUNT RIDER EVEL KNIEVEL (USA) HAD HAD 433 BONE FRACTURES BY THE END OF 1975. HIS LAST YEAR OF MAJOR STUNTS – THE **MOST BROKEN BONES IN A LIFETIME**.

EXTRA!
FOR THE LOWDOWN ON SOME BIZARRELY BIG BODY PARTS, GO TO P. 74!

HIGHEST PERCENTAGE OF BURNS TO THE BODY

• Tony Yarijanian (USA, right) underwent 25 surgeries after suffering burns to 90% of his body in an explosion at his wife's beauty spa on February 15, 2004.
• David Chapman (UK) also survived 90% burns after an accident with a gasoline canister on July 2, 1996.

ABDOMINOPLASTY:

The medical term for a tummy tuck. A small tummy tuck is called an apronectomy, after the "apron" of skin and fat removed.

★ NEW RECORD
★ UPDATED RECORD

★ LONGEST SURVIVING MULTI-ORGAN TRANSPLANT PATIENT

Mark Dolby (UK) received a heart-lung-liver transplant on August 21, 1987 and a kidney transplant in December 2005, all at Harefield Hospital, London, UK. As of April 22, 2009, he had survived 21 years 244 days as a multi-organ transplantee.

LEAST BLOOD TRANSFUSED IN A TRANSPLANT OPERATION

In June 1996, a team from St James University Hospital, Leeds, UK, performed a liver transplant on 47-year-old housewife Linda Pearson (USA) without any blood being transfused. Such an operation usually requires 4–6 pints (2.3–3.4 liters) of blood, but as a Jehovah's Witness Mrs Pearson chose to refuse the transfusion on religious grounds.

MOST HAND AMPUTATIONS ON THE SAME ARM

Clint Hallam (New Zealand) has had his right hand amputated a total of three times. He first lost his hand in 1984 after an accident with a circular saw. Surgeons managed to reattach the severed limb but an infection developed and it was removed in 1988. In September 1998, doctors gave him a hand transplant but Clint later requested that it be amputated.

YOUNGEST MULTI-ORGAN TRANSPLANT PATIENT

Sarah Marshall (Canada, b. February 14, 1997) became the youngest patient to receive a multi-organ transplant when, on August 7, 1997, she was given a liver, a bowel, a stomach, and a pancreas at the Children's Hospital in London, Western Ontario, Canada.

★ LARGEST TUMMY TUCK

According to Russian news website www.life.ru, in early 2010 a 49-year-old man known only as Petr F (pictured above, before and after) underwent a three-hour operation to remove 264 lb (120 kg) of fat and skin in Voronezh, Russia. Prior to the operation, Petr weighed 529 lb (240 kg), but his inability to walk for prolonged periods drove him to seek medical help.

★ LONGEST-LIVING HYDROCEPHALIC

The medical condition hydrocephalus is marked by excess cerebrospinal fluid in the skull, which puts pressure on the brain, often harming it. The most common treatment is a "shunt," a technique developed in 1952 that uses tubing inserted into the skull to carry the excess fluid safely to another part of the body. In 1985, the death rate for sufferers was 52%, making the case of Theresa Alvina Schaan (Canada, b. March 17, 1941) all the more striking. As of August 7, 2009, she's been living with the condition for 68 years 143 days.

JAN 2004   FEB 2004   AUG 2004   JAN 2007   OCT 2007

VARNA, BULGARIA
The **largest legal document** is an insurance policy measuring 29 ft 4 in x 19 ft 8 in (9 x 6 m), issued by ING Asigurari de Viata (Romania) and signed in Varna, Bulgaria, on March 15, 2008.

43°13'N
27°55'E

SUPER STUNTS

(SOME OF) ASHRITA'S ACHIEVEMENTS

1. Fastest 100-m egg-and-spoon race (19.90 seconds)
2. Fastest mile balancing a baseball bat on the finger (7 min 5 sec)
3. Fastest 1-mile sack race (16 min 41 sec)
4. Longest balance board duration (1 hr 49 min 5 sec)
5. Longest duration on an exercise ball (3 hr 38 min 30 sec)
6. Fastest 1-mile fireman's carry (15 min 11.87 sec)
7. Fastest 10-km hula hooping (1 hr 25 min 9 sec)
8. Fastest mile on a pogo stick while juggling balls (23 min 28 sec)
9. Fastest 1-mile piggyback race (13 min 1 sec)
10. Longest table-tennis-bat-and-ball duration (3 hr 7 sec)
11. Fastest mile on spring-loaded stilts (7 min 13 sec)
12. Fastest mile on a space hopper (15 min 3 sec)
13. Greatest distance traveled with a cue stick balanced on the chin (5,472 ft; 1,668 m)
14. Most star jumps in 1 minute (61)

NEW RECORD
UPDATED RECORD

JOHANNESBURG, SOUTH AFRICA

Vic Toweel (South Africa) knocked down Danny O'Sullivan (UK) 14 times in 10 rounds in their world bantamweight fight at Johannesburg, South Africa, on December 2, 1950, before the latter retired. You can hardly blame O'Sullivan for retiring – he'd just suffered the **most knockdowns in a boxing match**.

CONTENTS

★ MOST GUINNESS WORLD RECORDS HELD

Since 1979, Ashrita Furman of Queens, New York City, USA, has set or broken 259 official Guinness World Records, and at the time of going to press currently holds 100 records. Why is Ashrita – born Keith, but given the Sanskrit name Ashrita, meaning "protected by God," by his meditation teacher Sri Chinmoy – so passionate about record breaking? "I'm trying to show others that our human capacity is unlimited if we can truly believe in ourselves."

ISTANBUL, TURKEY

Ilker Yilmaz (Turkey) squirted milk from his eye a distance of 9 ft 2 in (279.5 cm) at the Armada Hotel, Istanbul, Turkey, on September 1, 2004, the **farthest distance to squirt milk from the eye**.

41°0'N 28°58'E

SUPER STUNTS
STUNTS

TIP THE BALANCE:
Michele uses a ramp to get the automobile up onto its side. He then uses his body weight to maintain the automobile's balance.

★ ★ ★ ★ ★ ★ ★ ★ ★ ★ ★ ★ ★ ☆

★ LONGEST DISTANCE COVERED BY AN AUTOMOBILE DRIVEN ON TWO SIDE WHEELS
Michele Pilia (Italy) drove his automobile for 230.57 miles (371.06 km) using only two side wheels at Sant'Elia Stadium in Cagliari, Italy, on February 26, 2009.

WHEELED WONDERS

MOST AUTOMOBILES DRIVEN ON TWO WHEELS SIMULTANEOUSLY
On November 26, 2000, a team of Renault drivers drove 16 automobiles on two wheels simultaneously, in a continuous line, at Evreux, France, for the TV show *L'Émission des Records*.

★ LONGEST VEHICLE DRIFT
Driving a 2010 Ford Mustang GT, Vaughn Gittin, Jr (USA) pulled off a drift of 6,280 ft (1,914.15 m) at the Speedway in Las Vegas, USA, on December 18, 2008.

★ LONGEST UTV RAMP JUMP
Junior Quisquis (USA) performed a jump of 47 ft 8 in (14.53 m) in a utility terrain vehicle (UTV) in Pauma Valley, California, USA, on October 31, 2009.

FASTEST SPEED DRAGGED BEHIND A MOTORCYCLE
Gary Rothwell of Liverpool, UK, was dragged behind a motorcycle at 156.3 mph (251.54 km/h) on 0.07-in (2-mm) titanium-soled boots at Bruntingthorpe Proving Ground, Leicester, UK, on April 18, 1999.

MOST MOTORCYCLISTS IN A GLOBE OF DEATH
On November 2, 1999, a team of five motorcyclists rode their vehicles around a person placed at the center of a 14-ft 3-in-diameter (4.33-m) steel sphere. The daredevil feat took place at The Riviera Hotel, Versailles Theater, Las Vegas, Nevada, USA, by a team led by Bela Tabak and featuring Gary Lurent, Humberto Fonseca Pinto, Kurtis Kunz, and Humberto H Fonseca Pinto, Jr (all USA). Bela's wife, Robin, was the person in the middle!

WALL OF DEATH – ENDURANCE
Martin Blume (Germany) performed on a "wall of death" for 7 hr 13 sec in Berlin, Germany, on April 16, 1983. He rode a Yamaha XS 400 for 12,000 laps on a wall with a diameter of 33 ft (10 m), averaging 30 mph (48 km/h) over 181 miles 880 yd (292 km).

★ MOST DONUTS IN ONE MINUTE
Emilio Zamora (Spain) achieved 24 donut (360°) spins on a motorbike in Cheste, Valencia, Spain, on November 6, 2009. This event took place during the 2009 World Grand Prix motorcycle championships.

★ MOST GYRATOR SPINS ON A BMX BIKE (ONE MINUTE)
Jason Plourde (Canada) performed 39 gyrator (360°) spins in a minute on the set of *Zheng Da Zong Yi – Guinness World Records Special* in Beijing, China, on November 22, 2009.

MISCELLANY

★ FASTEST TIME TO ESCAPE FROM THREE PAIRS OF HANDCUFFS UNDERWATER
Matthew "Matt the Knife" Cassiere (USA) escaped from three pairs of handcuffs while underwater in 44 seconds on the set of *Zheng Da Zong Yi – Guinness World Records Special* in Beijing, China, on December 17, 2006. (For more escapology, see p.96.)

★ NEW RECORD
★ UPDATED RECORD

★ LONGEST CABLE WALK
The longest walk on a cable-car cable is 3,624 ft (995 m) – the length of 14 jumbo jets – by Freddy Nock (Switzerland) at Zugspitze, near Garmisch-Partenkirchen, Germany, on August 30, 2009. The cable thickness was 1.96 in (50 mm), and the height difference was 1,141 ft (348 m) at the lowest point to 8,202 ft (2,500 m) above sea level at the highest!

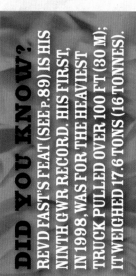

DID YOU KNOW?
REVD FAST'S FEAT (SEE P.89) IS HIS NINTH GWR RECORD. HIS FIRST, IN 1998, WAS FOR THE HEAVIEST TRUCK PULLED OVER 100 FT (30 M); IT WEIGHED 17.6 TONS (16 TONNES).

Reverend Fast's aircraft pulling record would not have been possible without the assistance of the Canadian Air Force.

TRIVIA

ANGLE
THE GRADIENT INVOLVED IN FREDDY'S CABLE WALK WAS 56%, WHERE 0% EQUALS A FLAT SURFACE AND 100% IS A VERTICAL WALL.

DANGLE
FREDDY NOCK IS A SWISS ARTIST AND HAILS FROM A FAMILY THAT HAS BEEN PERFORMING BALANCING ACTS SINCE 1770!

59°56'N 30°20'E

ST PETERSBURG, RUSSIA
The city of St Petersburg, Russia, has the **most extensive streetcar system**, with approximately 2,400 cars running on its routes and more than 430 miles (690 km) of track.

MOST BARS JUMPED ON THE BACK WHEEL OF A TRIAL BIKE

Benito Ros Charral (Spain) successfully jumped 48 gapping bars on the back wheel of a trial bike on the set of *Lo Show Dei Record* in Milan, Italy, on April 19, 2009.

★OLDEST WING WALKER

Thomas Lackey (UK) made a wing walk across the English Channel aged 89 years 33 days on July 25, 2009.

★HIGHEST BUNGEE JUMP RESTRAINED WITH THE HANDS

On September 28, 2008, Patrick Schurf (Austria) performed a bungee jump measuring 203 ft 4 in (61.99 m). He was secured only to strongman Frank Müllner (Austria), who held the bungee cord by hand!

★FASTEST TIME TO RUN THROUGH TEN LOCKED DOORS

Vennessa Mayer, aka Lady Fairy Floss (Australia), successfully ran through 10 locked doors in a time of 17.32 seconds on January 10, 2010. The record attempt took place on the set of *Australia Smashes Guinness World Records* in Sydney, New South Wales, Australia.

★HIGHEST AIR ON A MOTORCYCLE (QUARTER PIPE)

Ronnie Renner (USA) achieved a 35-ft 4-in (10.77-m) air – launching himself into the air off a quarter pipe – on a motorcycle (see below) during the Red Bull High Rise in Grant Park at Butler Field in Chicago, Illinois, USA, on July 25, 2009.

★MOST REPEATED BACKWARD FLIPS ON SPRING-LOADED STILTS

Yuan Shiwei (China) made 25 consecutive backward flips on spring-loaded stilts in Dengfeng city, Henan province, China, on September 17, 2008.

HIGHEST ALTITUDE REACHED USING HELIUM-FILLED TOY BALLOONS

Mike Howard (UK) and Steve Davis (USA) ascended to a height of 18,300 ft (5,580 m) by means of 1,400 helium-filled latex toy balloons near Albuquerque, New Mexico, USA, on August 4, 2001.

GREATEST DISTANCE FLOWN IN A WING SUIT

Adrian Nicholas (UK) flew 10 miles (16 km) in a wing suit over Yolo County, California, USA, on March 12, 1999. Exiting the airplane at 33,850 ft (10,317 m), he reached speeds of up to 150 mph (241 km/h) and "flew" for 4 min 55 sec.

★ HEAVIEST AIRCRAFT PULLED BY AN INDIVIDUAL

Revd Kevin Fast (Canada) pulled a CC-177 Globemaster III, weighing 416,299 lb (188.83 tonnes), a distance of 28 ft 10 in (8.8 m) on September 17, 2009.

"I still don't have the nerve to actually look that plane in the face."

Revd Kevin Fast, minutes after breaking his Guinness World Record

SUPER STUNTS
STRENGTH & BALANCE

★ ★ ★ ★ ★ ★ ★ ★ ★ ★ ★ ★ ★ ★ ★

★ GREATEST WEIGHT SUPPORTED WHILE SKIPPING A ROPE

The heaviest weight supported while simultaneously skipping a rope 10 times is 394 lb 10 oz (179 kg), by James Brewster Thompson (USA) in Milan, Italy, on April 18, 2009.

STRENGTH

★ FASTEST ICE CLIMBER

Pavel Gulyaev (Russia) climbed a 49-ft-high (15-m) vertical ice wall in a record time of 8.748 seconds at the Ice Climbing World Cup held in Bustemi, Romania, on February 8, 2009.

★ HEAVIEST VEHICLE PULLED BY THE HAIR

He Jianma (China) pulled a bus weighing 18,254 lb (8,280 kg), attached to his hair, for a distance of 98 ft (30 m) in You County, Hunan Province, China, on May 25, 2009.

★ LONGEST TIME TO RESTRAIN A VEHICLE ON AN INCLINE

Using a chain attached to a handle, Ervin Katona (Serbia) restrained an automobile weighing 2,160 lb (980 kg) while resting on a 45° incline for 1 min 2 sec in Milan, Italy, on April 25, 2009.

★ MOST TELEPHONE DIRECTORIES TORN BEHIND THE BACK IN THREE MINUTES (MALE)

Alexander Muromskiy (Russia) tore a total of six telephone directories (each 1,048 pages thick) behind his back in three minutes at the Moscow Center of Martial Arts in Moscow, Russia, on October 17, 2009.

★ FASTEST 20 M CARRYING 300 KG ON THE SHOULDERS

Agris Kazelniks (Latvia) covered a distance of 65 ft 7 in (20 m) carrying 661 lb 5 oz (300 kg) on his shoulders in a time of 11.4 seconds on the set of Lo Show dei Record in Milan, Italy, on April 18, 2009.

★ MOST ONE-FINGER PUSH-UPS IN 30 SECONDS

Fu Bing Li (China) managed 25 one-finger push-ups in 30 seconds in Beijing, China, on November 23, 2009.

★ FARTHEST THROW OF A PERSON

Jonathan Macfarlane threw Andrew Rainford (both New Zealand) 15 ft 11 in (4.87 m) in Auckland, New Zealand, on July 25, 2009.

★ HEAVIEST ROAD VEHICLE PULLED BY TEETH

Georges Christen (Luxembourg) pulled a bus weighing 19,982 lb (9,064 kg) using just his teeth in Beijing, China, on November 18, 2009.

★ FASTEST CAR PUSH OVER ONE MILE

On June 12, 2009, Mario Mlinaric (Croatia) pushed a 4,144-lb 11-oz (1,880-kg) automobile 1 mile (1.6 km) in a time of 15 min 21 sec in Zagreb, Croatia.

★ HEAVIEST WEIGHT LIFTED BY THE EAR

Using only one ear, Zafar Gill (Pakistan) lifted a weight of 160 lb 15 oz (73 kg) in Lahore, Pakistan, on January 3, 2009. Zafar lifted gym weights, which hung from a clamp that was attached to his right ear.

★ NEW RECORD
★ UPDATED RECORD

★ LONGEST DURATION BALANCING ON FOUR FINGERS

On November 9, 2008, Wang Weibao (China) managed to balance his entire body weight on just four fingers for a painful 19.23 seconds. He achieved his fantastic finger feat in Beijing, China.

EXTRA!
FOR SOME TRULY BREATHTAKING STUNTS, BACKFLIP JUST ONE PAGE.

GUINNESS WORLD RECORDS 2011

DID YOU KNOW?

THE TONGUE (SEE FAR RIGHT) IS MOSTLY MUSCLE. THIS ALTERS THE TONGUE'S SHAPE AND ATTACHES IT TO THE FLOOR OF THE MOUTH AND BACK OF THE THROAT.

Aneta Florczyk (right) has won 13 Polish Championship titles in powerlifting and bench press in all age categories.

TRIVIA

BALANCE

★ LONGEST TIME TO BALANCE A TIRE ON THE TEETH

Frank Simon (USA) held a 110-lb (50-kg) tire on his teeth for 31 seconds in Beijing, China, on June 21, 2009.

★ LONGEST TIME TO BALANCE A LAWN MOWER ON THE CHIN

On October 31, 2009, Preacher Muaddib (UK) balanced a 16-lb 4-oz (7.4-kg) lawn mower on his chin for 1 min 11 sec at the Spa Theatre, Whitby, UK.

★ MOST KNEE BENDS ON A SWISS BALL IN ONE HOUR

Balancing for one hour on an exercise ball, Stephen Buttler (UK) managed 1,716 knee bends at Hope House, Shropshire, UK, on November 12, 2009.

★ FARTHEST DISTANCE TRAVELED WITH A SOCCER BALL BALANCED ON THE HEAD

Yee Ming Low (Malaysia) covered 6.915 miles (11.129 km) with a soccer ball balanced on his head in Selangor, Malaysia, on August 21, 2009.

★ HEAVIEST WEIGHT BALANCED ON FEET

On November 20, 2009, Li Chunying (China) balanced 573 lb (260 kg) on his feet in Beijing, China.

★ MOST PEOPLE TO BE LIFTED AND THROWN IN TWO MINUTES (FEMALE)

Aneta Florczyk (Poland) picked up and threw 12 people in two minutes in Madrid, Spain, on December 19, 2008.

★ LONGEST HOLD OF THE "HUMAN SCALE"

Scott Fidgett and Cole Armitage (both UK) maintained the punishing "human scale" acrobalance position for an incredible 50.13 seconds, on the set of *Lo Show dei Record* in Rome, Italy, on April 1, 2010.

★ MOST DANCE SPINS BY A COUPLE (ONE MINUTE)

Lisa Anscomb-Smith and Giles Eadle (both UK) performed 125 dance spins in a minute at the Great British Salsa Experience in Manchester, UK, on November 22, 2008.

★ MOST REVOLUTIONS WITH HEAD AND FEET ON GROUND (ONE MINUTE)

Zhang Disheng (China) executed 52 body revolutions with head and feet on the ground on the set of *Lo Show dei Record* in Rome, Italy, on February 25, 2010.

★ MOST HORIZONTAL BAR BACKWARD SPINS (ONE MINUTE)

Wang Jue (China) achieved 164 spins on the set of *Lo Show dei Record* in Rome, Italy, on February 25, 2010.

★ LONGEST HUMAN SCALE

Scott Fidgett and Cole Armitage (both UK) held the acrobalance position for 48.17 seconds in London, UK, on April 21, 2009.

★ GREATEST WEIGHT LIFTED WITH THE TONGUE

Thomas Blackthorne (UK) attached a weight of 27 lb 8.96 oz (12.5 kg) to a hook that pierced his tongue on the set of *El Show Olimpico* in Mexico City, Mexico, on August 1, 2008.

MARINELLI:

The Marinelli bend is named after contortionist and theatrical agent H B Marinelli (1864–1924).

UNIQUE! IONA CLAIMS TO BE THE ONLY PERSON IN THE UK WHO CAN PERFORM THE MARINELLI BEND.

ARGH! "IT'S NOT PAINFUL – IF IT WAS I WOULDN'T BE HERE NOW. BUT THERE ARE VERY FEW PEOPLE THAT CAN DO IT." - IONA

★ LONGEST TIME TO HOLD THE MARINELLI BEND POSITION

The longest duration to maintain a Marinelli bend – a back bend in which the weight of the body is supported only by the teeth – is 50 seconds, set by Iona Oyungerel Luvsandorj (Mongolia) in Milan, Italy, on April 18, 2009.

SUPER STUNTS
PARTY TRICKS

★ ★ ★ ★ ★ ★ ★ ★ ★ ★ ★ ★ ★

"It all started at school, it just went from there. I never grew up."
Loudest burper Paul Hunn (right) talks about his emerging talent

★ MOST CARTWHEELS IN A MINUTE

Marcio Barbosa (Brazil) managed 55 cartwheels in one minute at the Arpoador beach in Rio de Janeiro, Brazil, on February 6, 2009.

★ LONGEST BURP

The lengthiest burp lasted 1 min 13 sec, and was achieved by Michele Forgione (Italy) at the 13th annual Hard Rock Beer festival "Ruttosound" competition held in Reggiolo, Italy, on June 16, 2009.

★ MOST BALLOONS BLOWN UP IN AN HOUR (INDIVIDUAL)

The greatest number of balloons blown up in an hour by an individual is 320 by Felipe Nascimento (Brazil) at Animasom Store, Leblon Shopping, Rio de Janeiro, Brazil, on February 4, 2009.

LOUDEST BURP (MALE)

Paul Hunn (UK) unleashed a burp of 109.9 dB at Butlins, Bognor Regis, UK, on August 23, 2009. The **loudest burp by a female** is 107.0 dB, by Elisa Cagnoni (Italy) at the 13th annual Hard Rock Beer festival "Ruttosound" competition in Reggiolo, Italy, on June 16, 2009.

WINDY
PAUL PRACTICES HIS STRANGE TALENT BY DRINKING COPIOUS AMOUNTS OF FIZZY DRINKS AND ALLOWING THE GAS TO BUILD UP IN HIS STOMACH!

★ FASTEST HOT WATER BOTTLE BURST

The fastest time to blow up a standard hot water bottle until it bursts is 18.81 seconds, a record set by Shaun Jones (UK) in London, UK, on November 3, 2009.

★ MOST MALTESERS THROWN AND CAUGHT WITH THE MOUTH (ONE MINUTE)

Bipin Larkin (USA) threw 59 Maltesers (chocolate malt balls) across a distance of 15 ft (4.5 m) into the mouth of catcher Ashrita Furman (USA) in a minute in New York City, USA, on 22 August 2009.

★ MOST ROPE JUMPS (ONE MINUTE)

Beci Dale (UK) performed 332 rope jumps in one minute at Pinewood Studios, UK, on April 4, 2009.

BLOW OUT
ANDREW CAN INFLATE TWO BALLOONS - ONE BY EACH NOSTRIL - AT THE SAME TIME.

★ MOST BALLOONS INFLATED BY THE NOSE IN THREE MINUTES

Andrew Dahl (USA) inflated 23 balloons using only his nose in three minutes on the set of *Lo show dei record* in Rome, Italy, on March 18, 2010.

DID YOU KNOW?
ANDREW ALSO HOLDS THE RECORD FOR THE MOST BALLOONS INFLATED BY THE NOSE IN ONE HOUR: 308 IN NEW YORK, USA, ON SEPTEMBER 16, 2008.

TRIVIA
Andrew found he could blow up balloons with his nose when he was seven years old and bored on a long automobile journey.

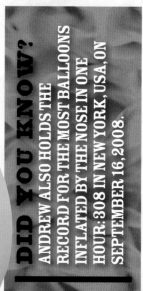

QUIZ!
ANSSI VANHALA SOLVED A RUBIK'S CUBE IN 36.77 SECONDS USING WHICH BODY PART?
SEE P.278 FOR THE ANSWER.

★ **NEW RECORD**
★ **UPDATED RECORD**

ERUCTATION:
The expulsion of air from the stomach through the mouth, better known as "burping."

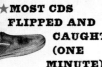

★ MOST SPOONS BALANCED ON THE FACE
The greatest number of spoons balanced on the face is 17, achieved by Aaron Caissie (Canada) on the set of *Lo Show dei Record* in Milan, Italy, on April 18, 2009.

MOST KICKS TO THE HEAD IN ONE MINUTE
Nick Gatelein (USA, above) matched Cody Warden's (USA) record of 77 kicks to the head while visiting X Games 15 in Los Angeles, California, USA, on August 2, 2009.

★ MOST TENNIS BALLS HELD IN THE HAND
The greatest number of tennis balls held in one hand is 21, achieved by Rohit Timilsina (Nepal) for 14.32 seconds in Kathmandu, Nepal, on June 14, 2008.

★ MOST CDS FLIPPED AND CAUGHT (ONE MINUTE)
Mohammad Rohail Riaz (Pakistan) successfully flipped and caught 58 CDs in one minute in Dubai, UAE, on February 21, 2009.

★ MOST GRAPES CAUGHT IN THE MOUTH (THREE MINUTES)
Ashrita Furman (USA) successfully caught a total of 182 grapes in his mouth from a distance of 15 ft (4.5 m) at the Grand National Park, Arizona, USA, on July 10, 2009.

★ MOST RUBBER BANDS STRETCHED OVER THE FACE
On September 20, 2009, at the Sylvia Park shopping mall in Auckland, New Zealand, Shay Horay (New Zealand) managed to stretch 71 regular elastic bands over his face on the set of *NZ Smashes Guinness World Records*.

★ FASTEST TIME TO DUCT-TAPE ONESELF TO A WALL
Ashrita Furman (USA) – aka Mr Versatility – stuck himself to a wall with duct tape in 6 min 32.87 sec in New York City, USA, on September 19, 2009.

★ MOST BRAS WORN AND REMOVED IN ONE MINUTE
Model Rosie Jones (UK) was able to put on and fully remove a bra seven times in a minute at the offices of *The Sun* newspaper in London, UK, on November 9, 2009.

★ FASTEST TIME TO SOLVE A RUBIK'S CUBE
• Hai Yan Zhuang (China) solved a Rubik's cube while blindfolded in just 30.90 seconds in Xi'an, China, on April 4, 2010.
• On November 7, 2009, at Kose in Estonia, Anssi Vanhala (Finland) solved a cube using his feet in 36.72 seconds.

EXTRA! FOR SOME SUPER-TALENTED CIRCUS ACTS, TURN TO PP. 98–99.

★ MOST STRAWS IN THE MOUTH
Mega-mouthed Simon Elmore (Germany) held 400 straws in his mouth for a regulation 10 seconds in Sollhuben, Bavaria, Germany, on August 6, 2009.

SUPER STUNTS
URBAN ARTS

★★★★★★

★MOST BACKFLIPS AGAINST A WALL IN ONE MINUTE

Miguel Marquez (Spain) made 29 backflips against a wall in a minute on the set of *Zheng Da Zong Yi – Guinness World Records Special* in Beijing, China, on June 19, 2009.

★LONGEST TIME TO CONTROL A SOCCER BALL

Dan Magness (UK) controlled a soccer ball for 24 hours during an event run by Sony PlayStation in Covent Garden, London, UK, on April 30 –May 1, 2009. Dan also holds the record for the ★**longest time to control a soccer ball on the back** – 3 min 40 sec – set on April 19, 2009.

★MOST DOUBLE DUTCH SKIPS IN ONE MINUTE

The greatest number of double Dutch skipping jumps carried out in 60 seconds is 202. It was set by Nobuyoshi Ando (Japan) at DoubleDutch Harbor Festival 09GW, Urban Dock Lalaport Toyosu, Tokyo, Japan, on May 3, 2009.

★The **most consecutive double Dutch style skips by a team** is 194, by the Blue and White Rope Skippers (all UK) on the set of *Guinness World Records Smashed* at Pinewood Studios, UK, on April 17, 2009.

The **most people skipping simultaneously on two ropes** is 38, at the studios of *El Show de los Récords* in Madrid, Spain, on December 5, 2001. They completed three full rotations of the ropes.

LONGEST CLIMB BY A HUMAN FLY

On May 25, 1981, Daniel Goodwin (USA) ascended 1,454 ft (443.2 m) up the outside of the Sears Tower in Chicago, USA, using only suction cups and metal clips.

EXTRA! FOR WORLD-BEATING WHEEL SKILLS AND DAREDEVIL FEATS, JUMP TO P.262.

NEW RECORD / UPDATED RECORD

GRAFFITI

★LARGEST SPRAY-PAINTED PICTURE

A 8,183.58-ft² (760.28-m²) picture, titled *There is Life on the Streets*, was spray-painted for Coca-Cola Ýcecek by 580 students from nine Turkish universities. It was completed at Hezarfen Airport, Istanbul, Turkey, on August 16, 2004.

LONGEST GRAFFITI SCROLL

On December 16, 2008, the children's charity "To hamogelo tou pediou" made a 2,299-ft 7-in-long (700.92-m) graffiti scroll in Kerkyra, Greece.

BASE JUMPING:

"BASE" stands for Buildings, Antennae, Spans (e.g. bridges), and Earth (e.g. cliffs) – all surfaces from which you can jump.

★FARTHEST BACKFLIP OFF A WALL

Chase Armitage (UK) achieved a backflip of 9 ft 11 in (3.04 m) off a wall on the set of *Guinness World Records Smashed* at Pinewood Studios, UK, on March 25, 2009. Chase is also able to clear an automobile driven in front of the wall, just as he is running up it.

BASE JUMPING

HIGHEST EXIT POINT

Dr Glenn Singleman and Heather Swan (both Australia) made a BASE jump from a ledge 21,666 ft (6,604 m) up Mount Meru in Garwhal Himalaya, India, on May 23, 2006. The husband-and-wife team wore wingsuits for their jumps.

★ MOST ONE-HAND JUMPS

Victor Mengarelli (Sweden) achieved 93 one-hand jumps at ICA Maxi in Haninge, Sweden, on November 2, 2007.

★ LONGEST HAND WAVE

Nana Mizuki fan club S C NANA NET (Japan) organized a breakdance hand wave involving 7,014 participants at the Tokyo Big Site, Japan, on November 21, 2009.

★ LONGEST MARATHON

Arulanantham Suresh Joachim, Troy Feldman, Jesse Catabog, Donald F Geraghty, Lance Johnson, Eva Nikitova, Damian Dobrowolski, Dan Rossignoli, Darren Bryan, Karl Alba, and Joseph Hersco (all Canada) breakdanced continuously for 24 hours at the Vaughan Mills shopping mall in Vaughan, Ontario, Canada, on March 23–24, 2007.

★ MOST POGO BACKFLIPS

The greatest number of consecutive backflips performed on a pogo stick is eight by Fred Grzybowski (USA) in Ohio, USA, in August 2009. Fred has been an avid pogoer since his school days.

MOST BUILDINGS CLIMBED SOLO

As of 2010, Alain "Spiderman" Robert (France) had scaled more than 100 towers, monuments, and skyscrapers without ropes, suction devices, or safety equipment. Alain uses pipes, window frames, cables, and the gaps between brickwork to scale structures often more than 1,300 ft (400 m) tall.

One of Alain's most notable endeavors was reaching the top of the Petronas Towers (pictured) in Kuala Lumpur, Malaysia, on September 1, 2009, after two failed attempts. In the picture above right, he is seen standing triumphantly atop the building's antenna.

JUMP? DID YOU KNOW IT IS PERMITTED TO BASE JUMP FROM THE PERRINE MEMORIAL BRIDGE (SEE BELOW)? BUT JUMP FROM A BRIDGE ELSEWHERE IN THE USA AND YOU COULD BE IN TROUBLE WITH THE LAW!

★ MOST HEADSPINS (ONE MINUTE)

B-Girl Roxy (aka Roxanna Milliner, UK) performed a dizzying 71 headspins during a warm-up session at the UK B-Boy Championships World Finals held at the O2 Academy Brixton in London, UK, on October 11, 2009.

★ LARGEST GROUP JUMP

A total of 30 skydivers from over seven different countries performed a BASE jump from the Ostankino television and radio tower in Moscow, Russia, on July 3, 2004.

MOST JUMPS IN 24 HR

Special Ops Officer Dan Schilling (USA) jumped off the 486-ft-high (148-m) Perrine Memorial Bridge over Snake River in Twin Falls, Idaho, USA, 201 times on July 7–8, 2006. He averaged one jump every 6 min 20 sec!

OLDEST BASE JUMPER

James Talbot Guyer (USA) parachuted off the Perrine Memorial Bridge on the north side of Twin Falls in Idaho, USA, on August 2, 2002 at the age of 74 years 47 days.

BREAKING

★ MOST FLARES IN ONE MINUTE

Victor Ortiz (Spain) performed 37 flares in a minute in the Spanish capital, Madrid, on January 9, 2009.

HIP! THE LONGEST TIME CONTINUOUSLY RAPPING IS 8 HR 45 MIN BY D O (AKA DUANE GIBSON, CANADA) ON JULY 5, 2003.

★ MOST WINDMILLS IN 30 SECONDS

LeeRoy Bailey (UK) carried out 46 "mills" in 30 seconds on the set of *Guinness World Records Smashed* at Pinewood Studios, UK, on March 31, 2009.

★ MOST BREAKDANCE ELBOW SPINS

Mark Dossenbach (Switzerland) performed 16 continuous spins on one elbow at Zug, Switzerland, on August 19, 2005. He's put the work in, though: Mark started practicing acrobatics at the age of eight, and he's had more than 20 years to perfect the art of elbow spinning!

HOP! JORDY (FRANCE) - THE YOUNGEST RAPPER - TOPPED THE FRENCH CHART WITH "DUR DUR D'ÊTRE BÉBÉ," AGED FOUR AND A HALF, IN SEPTEMBER 1993.

SUPER STUNTS
SIDESHOW ARTS

★ ★ ★ ★ ★ ★ ★ ★ ★ ★ ★ ★ ★

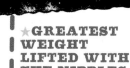

PETS! THE GREAT NIPPULINI OWNS TWO DOGS, THREE CATS, SEVEN REPTILES, A BLUE-FACED AMAZON PARROT, AND A MADAGASCAR HISSING COCKROACH.

★FASTEST STRAITJACKET ESCAPE

Jackson Rayne (USA) exited a Posey straitjacket in 7.26 seconds at the Hilton Convention Center, Las Vegas, USA, on November 17, 2009.

★FASTEST CHAINS ESCAPE

Matt "The Knife" Cassiere (USA) escaped from a set of chains in 49.67 seconds on the set of *Zheng Da Zong Yi* in Beijing, China, on November 13, 2008.

MOST KNIVES THROWN AROUND A HUMAN TARGET IN ONE MINUTE

Dr David R Adamovich (USA, aka The Great Throwdini) hurled 102 throwing knives, each 14 in (36 cm) long, around his partner in one minute in Freeport, New York, USA, on December 26, 2007. (See "Top 100," below right.) Throwdini also holds the record for the **fastest time to throw 10 knives around a human target:** 4.29 seconds.

★FASTEST HANDCUFF ESCAPE

Escapologist Zdenek Bradac (Czech Republic) escaped from a set of handcuffs in 1.66 seconds in Hamburg, Germany, on June 6, 2009.

On September 9, 2009, he escaped from a pair of handcuffs while underwater in a time of 10.66 seconds, in Jablonec nad Nisou, Czech Republic, the **★fastest escape from handcuffs underwater**.

★FASTEST TIME TO PASS THROUGH A TENNIS RACKET THREE TIMES

Ashrita Furman (USA) passed his body through a tennis racket three times in 8.1 seconds at the Panorama Café in New York City, USA, on October 4, 2009.

MOST LAYERED BED OF NAILS

Lee Graber, Todd Graber, Chris Smith, and Doreen Graber (all USA) formed a four-person bed of nails (6-in [15.25-cm] nails set 2 in [5 cm] apart) at Tallmadge, Ohio, USA, on October 8, 2000.

★GREATEST WEIGHT LIFTED WITH THE NIPPLES

On September 26, 2009, blacksmith, welder, and sculptor Sage Werbock (USA, aka The Great Nippulini) lifted a total weight of 70 lb 8 oz (31.9 kg) from piercings in his nipples. The weight comprised a 55-lb (24.9-kg) anvil, a 15-lb (6.8-kg) anvil, and chains weighing 8 oz (0.2 kg).

DID YOU KNOW? BY NIGHT, DR ADAMOVICH PERFORMS AS "IMPALEMENT ARTIST" THE GREAT THROWDINI. BY DAY, HE RUNS A WEDDING BUSINESS, AND HAS MARRIED THOUSANDS OF PEOPLE AS A CERTIFIED MINISTER!

TOP 100 VISITORS TO GWR'S WEBSITE HAVE VOTED THIS RECORD BY THE GREAT THROWDINI AS ONE OF THE TOP 100 GWR RECORDS OF ALL TIME!

★ **NEW RECORD**
★ **UPDATED RECORD**

GEEK: A term originally given to sideshow artists who indulged in sick acts such as biting the heads off small animals!

★MOST BEVERAGE CANS BROKEN WITH A WHIP IN THREE MINUTES

Adam Winrich (USA) split 23 beverage cans with a whip in three minutes on the set of *Lo Show dei Record* in Milan, Italy, on April 11, 2009. Winrich also set a record on June 20, 2009 when he achieved 257 cracks in a minute with a bullwhip at The Stone's Throw Bar in Eau Claire, Wisconsin, USA – the ★**most whipcracks in one minute**.

Lee Graber of Tallmadge, Ohio, USA, was sandwiched between two beds of nails, with a weight of 1,658 lb (752.5 kg) placed on top for 10 seconds on June 24, 2000 – the **heaviest weight endured on an "Iron Maiden" bed of nails**. The nails were spaced 2 in (5 cm) apart.

★HEAVIEST CONCRETE BLOCK BREAK ON A BED OF NAILS

Neal Hardy (Australia) had 16 concrete blocks weighing 1,173 lb 8 oz (532.3 kg) in total placed on his chest while he was lying on a bed of nails. The blocks were then broken with a sledgehammer at Vikings Auditorium, Erindale, Canberra, Australia, on February 16, 2008.

MOST PEOPLE SWALLOWING THE SAME OBJECT

A group of four sword swallowers – Thomas Blackthorne (UK), Chayne Hultgren (Australia), Captain Frodo (Norway), and Gordo Gamsby (Australia) – swallowed the four steel legs of the same bar stool. This gut-wrenching record was set in front of a live audience during a show at the Edinburgh Fringe Festival in Scotland, UK, on August 21, 2007.

★MOST SWORDS SWALLOWED AT ONCE

A group of 19 sword swallowers (from Italy, Sweden, and the USA) swallowed a total of 50 swords between them, simultaneously, in Wilkes-Barre, Pennsylvania, USA, on August 30, 2002.

GREATEST WEIGHT LIFTED BY THE BEARD

In the world of beard weightlifting, no one surpasses the achievements of Lithuania's Antanas Kontrimas. On September 16, 2007, he tied a 139-lb (63.2-kg) girl to his beard and lifted her 3.93 in (10 cm) off the ground on the set of *Zheng Da Zong Yi – Guinness World Records Special* in Beijing, China.

★YOUNGEST SWORD SWALLOWER

According to the Sword Swallowers Association International (SSAI), the youngest recorded sword swallower is Erik Kloeker (USA, b. October 27, 1989), who swallowed a solid-steel sword, up to the hilt, at the age of 16 years 267 days on July 21, 2006.

LONGEST SWORD SWALLOWED

Natasha Veruschka (USA) swallowed a sword 29.5 in (74 cm) in length on February 28, 2009. Natasha also holds the record for the **most swords swallowed simultaneously by a female**, at 13 blades.

SUPER STUNTS
CIRCUS SKILLS

★ NEW RECORD ★ UPDATED RECORD

★ THREE CONTORTIONISTS IN A BOX – DURATION

On September 20, 2009, Skye Broberg, Nele Siezen, and Jola Siezen (all New Zealand) climbed into a box with a 26 x 27 x 22-in (66.04 x 68.58 x 55.88-cm) interior and remained there for 6 min 13.52 sec on the set of *NZ Smashes Guinness World Records* at the Sylvia Park mall, Auckland, New Zealand.

EXTRA!
FOR SENSATIONAL STRONGMAN FEATS AND BREATHTAKING BALANCING, SEE P.90.

JUGGLING

The ★longest duration juggling four objects was 2 hr 23 min and was achieved by David Slick (USA) in North Richland Hills, Texas, USA, on March 1, 2009.

David also holds the record for the ★longest duration juggling three objects – 12 hr 5 min – set at North Richland Hills Public Library, Texas, USA, on July 22, 2009.

And just to make things even more challenging… the ★longest duration juggling three balls while suspended upside down by gravity boots is 5 min 20 sec and was set by Ashrita Furman (USA) in the hallway of the Sri Chinmoy Centre in Jamaica, New York City, USA, on November 21, 2009.

★HIGHEST STATIC TRAPEZE ACT

Amanda Vicharelli (USA, above), John "Chuck" Berry (New Zealand), and Johannes "Jojo" Rose (Germany) performed a static trapeze act at a height of 2,171 ft (662 m) in Xiaozhai Tiankeng Cave, China, on October 2, 2008.

★ MOST JUGGLING CATCHES (ONE MINUTE)

On July 12, 2009, Zdenek Bradac (Czech Republic) beat his own record for the most juggling catches in a minute, with 339, at the Prinzenraub Festival in Altenburg, Germany.

★ MOST HULA HOOPS SPUN SIMULTANEOUSLY

Paul "Dizzy Hips" Blair (USA) spun 136 hula hoops simultaneously on CBS's *The Early Show* in New York City, USA, on November 12, 2009, to celebrate Guinness World Records Day.

★ TALLEST STILTS

The tallest stilts ever mastered measured 53 ft 10 in (16.41 m) from ground to ankle. Saimaiti Yiming (China) walked 10 steps on them, without touching his safety lines, in Shanshan county, Xinjiang, China, on November 15, 2006.

★FASTEST TIGHTROPE WALK OVER 100 M

Aisikaier Wubulikasimu (China) covered 100 m on a tightrope in 44.63 seconds at Taimu Mountain Scenic Spot, Fuding city, Fujian province, China, on October 27, 2009. The attempt was an outdoor event for *Zheng Da Zong Yi – Guinness World Records Special 2009*.

DID YOU KNOW?

MIKE HOWARD (UK) PERFORMED THE HIGHEST AERIAL TRAPEZE ACT, SUSPENDED FROM A HOT-AIR BALLOON AT AN ALTITUDE OF 19,600–20,300 FT (6,000–6,200 M).

The "three-ring circus" can offer entertainment in three rings at once. The first, run by "Lord" George Sainger, was in 1860.

TRIVIA

CIRCUS STYLE

The ★most open umbrellas balanced is eight, by Liu Lina (China, right) for *Zheng Da Zong Yi – Guinness World Records Special* in Beijing, China, on June 21, 2009. Qiu Jiangning (China, far right) made the ★highest jump through a hoop – 10 ft 2 in (3.12 m) – on the show four days earlier.

FUNAMBULIST:

Another name for "tightrope walker." It comes from the Latin "funambulus," meaning "rope dancer."

HEAVIEST ELEPHANT LIFTED

In 1975, while performing with Gerry Cottle's Circus (UK), Khalil Oghaby (Iran) lifted an elephant off the ground using a harness and platform above the animal. At 4,400 lb (2 tonnes), this is the heaviest elephant ever lifted by a human.

LONGEST-RUNNING CIRCUS

Ringling Bros. and Barnum & Bailey Circus (USA) is the world's longest running, with Barnum Bailey's "Greatest Show on Earth" established in 1870 and later merging with the Ringling Brothers in 1919. At its height, the circus carried 150 clowns, traveling three trains with a staff of 1,500 to 2,500 people.

LARGEST CIRCUS AUDIENCE

A crowd of 52,385 people gathered to see the Ringling Bros.

and Barnum & Bailey Circus at the Superdome, New Orleans, Louisiana, USA, on September 14, 1975.

HIGHEST SHALLOW DIVE

On October 9, 2009, Darren Taylor (USA) performed a shallow dive from a height of 35 ft 9 in (10.9 m) at the Gwinnett Arena, Atlanta, Georgia, USA. In doing so, he broke his own record by 1 in (2.5 cm).

★MOST 360° SPINS ON A TIGHTROPE (TWO MINUTES)

On September 20, 2007, Maimaitiaili Abula (China) performed 41 full-circle spins on a tightrope on the set of *Zheng Da Zong Yi – Guinness World Records Special* in Beijing, China.

★MOST ROTATIONS HUNG FROM THE NECK OF ANOTHER PERSON (30 SECONDS)

Liu Xiaogao and Liu Jiangshan (both China), from the Shenyang Jinying Youth Acrobatic Troupe, performed 82 rotations suspended from each other's neck by a belt in 30 seconds on the set of *Zheng Da Zong Yi – Guinness World Records Special* in Beijing, China, on November 21, 2009.

★MOST BULLWHIP CRACKS (ONE MINUTE)

Adam Winrich (USA) carried out 257 bullwhip cracks in a minute at The Stone's Throw Bar in Eau Claire, Wisconsin, USA, on June 20, 2009.

MOST CONSECUTIVE SOMERSAULTS HORSEBACK RIDING

In 1856, James Robinson (USA) performed 23 consecutive somersaults on horseback at Spalding Rogers Circus, Pittsburgh, Pennsylvania, USA.

FARTHEST JUMP RIDING A LION

Edgard and Askold Zapashny (both Russia), of the Russian State Circus Company, performed a 7-ft 6-in (2.3-m) jump astride a lion named Michael on July 28, 2006.

HUMAN
BILLED AS "ALAR," THE FIRST HUMAN ARROW WAS TONY ZEDORAS (USA), AT THE BARNUM & BAILEY CIRCUS IN THE USA IN 1896.

ARROW
VESTA GUESCHKOVA (BULGARIA) WAS FIRED 75 FT (22.9 M) ON DECEMBER 27, 1995. THE FARTHEST A HUMAN ARROW HAS BEEN FIRED.

> *"Pain lasts for a minute. The glory lasts for a lifetime."*
> **Shallow dive supremo Darren Taylor, aka Professor Splash**

★LONGEST DISTANCE BY A HORSE ON HIND LEGS

The greatest distance covered by a horse walking on only two legs is 95 ft 5 in (30 m) and was achieved by a horse named Doc, ridden by Gregory Ancelotti (Italy), on the set of *Lo Show dei Record*, in Milan, Italy, on April 25, 2009.

KUWAIT CITY, KUWAIT

The **largest kite flown** had a lifting area of 10,225.7 ft² (950 m²). Laid flat, it had a total area of 10,968.4 ft² (1,019 m²) and was 83 ft 7 in (25.475 m) long and 131 ft 3 in (40 m) wide. The kite was made by Abdulrahman Al Farsi and Faris Al Farsi (both Kuwait) and flown at the Kuwait Hala Festival in Flag Square, Kuwait City, Kuwait, on February 15, 2005.

29°22'N 47°58'E

POPULAR CULTURE
MASS PARTICIPATION

LARGEST "THRILLER" DANCE

The largest Michael Jackson "Thriller" dance was performed by 13,597 participants at an event organized by the Instituto de la Juventud del Gobierno del Distrito Federal at the Monumento a la Revolución, Mexico City, Mexico, on August 29, 2009.

★ LARGEST BACKWARD RACE

The record for the largest backward race was achieved by 539 people at an event organized by Mater Salvatoris Institute in Kapellen, Belgium, on March 13, 2009.

★ LARGEST BIKINI PARADE

A bikini parade involving 287 women set a world record at an event held by Kellogg's Special K in Johannesburg, South Africa, on November 7, 2009.

★ MOST PEOPLE CRAMMED IN A SMART CAR

A total of 16 members of the Candy Lane Dancers troupe (all New Zealand) squeezed into a standard Smart Car at the Sylvia Park shopping mall in Auckland, New Zealand, on August 23, 2009.

★ LARGEST FAMILY REUNION

A reunion involving 2,585 people was achieved by the Lilly family at Flat Top, West Virginia, USA, on August 9, 2009.

★ LARGEST HUMAN BEATBOX ENSEMBLE

Michael Krappel (Austria) assembled a beatbox ensemble with 327 participants in Vienna, Austria, on September 27, 2009.

★ MOST PEOPLE GOLD PANNING

The greatest number of people gold panning at the same time was 100, at an event held by Primaria Rosia Montana in Rosia Montana, Romania, on August 30, 2009.

★ MOST PEOPLE CHANTING

At an event held in Gärdet Park, Stockholm, Sweden, 2,558 people chanted together on August 15, 2009.

★ LARGEST BOLLYWOOD DANCE

A Bollywood dance featuring 1,082 students and teachers of the Anglo Chinese School was performed in Singapore on April 29, 2009.

★ MOST PEOPLE DRESSED AS BEES

A total of 1,901 participants dressed up as bees on July 15, 2009 in Staffordshire, UK.

★ MOST PEOPLE HOLDING THEIR BREATH UNDERWATER

On October 11, 2009, a total of 280 people held their breath underwater in Torri del Benaco, Verona, Italy. The record was achieved by "La Scuola del Mare 2" (Italy).

★ LARGEST CHRISTMAS-CRACKER PULLING

A group of 1,478 people engaged in a mass Christmas-cracker pull in Tochigi, Japan, on October 18, 2009.

★ LARGEST CHARITY WALK

A charity walk by 1,903 participants took place at an event organized in Rathcoole Park, Rathcoole, County Dublin, Ireland, on September 5, 2009.

★ LARGEST GROUP HUG

A group of 9,758 people encircled the citadel of Alba Iulia in Transylvania, Romania, in a communal hug on May 29, 2009.

★ LARGEST DANCE CLASS

The biggest dance class was achieved by an unprecedented 7,770 participants at an event organized by DanceSport Team Cebu International Inc. at the Cebu City Sports Center in Cebu City, the Philippines, on June 27, 2009. The participants were trained more than three weeks prior to the event to ensure the success of the attempt.

MINI A GROUP OF 21 MALAYSIAN STUDENTS FITTED INTO AN OLD-STYLE MINI COOPER ON JUNE 17, 2006, THE MOST PEOPLE CRAMMED INTO A MINI COOPER.

MAXI THE MOST PEOPLE CRAMMED INTO A NEW-MODEL MINI IS 24, AT AN EVENT SET UP BY GRUPO LOGAX, S.A. DE C.V. IN MEXICO CITY, MEXICO, ON AUGUST 19, 2009.

TEHRAN, IRAN

35°41'N 51°25'E

Official Iranian estimates gave the size of the crowds lining the 20-mile (32-km) route to Tehran's Behesht-e Zahra cemetery on June 11, 1989, for the funeral of Ayatollah Ruhollah Khomeini, as 10,200,000 people. That figure represented one-sixth of Iran's population, the **largest percentage of a population to attend a funeral**.

LARGEST GATHERING OF SMURFS

The most people dressed as Smurfs was 2,510 and was achieved by Jokers' Masquerade with the help of Swansea University at Swansea Oceana in Swansea, UK, on June 8, 2009. Everyone's faces, arms, and legs had to be painted blue to qualify.

MOST KITES FLOWN SIMULTANEOUSLY

For an initiative organized by United Nations Relief and Works Agency (UNRWA), children at Al-Waha beach, Gaza Strip, on July 30, 2009, flew 3,710 kites, the greatest number in the air together at one time.

★ LARGEST COFFEE PARTY (SINGLE VENUE)

A coffee party comprising an incredible 8,162 participants was held by Krüger GmbH & Co. KG (Germany) at the Jugendpark in Cologne, Germany, on August 30, 2009.

★ MOST PEOPLE EXERCISING TO A VIDEOGAME

On May 22, 2009, 605 people performed an exercise routine to a videogame at the Electronic Arts Burnaby Campus Sports Field in Burnaby, British Columbia, Canada.

★ LARGEST MARTIAL ARTS DISPLAY

A martial arts display featuring 33,996 participants practicing tai chi took place at an event organized by Beijing Municipal Bureau of Sports in Beijing, China, on August 8, 2009.

★ MOST PEOPLE KNITTING

On August 7, 2009, at the "Sock Summit" in Portland, Oregon, USA, 937 people took part in a mass knitting event.

★ LARGEST ANNUAL GATHERING OF WOMEN

Attukal Pongala in Kerala, India, is a celebration of womenhood in which offerings (*pongala*) are made to Attukal Amma, the mother goddess. The 2010 event attracted more than three million women.

★ LARGEST PICNIC (MULTIPLE VENUE)

A total of 12,934 picnickers assembled across 79 venues in a record attempt organized in the UK for National Family Week on May 25, 2009.

★ MOST PEOPLE IN A MULTI-LEGGED RACE

The greatest number of participants in a multi-legged race was achieved by 261 people at an event held at the Nogata North Elementary School in Nogata, Japan, on November 21, 2008.

★ MOST PEOPLE DRESSED AS SUPERHEROES

The Children's Hospital at Dartmouth (CHaD)– in Hanover, New Hampshire, USA – hosted a record-beating 1,016 people dressed in a wide variety of superhero costumes on August 29, 2009.

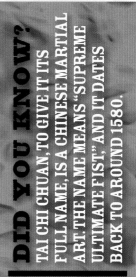

DID YOU KNOW?

TAI CHI CHUAN, TO GIVE IT ITS FULL NAME, IS A CHINESE MARTIAL ART. THE NAME MEANS "SUPREME ULTIMATE FIST," AND IT DATES BACK TO AROUND 1580.

Ken Dickenson and Kevin Bartolo performed a tai chi marathon lasting for 25 hr 5 min in Australia on March 17–18, 2006.

TRIVIA

SUPER STUNTS
MASS
PARTICIPATION

★ MOST PARTICIPANTS IN A BADMINTON RALLY

A total of 96 participants played in a badminton rally on May 23, 2009. The record was set by Aviva (Singapore), in Raffles City Mall, Singapore.

★ LARGEST SCUBA DIVING LESSON

A "class" of 2,465 people took part in a scuba lesson in the water of Malalayang beach in Manado, Indonesia, on August 16, 2009.

MOST...

★ MODELS IN A FASHION SHOW

The Muaa Summer 2010 show in Buenos Aires, Argentina, saw 260 models take to the runway on October 8, 2009.

★ BACKING DANCERS TO A SINGER

A total of 251 members of an audience were trained to perform a choreographed routine for singer Alesha Dixon (UK) in London, UK, on April 2, 2009.

★ AUTOMOBILES WASHED IN EIGHT HOURS (MULTIPLE VENUES)

During the Soaps It Up! National Car Wash Fundraiser event coordinated by Victory Management Group (USA) on June 20, 2009, 4,105 people gathered across the USA to wash automobiles and raise money for cystic fibrosis research.

★ GOLF BALLS HIT SIMULTANEOUSLY

A record 1,873 balls were hit simultaneously at the Real Federacion Español de Golf course in Madrid, Spain, on September 27, 2009.

★ CHAMPAGNE BOTTLES SABERED SIMULTANEOUSLY

At an event organized by International Sabrageurs Anonymous in Portarlington, Co. Laois, Ireland, on July 18, 2009, 152 participants simultaneously sabered bottles of champagne.

★ SKY LANTERNS FLOWN SIMULTANEOUSLY

An amazing 10,318 sky lanterns were launched at an event organized by Freedom Faithnet Global (Indonesia) in Ancol Carnaval Beach, Jakarta, Indonesia, on December 5, 2009.

★ KARAOKE PARTICIPANTS

The largest karaoke session took place at Bristol Motor Speedway in Bristol, Tennessee, USA, on August 22, 2009, when 160,000 people sang "Friends in Low Places," by Garth Brooks (USA), before the NASCAR Sharpie 500 race.

★ LARGEST PARADE OF MINIS

The London & Surrey Mini Owners Club organized a parade of Minis consisting of 1,450 vehicles as part of the London to Brighton Mini Run, in Crystal Palace, London, UK, on May 17, 2009.

MINIS: Made by British Motor Corporation (BMC), these old-style Minis were in production between 1959 and 2000.

ICON
THE MINI WAS VOTED THE SECOND MOST INFLUENTIAL AUTOMOBILE OF THE 20TH CENTURY IN 1999. THE FORD MODEL T CLAIMED FIRST PLACE.

MI 5YCO

GUINNESS WORLD RECORDS 2011

★LARGEST GATHERING OF SUPERHEROES

A record 1,091 people gathered at Twickenham Stadium, London, UK, while dressed as superheroes at an event organized by the Rugby Football Union and facilitated by event360 at the Emirates Airline London Sevens on May 23, 2010. Various hulks, bananamen, and ninja turtles attended, but Elvis and Santas were disqualified!

EXTRA! FOR MORE ECCENTRIC BEHAVIOUR, TURN TO PP.142-143 FOR SOME RECORD-BREAKING COLLECTORS!

LARGEST...

★HALLOWEEN GATHERING

A group of 508 people in scary costumes assembled in Bloomington, Indiana, USA, on Halloween 2009.

On September 24, 2009, the ★**largest gathering of skeletons** featured 197 people, in London, UK.

★GATHERING OF PEOPLE DRESSED AS STORYBOOK CHARACTERS

On November 12, 2009, 300 people dressed up as storybook characters for Guinness World Records Day. The record was set by Carr's Glen Primary School, in Belfast, Northern Ireland, UK.

★SPORTS LESSON

A record 882 students at Ballyclare High School in Northern Ireland took part in a sports lesson on November 12, 2009. Also top of the class were 5,401 participants who enjoyed the ★**largest physics lesson** in Denver, Colorado, USA, on May 7, 2009.

LONGEST CONGA ON ICE

An impressive 252 participants performed a conga on ice at the Alexandra Palace Ice Rink in London, UK, to celebrate Guinness World Records Day on November 11, 2009.

★LARGEST SOCCER TOURNAMENT

Copa Telmex 2009 was contested by 187,765 players, in 11,280 teams, and held in Mexico between May 1 and November 29, 2009. It was staged with the aim of providing a brighter future for Mexican youth.

ON ICE THE LARGEST ICE SKATING PINWHEEL WAS SET BY 70 PARTICIPANTS IN EINDHOVEN, THE NETHERLANDS, ON MARCH 14, 2010.

HUMAN ENDEAVORS

★ NEW RECORD
★ UPDATED RECORD

★ YOUNGEST FEMALE TO ROW THE INDIAN OCEAN

Sarah Outen (UK, b. May 26, 1985) single-handedly crossed the Indian Ocean, east to west, between April 1 and August 3, 2009 in her boat *Serendipity* (which she affectionately termed *Dippers*). At the start of her trip, Sarah was aged 23 years 310 days. Her journey began in Australia and ended 4,180 nautical miles (4,810 miles; 7,740 km) later in Mauritius. During the epic trip, she lost 44 lb (20 kg) in weight – despite scoffing a stomach-bulging 500 chocolate bars – and also broke two oars.

EXTRA!
IF YOU LOVE RECORD-BREAKING TALES OF THE HIGH SEAS, TURN TO P.118.

SSR 136912

SARAH OUTEN
SOLO ACROSS THE INDIAN - 2009
WWW.SARAHOUTEN.CO.UK

CONTENTS

{ *"If you're strong up top and have prepared well, then you have the best chance – stubborn and strong, and with a bit of luck, you'll weather the worst of the storms. It's all about attitude, endurance and keeping happy."*
Sarah Outen, ocean rower }

INDIAN OCEAN

The Indian Ocean is the planet's third largest
ocean, accounting for around 20% of the
planet's surface water. It is the second deepest
ocean – after the Pacific – with an average
depth of 12,260 ft (3,736 m).

The route from Australia to Mauritius stretches
for 3,100 nautical miles (see green line, right),
but Sarah clocked up 4,180 nautical miles (see
red line), thanks to "feisty currents, teasing
winds, and general unpredictable weather."

HUMAN ENDEAVORS
GRAND TOURS

★GREATEST DISTANCE ON A HAND-CRANKED CYCLE IN 24 HOURS

Thomas Lange (Germany) covered 403.80 miles (649.85 km) on a hand-cranked cycle in 24 hours during the Bike Sebring 12/24 Hours, in Sebring, Florida, USA, on February 14–15, 2009.

(8,008 km) by powered paraglider flying west to east across Canada from Tofino (British Columbia) to Bay St Lawrence (Nova Scotia) from May 15, 2009 to August 24, 2009. He landed and took off from Canadian schools along the way, where he gave presentations to the children to encourage them to challenge their fears and realize their own dreams.

PUNT

Aided by four other crew members, John Pearse (UK) traveled by punt from Oxford, UK, to Leeds, UK, and back to Oxford from June 19 to August 10, 1965, a total of 721 miles (1,160 km).

WALKING BACKWARD

Aged 36, Plennie L Wingo (USA) completed an 8,000-mile (12,875-km) backward walk from Santa Monica, California, USA, to Istanbul, Turkey, in 517 days between April 15, 1931 and October 24, 1932. Wingo averaged 15.47 miles (24.89 km) each day of his trip.

WHEELCHAIR

Rick Hansen (Canada) wheeled his wheelchair 24,901 miles (40,075 km) through four continents and 34 countries, starting from Vancouver, BC, Canada, on March 21, 1985 and returning there on May 22, 1987.

FASTEST...

PARIS–LONDON JOURNEY

On September 24, 1983, David Boyce of Stewart Wrightson (Aviation) Ltd traveled the 214 miles (344 km) from central Paris, France, to central London, UK (BBC TV Centre), in 38 min 58 sec. He traveled by motorcycle and helicopter to Le Bourget, France; then via Hawker Hunter jet (piloted by the late Michael Carlton) to Biggin Hill, UK; and lastly by helicopter to the TV Centre parking lot.

EXTRA!
MORE OF A HOMEBODY THAN A GLOBE-TROTTING GRAND TOURIST? THEN SWITCH TO P.168 TO FIND OUT WHAT'S ON TV.

★LONGEST JOURNEY SWIMMING

Martin Strel (Slovenia) covered a distance of 3,273.38 miles (5,268 km) when he swam the entire length of the Amazon River, in Peru and Brazil, from February 1 to April 8, 2007.

LONGEST JOURNEY BY...

carrying a 12-ft-tall (3.7-m) wooden cross and preaching from the Bible throughout.

★MOTORIZED BICYCLE

Eddie Sedgemore (UK) cycled 1,912.1 miles (3,077 km) on a motorized bicycle in 28 days from May 9 to June 5, 2009.

★ A PILGRIM

The greatest distance claimed for a "round the world" pilgrimage is 38,102 miles (61,319 km) by Arthur Blessitt (USA) since December 25, 1969. He has crossed 315 "nations, island groups, and territories"

POWERED PARAGLIDER

Benjamin Jordan (Canada) traveled 4,975.93 miles

FASTEST TIME TO CYCLE THE LENGTH OF THE PAN-AMERICAN HIGHWAY

Scott Napier (UK) cycled the Pan-American highway from Prudhoe Bay, Alaska, USA, to Ushuaia, Argentina, in 125 days from June 22 to October 25, 2009. Napier cycled a total of 14,099.11 miles (22,690.36 km) on his trip.

DID YOU KNOW?

GIAMPIETRO MARJON (ITALY) CYCLED THE SOUTH AMERICAN PORTION OF THE PAN-AMERICAN HIGHWAY, FROM CHIGORODO, COLOMBIA, TO USHUAIA, ARGENTINA, IN 59 DAYS IN 2000.

The Pan-American highway is broken by a small impassable section called the Darién Gap.

TRIVIA

CLASSIC JOURNEYS

On every continent there is a classic journey to be found; it may be from one extreme point to another, or it may be between two points that have an historical or even romantic association. Whatever the journey may be, you can be sure that someone is going to attempt to complete that journey using either an outlandish mode of transport, or in the quickest time possible, and more often than not both! These are a few of our favorite fastest journeys.

JOURNEY	FROM	TO	DISTANCE	HOW	WHO	TIME	WHEN
Cairo to Cape	Cairo, Egypt	Cape Town, South Africa	approximately 6,835 miles (11,000 km)	Bicycle	Chris Evans, David Genders, Michael Kennedy (all UK), Paul Reynaert (Belgium), Jeremy Wex, Steve Topham, Scotty Robinson, Andrew Griffin (all Canada), and Sascha Hartl (Austria)	119 days 1 hr 32 min	January 18 to May 17, 2003
John O'Groats to Land's End	John O'Groats, Scotland, UK	Land's End, England, UK	874 miles (1,407 km)	Foot	Andrew Rivett (UK)	9 days 2 hr 26 min	May 4–13, 2002
Land's End to John O'Groats	Land's End, England, UK	John O'Groats, Scotland, UK	874 miles (1,407 km)	Unicycle	Robert Ambrose (UK)	12 days 1 hr 59 min	August 13–25, 2000
Pan-American Highway	Ushuaia, Argentina	Prudhoe Bay, Alaska	19,019 miles (30,431 km)	Foot	George Meegan (UK)	2,426 days	January 26, 1977 to September 18, 2009
Trans-Australia	Perth, Western Australia	Sydney, New South Wales	approximately 2,485 miles (4,000 km)	Bicycle	Richard Vollebregt (Australia)	8 days 10 hr 57 min	October 13–21, 2006
Trans-USA	Jacksonville, Florida	San Diego, California	2,595 miles (4,175 km)	Inline skates	Russell "Rusty" Moncrief (USA)	69 days 8 hr 45 min	January 5 to March 15, 2002
Trans-USA	Newport, Oregon	Washington, DC	3,261 miles (5,248 km)	Unicycle	Akira Matsushima (Japan)	43 days	July 10 to August 22, 1992
Trans-USA	San Francisco, California	New York City	3,100 miles (4,989 km)	Foot	Frank Giannino, Jr (USA)	46 days 8 hr 36 min	September 1 to October 17, 1980

UNPOWERED CROSSING OF THE BERING STRAIT
The fastest crossing of the Bering Strait – the sea channel that separates Asia from North America -- on foot and skis was completed by Dmitry Shparo and his son Matvey (both Russia), achieved when they reached Chariot, Alaska, USA, on March 20, 1998.

They had begun their journey in Mys Dezhneva, East Cape, Russia, on March 1, and traveled a total distance of approximately 180 miles (290 km).

★TIME TO VISIT ALL SOVEREIGN COUNTRIES
Kashi Samaddar (India) visited all 194 United Nations member countries in 6 years, 10 months, and 7 days, between July 18, 2002 and May 24, 2009.

RELAY CYCLE AROUND AUSTRALIA
Starting and finishing in Brisbane, Queensland, a team of eight cyclists took 18 days 8 hr 39 min to cycle 8,894 miles (14,314 km) around Australia between October 22 and November 9, 2001, taking in 19 coastal cities along the way.

LONGEST JOURNEY BY SKATEBOARD
Starting in Leysin, Switzerland, on June 24, 2007 and finishing in Shanghai, China, on September 28, 2008, Rob Thomson (New Zealand) traveled a staggering 7,555 miles (12,159 km) on his skateboard in 463 days.

★LONGEST JOURNEY ON A POCKETBIKE (MINIMOTO)
Ryan Galbraith and Chris Stinson (both USA) traveled a record 445.26 miles (716.58 km) on pocketbikes (minimotos) from August 5 to August 8, 2009. Galbraith and Stinson began their journey in Colorado, USA, and ended in South Dakota, USA.

PUSH!
IN 2001, 30 SOUTH AFRICAN SCHOOL PUPILS PUSHED AN UNPOWERED SOAPBOX CART 1,280 MILES (2,061 KM) BETWEEN KOMATIPOORT AND CAPE TOWN, SOUTH AFRICA, IN 19 DAYS.

CRAWL!
ARULANANTHAM SURESH JOACHIM (CANADA) CRAWLED FOR A RECORD 35.18 MILES (56.62 KM) AROUND A CIRCUIT SYDNEY...

NEW RECORD
UPDATED RECORD

HUMAN ENDEAVORS
AROUND THE WORLD

★ ★ ★ ★ ★ ★ ★ ★ ★ ★ ★ ★ ★ ★

"There is no way they would send me off without me being fully prepared."

Michael Perham, on his parents' support for his record-breaking feat

★ YOUNGEST PERSON TO SAIL AROUND THE WORLD SOLO AND UNSUPPORTED

Michael Perham (UK, b. March 16, 1992) sailed non-stop around the world in *TotallyMoney.com*, starting and finishing at the Ushant/Lizard line, in 284 days from November 15, 2008 to August 27, 2009, arriving aged 16 years 7 months 30 days. It is a record that is unlikely to be beaten as GWR no longer accepts claims for this category by anyone under 16 years of age.

FIRST...

CIRCUMNAVIGATION BY AIRCRAFT WITHOUT REFUELING

Richard G "Dick" Rutan and Jeana Yeager (both USA) traveled the globe westward from Edwards Air Force Base, California, USA, in nine days from December 14 to 23, 1986 without refueling. The key to their success was their aircraft, *Voyager* -- created by Dick's brother Burt, the man behind *SpaceShipOne*, the vehicle used in the **first privately funded manned spaceflight.**

FIRST UNPOWERED EQUATORIAL CIRCUMNAVIGATION

Mike Horn (South Africa) circumnavigated the globe along the Equator by bicycle, dugout canoe, sailing trimaran, and on foot in 513 days between June 2, 1999 and October 27, 2000. His journey started and finished near Libreville in the west African state of Gabon, and proceeded in six legs that included crossing the Amazon and central Africa.

CIRCUMNAVIGATION BY BALLOON SOLO

Steve Fossett (USA) circled the globe in *Bud Light Spirit of Freedom*, a 140-ft-tall (42.6-m) mixed-gas balloon, from June 19 to July 2, 2002. He took off from Northam, Western Australia, and landed at Eromanga, Queensland, Australia, after covering 20,627 miles (33,195 km) over 14 days 19 hr 50 min – the **longest duration flown by a balloon solo.**

PERSON TO SAIL AROUND THE WORLD (SOLO AND NONSTOP)

Robin Knox-Johnston (UK) set sail from Falmouth, Cornwall, UK, in his yacht *Suhaili* on June 14, 1968 as one of nine participants in the *Sunday Times* Golden Globe Race. By the time he returned to Falmouth on April 22, 1969, he was the only remaining competitor and claimed both the record and the £5,000 ($8,070) prize money.

WOMAN TO SAIL NONSTOP AROUND THE WORLD IN BOTH DIRECTIONS

On February 16, 2009, former PE teacher Dee Caffari (UK) finished the Vendée Globe round-the-world yacht race in sixth place. This achievement means that Dee is the first woman to sail both ways around the world, alone and

FIRST CIRCUMNAVIGATION BY AIRCRAFT

Two US Army Douglas DWC seaplanes, the *Chicago*, piloted by Lt Lowell H Smith (right), and the *New Orleans*, flown by Leslie P Arnold, flew around the world in 57 "hops" between April 6 and September 28, 1924, beginning and ending at Seattle, Washington, USA.

EXTRA!
ALL THESE RECORD HOLDERS HAVE SKIPPED OVER OCEANS - MAKE SURE YOU DON'T BY SETTING SAIL FOR PP. 38-39.

VOCALINK

FIRST CIRCUMNAVIGATION BY AMPHIBIOUS VEHICLE

Ben Carlin (Australia) and his American wife Elinore left Montreal, Canada, in *Half-Safe*, a modified amphibious jeep, on July 24, 1950 intent on going around the world. It was an eventful trip – Elinore left her husband in India and filed for divorce – but eventually Ben arrived back in Montreal on May 8, 1958, after traveling 39,000 miles (62,765 km) over land and 9,600 miles (15,450 km) by water.

unaided. What's more, she is only the fourth person ever to do so. This remarkable feat is now added to her previous achievement of becoming the **first woman to circumnavigate westward solo and nonstop** in May 2006.

CIRCUMNAVIGATION BY PASSENGER AIRCRAFT

The fastest flight under the Fédération Aéronautique Internationale (FAI)

rules, which permit flights that exceed the length of the Tropic of Cancer or Capricorn (22,858.8 miles; 36,787.6 km), was one of 31 hr 27 min 49 sec, set by an Air France Concorde, flight AF1995 (Capts Michel Dupont and Claude Hetru, both France). The Concorde flew from JFK airport in New York, USA, eastbound via Toulouse, Dubai, Bangkok, Guam, Honolulu, and Acapulco on August 15–16, 1995 with a crew of 18 plus an additional 80 passengers.

Also according to the FAI rules, the **fastest time to fly around the world on scheduled flights** is 44 hr 6 min by David J Springbett (UK). His route took him over a course of 23,068 miles (37,124 km), from Los Angeles, California, USA, eastbound via London, Bahrain, Singapore, Bangkok, Manila, Tokyo, and Honolulu on January 8–10, 1980.

FASTEST TIME AROUND THE WORLD BY A SAILING CREW

Bruno Peyron (France) captained a crew of 14 around the world in 50 days 16 hr 20 min 4 sec aboard the maxi catamaran *Orange II* from January 24 to March 16, 2005. The journey started and finished in Ushant, France.

FIRST CIRCUMNAVIGATION

While Ferdinand Magellan is often credited with the first round-the-world voyage, he died on the way and never completed the journey. He led a fleet of five ships that left Spain on September 20, 1519. Of these, only the *Vittoria* returned, on September 8, 1522, under the command of navigator Juan Sebastián de Elcano and with just 17 of the original crew.

CIRCUMNAVIGATION BY HELICOPTER

John Williams and Ron Bower (both USA) flew west around the world (against the prevailing winds) in a Bell 430 helicopter in 17 days 6 hr 14 min 25 sec from August 17 to September 3, 1996, starting and finishing in Fair Oaks, London, UK.

CIRCUMNAVIGATION BY CAR

The record for the first and fastest man and woman to have circumnavigated the Earth by car covering six continents under the rules applicable in 1989 and 1991 embracing more than an Equator's length of driving (24,901 road miles; 40,075 km), is held by Saloo Choudhury and his wife, Neena Choudhury (both India). The journey took 69 days 19 hours 5 minutes from September 9 to November 17, 1989. The couple drove a 1989 Hindustan "Contessa Classic," starting and finishing in Delhi, India.

ON YER BIKE!
PHILIP WHITE (UK) WENT AROUND THE WORLD ON A BICYCLE BETWEEN JUNE 19, 2004 AND APRIL 24, 2005, AT THE RECORD-BREAKING AGE OF 24 YEARS & 125 DAYS.

NEW RECORD
★ UPDATED RECORD

LUCKNOW, INDIA
First established in 1959, the City Montessori School in Lucknow, India, had an enrolment of 32,114 pupils on February 5, 2008 for the 2007–08

26°51'N
80°55'E

HUMAN ENDEAVORS
ENDURANCE

★ ★ ★ ★ ★ ★ ★

★ MOST CONSECUTIVE POGO-STICK JUMPS (MALE)

The greatest number of consecutive jumps achieved on a pogo stick is 186,152, by James Roumeliotis (USA) in Massachusetts, USA, on September 22–23, 2007.

TREADMILL RUNS

The ★farthest distance run on a treadmill in 48 hours (team) is 539.86 miles (868.64 km), by the 12-strong Porsche Human Performance (UK) team at the Festival of Speed, Goodwood, UK, on July 3–5, 2009.

Lee Chamberlain (UK) traveled 468.04 miles (753.24 km) on a treadmill at the Camberley Shopping Centre, Surrey, UK, from July 18 to 25, 2009, the ★farthest distance run on a treadmill in a week.

FARTHEST...

★ DISTANCE TO SURF ON A RIVER BORE

On June 8, 2009, Sergio Laus (Brazil) surfed the Pororoca bore on the Araguari River, Amapa, Brazil, for 36 minutes, covering 7.33 miles (11.8 km).

★ LONGEST TIME TO HOLD THE BREATH VOLUNTARILY (FEMALE)

Karoline Mariechen Meyer (Brazil) held her breath underwater for an astonishing 18 min 32.59 sec at the Racer Academy swimming pool, Florianopolis, Brazil, on July 10, 2009. A professional freediver, Karoline trained for four months to try to break the record. Prior to the attempt, she inhaled oxygen for 24 minutes.

★ PADDLEBOARD JOURNEY (TEAM)

Stéphanie Geyer-Barneix, Alexandra Lux, and Flora Manciet (all France) completed a paddleboard journey extending 3,001 miles (4,830 km; 2,607 nautical miles), from the island of Cap Breton (Canada) to Capbreton (France) on August 28, 2009. The journey took 54 days to complete and the three women paddled from a kneeling or lying position using only their hands to propel them through the water.

★ DISTANCE BY MOTORCYCLE IN 24 HOURS

Omar Hilal Al-Mamari (Oman) rode 1,321.65 miles (2,127 km) on a motorcycle on a road between Marmool and Thamrait in Oman on August 18–19, 2009.

★ DISTANCE RUN IN ONE HOUR (FEMALE)

Dire Tune (Ethiopia) ran 60,751 ft (18,517 m) in one hour at the IAAF World Athletics Grand Prix meeting in Ostrava, Czech Republic, on June 12, 2008.

★ OPEN-WATER SWIM RELAY

A team of 200 participants swam a total of 425.48 miles (684.75 km) in an open-water relay at Lake Camlough, Camlough, Northern Ireland, UK, between September 9 and 19, 2009.

DISTANCE WALKED OVER HOT PLATES

Rolf Iven (Germany) walked 75 ft 1 in (22.90 m) over hot plates on the set of *Lo Show dei Record*, in Milan, Italy, on April 18, 2009.

★ FASTEST MILE IN A BOMB DISPOSAL SUIT

Lt Jonathan Kehoe (USA) ran a mile wearing a bomb disposal suit in a time of 10 min 16 sec at Camp ECHO in Diwaniyah provence, Iraq, on February 2, 2009. Jonathan is a lieutenant in the US Navy Explosive Ordnance Disposal (USN EOD). He wore a 75-lb (34-kg) EOD 9 bomb suit.

EXTRA! FOR AERIAL DAREDEVILRY, TAKE OFF FOR P.116. AND FOR TALES OF BRAVERY AND ENDURANCE ON THE WORLD'S OCEANS, WAVE HELLO TO P.118.

8°35'N
98°40'E

MEDAN, NORTH SUMATRA, INDONESIA

A young pointer puppy named Judy was captured by the Japanese in 1942 and interned at a makeshift POW camp at Medan, Indonesia, along with the captured crew of HMS *Grasshopper*, of which she was

DID YOU KNOW?

THE ★ MOST SANCTIONED TRIATHLONS COMPLETED IN ONE YEAR IS 123 AND WAS ACHIEVED BY BART M HACKLEY (USA) FROM FEBRUARY 21, 1988 TO FEBRUARY 19, 1989.

The ★**first modern triathlon** (a swim, cycle, and run) was held in San Diego, USA, in 1974.

TRIVIA

LONGEST STATIC CYCLING MARATHON

Switzerland's Mehrzad Shirvani rode a static cycle for a record eight days (192 hours) at the Kortrijk Xpo, Kortrijk, Belgium, from January 17 to 25, 2009. Shirvani beat the previous record by more than six hours.

★GREATEST DISTANCE RUN BY A RELAY TEAM

The longest distance run by a relay team is 1,923 miles (3,096 km) and was achieved by the Gillette Phenomenal Tour over 14 days, from September 21, 2009 to October 5, 2009.

IRON
IF CONVENTIONAL TRIATHLONS AREN'T TESTING ENOUGH, TRY AN IRONMAN: A 2.4-MILE (3.86-KM) SWIM AND A 112-MILE (180.25-KM) CYCLE, FOLLOWED BY A MARATHON!

LONGEST...

★READING-ALOUD MARATHON (TEAM)
Elizabeth Sánchez Vegas, Ana María Leonardi, María Cristina Alarcón, Lilly Blanco, Devorah Sasha, and Isabel Viera, from International Solidarity for Human Rights, read the Universal Declaration of Human Rights aloud at the InterAmerican Campus of the Miami Dade College in Miami, Florida, USA, for 240 hr 15 min 27 sec from November 3 to 13, 2009.

★DANCE MARATHON (INDIVIDUAL)
Dr Vattikotta Yadagiriacharya (India) danced for 108 hours continuously at the Ravindra Bharathi Auditorium, Hyderabad, India, from November 25 to 29, 2008.

TENNIS MARATHONS
The ★**longest doubles tennis match** lasted 50 hr 00 min 8 sec and was played between Vince Johnson, Bill Geideman, Brad Ansley, and Allen Finley (all USA) at the YMCA of Catawba Valley, Hickory, North Carolina, USA, from November 7 to 9, 2008.

The ★**longest singles tennis match** lasted 36 hours and was achieved by Dennis Schrader and Bart Hendriks (both Netherlands), in Zandvoort, the Netherlands, on September 10–11, 2009.

★STAND-UP COMEDY SHOW (INDIVIDUAL)
Comedian Tommy Tiernan (Ireland) performed a stand-up set lasting 36 hr 15 min at Nuns Island Theatre, Galway, Ireland. The event began at 3 p.m. on Friday, April 10, 2009, and ended two days later, at 3:15 a.m.

★TIME TO HOLD A LIVE SCORPION IN THE MOUTH
Kanchana Ketkaew (Thailand) held a living scorpion in her mouth for 2 min 23 sec on the set of *Lo Show dei Record* in Milan, Italy, on April 11, 2009. Her husband placed the scorpion in her mouth.

★FULL-BODY ICE CONTACT
Chen Kecai (China) spent 1 hr 48 min 21 sec in direct contact with ice in the frozen Jingbo Lake, Mudanjiang City, China, on March 14, 2010.

★HANDSHAKE
• On September 21, 2009, Jack Tsonis and Lindsay Morrison (Australia) shook hands for 12 hr 34 min 56 sec in Sydney, Australia.
• George Posner and John-Clark Levin (both USA) then shook for 15 hours in California, USA, on October 4, 2009.
• And on November 21, 2009, Matthew Rosen and Joe Ackerman (both UK) shook for 15 hr 30 min 45 sec in London, UK.

MAN
THE FASTEST TIME TO COMPLETE AN IRONMAN RACE IS 7 HR 50 MIN 27 SEC, BY LUC VAN LIERDE (BELGIUM) AT ROTH, GERMANY, ON JULY 13, 1997.

velofollies
www.velofollies.be

★ **NEW RECORD**
★ **UPDATED RECORD**

In its most scholarly transliteration, Krungthep Mahanakhon, the official name for Bangkok, the capital of Thailand, has 168 letters and is the **longest placename**. The official short version (without capital letters, which are not used in Thai) is: krungthephphramahanakhon

18°45'N
100°29'E

FEATURE
LAND SPEED RECORD

INTAKE DUCT
A single, central intake duct delivers airflow to the engine. The procedure is: 1. air enters; 2. air is compressed and pressurized; 3. fuel is added, then ignited; 4. expanded air is forced through the turbines; 5. gases are expelled through a nozzle out of the back of the engine.

COCKPIT
The driver is secured in a rigid carbon-fiber safety cell based on the design of a fighter plane cockpit. Its designer, Andy Green (who will drive the *Bloodhound*), calls it the "world's fastest office"!

WINGLETS
Dynamic (computer-controlled) winglets above the wheels help to maintain a constant wheel load – i.e., they keep the car on the ground!

BODYWORK
The carbon-fiber and aluminum shell can withstand an air pressure of more than 2,457 lb/ft² (12 tonnes/m²). Changes to the bodywork are constantly fed to the onboard computer.

★ ★ ★ ★ ★ ★ ★ ★ ★ ★ ★ ★

IN LATE 2011 (OR EARLY 2012), A NEW ATTEMPT WILL BE MADE AT THE LAND SPEED RECORD. THE TEAM BEHIND THE ATTEMPT IS LED BY THE UK'S RICHARD NOBLE (BELOW RIGHT) AND ANDY GREEN (BELOW LEFT), WHO SET THE CURRENT RECORD OF NEARLY 763 MPH (1,228 KM/H) IN 1997. THIS TIME, THE AIM IS TO BREAK THE 1,000 MPH (1,609 KM/H) BARRIER...

LAND SPEED RECORD
The official land speed record (measured over one mile) is 763.035 mph (1,227.985 km/h; Mach 1.020), set by Andy Green (UK) on October 15, 1997 in the Black Rock Desert, Nevada, USA, in *Thrust SSC* (SuperSonic Car).

Thrust SSC was the brainchild of former land speed record-holder Richard Noble (UK).

★ FIRST CAR TO BREAK THE SOUND BARRIER
When Andy Green set the land speed record in 1997 in the Black Rock Desert, it was the first time that anyone on land had gone faster than the speed of sound – around 768 mph (1,236 km/h) in dry air at 68°F (20°C). The resultant sonic boom shook a school and caused sprinkler covers to fall off in the nearby town of Gerlach. Pilot Green achieved the record 50 years and a day after the sound barrier was broken in the air by pilot Chuck Yeager (USA).

FASTEST SPEED ON A CONVENTIONAL MOTORCYCLE
John Noonan (USA) reached a speed of 252.662 mph (406.62 km/h) on a modified 1,350 cc Suzuki Hayabusa at Bonneville Salt Flats, Utah, USA, on September 7, 2005.

FASTEST ROCKET CAR
The highest speed ever attained in a rocket-powered car is 631.367 mph (1,016.084 km/h) over the first measured kilometer by *The Blue Flame*, on the Bonneville Salt Flats, Utah, USA, driven by Gary Gabelich (USA) on October 23, 1970. Momentarily, Gabelich exceeded 650 mph (1,046 km/h). The car was powered by a liquid natural gas/hydrogen peroxide rocket engine.

QUIZ!
HOW LONG AFTER THE SOUND BARRIER WAS FIRST BROKEN DID ANDY GREEN SET THE CURRENT LAND SPEED RECORD?
SEE P.278 FOR THE ANSWER.

GEE!
AS HE ACCELERATES, DRIVER ANDY GREEN WILL EXPERIENCE A G-FORCE OF 2.5 g, WHICH WILL PUSH HIM BACK INTO HIS SEAT AND FORCE THE BLOOD INTO HIS HEAD.

WHIZZ!
AS HE SLOWS DOWN, ANDY WILL FEEL A FORCE OF 3 g IN THE OPPOSITE DIRECTION, DRAINING THE BLOOD FROM HIS HEAD TO HIS FEET. HOPEFULLY, HE WON'T LOSE CONSCIOUSNESS!

★ **NEW RECORD**
★ **UPDATED RECORD**

KUALA LUMPUR, MALAYSIA
3°08'N 101°41'E
The 425-ft 1-tall (30-m) tower at Kuala Lumpur International Airport (KLIA) in Malaysia is the **tallest air traffic control tower** in the world. The design, by a local architect, is shaped like a giant Olympic torch.

PARACHUTE

After the attempt, the throttle is closed and airbrakes are deployed to begin *Bloodhound*'s deceleration. When the car slows to about 600 mph (950 km/h), a parachute is deployed, decreasing acceleration to 3 *g*. The car should stop within 4.5 miles (7 km).

FIN

Directional stability is provided by a relatively small fin – too big and the car can be affected by crosswinds; too small and it will be unstable.

EJ200 ENGINE

Approximately half of the thrust is provided by a 2,204-lb (1,000-kg) Rolls-Royce EJ200 engine – a military turbofan normally found in the engine bay of a Eurofighter Typhoon. And located beneath the engine is the...

HYBRID SOLID-FUEL ROCKET

At 350 mph (563 km/h), the 882-lb (400-kg) hybrid solid-fuel rocket kicks in; together, the jet and rocket has a power of 47,500 lb (212 kN) – equivalent to 180 Formula One cars.

REAR WHEELS

The 35.8-in (90-cm) solid-aluminum wheels turn 12,000 times a minute. They are protected by front- and rear-pointing covers that not only reduce drag but also protect the wheels from debris.

SUPER-SONIC CAR

Shown here is a CGI of the 14,148-lb (6,422-kg), 50-ft-long (12.8-m) *Bloodhound*, the SuperSonic Car (SSC) that Richard Noble hopes will jet driver Andy Green to over 1,000 mph (1,609 km/h) – faster than the current low-altitude air speed record. The target being set for *Bloodhound* is a 31% improvement on the team's previous record-breaking *Thrust SSC* time!

FASTEST WHEEL-DRIVEN VEHICLE

The fastest speed reached by a vehicle powered through its wheels – i.e., where the power of the engine is directed to the vehicle's wheels, as opposed to jet power – is 458.444 mph (737.794 km/h) by the turbine-powered *Vesco Turbinator*, driven by Don Vesco (USA) at Bonneville Salt Flats, Utah, USA, on October 18, 2001.

FASTEST CAR CRASH SURVIVED

In September 1960, during trials to set a new land speed record at Bonneville, multiple world-record-holder Donald Campbell (UK) crashed his car *Bluebird* while traveling at a speed of 360 mph (579 km/h). The vehicle rolled over and Campbell fractured his skull; against all the odds, the daredevil driver survived.

LONGEST SKIDMARK

The skidmark made by the jet-powered *Spirit of America*, driven by Norman Craig Breedlove (USA), after the car went out of control at Bonneville in Utah, USA, on October 15, 1964, was nearly 6 miles (10 km) long.

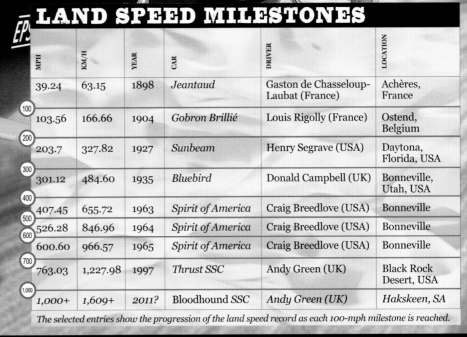

TRACK! THE *BLOODHOUND* TEAM HAVE CHOSEN TO ATTEMPT THE RECORD ON A DRIED-UP LAKE BED KNOWN AS THE HAKSKEEN PAN IN THE NORTHERN CAPE OF SOUTH AFRICA.

MACH NUMBER:

The speed of an object in relation to (i.e., divided by) the speed of sound – so a car at Mach 1 is traveling at the speed of sound. *Bloodhound* is designed to reach Mach 1.4.

LAND SPEED MILESTONES

MPH	KM/H	YEAR	CAR	DRIVER	LOCATION
39.24	63.15	1898	*Jeantaud*	Gaston de Chasseloup-Laubat (France)	Achères, France
103.56	166.66	1904	*Gobron Brillié*	Louis Rigolly (France)	Ostend, Belgium
203.7	327.82	1927	*Sunbeam*	Henry Segrave (USA)	Daytona, Florida, USA
301.12	484.60	1935	*Bluebird*	Donald Campbell (UK)	Bonneville, Utah, USA
407.45	655.72	1963	*Spirit of America*	Craig Breedlove (USA)	Bonneville
526.28	846.96	1964	*Spirit of America*	Craig Breedlove (USA)	Bonneville
600.60	966.57	1965	*Spirit of America*	Craig Breedlove (USA)	Bonneville
763.03	1,227.98	1997	*Thrust SSC*	Andy Green (UK)	Black Rock Desert, USA
1,000+	*1,609+*	*2011?*	Bloodhound *SSC*	*Andy Green (UK)*	*Hakskeen, SA*

The selected entries show the progression of the land speed record as each 100-mph milestone is reached.

HUMAN ENDEAVORS
HIGH ACHIEVERS

★ ★ ★ ★ ★ ★ ★ ★ ★ ★ ★

"It will be a case of mind over matter. We want to show people that if we can do it anyone can."

Amputee John Sandford Hart (UK), preparing to climb Kilimanjaro on crutches

FEMALE
TAMAE WATANABE (JAPAN) REACHED THE SUMMIT OF MOUNT EVEREST AT THE AGE OF 63 YEARS 177 DAYS ON MAY 16, 2002, BECOMING THE OLDEST WOMAN EVER TO DO SO.

★ MOST CONQUESTS OF MOUNT EVEREST

Apa Sherpa (Nepal) reached the summit of Mount Everest, on the Nepal–Tibet border, for the 19th time on May 21, 2009, the most times anyone has ever successfully climbed the world's highest mountain.

Apa began climbing in the late 1980s because he, like many other Sherpa people, found that being a guide was a good way to make money to support a family.

★ OLDEST MAN TO CLIMB MOUNT KILIMANJARO

Reginald W Alexander (UK, b. October 1, 1930) reached the summit of Mount Kilimanjaro, Tanzania, on August 3, 2009, aged 78 years 306 days.

★ **NEW RECORD**
★ **UPDATED RECORD**

★ HIGHEST ALTITUDE SCUBA DIVING

Scuba dives have been made on several occasions at an altitude of 19,357 ft (5,900 m), in a lagoon in the crater of Licancabur, a volcano on the border between Chile and Bolivia. One diver to investigate the lagoon was Henri Garcia of the Chilean Expedición America team; he spent 1 hr 8 min at depths of 16–23 ft (5–7 m) on January 16, 1995.

★ HIGHEST ALTITUDE REACHED BY MOTORCYCLE

A team of six from the North Calcutta Disha Motorcycle Club (all India) rode their Hero Honda motorcycles to an altitude of 20,488 ft (6,245 m) on the Changchemno Range near Marsemikla, India, on August 29, 2008.

★ HIGHEST MARATHON

The Everest Marathon, first run on November 27, 1987, begins at Gorak Shep, (17,100 ft; 5,212 m) and ends at Namche Bazar, (11,300 ft; 3,444 m). The fastest time for a man to complete this race is 3 hr 50 min 23 sec by Hari Roka (Nepal) in 2000, and the fastest time for a woman is 4 hr 35 min 4 sec by Anna Frost (New Zealand) in 2009.

★ FIRST WOMAN TO CLIMB MOUNT EVEREST

Junko Tabei (Japan) reached the summit of Mount Everest on May 16, 1975.

MALE
ACCORDING TO THE SENIOR CITIZEN MOUNT EVEREST EXPEDITION, MIN BAHADUR SHERCHAN (NEPAL) REACHED THE TOP OF EVEREST ON MAY 25, 2008 AT THE RECORD AGE OF 76 YEARS 340 DAYS.

DID YOU KNOW?

EIGHT RAF FIREFIGHTERS CLIMBED THE HEIGHT OF EVEREST (29,028 FT; 8,848 M) ON A "VERSACLIMBER" MACHINE IN A RECORD 1 HR 56 MIN 8 SEC AT MOUNT PLEASANT AIRFIELD, FALKLAND ISLANDS, ON APRIL 27, 2004.

The first published height of Everest, then known as Peak XV, was 29,002 ft (8,840 m) in 1856.

★ FIRST MARRIED COUPLE TO REACH THE SUMMIT OF MOUNT EVEREST

Phil and Susan Ershler (USA) were the first married couple to successfully climb Mount Everest, reaching the summit on Thursday May 16, 2002 – the same day that a record 54 people reached the top.

TRIVIA

FIRST PEOPLE TO CLIMB EACH OF THE 8,000ERS

The 8,000ers are the 14 mountains on Earth that rise to more than 26,247 ft (8,000 m) above sea level. They are all located in the Himalayan and Karakoram mountain ranges in Asia. Reinhold Messner (Italy) became the **first person to climb all of the 8,000ers** when he summited Lhotse on the Nepal–Tibet border on October 16, 1986, having begun his quest in June 1970 – a total of 16 years 3 months 19 days. By the end of 2009, only 18 people had completed the feat. The ★**fastest person to climb all 8,000ers** is Jerzy Kukuczka (Poland), who took 7 years 11 months 14 days to complete the feat, between October 4, 1979 and September 18, 1987.

(source for table: www.8000ers.com)

MOUNTAIN	HEIGHT	DATE	EXPEDITION NATIONALITY	FIRST TO CLIMB (nationality as Expedition unless stated)
Everest	29,028 ft (8,848 m)	May 29, 1953	British	Edmund Hillary (New Zealand), Tenzing Norgay (India/Sherpa)
K2	28,251 ft (8,611 m)	July 31, 1954	Italian	Achille Compagnoni, Lino Lacedelli
Kangchenjunga	28,169 ft (8,586 m)	May 25, 1955	British	George Band, Joe Brown
Lhotse	27,939 ft (8,516 m)	May 18, 1956	Swiss	Fritz Luchsinger, Ernst Reiss
Makalu	27,837 ft (8,485 m)	May 15, 1955	French	Jean Couzy, Lionel Terray
Cho Oyu	26,863 ft (8,188 m)	May 19, 1954	Austrian	Josef Jöchler, Herbert Tichy, Pasang Dawa Lama (India/Sherpa)
Dhaulagiri I	26,794 ft (8,167 m)	May 13, 1960	Swiss	Kurt Diemberger (Austria), Peter Diener (Germany), Ernst Forrer, Albin Schelbert, Nawang Dorje (Nepal/Sherpa), Dorji (Nepal/Sherpa)
Manaslu	26,781 ft (8,163 m)	May 9, 1956	Japanese	Toshio Imanishi, Gyalzen Norbu (India/Sherpa)
Nanga Parbat	26,656 ft (8,125 m)	July 3, 1953	Austro-German	Hermann Buhl (Austria)
Annapurna I	26,545 ft (8,091 m)	June 3, 1950	French	Maurice Herzog, Louis Lachenal
Gasherbrum I	26,509 ft (8,080 m)	July 5, 1958	American	Andrew Kauffman, Peter Schoening
Broad Peak	26,414 ft (8,051 m)	June 9, 1957	Austrian	Hermann Buhl, Kurt Diemberger, Marcus Schmuck, Fritz Wintersteller
Gasherbrum II	26,362 ft (8,035 m)	July 7, 1956	Austrian	Josef Larch, Fritz Moravec, Johann Willenpart
Shisha Pangma	26,335 ft (8,027 m)	May 2, 1964	Chinese	Hsu Ching, Chang Chun-yen, Wang Fu-zhou, Chen Sam, Cheng Tien-liang, Wu Tsung-yue, Sodnam Doji, Migmar, Trashi, Doji, Yonten

★FASTEST ASCENT OF MOUNT KILIMANJARO ON CRUTCHES

John Sandford Hart (UK, below center) completed an ascent of Mount Kilimanjaro on crutches in 4 days 20 hr 30 min. Sandford Hart, who had his right leg amputated as the result of a boating accident, completed the challenge on October 24–29, 2009.

★HIGHEST ALTITUDE CYCLING

Gil Bretschneider and Peer Schepanski (both Germany) rode their mountain bikes at an altitude of 23,658 ft (7,211 m) on the slopes of the Muztagata peak in Xinjiang province, China, on July 10, 2009.

The challenge started on June 23, 2009, when the pair were at an altitude of 17,552 ft (5,350 m), and it took them 17 days to reach their goal.

HO CHI MINH CITY, VIETNAM

The **largest T-shirt** measured 187 ft 7 in (57.19 m) long and 134 ft 1 in (40.88 m) wide. The T-shirt was made by OMO Safe Detergent in Ho Chi Minh City, Vietnam, and displayed on March 9, 2006.

10°48'N
106°41'E

HUMAN ENDEAVORS

REACH FOR THE SKIES

★ ★ ★ ★ ★ ★ ★ ★ ★ ★ ★ ★

EXTRA!
WANT TO LOOK EVEN FARTHER AFIELD? CHECK OUT THE SPACE CHAPTER, FROM P.22.

★ MOST TANDEM JUMPS BY ONE INSTRUCTOR IN 24 HOURS

Harold "Chip" Bowlin, with his passenger Kristine Gould (both USA), achieved 103 tandem parachute jumps in 24 hours, the record for a single instructor. The attempt was undertaken in Zephyrhills Skydive City, Florida, USA, on April 14–15, 2009.

★ FIRST CORPS OF MILITARY BALLOONISTS

The French Army established a corps of balloonists – known as The Aérostiers – on April 2, 1794. The corps was a reconnaissance unit that used its elevated position to plot the location of the enemy on the battlefield.

FIRST AIRCRAFT FLIGHT OVER THE NORTH POLE

Roald Amundsen (Norway) made the first verified flight over the North Pole on May 12, 1926 in the airship *Norge*. Amundsen was accompanied on the flight from Spitzbergen, Norway, to Alaska, USA, by 15 crew members, including Umberto Nobile (Italy), the airship's designer and pilot, American explorer Lincoln Ellsworth, and Oscar Wisting (Norway), a polar explorer who was also the helmsman.

★ FIRST LANDING ON AN AIRCRAFT CARRIER

Flying a Sea Vampire of the Royal Navy registration LZ551/G, Eric "Winkle" Brown (UK) became the first person to land and take off a jet aircraft from an aircraft carrier (HMS *Ocean*) on December 3, 1945.

★ FARTHEST FLIGHT BY A PARAGLIDER (FEMALE)

Kamira Pereira (Brazil) flew her paraglider 201.63 miles (324.5 km) in a straight line west from Quixada, Brazil, on November 14, 2009. In doing so, she beat her own record of 200.7 miles (323 km), which she had set just six days earlier.

★ OLDEST SOLO PILOT HELICOPTER FLIGHT

Peter Chantler (UK) completed a solo helicopter flight over Rosebank Farm in Tarporley, UK, on April 8, 2009 at the age of 83 years 2 months and 11 days.

★ GREATEST VERTICAL DISTANCE FREEFALLING IN 24 HOURS

The greatest accumulated vertical distance covered while freefalling in 24 hours is 63.38 miles (102 km) and was achieved by the Nagual Freefly Team – Daniele Fraternali, Cristian Giorgi, and Alessandro Mitrugno (all Italy) – in Fano, Italy, on June 28, 2009.

DID YOU KNOW?
CAPTAIN ELGEN M LONG (USA) MADE THE FIRST CIRCUMPOLAR FLIGHT IN A PIPER PA-31 NAVAJO FROM NOVEMBER 5 TO DECEMBER 3,1971. HE FLEW 38,896 MILES (62,597 KM) IN 215 FLYING HOURS.

Mark Malkoff (USA) completed a record 135 scheduled flight journeys in 30 days on June 1–30, 2009.

TRIVIA

"Once you've learned the skills, your muscles remember."
Peter Chantler (right)

22°18'N 114°12'E

HONG KONG, CHINA

The world's **longest escalator system** is Hong Kong's Central Hillside Escalator Link. The 2,624-ft-long (800-m) system carries commuters between the Mid-Levels district and Central Market on Hong Kong Island.

HEAVIEST ITEM AIRLIFTED

A power plant generator weighing 206.7 tons (187.6 tonnes) was airlifted by an Antonov Airlines 225 "Mriya" aircraft at Frankfurt Hahn Airport, in Frankfurt, Germany, on August 11, 2009.

★LARGEST CIVILIAN FORMATION FLIGHT

A record 37 Van's RV Aircraft led by Stu McCurdy (USA) flew in different close formations during the AirVenture09 Airshow in Oshkosh, Wisconsin, USA, on July 28–29, 2009.

FIRST FLIGHT OVER EVEREST

On April 3, 1933, two aircraft, a Houston-Westland and a Westland-Wallace -- both open-cockpit biplanes fitted with Bristol Pegasus SIII engines -- made the first manned flights over Mount Everest (29,029 ft; 8,848 m), the **highest mountain in the world**. The aircraft took off from Lalbalu aerodrome, near Purnea, India, crewed by Colonel L V S Blacker and Squadron Leader the Lord Clydesdale in one and Flight Lieutenant D F MacIntyre and S R Bonnet (all UK) in the other.

The flight cleared the mountain by a reported 100 ft (30.48 m). Close-range photographs of Everest proved the achievement.

★FASTEST ELECTRIC AIRCRAFT

On June 12, 2009, Maurizio Cheli (Italy) piloted the electrically powered SkySpark light aircraft at the World Air Games 2009 in Turin, Italy. During the eight-minute flight, Cheli achieved a record-breaking maximum speed of 155 mph (250 km/h).

★ NEW RECORD
UPDATED RECORD

QUIZ!
IN 1911, NORWAY'S ROALD AMUNDSEN BECAME THE FIRST MAN TO REACH THE SOUTH POLE. WHAT OTHER POLAR RECORD DID HE ACHIEVE 15 YEARS LATER?

SEE P.278 FOR THE ANSWER.

★FASTEST HANG GLIDER

Dustin Martin (USA) completed a circuit of a 62.14-mile (100-km) triangular course in a hang glider at an average speed of 30.45 mph (49 km/h). A US national hang-gliding team member, Martin completed his flight over Zapata, Texas, USA, on July 26, 2009 in his Wills Wing T2C 144.

★FIRST PUBLIC DEMONSTRATION OF A STEERABLE LIGHTER-THAN-AIR CRAFT

On September 24, 1852, engineer Henri Giffard (France) traveled 16.7 miles (27 km), from Paris to Trappes (both France), in his hydrogen-filled dirigible. He controlled the aircraft using a tiny steam engine, and maintained a speed of just 3 mph (5 km/h).

★LONGEST HOT-AIR BALLOON FLIGHT BY A FEMALE TEAM

On September 8, 2009, Dr Ann Webb and Dr Janet Folkes (both UK) set a new world record for the longest balloon flight by an all-female team, breaking the previous record of 60 hr 12 min by just over nine hours. They set the record during the annual Coupe Aéronautique Gordon Bennett.

FASTEST TIME TO FLY A HELICOPTER AROUND THE WORLD (EASTBOUND)

Simon Oliphant-Hope (UK) flew around the world in a time of 17 days 14 hr 2 min 27 sec, at an average speed of 55.2 mph (88.9 km/h), in a MD Hughes HU/50 - MD500E single-engined helicopter from June 3–21, 2004. His start and finishing point was Shoreham, West Sussex, UK.

HIGHEST FLIGHT BY AN AIRSHIP

David Hempleman-Adams (UK) flew a Boland Rover A-2 airship over Rosedale, Alberta, Canada, reaching an altitude ratified by the Fédération Aéronautique Internationale (FAI) at 21,699 ft (6,614 m) on December 13, 2004.

LONGEST TIME FLYING AN AIRSHIP

In November 1928, Hugo Eckener (Germany) flew the Graf Zeppelin for 71 hours, covering a total of 3,967 miles (6,384.5 km), between Lakehurst, New Jersey, USA, and Friedrichshafen, Germany. This is the longest nonstop flight by an airship, both in distance and duration.

NORTH!
IVAN ANDRÉ TRIFONOV (AUSTRIA) FLEW A ONE-MAN THUNDER AND COLT CLOUDHOPPER BALLOON OVER THE GEOGRAPHIC NORTH POLE ON APRIL 20, 1996...

SOUTH!
...ON JANUARY 8, 2000, TRIFONOV BALLOONED OVER THE GEOGRAPHIC SOUTH POLE, ANTARCTICA. HE IS THE FIRST MAN TO ACHIEVE BOTH FEATS.

HUMAN ENDEAVORS
ALL AT SEA

★ NEW RECORD ★ UPDATED RECORD

★ ★ ★ ★ ★ ★ ★ ★ ★ ★ ★ ★ ★ ★

ATLANTIC OCEAN

The **first person to row any ocean solo** is John Fairfax (UK), who rowed the Atlantic east to west in *Britannia* from January 20 to July 19, 1969. He and Sylvia Cook (UK) were also the **first team to row the Pacific Ocean**, in *Britannia II*, between April 26, 1971 and April 22, 1972.

John Fairfax also holds the record for the **first person to row two oceans**.

The **youngest person to sail the Atlantic Ocean solo** is David Sandeman (UK), who, in 1976, sailed between Jersey, UK, and Newport, Rhode Island, USA, aged 17 years 176 days.

★ FIRST TANDEM ROW ACROSS THE INDIAN OCEAN

Guy Watts and Andrew Delaney (both UK) rowed across the Indian Ocean aboard their boat *Flying Ferkins* in 102 days 13 hr 40 min between April 19 and July 30, 2009. Guy and Andrew's incredible achievement secured the pair Guinness World Records recognition for the **first** and the **★ fastest tandem row across the Indian Ocean**.

David's boat was the 35-ft-long (10.67-m) *Sea Raider* and his voyage lasted 43 days. *Guinness World Records does not endorse or sanction any attempts under the age of 16 for this category.*

INDIAN OCEAN

The **★ first row across the Indian Ocean by a four-man-strong team** was completed by team Row 4 Charity – Phil McCorry, Matt Hellier, Ian Allen and Nick McCorry (all UK) – who completed the journey aboard the *Bexhill Trust Challenger* between April 19 and June 26, 2009.

The **★ first row across the Indian Ocean by a female team of four** was by the Ocean Angels – Sarah Duff, Fiona Waller, Elin Haf Davis and Joanna Jackson (all UK) – who made the crossing from April 19 to July 6, 2009 in the *Pura Vida*.

The Ocean Angels quartet completed their trip in 78 days – making it the **★ fastest row across the Indian Ocean by a team of four (female)**.

The **★ fastest row across the Indian Ocean** took 58 days 15 hr 8 min, between April 28 and June 25, 2009. The feat was accomplished by team Pirate Row – Angela Madsen, Doug Tumminello, Brian Flick (all USA), Helen Taylor, Paul Cannon, Ian Couch, Simon Chalk (all UK) and Bernard Fissett (Belgium) – in their boat *Aud Eamus*. The trip also gave them another record – see p.119!

PACIFIC OCEAN

Mick Dawson and Chris Martin (UK) were the **★ first team to row the Pacific Ocean (west to east)**. They made the journey from Choshi, Japan, to the Golden Gate Bridge, San Francisco, California, USA, aboard their craft, *Bojangles*, in 189 days 10 hr 39 min, between May 8 and November 13, 2009.

WORLD APPROXIMATELY 70% OF THE EARTH'S SURFACE IS COVERED BY WATER – AROUND 138,000,000 MILES² (360,000,000 KM²).

WATER AT 64,186,000 MILES² (166,241,000 KM²), THE PACIFIC OCEAN IS ABOUT TWICE THE SIZE OF THE ATLANTIC (33,420,000 MILES², 86,557,000 KM²).

FASTEST ATLANTIC CROSSING WALK ON WATER

Rémy Bricka (France) "walked" across the Atlantic Ocean between Tenerife, Canary Islands, and Trinidad on 13-ft 9-in-long (4.2-m) skis in 59 days, from April 2 to May 31, 1988. He covered 3,502 miles (5,636 km), towing a platform housing supplies and essentials such as a water still. Rémy is also a seasoned musician, and has produced a string of albums and singles since the 1970s.

The Pacific Ocean is the **oldest ocean**. The rocks at the bottom are around 200 million years old.

TRIVIA

Born on February 19, 1947, Peter Bird (UK) was the ★**youngest person to row solo (east to west) across the Pacific Ocean** in his boat, *Hele-on-Britannia*. He left San Francisco, USA, on August 23, 1982 and arrived at the Great Barrier Reef, Australia, on June 14, 1983 at the age of 36 years 114 days. In doing so, he also became the **first person to row the Pacific Ocean solo**.

The **fastest solo row (west to east) across the Pacific Ocean** is 134 days 12 hr 15 min, by Gerard d'Aboville (France). He departed from Choshi, Japan, on July 11, 1991 and arrived in Ilwaco, Washington, USA,

on November 21, 1991, after covering 6,200 nautical miles (7,134 miles; 11,482 km).

The raft *Nord*, captained by Andrew Urbanczyk (USA), sailed from Half Moon Bay, California, USA, to the Pacific island of Guam, a straight-line distance of 5,110 nautical miles

KAYAK: From the Inuit "qayak," describing a wooden canoe covered in sealskin and propelled with a paddle.

(5,880 miles; 9,463 km), in 136 days from August 26, 2002 to January 28, 2003. This represents the **longest nonstop journey by raft**.

ENGLISH CHANNEL

The **fastest swim of the English Channel**, and the **fastest swim of the England–France route**, is 6 hr 57 min 50 sec and was achieved by Petar Stoychev (Bulgaria), who crossed from Shakespeare Beach, Dover, UK, to Cap Gris Nez, France, on August 24, 2007.

On May 24, 2007, Micha Robyn (Belgium) achieved the

★**fastest crossing of the English Channel by waterski**, in 29 min 26 sec.

The **oldest person to swim the English Channel** was George Brunstad (USA, b. August 25, 1934), who was aged 70 years 4 days when he completed the crossing, in a time of 15 hr 59 min, on August 29, 2004.

Simon Paterson (UK) traveled underwater from France to England with an air hose attached to a pilot boat in 14 hr 50 min

★FASTEST NORTH SEA CROSSING BY A DOUBLE SEA KAYAK (CANOEING)

On July 4, 2009, Ian Castro and Simon Worsley (both UK) crossed the North Sea in a double kayak in 17 hr 53 min. They began in Southwold, UK, and ended in Zeebrugge, Belgium. The pair also achieved the **fastest North Sea crossing in single sea kayaks**: 24 hr 20 min, ending on August 28, 1999.

on July 28, 1962, the **fastest time to swim the English Channel underwater**.

The ★**fastest crossing of the English Channel by a single canoe/kayak** is 2 hr 59 min, by Ian Wynne (UK), between Shakespeare Beach, Dover, UK, and Cap Gris Nez, France, on October 5, 2007.

★FIRST CROSSING OF THE INDIAN OCEAN (TEAM)

The eight-strong team Pirate Row — comprising one Belgian, four Britons, and three Americans – rowed across the Indian Ocean between April 28 and June 25, 2009 in their craft, *Aud Eamus*.

EXTRA!

IF WE'VE WHETTED YOUR APPETITE FOR ADVENTURE, TURN TO P.110 FOR MORE AMAZING FEATS OF ENDURANCE.

HUMAN SOCIETY

EXTRA!
TURN TO PP.126–127
FOR MORE ON
NATIONS &
POLITICS.

★ NEW RECORD
★ UPDATED RECORD

UNICEF: After World War II, children in Europe were at great risk of famine and disease, so the United Nations Children's Fund (UNICEF) was created in December 1946 to provide them with food, clothing, and health care. Today, the organization provides humanitarian aid to children in developing countries worldwide.

WHO?
IN JULY 2009, THE
POPULATION OF
AFGHANISTAN WAS
ESTIMATED AT 28,395,716,
OF WHOM 43.6% ARE AGED
BETWEEN 0 AND 14 YEARS.
(MALE, 6,343,611;
FEMALE, 6,036,673.)

WHERE?
AFGHANISTAN IS SITUATED
IN SOUTHERN ASIA, NORTH
AND WEST OF PAKISTAN
AND EAST OF IRAN. IT HAS
AN AREA OF 251,827 MILES²
(652,230 KM²), WHICH IS
SLIGHTLY SMALLER THAN
TEXAS, USA.

★ MOST DANGEROUS COUNTRY IN WHICH TO BE BORN

According to the UNICEF Annual Report *The State of the World's Children*, Afghanistan is the worst country in which a child can be born. The infant mortality rate in the country is 257 deaths for every 1,000 live births. Apart from the danger posed by military operations against Taliban insurgents, the lack of access to clean water and growing insecurity in the country often make it impossible to carry out vital life-saving vaccination programs against diseases such as poliomyelitis and measles. Afghanistan also has the world's ★**lowest adult life expectancy**: 43.8 years.

CONTENTS

HUMAN SOCIETY
THAT'S LIFE

★ **NEW RECORD**
★ **UPDATED RECORD**

★ LONGEST MARRIAGE

Herbert Fisher (USA, b. June 10, 1905) and Zelmyra Fisher (USA, b. December 10, 1907) were married on May 13, 1924 in North Carolina, USA. They had been married for 85 years, 10 months, and 8 days as of March 21, 2010.

MOST PROLIFIC MOTHER

The greatest recorded number of children born to one mother is 69, to the first wife of Feodor Vassilyev (Russia). In 27 pregnancies between 1725 and 1765, she gave birth to 16 pairs of twins, seven sets of triplets, and four sets of quadruplets. Only two of the children failed to survive their infancy.

The mother also holds the records for giving birth to the most sets of twins and the most sets of quadruplets.

MOST SETS OF TRIPLETS

Maddalena Granata (Italy, 1839–1886) gave birth to 15 sets of triplets during her lifetime.

EXTRA!
FOR MORE BIZARRE BODY RECORDS, VISIT "SKIN DEEP" ON PP.78-79.

MOST ALBINO SIBLINGS

All four children of Canada's Mario and Angie Gaulin – Sarah (b. 1981), Christopher (b. 1983), Joshua (b. 1987), and Brendan (b. 1989) – were born with the rare genetic condition oculocutaneous albinism. Their father also has the condition and their mother carries the gene. Pictured above are the family's three brothers.

MOST GENERATIONS BORN ON THE SAME DAY

Five families hold the record for having four generations born on the same day: Ralph Betram Williams (USA, b. July 4, 1982), Veera Tuulia Tuijantyär Kivistö (Finland, b. March 21, 1997), Maureen Werner (USA, b. October 13, 1998), Jacob Camren Hildebrandt (USA, b. August 23, 2001), and Mion Masuda (Japan, b. March 26, 2005) all share their birthday with a parent, grandparent, and great-grandparent.

MOST TWINS BORN ON THE SAME DAY

There are only two verified examples of a mother producing two sets of twins with coincident birthdays. The first is that of Laura Shelley (USA), who gave birth to Melissa Nicole and Mark Fredrick Julian, Jr on March 25, 1990 and Kayla May and Jonathan Price Moore on the same date in 2003. The second is that of Caroline Cargado (USA), who gave birth to Keilani Marie and Kahleah Mae on May 30, 1996 and Mikayla Anee and Malia Abigail on the same date in 2003.

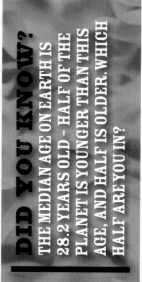

DID YOU KNOW? THE MEDIAN AGE ON EARTH IS 28.2 YEARS OLD – HALF OF THE PLANET IS YOUNGER THAN THIS AGE, AND HALF IS OLDER. WHICH HALF ARE YOU IN?

There are, on average, 6,200 weddings every day in the USA; one-third have been married before.

TRIVIA

SILVER SURFERS
FOR TIPS ON A LONG, HEALTHY MARRIAGE, FOLLOW HERBERT AND ZELMYRA'S TWITTER FEED AT HTTP://TWITTER.COM/LONGESTMARRIED

★ MOST "MULTIPLES" IN ONE CLASS

The 2009–10 tenth-grade class (above) at J J Pearce High School in Richardson, Texas, USA, boasts 10 sets of twins and one set of triplets. Having 10 sets of twins in one academic year is also a record, shared with the 7th grade of the 2006–07 year at Raymond J Grey Jr High School in Acton, Massachusetts, USA. At the Louis Marshall School in Brooklyn, New York City, USA, there were 29 sets of twins for the 1999–2000 school year (the **most twins in one school**).

★ MOST COUPLES MARRIED IN 24 HR

A total of 163 couples were married, one after the other, at the Singapore Botanic Gardens in Singapore on September 20, 2009.

★ LARGEST VOW RENEWAL CEREMONY

On June 20, 2009, 1,087 married couples amassed at Miami University in Oxford, Ohio, USA, for the "Miami Merger Moment," a wedding-vow-renewal event that formed part of the university's Alumni Weekend.

★ LONGEST BRIDAL VEIL

A wedding veil measuring 11,017 ft (3,358 m) long was worn by Sandra Mechleb at her wedding to Chady Abi Younis (both Lebanon) in Arnaoon, Lebanon, on October 18, 2009. The veil was longer than 140 tennis courts laid end to end.

★ SMALLEST AGE DIFFERENTIAL IN A MARRIED COUPLE

The married couple with the smallest known age difference is Allan Ramirez (b. December 19, 1980,

12:14 p.m.) and Elizabeth Ramirez (b. December 19, 1980, 12:16 p.m.) of Texas, USA, who were born just two minutes apart. They were married on November 4, 2000 in Plantersville, Texas, USA.

★ MOST EXPENSIVE DIVORCE

When media mogul Rupert Murdoch and his wife Anna (both Australia) divorced in 1999 – after 32 years of marriage – he agreed to let his ex-wife have $1.7 billion worth of his assets as well as $110 million in cash. He remarried soon after.

★ FIRST ZERO-GRAVITY WEDDING

On June 23, 2009, Erin Finnegan and Noah Fulmor (both USA) wed in zero-gravity in a modified Boeing 727-200. Weightlessness was achieved by flying the plane in repeated dives from 36,000 ft (10,970 m) to 24,000 ft (7,315 m).

★ MOST SETS OF MIXED TWINS

Lightning struck twice for mixed-race parents Dean Durrant (UK, of West Indian descent) and Alison Spooner (UK) when, in March 2009, Alison delivered her second set of mixed twins: Leah and Miya. In 2001, she gave birth to mixed twins – the dark-skinned Hayleigh and fair-skinned Layren.

ODDS
A MIXED-RACE COUPLE HAS A 1-IN-500,000 CHANCE OF HAVING A SET OF MIXED TWINS, BUT NO STATISTICS EXIST FOR ... AND MIYA – TWO ...

DEATH

★ ★ ★ ★ ★ ★ ★ ★ ★ ★ ★ ★ ★

★ MOST EXPENSIVE GHOSTS

Two vials supposedly containing the exorcized spirits of an old man and a young girl were sold at an online auction in March 2010 for NZ$2,830 ($1,990). New Zealander Avie Woodbury claimed to have enlisted the help of an exorcist and a ouija board to contact and trap the spirits in July 2009.

★ OLDEST KNOWN CATACOMBS

The first burial chambers to be referred to directly as catacombs were those beneath San Sebastiano ad Catacumbas (aka Sebastiano fuori le mura) in Rome, Italy, which was built in the early 4th century. There are many such tombs along the Via Appia (Appian Way) – the ancient road that leads from Rome to Brindisi – as burials were considered Christian and outlawed within the walls of Rome.

★ LARGEST AUTOMATED TOMB FACILITY

The six-story Kouanji Buddhist Temple in Tokyo, Japan, is an automated tomb facility that, as of January 1, 2010, houses 6,850 human remains. Square marble boxes – which can contain the cremated remains ("cremains") of up to nine relatives – are accessed by visitors using a swipe card that identifies the location of the remains and delivers them via a conveyor-belt system. Each burial costs around Y800,000 ($8,800).

GENEROUS SPIRITS
PROCEEDS FROM THE SALE OF THE EXPENSIVE SPIRITS – TRAPPED IN BOTTLES WITH HOLY WATER – WILL GO TO AN ANIMAL CHARITY... ONCE THE EXORCIST'S FEE HAS BEEN PAID.

QUIZ!
ON AVERAGE, HOW MANY GRAVES DID JOHANN HEINRICH KARL THIME DIG IN HIS 50-YEAR CAREER?
SEE P.278 FOR THE ANSWER.

★ LARGEST GATHERING OF ZOMBIES

The Big Chill music festival in Ledbury, Herefordshire, UK, was swamped by 4,026 zombies on August 6, 2009. The living dead were taking part in filming for the forthcoming Film4/Warp Films production *I Spit on Your Rave*. Set nine years in the future, the movie stars comedian Noel Fielding (UK) as a zombie king in a Britain wiped out by a virus.

CATACOMB: Underground tomb or burial chamber, suspected to derive from the Latin cata tumbas – "among the tombs."

LARGEST COMMUNAL TOMB

A communal tomb housing 180,000 World War II dead on Okinawa, Japan, was enlarged in 1985 to accommodate another 9,000 bodies thought to be buried on the island.

FARTHEST RESTING PLACE

On July 31, 1999, America's *Lunar Prospector* spacecraft crashed into the Moon after 18 months of successful mission operations. Incorporated into this orbiter was a small (1.5-in; 3.8-cm) polycarbonate container holding 1 oz (28.3 g) of the remains of the pioneering planetary scientist Dr Eugene Shoemaker (USA). Wrapped around the container was a piece of foil inscribed with some of Shoemaker's work.

LARGEST MASS CREMATION

In December 1997, at a temple in Smut Scom, Thailand, tons of bones (including 21,347 skulls) were cremated to mark the end of urban burials in Bangkok, the overcrowded Thai capital. The bones represented unclaimed remains from a Chinese cemetery in Bangkok.

★LARGEST OSSUARY

The skeletal remains of 6 million people lie, neatly arranged, in subterranean catacombs – aka ossuaries or charnel houses – beneath the streets of Paris, France. The city is riddled with an estimated 186 miles (300 km) of tunnels and pathways, of which 3 acres (nearly 11,000 m²) are packed tightly with the bones of those reinterred from the city's overflowing cemeteries in the late 1700s.

LARGEST LIVE TV AUDIENCE

The worldwide TV audience for the funeral of Diana, Princess of Wales (UK, 1961–97) on September 6, 1997 at Westminster Abbey, London, UK, was watched by an estimated global audience of 2.5 billion.

LARGEST VIRTUAL FUNERAL

In October 2005, an avid computer gamer known only as Snowly (China) indulged in a three-day nonstop marathon of the Massively Multiplayer Online Role-Playing Game *World of Warcraft* (Blizzard, USA). While attempting a particularly challenging task in the game, Snowly died of fatigue in the real world. More than 100 gamers visited a virtual cathedral inside the game, where a service was held in her memory.

FASTEST HEARSE

Joe Gosschalk (Australia) covered a quarter-mile in his 1979 Ford LTD P6 hearse in 13.7 seconds at 98 mph (158 km/h) at Willowbank Raceway in Queensland, Australia, on June 10, 2005. The hearse has a 351-cu-in (5.7-liter) engine with nitrous oxide boost. Its license plates read "Undead."

LONGEST CAREER AS A GRAVE DIGGER

It is recorded that Johann Heinrich Karl Thieme, sexton of Aldenburg, Germany, dug 23,311 graves during a 50-year career. After his death in 1826, his understudy dug *his* grave!

LARGEST FUNERALS

The funeral of India's charismatic C N Annadurai (above, d. Feb 3, 1969), a Chennai Chief Minister, was attended by 15 million people, according to police sources.

• The queue at the grave of the popular Russian singer Vladimir Visotsky (d. Jul 28, 1980) stretched for 6 miles (10 km).

★LONGEST-RUNNING FESTIVAL OF THE DEAD

In one form or another, Día de los Muertos (Day of the Dead) in Mexico has been celebrated in this part of the world for more than 3,500 years. To honor their dead, and the goddess Mictecacihuatl (the "Lady of the Dead"), the Aztecs and other Meso-Americans would perform rites and rituals, often involving skulls. Today, the tradition continues on November 1 and 2 each year, with the emphasis on partying and celebrating with the family, often in flamboyant costumes and masks.

DEATH
IN THE 16TH CENTURY, THE SPANISH CONQUISTADORS, UNABLE TO STOP THE "PAGAN" CEREMONY, MOVED DAY OF THE DEAD TO COINCIDE WITH HALLOWEEN, BUT THE TWO ARE NOT REALLY CONNECTED.

MASK
REVELERS WISHING TO COMMEMORATE DECEASED RELATIVES AND FRIENDS DON WOODEN SKULL MASKS, OR CALACAS, AND TAKE PART IN FEASTING AND DANCING.

HUMAN SOCIETY
NATIONS & POLITICS

★LONGEST-SERVING DEMOCRATIC HEAD

Lee Kuan Yew was Prime Minister of Singapore from 1959 to 1990 — a total of 31 consecutive years. Despite leaving power, Kuan Yew remains an important political figure in Singapore and is "Minister Mentor" to the current Prime Minister, his son Lee Hsien Loong.

★HIGHEST DEATH RATE FROM AIDS (COUNTRY)

In 2007, incidence of AIDS-related deaths in Zimbabwe reached a shocking 1,060 people per 100,000 population. An estimated 15.3% of Zimbabwe's population is living with AIDS but drought, famine, and a poor economy have all made matters worse.

★LARGEST COUNTRY WITHOUT AN AIRPORT

With an area of 180 miles^2 (468 km^2) and a population of 71,822, Andorra is the largest country without an airport. Visitors wishing to travel there by air are advised to fly to Barcelona and take a bus the rest of the way.

★MOST CORRUPT COUNTRY

According to Transparency International's most recent Corruption Perceptions Index, in 2009 Somalia scored 1.1 on its 10-point corruption scale. By contrast, New Zealand rated as the **least corrupt country** with a score of 9.4.

★COUNTRY WITH MOST POLITICAL ARMED GROUPS

On January 7, 2010, an independent commission in the Philippines began work on disbanding politicians' private armies. According to the Philippines' Defense Secretary Norberto Gonzales, there are 132 armed groups, many led by politicians, totaling some 10,000 armed individuals spread throughout the country. Such private armies are typically used to assist the official security forces and to defend communities endangered by communist or Muslim separatist guerrillas, but are also often used to maintain local politicians in power by intimidating rivals, voters, and journalists.

★LEAST STABLE STATE

Somalia has lacked an effective central government since 1991, when the previous president was overthrown. Since Ethiopian troops left Somalia in January 2009, its stability rating has fallen further according to *Jane's Intelligence Review*.

★COUNTRIES MOST THREATENED BY INUNDATION

The collection of reef islands and atolls (such as Funafuti Atoll, above) that constitute the low-lying nations of Tuvalu and the Maldives are under imminent threat of disappearing under the waves due to a combination of factors including rising sea levels due to global warming. At their highest elevations, Tuvalu and the Maldives are 16 ft 3 in (5 m) and 8 ft (2.4 m) above sea level respectively.

★LARGEST MARCH AGAINST ILLEGAL DRUGS

The "Grand BIDA March" against illegal drugs included 332,963 people and was held in Manila, in the Philippines, on March 21, 2009.

★LARGEST OPIUM PRODUCER

Despite a reduction in recent years, Afghanistan still had the largest opium harvest in 2008, according to United Nations statistics, with an 8,480-ton (7,700-tonne) crop, worth $3.4 billion in the illegal heroin trade.

★LARGEST OPIUM SEIZURE

According to the 2009 report of the United Nations Office on Drugs and Crime (UNODC), Afghanistan's eastern neighbor Iran seized 941,698 lb (427,147 kg) of opium in 2007, a figure that constitutes 84% of all opium seizures worldwide in that year.

Iran also registered the largest seizures of heroin and morphine in 2007 with 56,394 lb (25,580 kg) – representing 28% of the global total.

★LARGEST DONOR OF FOREIGN AID

The USA donated $21.7 billion worth of aid to foreign countries in 2007, according to figures published by *The Economist*. The ★largest recipient of foreign aid in 2007 was Iraq, which received $9.1 billion.

★MOST HUMAN RIGHTS ACTIVISTS KILLED

The 2010 Human Rights Watch World Report revealed that eight murders were perpetrated against human rights supporters in Russia during 2009.

★HIGHEST NATURAL POPULATION INCREASE

The population of the East African state of Niger is currently estimated to grow 3.73% between 2010 and 2015, largely thanks to the country's high fertility rate. It's estimated that there will be 6.86 children for each woman of childbearing age over the same period.

★LAST SPEAKER OF BO

Bo, the tongue of the Bo tribe of the Andaman Islands in the Bay of Bengal, is said to have emerged 10,000 years ago. In January 2010, it ceased to be a living language when its last native speaker, Boa Sr (pictured above), died.

QUEEN... THE LONGEST-REIGNING LIVING QUEEN IS HER MAJESTY QUEEN ELIZABETH II (B. APRIL 21,1926), WHO SUCCEEDED TO THE THRONE ON FEBRUARY 6,1952.

...VIC THE LONGEST-REIGNING QUEEN EVER IS VICTORIA (UK), QUEEN OF GREAT BRITAIN FROM 1837 TO 1901 AND EMPRESS OF INDIA FROM 1876, WHO REIGNED FOR 63 YEARS 216 DAYS.

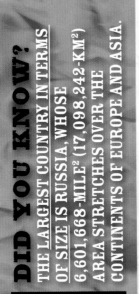

DID YOU KNOW? THE LARGEST COUNTRY IN TERMS OF SIZE IS RUSSIA, WHOSE 6,601,668-MILE² (17,098,242-KM²) AREA STRETCHES OVER THE CONTINENTS OF EUROPE AND ASIA.

According to the CIA World Factbook, China has a record population of 1.3 billion citizens.

TRIVIA

LONGEST-REIGNING LIVING MONARCH

Born on December 5, 1927, King Bhumibol Adulyadej, King Rama IX of the Chakri dynasty, of Thailand ascended to the throne on June 9, 1946 following the death of his older brother. His formal coronation did not take place until May 5, 1950, and has since reigned without interruption for more than 63 years.

HUMAN SOCIETY
CONFLICT

National Union of Journalists of the Philippines

★ LARGEST CONTRIBUTOR TO UN PEACEKEEPING FORCES

As of February 28, 2010, Bangladesh is the largest contributor of uniformed personnel to UN peacekeeping missions, with a total of 10,852 blue-hatted personnel deployed worldwide.

★ MOST DANGEROUS COUNTRY FOR THE MEDIA

According to the International Federation of Journalists, 74 journalists have been killed in the Philippines since 2002, with 36 being killed in 2009, in the ongoing bloody conflict between the Moro Islamic Liberation Front (MILF) separatists and government forces.

★ LARGEST ARMY

According to 2008 estimates published in the CIA World Factbook, the manpower available for military service in China is 375,009,345 people, with 218,459,000 active military personnel.

★ LARGEST SCUTTLING OF SHIPS

On November 27, 1942, the French fleet in Toulon, France, was scuttled on the orders of the French Admiralty to avoid their capture by German forces. Of the 73 ships sunk in the action, 57 were major vessels. Only three submarines managed to escape Toulon and join up with the Allies.

★ YOUNGEST SERVICEMAN TO DIE IN WORLD WAR II

On February 5, 2010, on what would have been his 83rd birthday, Reginald Earnshaw (UK) was named by the Commonwealth War Graves Commission as the youngest serviceman to have been killed in World War II. He had lied about his age in order to join the British Royal Navy, claiming to be 15 years old, and went on to serve as a cabin boy. Reginald was killed on July 6, 1941 at the age of 14 years and 152 days – just five months after joining up – when his ship, the *SS Devon*, was attacked

★ HIGHEST AWARD FOR ANIMAL GALLANTRY

Introduced in 1943 by Maria Dickin (UK), the founder of the People's Dispensary for Sick Animals (PDSA), the Dickin Medal is the highest honor for animals serving in a military conflict. On February 24, 2010, an eight-year-old black Labrador named Treo became the latest animal to be awarded the medal in recognition of the numerous lives he had saved in Afghanistan sniffing out and locating roadside bombs.

FIRST CONFIRMED SURVIVOR OF TWO NUCLEAR ATTACKS

Tsutomu Yamaguchi (Japan) was in Hiroshima, Japan, on a business trip on August 6, 1945, when US forces dropped the "Little Boy" atomic bomb on the city, killing 140,000 people. Suffering burns to his upper body, Tsutomu returned to his hometown of Nagasaki on August 8. The next day, the US Army dropped "Fat Boy" on the city, killing a further 73,000 people. Tsutomu again managed to survive with minor injuries, despite living within 3 km (1.8 miles) of ground zero each time.

★SMALLEST ARMY

The smallest and **oldest standing army** is the Pontifical Swiss Guard in the Vatican City, which was created in its current form on January 21, 1506 and had 110 active guards as of 2006. Swiss Guardsmen must be single Swiss-Catholic men taller than 5 ft 8 in (1.7 m).

by a German aircraft.

★OLDEST LIVING WORLD WAR I VETERAN

Frank Woodruff Buckles was born in Harrison County, Missouri, USA, on February 1, 1901 and became the oldest surviving World War I veteran on July 28, 2009, aged 108 years 168 days. Mr Buckles served as an ambulance driver in the Army from 1917 to 1919; he is also the last of 4.7 million Americans who served during the conflict.

★MOST PEOPLE KILLED BY FRIENDLY FIRE

During their 1788 campaign against the Turks, the Austrian Army crossed a bridge at Karansebes,

★ NEW RECORD
★ UPDATED RECORD

Turkey. An advance guard of cavalrymen stopped to buy alcohol from local peasants. The infantrymen bringing up the rear wanted a share of the booze. When the cavalry refused, the infantry tried to frighten them, firing their rifles in the air. The surrounding Austrian forces were confused by this and opened fire on their colleagues, causing the utility horses at the rear to stampede. The fighting raged for hours, resulting in more than 10,000 dead and injured Austrians.

★LARGEST CONTRIBUTOR TO THE UN PEACEKEEPING BUDGET

The UN's Peacekeeping budget between July 1, 2009 and June 30, 2010 is $7.9 billion. The largest single contributor to this figure is the USA, which donates 27.17% of the total; next donor is Japan, which provides 12.53% of the total peacekeeping budget.

★MOST PEOPLE DEPLOYED IN PEACEKEEPING OPERATIONS

According to the Stockholm International Peace Research Institute (SIPRI), a total of 187,586 people were deployed on peacekeeping missions in 2008. Military forces accounted for 166,146 of those deployed. The largest peace operation occurred – not surprisingly – in Afghanistan.

★MOST LAND-MINED COUNTRY

According to the United Nations, Afghanistan now shares with Iraq the record for the most mined country in the world with an estimated total of 10,000,000 mines each. In Afghanistan, more than 60 Afghans fall victim to land mines every month.

LONG...
THE LONGEST WAR THAT COULD BE DESCRIBED AS CONTINUOUS WAS THE THIRTY YEARS WAR FOUGHT BETWEEN THE HOLY ROMAN EMPIRE AND VARIOUS EUROPEAN COUNTRIES FROM 1618 TO 1648.

...SHORT
THE SHORTEST WAR WAS FOUGHT BETWEEN BRITAIN AND ZANZIBAR (NOW PART OF MODERN TANZANIA). IT LASTED FROM 9:00 A.M. TO 9:45 A.M. ON AUGUST 27, 1896 AND ENDED IN A SWIFT BRITISH VICTORY.

OSAKA, JAPAN
The **longest monorail** is the Osaka Monorail, in Osaka, Japan, which has a total length of 13.8 miles (22.2 km). Fully operational since August 1997, its main line runs between Osaka International Airport and Hankyu Railway Minami Ibaraki Station.

34°40'N
135°30'E

HUMAN SOCIETY
CRIME

★ ★ ★ ★ ★ ★ ★ ★ ★ ★ ★ ★ ★ ★ ★ ★

★ WORST WAR CRIMINAL CONVICTED IN THE 21ST CENTURY

Kang Kek leu, or "Comrade Duch," ran the Tuol Sleng prison in Cambodia, southeast Asia, when the country was under the control of Pol Pot's regime. Between 1977 and 1979, of the 15,000 people who entered the prison, only around 15 emerged alive. This figure makes Kang Kek leu the worst war criminal convicted in the 21st century.

★ LARGEST SPEEDING FINE

In January 2010, an unnamed Swiss millionaire was given a record fine by the regional court in St Gallen, Switzerland, of 307,496 Swiss Francs ($290,000) for speeding. He was caught driving his red Ferrari Testarossa 35 mph (57 km/h) faster than the legal speed limit allowed. The huge fine was based on the driver's wealth, which was assessed at 24 million Swiss Francs ($22.7 million), and the fact that he was a repeat traffic offender.

★ HIGHEST PRISON RIOT DEATH TOLL

The war for supremacy between different drug cartels in Mexico, which saw over 5,400 people killed in 2008, has been carried into Mexican jails. At least 83 prisoners were killed and many more injured in a number of riots during a six-month period covering part of 2008 and part of 2009. The trend appears to have continued into 2010, with the latest riot on January 20, 2010, when at least 23 inmates of rival drug trafficking gangs in a prison in the northern Mexican state of Durango were killed.

★ MOST MURDERS

According to the 10th United Nations Survey of Crime Trends and Operations of Criminal Justice Systems, covering the period 2005–06, India has the greatest number of murders of any of the 86 countries listed in the report. It had a total of 32,481 homicides in 2006.

★ LARGEST BACKLOG OF COURT CASES

According to an annual report for the Delhi High Court, India, by Chief Justice A P Shah, there is such a backlog of cases that it could take the court 466 years to clear. The court hears cases in an average time of 4 min 55 sec, but has 700,000 cases waiting to be heard out of a national backlog reported by the United Nations Development Programme to be in the order of 20 million. The court has 629 civil cases and around 17 criminal cases pending that are over 20 years old.

★ MOST PRISONERS ON DEATH ROW

According to Amnesty International's Annual Report 2009, the country with the most prisoners awaiting execution in 2008 is Pakistan, with over 7,000 – almost one third of the estimated 24,000 on Death Row around the world. In the same year, Pakistan executed at least 36 people and reportedly sentenced 236 to death.

★ LARGEST PASSPORT FORGERY

On May 8, 2009, Mandip Sharma (India) and Brando Sibayan (Philippines) received jail terms of four years each from a UK court for running the largest known passport forgery factory. On searching a property in Leicester, UK, officers from the Border Agency found up to 4,000 counterfeit passports for several EU countries.

WORST PHOTOFIT...?

A contender for worst photofit was considered in early 2010, but was rejected by GWR as it actually achieved its purpose. The extremely basic picture of an alleged murderer – drawn for Bolivian police by a neighbor of the victim, Rafael Vargas, who was stabbed seven times – has led to two arrests so far.

EXTRA! FOR THE LATEST DEFENSE TECHNOLOGY, SHOOT TO PP.210-211.

ADELAIDE, AUSTRALIA
The record for the **most jokes told in an hour** is held by Anthony Lehmann (Australia), who cracked 549 jokes against the clock at the Rhino Room club, Adelaide, South Australia, on May 25, 2005.

★OLDEST CRIMINAL GANG (AVERAGE AGE)

In March 2009, a group of British criminals with an average age of 57 (the oldest being 83) pleaded guilty to counterfeiting charges and were sentenced to a total of 13 years. They had been able to produce a finished batch of notes worth £800 ($1,600) in just half an hour.

★OLDEST PERSON ACCUSED OF MURDER (FEMALE)

A post mortem examination determined that Elizabeth Barrow (USA), aged 100, had been strangled in her nursing home in Massachusetts, USA, on September 24, 2009. The accused is Laura Lundquist (USA), the victim's roommate, who is 98 years old and a dementia sufferer.

★FIRST JUDICIAL SINGLE-DRUG EXECUTION

On December 8, 2009, convicted murderer Kenneth Biros was executed in Ohio, USA, using a single, large injection of anesthetic. It is the first time that a single injection has been used in a legal, judicial execution in a democratic state. Normally, a mixture of three drugs is used.

★MOST PRISONERS

According to data from the International Centre for Prison Studies, King's College, London, UK, the USA has 2.3 million prisoners behind bars, of whom 1,610,446 were sentenced prisoners at the end of 2008. China, with four times the population of the USA, has 1.6 million prisoners. The ★country with least prisoners, out of a list of 218 countries for which data was available, was San Marino, with only one.

★LARGEST FINE

In September 2009, US pharmaceutical giant Pfizer Inc. and its subsidiary Pharmacia & Upjohn Company Inc. agreed to pay $2.3 billion, the largest-ever health-care fraud settlement, to resolve criminal and civil liability arising from the illegal promotion of certain pharmaceutical products. Of the total, Pfizer will pay a $1.195 billion fine – the largest criminal fine in US history.

★HIGHEST BAIL SET

In New York, USA, on October 16, 2009, bail for the billion-dollar hedge fund owner Raj Rajaratnam (Sri Lanka) was set at a record $100 million after his arrest on criminal charges for alleged insider trading.

★LONGEST JURY DELIBERATION

In a 1992 lawsuit in Long Beach, California, USA, which took 11 years and 6 months to reach trial, Shirley and Jason McClure (USA) accused city officials of violating the US Fair Housing Act by conspiring to prevent them from opening a chain of residential homes. The jury deliberated for four and a half months and eventually awarded the McClures $25.5 million in damages.

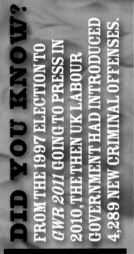

DID YOU KNOW?

FROM THE 1997 ELECTION TO *GWR 2011* GOING TO PRESS IN 2010, THE THEN UK LABOUR GOVERNMENT HAD INTRODUCED 4,289 NEW CRIMINAL OFFENSES.

As UK PM, Gordon Brown introduced an average of 33 new offenses per month.

TRIVIA

LARGEST PRISON

Housing about 5,000 inmates but with a total capacity of 6,750, the Twin Towers Correctional Facility in Los Angeles, USA, has a 1.5 million-ft² (140,000-m²) floor area and is situated on a 10-acre (4-ha) site. In 2004, it cost around $50 million a year to run – $61.21 a day for each inmate.

★ NEW RECORD
★ UPDATED RECORD

QUIZ!
HOW OLD WAS THE OLDEST PERSON TO BE ACCUSED OF MURDER?
SEE P.278 FOR THE ANSWER.

IN...
THE PRISON OPENED IN 1997 BUT THERE WAS NO BUDGET TO RUN IT SO IT REMAINED EMPTY. THE GUARDS EMPLOYED THERE ACTUALLY HAD TO STOP PEOPLE BREAKING IN!

...OUT
INMATE KEVIN PULLUM WALKED OUT OF A TWIN TOWERS EMPLOYEE EXIT ON JULY 6, 2001, TWO HOURS AFTER BEING CONVICTED OF ATTEMPTED MURDER. HE WAS RECAPTURED 18 DAYS LATER.

LOS ANGELES COUNTY SHERIFF'S DEPARTMENT
TWIN TOWERS CORRECTIONAL FACILITY
INMATE RECEPTION CENTER • MEDICAL SERVICES
450 BAUCHET ST

HUMAN SOCIETY
WEALTH & COMMERCE

★ LARGEST LOTTERY PRIZE FUND

Spain's Christmas lottery, nicknamed "El Gordo" (Fat One), is a Christmas tradition in the country and is the world's biggest lottery in terms of the total sum paid out. The 2009 lottery showered €2.3 billion ($3.3 billion) on its winners. The top prize went to the 1,950 lucky ticket holders who won €300,000 ($430,797) each.

★ LARGEST FIND OF ANGLO-SAXON TREASURE

Metal detectorist Terry Herbert (UK) found more than 1,500 gold and silver pieces, estimated to date from the 7th century, in a farmer's field in Staffordshire, UK. The find, announced on September 24, 2009, included at least 650 items of gold, weighing more than 11 lb (5 kg), and 530 silver objects, weighing more than 2.2 lb (1 kg).

OOH!
THE ORAPA DIAMOND MINE, BOTSWANA, IS THE WORLD'S LARGEST BY AREA. IT COVERS 0.45 MILES² (1.18 KM²) AND IN 2003 PRODUCED 16.3 MILLION CARATS (3,260 KG) OF DIAMONDS.

★ RICHEST PERSON (PRESENT DAY)

Mexico's Carlos Slim Helú's estimated worth of $53.5 billion sees him top the 2010 *Forbes* list of the World's Billionaires.

Slim has amassed a fortune that includes fixed-line telephone assets and a construction conglomerate, plus stakes in financial group Inbursa, Bronco Drilling, Independent News & Media, Saks, and New York Times Co. He increased his wealth by $18.5 billion in 2009, which helped knock Bill Gates (USA) off the top spot.

★ RICHEST WOMAN

Christy Walton (USA), former daughter-in-law of deceased Wal-Mart founder Sam Walton, has a fortune estimated by *Forbes* at $22.5 billion. Her sister-in-law Alice Walton (USA) is runner-up, with $19.5 billion.

LARGEST PRIVATELY OWNED YACHT

The *Eclipse*, which is owned by Chelsea Football Club (UK) owner Roman Abramovich (Russia), measures 560 ft (170 m) long and was constructed by German shipbuilding company Blohm + Voss. The price of the yacht is estimated at $485 million. It is equipped with two helicopter pads, 11 luxurious guest cabins, a mini-submarine, and its own missile-defense system.

OW!
IN THE FINANCIAL YEAR ENDING 2009, THE WORLD'S 1,125 BILLIONAIRES LOST AN ESTIMATED $1.4 TRILLION BETWEEN THEM.

QUIZ!
WHO DID CARLOS SLIM HELÚ REPLACE AS THE WORLD'S RICHEST MAN?
SEE P. 278 FOR THE ANSWER.

CASH: The word "cash" comes from the French word "caisse," meaning "money box."

★LARGEST LOSS OF PERSONAL FORTUNE

The collapse of the world's economy saw a decline in many fortunes, but none more dramatic than that of Anil Ambani (India). By March 2009, he had lost an estimated $32 billion – 76% of his fortune – owing to the crumbling value of shares in his companies Reliance Power, Reliance Communications, and Reliance Capital.

annual list, the world lost 332 billionaires, leaving just 793 of these rare creatures compared to 1,125 in the previous year.

★LARGEST DECLINE IN BILLIONAIRES IN ONE YEAR

The financial year ending 2009 saw billionaires melting away like snow in spring. According to *Forbes'*

★WEALTHIEST UNIVERSITY

Harvard University, located in Cambridge, Massachusetts, is America's oldest university (established 1636) and is also the world's wealthiest. When assessed in June 2009, Harvard's endowment was $26 billion, down from $36.9 billion the previous year.

★LARGEST DEPOSIT LOST

In 2008, Mikhail Prokhorov (Russia) agreed to pay €390 million ($528.9 million) for the villa *Leopolda de Villefranche-sur-Mer*, owned by heiress Lily Safra (Brazil), and located outside Nice, France. Prokhorov withdrew from the sale in 2009, losing his €40-million ($54.2-million) deposit in the process.

LARGEST LIFE INSURANCE POLICY

July 2010 marked the 20th anniversary of Peter Rosengard's (UK) record insurance sale. In 1990, he sold the largest-ever single life insurance policy for $100 million on the life of a well-known US entertainment industry figure. Incredibly, he made the sale during a cold call from a telephone booth!

INSTANT EXPERT

★ THE WORLD'S ★FIRST DOLLAR BILLIONAIRE WAS JOHN D ROCKEFELLER (USA, 1839-1937). HE MADE HIS FORTUNE IN THE OIL BUSINESS AND WAS WORTH AN ESTIMATED $1.4 BILLION.

✿ IT IS ESTIMATED THAT ROCKEFELLER'S WEALTH WOULD BE THE EQUIVALENT OF $210 BILLION TODAY (MEASURED AS A PERCENTAGE OF GDP), WHICH WOULD MAKE HIM, ARGUABLY, THE RICHEST PERSON EVER.

✿ ROCKEFELLER GAVE AWAY THE VAST MAJORITY OF HIS WEALTH TO WORTHY CAUSES.

★LARGEST CORPORATE BANKRUPTCY

On September 15, 2008, US investment bank Lehman Brothers Holdings Inc. filed for bankruptcy to the tune of $613 billion, having succumbed to the subprime mortgage crisis that started the worldwide recession in 2008.

DID YOU KNOW?

IN 2009, NEW YORK CITY, USA, REGAINED THE TITLE OF ★CITY WITH THE MOST BILLIONAIRES FROM MOSCOW, RUSSIA. THERE ARE CURRENTLY 55 MEMBERS OF THE BIG APPLE BILLIONAIRES CLUB.

The world's highest average net income in relation to cost of living is earned by the citizens of Zürich, Switzerland.

TRIVIA

★ NEW RECORD
★★ UPDATED RECORD

FULD
PICTURED IS RICHARD FULD - CHAIRMAN AND CHIEF EXEC OF LEHMAN BROTHERS HOLDINGS - WITH PROTESTERS IN WASHINGTON, DC, USA, ON OCTOBER 6, 2008.

SHAME

CAP GREED

HUMAN SOCIETY
CONSUMPTION & WASTE

EXTRA!
FOR A DIFFERENT KIND OF CONSUMPTION, LOOK AT EXTREME CUISINE ON P.140.

★ NEW RECORD
★ UPDATED RECORD

LONGEST-SURVIVING GREENHOUSE GAS

Of all the gases emitted by mankind that add to global warming, the longest lived is the refrigerant gas tetrafluoromethane. It can last for 50,000 years in the atmosphere.

★ LARGEST CONSUMER OF ENERGY

The country that consumes more energy than any other is the USA, which was shown to have used 2,321 Mtoe (million tonnes of oil equivalent) in 2006, the latest year for which records exist.

★ LARGEST PRODUCER OF ENERGY (COUNTRY)

China produces more energy annually than any other nation, with 1,749 Mtoe (million tonnes of oil equivalent) as of 2006.

★ LARGEST CONSUMPTION OF ENERGY PER HEAD

The people of Qatar each consumed an average of 48,627 lb (22,057 kg) in 2006. Iceland was in second place with 31,387 lb (14,237 kg) per head, while the USA, which is the greatest annual consumer of energy, is 10th on the list with 17,125 lb (7,768 kg).

★ HIGHEST CARBON DIOXIDE EMISSIONS PER CAPITA

Citizens of Kuwait emitted 40.6 tons (36.9 tonnes) of carbon dioxide per person in 2005.

★ FIRST CLIMIGRATION

In 2009, Alaskan human rights lawyer Robin Bronen coined the word "climigration" to describe the forced migration of people resulting from climate-induced ecological changes in a community's environment.

Bronen used the term in a report on Alaskan indigenous communities who were having to relocate due to climate change. The Intergovernmental Panel on Climate Change (IPCC) has estimated that there will be 150 million such "climate refugees" seeking new homes by 2050.

★ LARGEST PRODUCER OF CARBON DIOXIDE EMISSIONS (COUNTRY)

According to a report compiled by the Netherlands Environmental Assessment Agency, as of 2006 the country responsible for the greatest carbon dioxide emissions is China, which produced 6,200 million tonnes of CO_2 compared with 5,800 million tonnes produced by the USA. By comparison, the UK produced 600 million tonnes.

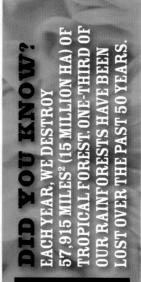

DID YOU KNOW? EACH YEAR, WE DESTROY 57,915 MILES^2 (15 MILLION HA) OF TROPICAL FOREST ONE-THIRD OF OUR RAINFORESTS HAVE BEEN LOST OVER THE PAST 50 YEARS.

According to a report by The Prince's Rainforests Project, 137 species of plant, insect, or animal are wiped out every day.

TRIVIA

MOST TREES PLANTED IN AN HOUR (TEAM)

A team of 100 people planted 26,422 trees at Gransha Park, Derry, UK, on December 5, 2009. BBC Breathing Places achieved the feat in partnership with Conservation Volunteers NI, Western Health & Social Care Trust, Northern Ireland EA, and Derry City Council.

★LARGEST ISLAND EVACUATION AS A RESULT OF CLIMATE CHANGE

In 1995, more than 500,000 inhabitants of Bhola Island, Bangladesh, were forced to evacuate when rising seas, attributed to climate change, threatened to flood the island.

★GREENEST CITY

Masdar City in Abu Dhabi, UAE, designed by the British architect firm Foster and Partners, is the world's first city designed to be zero-carbon and zero-waste. All of its power is generated from renewable resources, and all waste material is recycled. Automobiles are banned in favor of electric, driverless, underground vehicles, so the city's projected 50,000 citizens should leave no carbon footprint.

★MOST STEEL CANS COLLECTED IN ONE MONTH

South African recycling venture Collect-a-Can collected 2,122,238 steel cans weighing 146,210 lb 7 oz (66,319.95 kg) from schools across South Africa between October 1 and 31, 2009, in an initiative to promote the recycling of cans in the country.

★LARGEST COLLECTION OF CLOTHES TO RECYCLE

On August 12, 2009 at Union Station, Washington, DC, USA, *National Geographic Kids* magazine announced that it had collected 33,088 pairs of jeans for recycling through its denim drive event.

All the denim collected will be donated to the organization COTTON. FROM BLUE TO GREEN, which recycles jeans into UltraTouch Natural Cotton Fiber Insulation, a product that is used to help build houses in places that have been damaged by hurricanes and other natural disasters.

It takes about 500 pairs of jeans to recycle enough denim to insulate one average-size house.

★MOST BOTTLES RECYCLED BY A DOG

A Labrador called Tubby, owned by Sandra Gilmore of Pontnewydd, Torfaen, UK, has helped recycle an estimated 26,000 plastic bottles over the past six years by collecting them on his daily walks, crushing them, and passing them to his owner.

LARGEST PLASTIC BAG SCULPTURE

A sculpture of a globe made of 17,773 plastic bags measuring 36 ft 1 in (11 m) in circumference was revealed at the Ministerio de Medio Ambiente in Madrid, Spain, by the charity InspirAction to promote recycling and environmental issues on December 12, 2009.

OUCH! ACCORDING TO A REPORT BY THE GARTNER GROUP AND HEWLETT-PACKARD, THE AVERAGE INTERNET USER PRINTS 28 PAGES EVERY DAY.

OH! THE ENERGY NEEDED TO MELT RECYCLED GLASS IS 30% LESS THAN THAT NEEDED TO MELT RAW MATERIALS USED TO MAKE NEW JARS AND BOTTLES.

HUMAN SOCIETY
AMERICAN HEROES

APOLLO 11 CREW

Neil Alden Armstrong and Edwin "Buzz" Aldrin became the **first men on the Moon** on July 21, 1969. The third man in the Apollo 11 team – Michael Collins (Italy/USA) – remained behind in the command module *Columbia*.

NYC FIREFIGHTERS

The **single largest loss of firefighters** occurred on September 11, 2001, when 341 New York City Fire Department staff – plus two paramedics – who attended the World Trade Center attacks died. In all, 411 emergency workers lost their lives.

MICHAEL JORDAN

The NBA's **highest point-scoring average** for players exceeding 10,000 points is 30.1 by Michael Jordan, who scored 32,292 points in 1,072 games for the Chicago Bulls (1984–98) and the Washington Wizards (2001–03).

AMELIA EARHART

On May 20–21, 1932, Amelia Earhart became the **first woman** (and second person) **to make a solo transatlantic flight** when she piloted her Lockheed Vega from Harbour Grace in Newfoundland, Canada, to Londonderry, Northern Ireland, UK, in 13 hr 30 min.

RONALD REAGAN

In a poll of 2.4 million Americans conducted by AOL and the Discovery Channel in 2005, 40th US President Ronald Reagan was voted the **greatest American of all time**. His two terms in office (1981–89) are associated with the end of the Cold War and economic prosperity, a period of much-needed stability following the Vietnam War.

EXTRA!
FOR THE LATEST RECORDS FROM AMERICA'S "FAVORITE PASTIME,"
SEE P.232.

STEPHEN SONDHEIM

Recipient of the **most Tony Awards won by a composer** (seven), Stephen Sondheim (b. 1930) is also the greatest living Broadway lyricist (for *West Side Story* and *Gypsy*, among others) and composer (credits include *Company*, *Follies*, *Sweeney Todd*, and *Into the Woods*).

BARACK
CHIEF AMONG OUR HEROES IS BARACK OBAMA (B. 1961), WHO MADE HISTORY IN 2009 BY BECOMING THE FIRST BLACK AMERICAN PRESIDENT.

OBAMA
HE'S ALSO THE FIRST US PRESIDENT TO HAVE REGULAR EMAIL ACCESS, AND HE RIDES IN THE MOST SECURE PRESIDENTIAL LIMOUSINE.

NEW RECORD
★ UPDATED RECORD

OPRAH WINFREY

Undoubtedly the ★**most powerful person in television** (11 places ahead of Dr Phil and 13 ahead of Letterman!), Oprah Gail Winfrey (b. 1954) is also the **highest paid TV personality** ($275 million earned in 2008–09, thanks to her TV and radio shows, magazine, and Oprah Winfrey Network). A self-made billionaire (worth $2.3 billion as of September 2009), the philanthropist/actress/producer is arguably the most influential woman in the world.

JOHN F KENNEDY

John Fitzgerald Kennedy (1917–63), Democratic victor in the 1960 US presidential election, was, at age 43, the **youngest man ever to win the American presidency**. He was also the ★**youngest US president to die in office**, when he was assassinated on November 22, 1963. An advocate of civil rights, JFK remains one of the most popular figures in the White House, having survived the Bay of Pigs debacle and the Cuban Missile Crisis.

BILLIE-JEAN KING

Between 1961 and 1979, Billie-Jean King (b. 1943) achieved the **most Wimbledon victories by a woman**, winning 20 titles (six singles, 10 women's doubles, and four mixed doubles) – a record she shares with Martina Navratilova (USA, b. Czechoslovakia).

MARTIN LUTHER KING, JR

On August 28, 1963, civil rights leader Martin Luther King, Jr (1929–68) led more than 250,000 demonstrators down the Mall in Washington, DC, to promote equal civil rights for all Americans – the **largest racial-equality rally** ever held. From the steps of the Lincoln Memorial, King delivered his legendary "I have a dream" speech.

MEDIA TODAY, THE WALT DISNEY COMPANY IS THE ★**LARGEST MEDIA AND ENTERTAINMENT CONGLOMERATE IN THE WORLD**, WITH A NET INCOME IN 2008-09 OF $4.4 BILLION!

WALT DISNEY

The Disney brothers Roy (1893–1971) and Walter (1901–66) might have been cofounders of the world's **largest theme park operator**, but it's Walt whose name lives on as a synonym for fun. He holds the record for the **most Oscar nominations** (64), and between 1942 and 1950, he was nominated every single year, also a record. In addition, he holds the record for the **most Oscar wins** (26), and in 1953, he was awarded the **most Oscar wins in a year** (4).

BILL GATES

William Gates III, who is worth an estimated $40 billion, was the richest person alive from 1995 to 2010, excluding 2007. In 2009, he and his wife donated $3.8 billion to the Bill and Melinda Gates Foundation, the world's **richest charitable group**.

CHESLEY B SULLENBERGER

Although there have been previous incidents of commercial airliners ditching in which 100% of the passengers have survived, the **largest number of survivors** in such a scenario were the 155 passengers and crew involved in the ditching of US Airways Airbus A320 Flight 1549 from LaGuardia into the Hudson, by Captain Chesley B "Sully" Sullenberger, on January 15, 2009.

"BABE" RUTH

During his career, George Herman "Babe" Ruth (1895–1946) hit 714 homers from 8,399 times at bat: a success rate of 8.5% and the **highest home run percentage in MLB history**. He also hit the longest home run – 575 ft (175 m) for the Yankees against the Detroit Tigers on July 18, 1921.

MORE AMERICAN HEROES

These pages are a warm tribute to those great Americans who hold Guinness World Records. Here are some more candidates worthy of inclusion in any American Hall of Fame:

Franklin Delano Roosevelt, "FDR" (1882–1945)	*32nd President of United States (1933–45)*	Led the country through economic depression and World War II; only president elected to more than two terms.
Abraham Lincoln (1809–65)	*16th President of United States (1861–65)*	Preserved the Union through the Civil War; abolished slavery; Gettysburg Address.
David "Davy" Crockett (1786–1836)	*Frontiersman, soldier, folk hero*	Tennessee Member of House of Representatives; fought for independence of Texas; killed at the Alamo.
George Washington (1732–1799)	*1st President of United States (1789–97)*	"Father of our Country," Commander-in-Chief of colonial armies in American Revolution, stabilized country after political chaos.
Jonas Salk (1914–95)	*Virologist*	Developed polio vaccine (announced April 12, 1955).

MICHAEL NO LIST OF ICONIC AMERICANS WOULD BE COMPLETE WITHOUT THE KING OF POP HIMSELF, MICHAEL JACKSON. CHECK OUT OUR SPECIAL TRIBUTE TO THE LEGEND ON P.189

MADONNA AND FOR HER ENDURING APPEAL, HER CONSTANT REINVENTION, HER DECADENCE, AND HER ENDLESS STRING OF HIT ALBUMS, SINGLES, AND TOURS, HATS OFF TO THE MATERIAL GIRL – SEE P.186

SYDNEY, AUSTRALIA

The Panasonic IMAX Theatre at Darling Harbour, Sydney, Australia, holds the **largest fixed projection screen** in the world, measuring 117 x 97 ft (35.72 x 29.57 m). It opened in September 1996 and can seat 540 people.

33°51'S 151°12'E

HUMAN SOCIETY
MOST EXPENSIVE

EXTRA!
TO FIND OUT MORE ABOUT THE WORLD'S RICHEST AND POOREST, FLICK BACK TO P. 132.

★ **SCULPTURE SOLD AT AUCTION**

Alberto Giacometti's (Switzerland) bronze sculpture entitled *Walking Man I* (1960) sold to an anonymous bidder at Sotheby's in London, UK, for a record £65,000,000 ($104,300,000) on February 3, 2010. The sculpture stands 6 ft (1.82 m) tall.

DOLLAR: From the Low German "Thal"/"Thaler," meaning "valley." In the 15th century, silver was mined in a place called Joachim's Thal; the coins minted from this silver were known as Thalers.

★ **DRAWING BY AN OLD MASTER**

Head of a Muse by Raphael (Italy, 1483–1520) sold for £29,200,000 ($46,700,000) at Christie's, London, UK, on December 9, 2009.

COST!
TEN YEARS AGO, ANOTHER GIACOMETTI HELD THE MOST EXPENSIVE SCULPTURE RECORD – HIS *GRANDE FEMME DEBOUT 1* SOLD AT CHRISTIE'S FOR $14 MILLION.

ICE-CREAM MAKER

The G Series ice-cream makers launched by NitroCream (USA) are customized and signed by the artists Robert Kennedy and Ward Goodell and sell for $75,000. The G Series uses liquid nitrogen to create desserts almost instantly by mixing the cold nitrogen – which turns into gas at -321°F (-196°C) – directly with the ice-cream or sorbet mixture.

★ **MUSIC SINGLE**

A rare seven-inch copy of the unreleased 1965 single "Do I Love You (Indeed I Do)" by Frank Wilson (USA) sold for $39,294 in April 2009 to a buyer who wishes to remain anonymous.

★ **BED**

The K.mooi Crystal Noir Limited Edition bed created by Maxxa International Limited (China) is covered with 802,903 CRYSTALIZED™ Swarovski crystals and is on sale for RMB 3,000,000 ($440,000). It was first unveiled at the 100% Design show in Shanghai, China, on October 15, 2009.

★ **CHOCOLATE BAR**

A Wispa Gold bar covered in edible gold leaf was created by Cadbury's (UK) in 2009 to celebrate its comeback after six years. The chocolate treat – which usually sells for 55p (82¢) – is available to buy from Selfridges in London, UK, for £961.48 ($1,441).

★ **CITY COMMUTE**

Based upon an average downtown commuter journey by the most popular public means, London is the most expensive city for commuters, averaging £2.62 ($4.33) per single journey. The results were drawn from Mercer's Worldwide Cost of Living 2009.

★ **NEW RECORD**
★ **UPDATED RECORD**

★ DIAMOND PER CARAT

A 7.03-carat fancy vivid-blue modified rectangular brilliant-cut diamond sold for a record per-carat price of $1,375,938 at Sotheby's in Geneva, Switzerland, on May 12, 2009.

★ LETTER

A letter written by George Washington in 1787 to his nephew Bushrod Washington, urging adoption of the country's new constitution, sold for $3,200,000 on December 5, 2009 at Christie's, New York, USA – the highest price ever paid for a single signed letter.

★ SPA PACKAGE

On sale at the Vitality Show in London's Earls Court, UK, in March 2010: spa therapy for £5,000 ($7,560). Included was a hot-rock spinal massage using diamonds; a 24-carat-gold facial wrap; a chocolate body wrap; and a caviar-and-coffee hair wash.

disappearance, and the calendar – which was bought by Duncan Mackay (UK) – featured a variety of drawings made by Madeleine and her siblings, Sean and Amelie.

★ HOTEL SUITE

The Royal Penthouse Suite at the President Wilson Hotel in Geneva, Switzerland, costs $65,000 per day, although for that price you do get access to 18,000 ft² (1,670 m²) of space plus views of Mont Blanc (through 2-in-thick [6-cm] bullet-proof windows), a private cocktail lounge, a Jacuzzi and fitness center, and a conference room.

★ SUIT

It took Alexander Amosu (UK) more than 80 hours – and 5,000 stitches – to create a suit from gold thread and the wool of Himalayan pashmina goats, Arctic musk oxen, and Peruvian vicuñas. The suit, finished with nine 18-carat-gold-and-pavé-set-diamond buttons, sold for $113,000 in April 2009 and was delivered to the buyer in an armored Land Rover.

★ ROUGH DIAMOND

Petra Diamonds Ltd (UK) sold a 507.9-carat rough diamond – the 19th largest gem ever discovered – for $35.5 million to the Chow Tai Fook Jewellery Co., Ltd (Hong Kong) on February 26, 2010. The stone, named the Petra Heritage, weighed just over 3.3 oz (100 g) and is as big as a chicken's egg. It was found in September 2009 in South Africa's Cullinan mine.

★ WALL CALENDAR

A wall calendar entitled *Still Missing Still Missed* was sold for £20,000 ($30,000) at an auction held on January 27, 2010 in London, UK. The auction was in aid of three charities: Missing Children Europe; Missing People; and Madeleine's Fund: Leaving No Stone Unturned, the charity established to find Madeleine McCann (UK), who went missing during a family holiday in Portugal on May 3, 2007. The fund-raiser was held on the 1,000th day of Madeleine's

MOVE
IN 2003, RONALDO MOVED FROM SPORTING LISBON (PORTUGAL) TO MANCHESTER UNITED (ENGLAND) FOR A MODEST €12.2 MILLION ($15.3 MILLION).

MOVIES
RONALDO – AKA CRISTIANO RONALDO DOS SANTOS AVEIRO – WAS NAMED AFTER US PRESIDENT RONALD REAGAN, HIS FATHER'S FAVORITE MOVIE ACTOR!

The ★ **most expensive manmade object** is the International Space Station – its final cost will be more than $100 billion!

TRIVIA

★ SOCCER PLAYER

The highest transfer fee for a player is a reported €80 million ($131.86 million) for Cristiano Ronaldo (Portugal) by Real Madrid (Spain) to English Premiership club Manchester United on July 1, 2009. According to Spanish newspaper *El Mundo*, Ronaldo cost Real Madrid 57 times his own weight in gold!

HUMAN SOCIETY
EXTREME CUISINE

★ ★ ★ ★ ★ ★ ★ ★ ★ ★ ★ ★

MOST EXPENSIVE...

★**Fishsticks**: In 2004, Barry Coutts' Bistro in Aberdeen, UK, added to their menu haute cuisine fishsticks – made with smoked halibut, king scallops, crayfish, monkfish (goosefish), and Beluga caviar – at a cost of £100 ($167.58) each.

★**Bottle**: Tequila Ley .925 sold a Platinum & White Gold Tequila bottle to a private collector in Mexico City, Mexico, on July 20, 2006 for $225,000.

★**Cherries**: In October 2007, Nick Moraitis (Australia) paid A$35,000 ($31,771) to Variety, the children's charity of New South Wales, for a box of cherries sold by Sydney Markets, Australia.

★**Cognac**: A 1788 bottle of Vieux Cognac sold at auction by the Tour d'Argent restaurant (France) in December 2009 raised €25,000 ($35,364).

★ LARGEST SERVING OF HUMMUS

On May 10, 2010, 300 Lebanese chefs prepared a serving of hummus that weighed 59,992 lb (23,130 kg) in Ain Saadeh, northeast of Beirut. The dish, which beat the previous effort from neighbouring Israel, required 22,046 lb (10 tons) of chickpeas.

THE CHOMP-IONS

FOOD	MOST EATEN IN 1 MIN	WHO
After Eight Thin Mints (no hands)	8	Ashrita Furman (USA) James Graham Boyd (UK)
Bananas (peeled & eaten)	6	Robert Godfrey (USA)
Brussels sprouts	31	Linus Urbanec (Sweden)
Garlic cloves	22	Ashrita Furman (USA)
Cockroaches	5	Alexis Chambon (France)
Ferrero Rocher (chocolates)	8	Chris Vollmershausen (Canada)
Jaffa Cakes	8	Gustav Schulz (Germany)
Jalapeño chilis	16	Alfredo Hernandes (USA)
Gelatin (jello)	16 oz (455 g)	Ashrita Furman (USA)
M&Ms (with chopsticks)	42	Fero Andersen (Germany)
Meatballs	27	Nick Marshall (UK)
Sausages	8	Stefan Paladin (NZ)

FOOD	MOST EATEN IN 3 MIN	WHO
Doughnuts (jelly)	6	Lup Fun Yau (UK)
Doughnuts (powdered)	5	Christopher "Big Black" Boykin (USA)
Grapes (with teaspoon)	151	Ashrita Furman (USA)
Hot dogs	6	Takeru Kobayashi (Japan)
Oysters	233	Colin Shirlow (UK)
Corn kernels (with cocktail stick)	236	Ian Richard Purvis (UK)

MOST PIZZA ROLLS

The **most continuous pizza rolls across the shoulders in 30 seconds** using 20 oz (567 g) of dough is 37 by Tony Gemignani (USA) at the Mall of America, Minneapolis, Minnesota, USA, on April 20, 2006 for the Food Network channel.

QUIZ!

ON MAY 2, 2007, LUP FUN YAU (UK) SET A NEW RECORD FOR THE MOST JELLY DOUGHNUTS EATEN IN THREE MINUTES. BUT HOW MANY DID HE EAT?

SEE P.278 FOR THE ANSWER.

BANANA: They don't grow on trees – the banana plant is actually one of the world's biggest herbs!

★ MOST BANANAS SNAPPED (ONE MINUTE)

Graheme Celledoni (Australia) snapped a total of 96 bananas in half, using only his hands, at the Innisfail Society Show in Queensland, Australia, on July 9, 2009.

★ MOST ICE-CREAM SCOOPS STACKED ON ONE CONE

Terry Morris (New Zealand) balanced 25 scoops of ice cream on a single cone on the set of *NZ Smashes Guinness World Records* at Sylvia Park shopping mall, Auckland, New Zealand, on September 20, 2009.

★ MOST NAANS MADE (ONE HOUR)

A team of five from the Indian Ocean restaurant in Ashton-under-Lyne, UK, made 640 naans on September 29, 2009.

★ FIRST COCKTAIL

In September 2005, archaeochemist Patrick McGovern from Pennsylvania University, USA, announced the discovery of 5,000-year-old earthenware from the banks of the Tigris, between Iran and Iraq, containing traces of tartaric acid, honey, apple juice, and barley.

★ LARGEST PIE FIGHT

Shaw Floors in Grapevine, Texas, USA, organized a pie fight between 434 employees on 7 January 2010. The flan fighters flung a total of 1,200 chocolate, apple and cherry pies at a Shaw sales meeting to demonstrate the strain resistance of a premium nylon carpet.

FASTEST TIME TO...

★ **Carve a turkey**: Paul Kelly (UK) carved a turkey in 3 min 19.47 sec at Little Claydon Farm, Essex, UK, on June 3, 2009.

Pluck a turkey: Vincent Pilkington (Ireland) plucked a turkey in 1 min 30 sec on November 17, 1980.

★ MOST CUSTARD PIES IN THE FACE

James Kerley "pied" Damien Bignell (both Australia) with 46 custard pies in a minute on the set of *Australia Smashes Guinness World Records* at the Warringah Mall in Sydney, Australia, on January 15, 2010.

★ MOST PANCAKES MADE (EIGHT HOURS)

A total of 175 volunteers from Batter Blaster (USA) used 37 griddles to prepare a record 76,382 pancakes on May 9, 2009 – and serve them to 20,000 people for breakfast – on the Great Lawn of the Centennial Olympic Park in Atlanta, Georgia, USA. Each recipient paid $1 toward two charities: Homeless and Hosea Feed the Hungry.

★ LARGEST DISPLAY OF TEQUILA

The Tequila Regulatory Council of Mexico displayed a record 1,201 varieties of tequila at Hospicio Cabañas, Guadalajara, Mexico, on November 6, 2009.

TALLEST...

★ **Poppadom stack**: A freestanding tower of 1,052 poppadoms (thin and crispy Indian flatbreads) measured 4 ft 11 in (1.51 m) at the Curry Lounge in Nottingham, UK, on July 22, 2009.

★ **Sugar cube tower**: Paul Van den Nieuwenhof (Belgium) took 2 hr 12 min to build a record-breaking 6-ft 2-in tall (1.9-m) tower from 1,753 sugar cubes on November 12, 2009.

Don't try this at home!

★ MOST EGGS HELD IN ONE HAND

Zachery George (USA) held 24 eggs in one hand at the Subway restaurant in Parsons, West Virginia, USA, on March 21, 2009. As stipulated in the guidelines, Zachery had 30 seconds to position all the eggs in his hand and then held them there for 10 seconds.

★ **NEW RECORD**
★ **UPDATED RECORD**

COCO...

THE FASTEST TIME TO CLIMB A 29-FT 6-IN (9-M) COCONUT TREE IS 4.88 SECONDS, BY FUATAI SOLO (FIJI) ON AUGUST 22, 1980.

NUTS!

A RECORD COCONUT ENSEMBLE OF 5,877 PEOPLE KNOCKED THEIR NUTS TOGETHER TO THE TUNE OF MONTY PYTHON'S "ALWAYS LOOK ON THE BRIGHT SIDE OF LIFE" IN LONDON, UK, ON APRIL 23, 2007.

★ MOST COCONUTS SMASHED WITH ONE HAND IN ONE MINUTE

Nut cracker Muhamed Kahrimanovic (Germany, pictured) crushed 82 coconuts by hand during the Vienna Recordia event in Vienna, Austria, on September 27, 2009. In a similar event held in Malaysia on June 21, 2009, Ho Eng Hui (Malaysia) pierced four coconuts with his right index finger – the ★ **most coconuts pierced by finger in one minute**.

WELLINGTON, NZ
Wellington, North Island, New Zealand, with a population of 179,436, is the **most southerly capital city** of an independent country.
41°17'S 174°46'E.

HUMAN SOCIETY
ENORMOUS NOSH

★ LARGEST CUPCAKE

A colossal cupcake weighing 1,315 lb (596.47 kg) was made by Global TV Concepts (USA) during the second annual THINK PINK ROCKS charity concert at Mizner Park in Boca Raton, Florida, USA, on October 3, 2009.

FANTASTIC FEASTS

LARGEST...	RECORD	ORGANIZER/VENUE	DATE
★ Birth feast	819	Council of Utrecht/Vinkenburgstraat, the Netherlands	Jan 24, 09
Breakfast (cooked)	18,941	The Cowboy Breakfast Foundation, San Antonio, USA	Jan 26, 01
Breakfast (noncooked)	27,854 in 1 hr	Nutella/Arena AufSchalke, Gelsenkirchen, Germany	May 29, 05
Coffee morning (multi-venue)	576,157	Macmillan Cancer Relief (UK)	Sep 26, 03
★ Picnic (single-venue) (see also p.101)	22,232	Modelo/Parque da Bela Vista, Lisbon, Portugal	Jun 20, 09
Tea party (multi-venue)	280,246	The Cancer Council/6,062 locations across Australia	May 26, 05

★ NEW RECORD   UPDATED RECORD

LARGEST...

★ CRAB CAKE

The largest crab cake on record weighed 253 lb (114.75 kg) and was made by Special Olympics Maryland in conjunction with Handy International and Graul's Market (all USA) in Hampden, Maryland, USA, on June 13, 2009.

★ FISHSTICK

A 16-ft 6-in-long (2-m) fishstick weighing 299 lb 13 oz (136 kg) was prepared by Michael Gorich (Germany) in Bremerhaven, Germany, on January 22, 2009.

★ FUDGE

On June 29, 2009, William Nicklosovich and Peppermint Jim Crosby (both USA) made a slab of fudge weighing 5,200 lb (2.35 tonnes) at Lansing Community College West Campus, Delta Township, Michigan, USA.

★ HAGGIS

The national dish of Scotland, haggis, is a sausage of minced offal with oatmeal, beef suet, and spices. The largest ever weighed 1,234 lb 9 oz (560 kg) – about the same as a Jersey cow – and was made by the Mauchline Burns Club in Ayrshire, UK, in May 2009.

★ HALVA

A halva – a Middle East dessert – weighing 8,402 lb (3,811 kg) was created by the Nazareth Halva Factory in Israel on October 14, 2009. It contained an estimated 20 million calories!

★ LOLLIPOP

On August 27, 2009, Ashrita Furman (USA) and members of the New York Sri Chinmoy Centre created a 25-ft-tall (7.62-m) lollipop weighing 6,514 lb (2.95 tonnes) – equal to 165,070 regular lollipops!

LARGEST DISH OF MUSSELS

A mussels dish weighing 4.07 tons (3,692 kg) was prepared for the public in the streets of Taranto, Italy, on August 1, 2009.

WHAT?

MUSSELS: 7,275 LB 4 OZ
RED TOMATOES: 661 LB 6 OZ
GARLIC: 66 LB 2 OZ
SALT: 6 LB 10 OZ
OLIVE OIL: 330 LB 11 OZ
PEPPER: 44 LB 2 OZ
PARSLEY: 44 LB 2 OZ
WINE: 33 GAL
BREAD CROUTONS: 661 LB 6 OZ

WHO?

THE FISHY DISH WAS ORGANIZED BY THE SHOPPING MALL MONGOLFIERA AND COOP ESTENSE AND THE "SOCIETA" SVILUPPO COMMERCIALE IN TARANTO, ITALY.

AUCKLAND, NEW ZEALAND

36°51'S 174°47'E

On February 19, 1998, the four main power cables to downtown Auckland, New Zealand, failed, in the **longest peacetime blackout**. The disruption lasted for 66 days, affected 7,500 business and residential customers, and cost businesses some NZ$300 million (US $156 million).

★ LARGEST "FULL ENGLISH" BREAKFAST

A "full English" on the menu at Mario's Cafe Bar in Bolton, Lancashire, UK, weighs on average 6 lb 7 oz (2.9 kg) and costs £10.95 ($17.87). The melee of bacon, sausages, eggs, bread, mushrooms, blood sausage, beans, and tomatoes is free if eaten within 20 minutes.

★ PORRIDGE

The largest bowl of porridge weighed 378 lb 15 oz (171.9 kg) and was prepared by Mornflake Oats (UK) at the Lowry Theatre, Salford, UK, on September 10, 2009. The 55 lb 1 oz (25 kg) of porridge oats and 32.9 gal (150 liters) of water was sufficient to cater for 830 individual servings.

★ SOUP

DENK Communicatie prepared a 5,863-gal (26,658-liter) vegetable soup in Poeldijk, the Netherlands, on May 16, 2009.

LONGEST...

★ GARLIC BREAD

A garlic bread measuring 12 ft 6 in (3.81 m) was baked by Cole's Quality Foods in Muskegon, Michigan, USA, on June 12, 2009.

★ SAUSAGE CHAIN

On June 28, 2009 at Gelsenkirchen, Germany, more than 10,000 Fleischwurst sausages were linked in a 4,921-ft 3-in-long (1,500-m) chain. The **fastest man to run 1,500 m** – Hicham El Guerrouj (Morocco) – would take 3 min 26 sec to run from end to end!

★ RICE NOODLE

A 1,800-ft 2-in (548.7-m) noodle – as long as five football fields – was unveiled at Taipei County Hakka Museum, Taiwan, on December 28, 2008.

★ MEATBALL

A meatball weighing 222 lb 8 oz (100.92 kg) was created by Nonni's Italian Eatery in Concord, New Hampshire, USA, on November 1, 2009.

★ MEAT STEW

A stew weighing 5,132 lb 15 oz (2,328.2 kg), containing 2,854 lb (1,294.6 kg) of lamb meat (from an estimated 75 lambs), was cooked in Badajoz, Spain, on October 25, 2009.

★ MOJITO

The largest glass of mojito – a Cuban cocktail of rum, sugar, mint, and lime juice – contained 156 gal (713 liters) and measured 4 ft 4 in (1.34 m) tall and 4 ft 1 in (1.25 m) at its widest. It was made by the bar-ristorante Sirio in Spotorno, Savona, Italy, on August 28, 2009, and required at least 200 lb (90 kg) of limes.

LARGEST CHOCOLATE RABBIT

A chocolate rabbit weighing in at 6,172 lb 15 oz (2,800 kg) was made by Supermercados Imperatriz Ltda and Nestlé FoodServices (both Brazil) in São José, Santa Catarina, Brazil, on March 30, 2009.

LONGEST BAR

The 405-ft 10-in (123.7-m) counter in the Beer Barrel Saloon at Put-in-Bay, South Bass Island, Ohio, USA, is fitted with 56 beer taps and features 160 bar stools, and is the longest continuious bar in the world.

HIGH! IF STOOD ON ITS SIDE, THE BEER BARREL BAR WOULD BE TALLER THAN THE STATUE OF LIBERTY (INCLUDING HER CONCRETE PLINTH)!

DRY! ROBERT BEGLEY (USA) HAS THE GUINNESS WORLD RECORD FOR THE LARGEST COLLECTION OF BAR TOWELS – HE OWNS 2,372 TOWELS FROM 27 COUNTRIES.

HONOLULU, HI, USA
On December 19, 1992, local citizens made a 14,550-ft (4,434-m) paper lei at the Hyatt Regency Waikiki, Honolulu, Hawaii, USA -- the **largest artificial garland**.

21°18'N
157°49'W

HUMAN SOCIETY
COLLECTORS' ITEMS

★ ★ ★ ★ ★ ★ ★ ★ ★ ★ ★ ★ ☆

★ BOTTLED WATER LABELS

Lorenzo Pescini of Florence, Italy, had a collection of 8,650 different bottled water labels from 185 different countries of 1,683 different springs, as of January 12, 2009. He started his collection in 1992.

★ BUS TICKETS

Ladislav Šejnoha (Czech Republic) had 200,000 bus tickets from 36 countries as of September 30, 2008.

★ CALENDARS

Yakov L Kofman (USA) had put together a collection of 16,552 different calendars as of October 26, 2008. His collection began in 1945.

★ MOVIE CAMERAS

Since 1960, Richard LaRiviere (USA) has built up a collection of 894 movie cameras. The oldest is a 1907 Darling with hand crank.

★ HEARTS

Dr Diana Reser (Switzerland) has collected 775 heart-shaped motifs and items since becoming a cardiac surgeon in 2006.

★ TROLLS

Sophie Marie Cross (UK) began collecting trolls in 2003 and, as of December 3, 2009, had amassed a set of 633 unique items.

NEW COLLECTIONS

	ITEM	COLLECTOR	QUANTITY	DATE ACHIEVED
★	Airline boarding passes	Miguel Fernandez (Spain)	1,020	Aug 2009
★	Banknotes	Anil Bohora (India)	10,025	Jan 2009
★	Cachaça bottles	Messias Soares Cavalcante (Brazil)	12,800	Aug 2009
★	Casino chips and tokens	Bruce and Sue Wunder (both USA)	554	May 2009
★	Chicken memorabilia	Cecil and Joann Dixon (both USA)	6,505	Jun 2006
★	Christmas brooches	Adam Wide (UK)	1,329	Jun 2009
★	Cow memorabilia	Denise Tubangui (USA)	2,261	Oct 2009
★	Hedgehog memorabilia	Bengt W Johansson (Sweden)	468	Nov 2009
★	Joker playing cards	Tony De Santis (Italy)	8,520	Mar 2009
★	Kappa (Japanese river sprite) memorabilia	Tatsuo Kitano (Japan)	7,845	Jun 2009
★	Millstones	He Hengde (China)	39,052	Jul 2009
★	Oil lamps	Gerd Bonk (Germany)	356	Nov 2009
★	Panda memorabilia	Miranda Middleton (USA)	1,175	Jan 2009
★	Stamps (postal covers)	Joshua Steinberg (UK)	6,037	Nov 2004
★	Sugar packets	Pavlina Yotkova (Bulgaria)	3,384	Apr 2009
★	Surfboards	Donald Dettloff (USA)	647	Nov 2009
★	Tea-bag holders	Mimi Wilfong (USA)	116	Jun 2009

D'OH!
CAMERON GIBBS (AUSTRALIA) HAD AMASSED A TOTAL OF 2,580 DIFFERENT SIMPSONS ITEMS, AS OF MARCH 20, 2008.

★ SMURF MEMORABILIA

Stephen Parkes (UK) began collecting Smurfs as a child, when they were sold by a chain of filling stations across the UK. As of January 28, 2010, his collection totals 1,061 and includes Christmas Smurfs, Easter Smurfs, Smurfs dressed as historical figures, and Smurfs doing almost every occupation you can imagine. And he's still collecting...

★ NEW RECORD
★ UPDATED RECORD

CLASSIC COLLECTIONS

	ITEM	COLLECTOR	QUANTITY	DATE ACHIEVED
★	Airsickness bags	Niek Vermeulen (Netherlands)	6,016	Jan 2010
	Barbie dolls	Bettina Dorfmann (Germany)	7,246	Feb 2010
	Bells	Myrtle B Eldridge (USA)	9,638	Mar 2005
	Board games	Brian Arnett (USA)	1,345	Feb 2007
★	Bookmarks	Frank Divendal (Netherlands)	103,009	Feb 2010
★	Candles	Véronique Salmont (France)	2,119	Jun 2009
★	Clocks	Jack Schoff (USA)	1,509	Feb 2010
	Coffeepots	Robert Dahl (Germany)	13,267	Sep 2009
	Colored vinyl records	Alessandro Benedetti (Italy)	1,507	Mar 2010
	"Do Not Disturb" signs	Jean-François Vernetti (Switzerland)	10,000	Jun 2009
★	Hats	Roger Buckey Legried (USA)	100,336	Mar 2010
★	Ladybird memorabilia	Carine Roosen (Belgium)	3,531	Sep 2009
★	Magic sets	Manfred Klaghofer (Austria)	2,401	Feb 2010
★	Masks	Gerold Weschenmoser (Germany)	5,385	Mar 2010
★	Mobile (cell) phones	Carsten Tews (Germany)	1,563	Feb 2010
★	Model cars	Nabil Karam (Lebanon)	22,222	Nov 2009
★	Pencils	Vladimir Jindra (Czech Republic)	11,068	Nov 2009
★	Registration (license) plates	Shahin Ebrahim Mohajer (Oman)	561	May 2009
★	Rubber ducks	Charlotte Lee (USA)	5,429	Feb 2010
	Santa Claus memorabilia	Jean-Guy Laquerre (Canada)	23,947	Feb 2010
	Sports mascots	Adina and Falk Hinneberg (both Germany)	874	Feb 2010
★	Stickers for bumpers	Bill Heermann (USA)	4,131	Apr 2009
	Teapots	Tang Yu (China)	30,000	Oct 2008
★	Toothbrushes	Grigori Fleicher (Russia)	1,320	Nov 2008
★	Yo-yos	John "Lucky" Meisenheimer (USA)	4,586	Feb 2010

★SOAPS

Carol Vaughan (UK) has collected 1,331 individual soap bars since 1991. She is always on the lookout for new, unusual soaps – though, of course, she never uses items in her collection to wash with...

MICKEY MOUSE MEMORABILIA

As of December 11, 2008, Janet Esteves (USA) had collected 2,760 different Mickey Mouse items. Janet started her collection in 1960, when she was a child. Her father made regular business trips to California and would bring back Disney products for her.

QUACK! AS OF MAY 28, 2008, MARY BROOKS (USA) HAD 1,285 ITEMS OF DONALD DUCK MEMORABILIA. SHE HAS BEEN COLLECTING FOR MORE THAN 30 YEARS.

FAIRBANKS, AL, USA

64°50 N
147°42 W

The Pan-American Highway, the **longest motorable road**, starts at Fairbanks, Alaska, USA, and stretches to Santiago, Chile; it then turns eastward to Buenos Aires, Argentina,

HUMAN SOCIETY
TOYS & GAMES

★ ★ ★ ★ ★

LARGEST PARTY GAMES

★OLD MacDONALD HAD A FARM
A record 332 people played the largest game of "Old MacDonald Had a Farm" on the set of *Lo Show dei Record*, in Milan, Italy, on April 25, 2009.

★MOST SIMULTANEOUS CHESS GAMES
Morteza Mahjoob (Iran) played 500 games of chess simultaneously against different opponents at the Engelab Sports Complex in Tehran, Iran, on August 13–14, 2009. Only 13 of his opponents beat him.

★FASTEST JENGA TOWER
Mitchell Bettell (UK) built 10 levels on a Jenga tower in 43.94 seconds at the GWR Live! event held at Butlins, Bognor Regis, UK, on August 26, 2009.

★HEAD, SHOULDERS, KNEES, AND TOES
A mammoth 1,461 participants from Gladesmore Community School and Crowland Primary School got together to play the largest game of "Head, Shoulders, Knees, and Toes" at Markfield Park, Tottenham, London, UK, on October 23, 2009.

★MUSICAL STATUES
A record 987 people tried to keep very still when the music stopped as they took part in the largest game of musical statues at an event organized by Sir Thomas Boteler Church of England High School in Latchford, Warrington, UK, on July 10, 2009.

★MUSICAL BUMPS
On July 15, 2009, 348 people gathered at St Thomas of Aquin's High School in Edinburgh, UK, to play the largest-ever game of musical bumps.

MUSICAL CHAIRS
On August 5, 1989, the largest game of musical chairs began with 8,238 participants at the Anglo-Chinese School in Singapore. Three-and-a-half hours later, 15-year-old Xu Chong Wei (Singapore) was left sitting on the last chair.

★IF YOU'RE HAPPY AND YOU KNOW IT
During the SkyFest family festival held in Edinburgh, UK, on September 6, 2009, 755 people took part in the largest-ever game of the children's favorite "If You're Happy and You Know it."

STACK!
THE LARGEST NUMBER OF DOMINOES STACKED ON ONE SINGLE PIECE WAS 1,002, ACHIEVED BY MAXIMILIAN POSER (GERMANY) IN BERLIN, GERMANY, ON FEBRUARY 6, 2009.

SPIRAL!
THE LARGEST NUMBER OF DOMINOES TOPPLED IN A SPIRAL WAS 28,800, BY MAXIMILIAN POSER (GERMANY) IN BERLIN, GERMANY, ON APRIL 14, 2009.

★LARGEST GAME OF DODGEBALL
San Diego State University (USA) organized a game of dodgeball for 450 participants at the Aztec Recreation Center in San Diego, California, USA, on September 5, 2009.

DID YOU KNOW?
THE FARTHEST A PAPER AIRPLANE HAS FLOWN IS 207 FT 4 IN (63.19 M).

A record 12,672 paper planes were launched at once on November 2, 2009.

TRIVIA

★ **GREATEST DISTANCE TRAVELED BY A RADIO-CONTROLLED MODEL VEHICLE ON A SET OF BATTERIES**

A battery-operated radio-controlled model vehicle in the shape of a robot pedaling a three-wheeled cycle covered 14.742 miles (23.726 km) using just one set of Panasonic Evolta batteries in Le Mans, France, on August 5–6, 2009.

EXTRA! FOR VIDEO GAME RECORDS, TAKE A LOOK AT P.162.

CLASSIC TOYS

★ **LONGEST SLOT CAR TRACK**
A fully working slot car track measuring 2.953 miles (4.752 km) was built by James May (UK) and 300 volunteers at Brooklands, UK, on August 16, 2009.

★ **MOST RUBIK'S CUBES SOLVED UNDERWATER**
David Calvo (Spain) solved four Rubik's Cubes while holding his breath underwater in Madrid, Spain, on January 16, 2009.

★ **LONGEST MODEL TRAIN**
An HO (that is, 1:87.1) scale model train measuring 892 ft 3 in (271.97 m) made up of eight locomotives and 2,212 cars was constructed by Miniature Wunderland in Hamburg, Germany, on July 25, 2008.

★ **LARGEST SIMULTANEOUS YO-YO**
On March 13, 2009, a group of 662 people "yo-yo'd" together at an event organized by CTC Kingshurst Academy in Birmingham, UK.

SCHOOL FAVES

★ **LONGEST HOPSCOTCH GAME**
A hopscotch game measuring 15,762 ft (4,804.55 m) – equal in length to about 45 soccer pitches – was created by Victory Baptist Church in co-operation with Toms Shoes (both USA) in Ladd Landing, Kingston, Tennessee, USA, on September 26, 2009.

★ **FASTEST GAME OF HOPSCOTCH**
Ashrita Furman (USA) completed a game of hopscotch in 1 min 8 sec in New York City, USA, on December 29, 2009.

★ **LARGEST LEGO HOUSE**
A full-scale LEGO house measuring 15 ft 4 in (4.69 m) high, 30 ft 9 in (9.39 m) long, and 18 ft 10 in (5.75 m) wide was built by 1,200 volunteers and television presenter James May (UK) for the program *James May's Toy Stories* in Dorking, UK, on September 17, 2009. In all, 2.4 million LEGO bricks were used in the construction.

★ **LARGEST GAME OF TAG**
On April 29, 2009 465 people took part in a game of tag at an event organized by Marcia LeVatte (Canada) in Sherwood Park, Canada.

★ **LARGEST GAME OF HE LOVES ME, HE LOVES ME NOT**
On the set of *Lo Show dei Record*, in Milan, Italy, on April 18, 2009, 331 people picked petals off daisies in a game of He Loves Me, He Loves Me Not.

★ **LARGEST MARIONETTE**
A marionette measuring 58 ft 5.5 in (17.82 m) in height was presented by the Villa Marconi Long-Term Care Centre as the mascot to the annual Ital-Fest in Ottawa, Canada, on September 6, 2008.

WHITEHORSE, YT, CANADA
On October 22, 2000, in the city of Whitehorse in the Yukon Territory of Canada, 210 dogs pulled a sled attached to a weight of 145,302 lb (65,910 kg), **the heaviest weight pulled by a dog sled** team. The vehicle reached a top speed of 2 mph (45 km/h) and traveled a distance of six blocks

60°43'N, 135°03'W

FEATURE
ROUTE 66

RUNNING NEARLY 2,500 MILES (4,020 KM) FROM SANTA MONICA ON THE WEST COAST TO THE WINDY CITY OF CHICAGO, ROUTE 66 IS AN INHERENT PART OF AMERICAN FOLKLORE. INSPIRED BY THIS HISTORIC HIGHWAY, GWR TAKES YOU ON A RECORD-BREAKING ROAD TRIP...

4. LAKE HAVASU CITY-WINSLOW (AR), 270 MILES

We continue on another four hours or so to Coon Butte (or Barringer Crater), the **largest meteor crater in the Americas**. Discovered in 1891, near Winslow, Arizona, it's 4,150 ft (1,265 m) wide and 575 ft (175 m) deep.

★ ★ ★

3. SAN DIMAS-LAKE HAVASU CITY (AR), 270 MILES

It's just a four-and-a-half-hour drive to see London Bridge... in Arizona? Yes, it's the record for the **farthest distance to move a bridge**. The British bridge was auctioned in 1962 to Robert McCulloch (USA) for $2,460,000 and dismantled and moved 5,300 miles (8,530 km) to Arizona!

1. SANTA MONICA-IRWINDALE (CA), 36.7 MILES

The first leg of the journey takes us from the starting point at Santa Monica to the Irwindale Speedway to ride the **fastest monowheel**. Designed by Kerry McLean, this is no ordinary unicycle: powered by a 340 cc snowmobile engine generating 40 hp (30 kW), it can reach up to 57 mph (91.7 km/h)!

2. IRWINDALE-SAN DIMAS (CA), 10.1 MILES

From Irwindale to San Dimas should take just 15 minutes by car, so pop on over and say hello to Bert, the world's **highest-ranking camel** (he's officially a Reserve Deputy Sheriff!).

5. WINSLOW-ALBUQUERQUE (NM), 269 MILES

Another four hours on and you'll come to the New Mexico capital of Albuquerque, where, if you time your trip correctly, you'll witness the International Balloon Fiesta and the **largest combined ascent of hot-air balloons**. The biggest ever launch took place on October 7, 2000, when 329 balloons took to the skies in the space of an hour.

JUNEAU, AL, USA

In a 24-hour period between July 20 and 21, 2005, Isabel Bush (USA) skipped an incredible 151,036 jumps of a rope in Juneau, Alaska, USA -- the **most skips in 24 hours**.

10. ST LOUIS–CHICAGO (IL), 298 MILES

So, 2,231 miles and 37 hours of solid driving later and we're here, two blocks from Lake Shore Drive, at the John Hancock Center, the **highest residential apartments** in the world. From 1,127 ft (343.5 m) and 100 stories up, you can almost see all the way back toward Santa Monica!

6. ALBUQUERQUE–OKLAHOMA CITY (OK), 541 MILES

After a nine-hour drive, you'll be grateful for Carl C Magee's (USA) invention: the **first parking meter** was installed on Park and Robinson Avenues, Oklahoma City, Oklahoma, on July 19, 1935.

7. OKLAHOMA CITY–SHAWNEE (OK), 39 MILES

A 40-minute detour is worth the drive to see the world's **largest pair of bib overalls**. They boast an 8-ft (2.46-m) inseam, a 15-ft (4.54-m) waist, and buttons 8 in (20.3 cm) wide!

9. CUBA–ST LOUIS (MO), 83 MILES

No trip to St Louis should be without a visit to the biggest thing you can see for miles around: the 630-ft-tall (192-m) stainless-steel Gateway Arch, the world's **tallest commemorative monument**. It was completed in 1965, cost $29 million to build, and celebrates the westward expansion after the Louisiana Purchase of 1803.

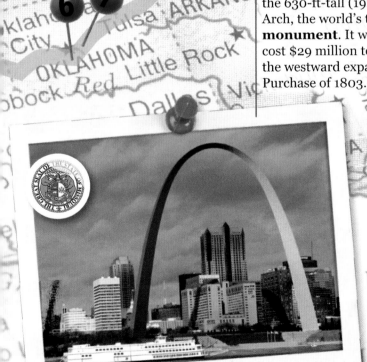

8. SHAWNEE–CUBA (MO), 417 MILES

From Oklahoma, you can hook up with I-44 East or, more enjoyably, join the original "historic" Route 66 and ride it most of the way to Cuba, MO, and the **largest rocking chair**. At 42 ft 1 in (12.83 m) tall and 20 ft 3 in (6.17 m) wide, you can't miss it!

ANIMAL MAGIC

★ **NEW RECORD**
★ **UPDATED RECORD**

★ LONGEST TONGUE ON A DOG

The longest recorded canine tongue measures 4.5 in (11.43 cm) and belongs to Puggy, a Pekingese owned by Becky Stanford (USA). The record-breaking muscle was measured at Avondale Haslet Animal Clinic in Texas, USA, on May 8, 2009.

CONTENTS

ACTUAL SIZE

EXTRA!
FOR MORE CANINE
CHAMPIONS, SIMPLY
TURN THE PAGE...

ANIMAL MAGIC
BARKING MAD

★ ★ ★ ★ ★ ★ ★ ★ ★ ★ ★ ★

LOUDEST BARK

The loudest bark by a dog measured 108 dB and was produced by a white German shepherd dog named Daz, owned by Peter Lucken (UK), in Finsbury Park, London, UK, on June 15, 2009.

★ MOST DOGS IN FANCY DRESS

A total of 123 dogs took to the runway for the "101 Chihuahua Fashion Show" in the downtown of Oosterhout, the Netherlands, on May 3, 2009. To qualify for this record, each dog had to be dressed for the occasion and walk at least one length of the platform with their owner by their side, as per Guinness World Records guidelines.

★ NEW RECORD
★ UPDATED RECORD

★ FIRST AIRPLANE CRASH CAUSED BY A DOG

At 2:20 p.m. on November 29, 1976, an unrestrained German shepherd dog on board a Piper 32-300 Air Taxi operated by Grand Canyon Air interfered with the controls, causing the airplane to crash. The dog perished along with the pilot and lone passenger.

This is the first and, to date, only known accident in which a pet has caused the crash of an aircraft.

★ MOST EXPENSIVE KENNEL

In 2008, UK architect Andy Ramus designed a £250,000 ($384,623) kennel – nicknamed Barkingham Palace – complete with high-tech gadgets such as a plasma TV and a retina-controlled dog door.

FASTEST CANINE RAT CATCHER

In the 1820s, a 26-lb (11.8-kg) "bull and terrier" dog named Billy killed 4,000 rats in 17 hours, a remarkable achievement considering that he was blind in one eye. His most notable feat was the killing of 100 rats in 5 min 30 sec at the Cockpit in Tufton Street, London, UK, on April 23, 1825. He died on February 23, 1829 at the age of 13 years.

DEEPEST SCUBA DIVE BY A DOG

You've heard about the doggy paddle, but what happens when you take this to an extreme? Dwane Folsom (USA) regularly takes his dog, Shadow, scuba diving off the coast of Grand Cayman Island, going as deep as 13 ft (4 m). Shadow wears a diving suit comprising a helmet, weighted dog jacket, and breathing tube connected to his owner's air tank.

★ MOST FRISBEES CAUGHT AND HELD

Edward Watson's (USA) dog Rose can catch seven flying discs thrown one at a time and hold them all in her mouth at once!

LOW! THE SHORTEST DOG LIVING MEASURES JUST 4 IN (10.16 CM) TALL. TURN THE PAGE TO FIND OUT MORE ABOUT THIS PINT-SIZED POOCH!

LOWER! THE SMALLEST DOG EVER WAS A FIST-SIZED, DWARF YORKSHIRE TERRIER OWNED BY ARTHUR MARPLES (UK). FULL GROWN, IT STOOD 2.8 IN (7.11 CM) TALL.

GUINNESS WORLD RECORDS 2011

EXTRA!
FIND MORE PECULIAR PETS ON P.154.

★ FASTEST SPEED ON A SKATEBOARD BY A DOG

Meet Tillman, the skateboarding, body-boarding, surfing action dog. The California-based bulldog loves to board, and set a new Guinness World Record – at X Games 15 in Los Angeles, no less – as the fastest skateboarding dog! Tillman's average time across a two-way 100-m (328-ft) stretch in a parking lot was 19.678 seconds.

INSTANT EXPERT

✪ ACCORDING TO BIOLOGIST DR RAYMOND COPPINGER, THERE ARE AN ESTIMATED 400 MILLION DOGS IN THE WORLD!

✪ DOGS WERE THE FIRST ANIMALS TO BE DOMESTICATED.

✪ THE SCIENTIFIC NAME FOR DOG IS *CANIS LUPUS FAMILIARIS*, REFERRING TO A DOMESTICATED FORM OF GRAY WOLF.

✪ IN SOME COUNTRIES, DOG MEAT IS ACCEPTABLE FARE, WITH *ANIMAL PEOPLE* NEWSPAPER ESTIMATING THAT A TOTAL OF 13-16 MILLION DOGS ARE EATEN IN ASIA EVERY YEAR.

LONGEST JOURNEY HOME BY A LOST DOG

The farthest distance a lost pet dog has walked in order to find his way home is 2,000 miles (3,218 km).

Jimpa, a Labrador/boxer cross, turned up at his old home in Pimpinio, Victoria, Australia, after walking across the entire country. His owner, Warren Dumesney (Australia), had taken the dog with him 14 months earlier but lost him when he worked on a farm at Nyabing, Western Australia. During Jimpa's trek, the dog negotiated the almost waterless Nullarbor Plain.

LONGEST TIME ON DEATH ROW FOR A DOG

A dog named Word was held on doggy death row for a total of eight years and 190 days. Word, a Lhasa apso owned by Wilton Rabon of Seattle, Washington, USA, was initially incarcerated at the Seattle Animal Control Shelter, USA, on May 4, 1993 following two biting incidents. He was later released on November 10, 2001 and transported to the Pigs Peace Sanctuary in Washington, USA. Word ended his days as a seeing dog to a visually impaired potbellied pig!

LARGEST DOG WEDDING

The record for the largest dog "wedding" ceremony was achieved by 178 dog couples who sealed their marriage at the Bow Wow Vows event at the Aspen Grove Lifestyle Center in Littleton, USA, on May 19, 2007.

HARDIEST DOG

On April 15, 2003, a mixed-breed named Dosha slipped out of her home in Clearlake, California, USA, only to be run over by a truck. A concerned police officer decided to end her pain and shot her in the head; she was then sealed in a bag and placed in a freezer at an animal center. Two hours later, staff at the clinic looked inside the freezer – and found Dosha alive and sitting up!

LARGEST SOLID OBJECT SWALLOWED BY A DOG

Kyle, a collie/Staffordshire bull terrier, who was 18 in (45.7 cm) long at the time, swallowed a 15-in (38-cm) bread knife in December 2000. The knife was stuck in his stomach, pointing toward his throat. The dog was taken to the People's Dispensary for Sick Animals in Leeds, UK, where Dr Ann Draper carefully removed the knife.

Kyle now lives a normal life back at home with owner Eva Oliver (UK). Let's hope he sticks to a more sensible diet from now on!

DID YOU KNOW?

• A DOG'S NOSEPRINT IS AS UNIQUE AS A HUMAN FINGERPRINT!
• HUMANS HAVE 5 MILLION SMELL (OLFACTORY) CELLS; DOGS HAVE 220 MILLION!

Dogs sweat in just one place: between their paw pads. When they need to cool down, they hang out their tongues!

TRIVIA

FASTEST TIME TO POP 100 BALLOONS BY A DOG

The fastest time to pop 100 balloons by a dog is 44.49 seconds by Anastasia (a Jack Russell terrier), owned by Doree Sitterly (USA), on the set of *Live with Regis and Kelly* in Los Angeles, USA, on February 24, 2008.

ANIMAL MAGIC
PETS

★ ★ ★ ★ ★ ★ ★ ★ ★ ★ ★ ★ ★ ★ ★

★ **NEW RECORD**
★ **UPDATED RECORD**

SMALLEST LIVING DOG

The smallest dog living, in terms of height, is a long-haired female Chihuahua called Boo Boo, who measured 4 in (10.16 cm) tall on May 12, 2007. Boo Boo is owned by Lana Elswick of Raceland, Kentucky, USA.

★ EARLIEST DOMESTICATED CAT

The oldest archaeological evidence of the domestication of the cat dates back 9,500 years. The bones of a cat were discovered in the neolithic village of Shillourokambos on Cyprus.

MOST INTELLIGENT DOG BREED

Research by Stanley Coren (USA), Professor of Psychology at the University of British Columbia – and the polling of professional dog obedience judges -- reveals the smartest dog breed to be the Border collie, followed by the poodle and German shepherd.

★ FARTHEST JUMP BY A GUINEA PIG

The longest leap by a guinea pig was achieved by Diesel (above), who cleared a gap of 8.07 in (20.5 cm) in London, UK, on July 27, 2009. The **highest jump by a guinea pig** was achieved by Puckel Martin, who jumped 7.8 in (20 cm), on March 16, 2003.

★ LONGEST JUMP BY A RABBIT

The world record for the longest rabbit jump is 9 ft 9.6 in (3 m) and was achieved by Yabo, handled by Maria Brunn Jensen (Denmark), on June 12, 1999 in Horsens, Denmark. That's some bunny hop...

★ HIGHEST RATE OF PET OWNERSHIP (COUNTRY)

The country with the highest rate of pet ownership per household as of 2010 is Australia, with more than 60% of households having at least one animal as a companion (typically a cat or dog) and 83% of Australians having owned a pet at some point in their life.

LONGEST EARS ON A RABBIT

Nipper's Geronimo, an English lop owned by Waymon and Margaret Nipper (USA), has ears that were measured at 31.125 in (79 cm) in a complete span on November 1, 2003 at the American Rabbit Breeders Association National Show in Wichita, Kansas, USA.

★ NEWEST BREED OF CAT

Finally recognized as an official cat breed in 2002, though it was first reported in Toronto, Canada, in the mid-20th century, the hairless sphynx cat can trace its origin to a number of cats with a recessive gene that causes hairlessness.

FUR!
THE SPHYNX CAT DOES NOT HAVE ANY FUR, BUT ITS SKIN IS THE SAME COLORATION AS FUR AND ALSO FEATURES THE USUAL CAT MARKING PATTERNS, SUCH AS SOLID, TABBY, OR TORTIE!

★LONGEST RABBIT

Darius, a Flemish giant rabbit owned by Annette Edwards (UK, pictured with her big bunny), was found to be 4 ft 3 in (129 cm) long when measured for an article in the UK's *Daily Mail* newspaper on April 6, 2010.

SMALLEST RABBIT

Both the Netherlandish and Polish dwarf breeds of rabbit have a weight range of 2–2 lb 7 oz (0.9–1.13 kg). In 1975, Jacques Bouloc of Coulommiere, France, announced a new hybrid of these two breeds weighing just 13.9 oz (396 g).

OLDEST DOG EVER

The greatest recorded age for a dog is 29 years 5 months for an Australian cattle dog named Bluey, owned by Les Hall (Australia). Bluey was obtained as a puppy in 1910 and lived until November 14, 1939.

OLDEST CAT EVER

Born on August 3, 1967, Creme Puff lived with her owner, Jake Perry, in Austin, Texas, USA, until August 6, 2005 – an amazing 38 years 3 days!

OLDEST GOLDFISH EVER

In 1956, seven-year-old Peter Hand of Carlton Minniot, North Yorkshire, UK, won a goldfish (which he named Tish) at a fairground stall. For the next 43 years, Peter's parents, Hilda and Gordon, cared for Tish until the fish died in 1999.

OLDEST CAGED GERBIL

A Mongolian gerbil called Sahara, born in May 1973 and belonging to Aaron Milstone of Lathrup Village, Michigan, USA, died on October 4, 1981 aged eight years and four-and-a-half months old.

SMALLEST BREED OF DOMESTIC HAMSTER

The Roborovski (*Phodopus roborovskii*) typically grows to a length of 1.5–2 in (4–5 cm). These hamsters originate from Mongolia and northern China.

MOST TOES ON A CAT

Jake, a male ginger tabby cat owned by Michelle and Paul Contant (both Canada), had 28 toes – seven per paw – with each toe having its own claw, pad, and bone structure, on September 24, 2002.

PURR! THE F1 SAVANNAH IS A FIRST-GENERATION SERVAL (WILD CAT)/DOMESTIC CAT HYBRID, WHICH IS CONSIDERED A DOMESTICATED CAT BY THE INTERNATIONAL CAT ASSOCIATION (TICA).

★TALLEST DOMESTIC CAT

Scarlett's Magic, an F1 Savannah cross owned by Kimberly and Lee Draper (USA), measured 16.48 in (41.87 cm) tall on December 17, 2009.

TALLEST LIVING DOG

Giant George is a Great Dane who measured 43 in (1.092 m) tall on February 15, 2010. The huge hound weighs 245 lb (111 kg) and is owned by David Nasser of Tucson, Arizona, USA.

SACRAMENTO, CA, USA

The **longest table tennis doubles marathon** lasted 101 hr 1 min 11 sec and was carried out by Lance, Phil and Mark Warren and Bill Weir (all USA) in Sacramento, California, USA, on April 9–13, 1979.

38°33'N 121°28'W

ANIMAL MAGIC
ZOOS & SANCTUARIES

★ ★ ★ ★ ★ ★ ★ ★ ★ ★ ★ ★ ★ ★

LONGEST SNAKE

Fluffy, a reticulated python (*Python reticulatus*), lives in Columbus Zoo and Aquarium, Powell, Ohio, USA. When measured on September 30, 2009, she was found to be more than 24 ft (7.3 m) long. The **longest snake ever** was found in Indonesia in 1912 and measured 32 ft 9.5 in (10 m).

OLDEST ZOO

The **earliest known collection of animals** was established at modern-day Puzurish, Iraq, by Shulgi, a 3rd-dynasty ruler of Ur from 2097 BC to 2094 BC. In the early 13th century, English monarch King John began the most extensive animal collection of the medieval era, which was housed in the Tower of London.

The ★**oldest continuously operating zoo** is the Tiergarten Schönbrunn, part of the Schönbrunn Palace in Vienna, Austria. Created in 1752 by order of Holy Roman Emperor Francis I, initially as a crown menagerie, it was first opened to the public in 1779. The first elephant born in captivity was born here in 1906.

★LARGEST PEDICURES

Elephants in captivity are the largest animals to receive pedicures. Pictured above is a (sedated) 39-year-old Asian elephant named Boy, receiving a pedicure from a German vet on May 23, 2009, at Kiev Zoo, Ukraine.

LARGEST ZOO

In terms of numbers of different species in captivity, the largest zoo is the Zoologischer Garten Berlin (Berlin zoological garden), also the first zoo in Germany, which opened on August 1, 1844. The 86-acre (35-ha) site currently houses 14,000 animals from 1,500 different species, and receives some 2.6 million visitors each year.

AQUARIUMS

Sea Life in Brighton, East Sussex, UK, is the world's ★**oldest aquarium**, dating back to 1872. Combining Victorian architecture with modern-day, high-tech exhibits, it contains more than 150 species of marine life, which are exhibited in 57 separate displays.

In terms of water volume, the Georgia Aquarium in Atlanta, Georgia, USA, is the **largest aquarium**, with 8 million gal (30.28 million liters) of fresh and salt water. The attraction opened in November 2005, covers 500,000 ft² (51,096 m²), and contains 120,000 fish and animals from 500 species. It has 60 different habitats, the largest of which contains 6.2 million gal (23.47 million liters) and was designed to house whale sharks.

EXTRA!
GWR'S TOUR AROUND OUR INCREDIBLE LIVING PLANET STARTS ON P.46.

LOS ANGELES, CA, USA

The **first movie shot in Hollywood** was *In Old California* (USA, 1910), which was filmed in Los Angeles in 1907 by a Chicago production that had moved to California to take advantage of the state's sunnier weather.

DID YOU KNOW?

THE LARGEST LION WAS SIMBA, A BLACK-MANED MALE 44 IN (1.11 M) AT THE SHOULDER, WHO LIVED AT ZOOS IN COLCHESTER AND KNARESBOROUGH, UK.

★MOST GIRAFFE OFFSPRING BORN IN CAPTIVITY

Denisa, a female giraffe living in the Safari Park zoo in Ramat Gan, Israel, has given birth to a record 11 offspring. She is pictured with her latest, in July 2009.

TRIVIA

The largest of the "big cats" is the tiger. Size apart, "big cats" are also distinguished from other cats by their ability to roar.

LARGEST LITTER OF TIGERS

On April 15, 1979, eight tigers were born at Marine World Africa USA, Redwood City, California, USA, to a Bengal tiger (*Panthera tigris tigris*) named Baghdad. This is the greatest recorded number of tigers born in captivity.

★ LARGEST WALK-IN AVIARY

Part of Singapore's Jurong Bird Park – the world's largest bird park, with 8,000 birds – the world's largest walk-in aviary is the African Waterfall Aviary, containing more than 1,500 free-flying birds belonging to more than 50 different species.

★ OLDEST GORILLA IN CAPTIVITY

Colo (b. December 22, 1956) the first gorilla ever born in captivity, currently lives in Columbus Zoo in Powell, Ohio, USA. She has now reached the grand old age of 53 years.

★ NEW RECORD
★ UPDATED RECORD

GORILLA

THE LARGEST MAMMAL TO BUILD A NEST IS THE AFRICAN GORILLA (*GORILLA GORILLA*), WHICH GROWS UP TO 6 FT (1.8 M) TALL AND WEIGHS UP TO 500 LB (227 KG).

GORILLA

THE GREATEST HEIGHT RECORDED FOR A PRIMATE IN THE WILD IS 6 FT 5 IN (1.95 M) FOR A MOUNTAIN BULL GORILLA FOUND IN THE EASTERN CONGO IN MAY 1938.

ANIMAL MAGIC
DOWN ON THE FARM

★★★★★★★★★★★★

★ SMALLEST COW

Swallow, a Dexter cow owned by Martyn and Caroline Ryder (both UK) – pictured here with Freddie, a full-size British shorthorn – was measured at 33.5 in (85 cm), from rear foot to hind, at Pike End Farm, Rishworth, Halifax, UK, on July 22, 2009.

NEW RECORD
UPDATED RECORD

MENTAL!
A "MANTLE" OF BEES IS A GIANT CLUSTER OF BEES THAT FORMS A PROTECTIVE LAYER AROUND THE QUEEN. BY WEARING THE QUEEN IN A LOCKET, AN INDIVIDUAL CAN ENCOURAGE A MANTLE OF BEES TO FORM AROUND THEMSELVES!

★ HEAVIEST MANTLE OF BEES

On March 9, 2009, at the Indian Agriculture Research Institute in New Delhi, India, Vipin Seth (India) was covered by a mantle of bees weighing 136 lb 4 oz (61.4 kg) and comprising an estimated 613,500 bees.

LARGEST FARM

The farm owned by Laucídio Coelho (Brazil) in Mato Grosso, Brazil, covered 3,360 miles² (8,700 km²) and supported 250,000 cattle at the time of Coelho's death in 1975. The smallest US state, Rhode Island, would fit into the farm three times.

★ FIRST MOOSE FARM

The first farm devoted to the domestication and rearing of the moose (*Alces alces*) – the world's **largest species of deer** – is the Kostroma Moose Farm (established 1963) in Kostroma Oblast, Russia. It includes 10 to 15 milk-producing moose cows, with more than 800 moose having lived on the farm during its existence.

★ LARGEST ANT FARM

An ant farm measuring 3 ft 11 in x 2 ft 11 in x 3 in (1.2 x 0.9 x 0.08 m) and housing between 200 and 300 ants was unveiled on December 28, 2008 by Colgate Palmolive Ltd as part of a toothpaste advert on the side of a bus stop in Singapore.

★ MOST HORNS ON A SHEEP

Both ewes and rams of the Jacob sheep – a rare breed produced in both the USA and UK – typically grow two or four horns; however, some six-horned specimens have been recorded.

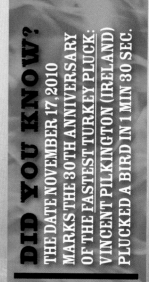

DID YOU KNOW?
THE DATE NOVEMBER 17, 2010 MARKS THE 30TH ANNIVERSARY OF THE FASTEST TURKEY PLUCK: VINCENT PILKINGTON (IRELAND) PLUCKED A BIRD IN 1 MIN 30 SEC.

Vincent also killed 100 turkeys in 7 hr 32 min on December 15, 1978 – an average of one every four-and-a-half minutes!

TRIVIA

LARGEST HORN CIRCUMFERENCE

The African ankole watusi breed of cattle are famed for their thick horns. For **steers**, Lurch (pictured) is the record holder, with a horn 37.5 in (95.25 cm) in circumference. For **bulls**, C T Woodie takes the title with a 40.75-in (103.5-cm) horn.

FAST!
THE FASTEST TIME TO SHEAR A SINGLE MERINO LAMB IS 53.88 SECONDS BY DWAYNE BLACK (AUSTRALIA) IN BEIJING, CHINA, ON SEPTEMBER 20, 2007.

FASTER!
THE FASTEST TIME TO SHEAR A SINGLE SHEEP IS 45.41 SECONDS ALSO BY DWAYNE BLACK (AUSTRALIA) IN SYDNEY, NEW SOUTH WALES, AUSTRALIA, ON APRIL 17, 2005.

★MOST PROLIFIC CHICKEN

The highest authenticated rate of egg-laying is 371 eggs in 364 days, laid by a White Leghorn (No. 2988) in an official test conducted by Prof. Harold V Biellier and ending on August 29, 1979 at the College of Agriculture, University of Missouri, USA.

★OLDEST LIVING SHEEP

Lucky, a Dorset cross owned by Delrae and Frank Westgarth (both Australia) of Lake Bolac, Australia, was born on April 25, 1986.

OLDEST LIVING PIG

The oldest pig is Oscar, who turned 20 years old on October 29, 2009. He lives with his owner, Stacy Leigh Kimbell (USA), in Dallas, Texas, USA.

MOST EXPENSIVE...

★Cow: A Friesian fetched $1.3 million at auction in East Montpelier, Vermont, USA, in 1985.

Goat: An Angora buck bred by Waitangi Angoras of Waitangi, New Zealand, was sold to Elliott Brown Ltd of Waipu, New Zealand, for NZ$140,000 ($82,600) on January 25, 1985.

Horse: The highest price paid for a thoroughbred at public auction is $16 million for a two-year-old colt who had yet to even race.

He was bought at an auction held at Calder Race Course, Florida, USA, on February 28, 2006.

★Pig: E A Bud Olson and Phil Bonzio paid $56,000 to Jeffrey Roemisch of Texas, USA, for Bud, a crossbred barrow, on March 5, 1983.

★Sheep: Jimmy Douglas paid £231,000 ($369,000) for an eight-month-old Texel tup in Lanark, Scotland, UK, in August 2009. This valuable sheep was purchased for breeding purposes.

★TALLEST HORSE

Big Jake, a nine-year-old Belgian gelding horse, measured 20 hands 2.75 in (82.75 in; 210.19 cm), without shoes, at Smokey Hollow Farms in Poynette, Wisconsin, USA, on January 19, 2010.

EXTRA!
WANT EVEN MORE TALL TALES? WHY NOT TRY PP. 76–77 ON FOR SIZE

POPULAR CULTURE

★ **NEW RECORD**
★ **UPDATED RECORD**

CONTENTS

HIGHEST BOX-OFFICE MOVIE GROSS

James Cameron's (Canada) sci-fi extravaganza *Avatar* (USA/UK, 2009) sailed past his own *Titanic* (USA, 1997) to become the biggest movie in box-office history, grossing $2.05 billion worldwide as of February 2010. *Avatar* – starring Sam Worthington (UK) and Zoe Saldana (USA), pictured – is the ★**first movie to gross more than $2 billion** and makes Cameron the director of the ★**most movies to gross more than $1 billion**. It also claims the record for the ★**fastest-selling Blu-ray disc**, with 2.7 million copies purchased in its first four days on sale in North America alone. For more *Avatar* achievements, see below.

AVATAR RECORDS

	RECORD	NOTES	DATE
★	Highest grossing movie	Beating *Titanic* (USA, 1997)	Jan 26, 2010
★	Fastest to $500 million	Achieved in 32 days; *Titanic* took 45 days	Jan 19, 2010
★	Highest grossing PG-13	Beating *Titanic* (USA, 1997)	Mar 1, 2010
★	Highest grossing 3D movie	Beating *Up* (USA, 2009, now in 3rd place) and staying ahead of *Alice in Wonderland* (USA, 2010, in 2nd place)	Mar 1, 2010
★	Highest grossing sci-fi movie	$2.69 billion (£1.80 billion)	Mar 1, 2010
★	Highest grossing New Year's Day	Took $25.2 million (£16.8 million)	Jan 1, 2010
★	Largest motion-capture project	Three years of motion-capture by Giant Studios (Los Angeles, USA)	NA
★	Largest area to be motion-captured	The Kong stage (Wellington, NZ): 150 x 80 x 40 ft (45 x 24 x 12 m)	NA
★	Most actors motion-captured for a movie	Giant Studios captured 80 people	NA
★	First 3D movie to win Best Cinematography Oscar	*Avatar* (USA, 2010)	Mar 7, 2010

SLOW!
AVATAR WAS IN PRODUCTION FOR SO MANY YEARS THAT EACH FRAME OF THE MOVIE (1/24TH OF A SECOND) TOOK AN AVERAGE OF 47 HOURS TO SHOOT!

FAST!
THE MOVIE CROSSED THE $1 BILLION MARK IN A RECORD 17 DAYS – A VAST IMPROVEMENT ON THE 197 DAYS THAT IT TOOK *THE DARK KNIGHT* TO ACHIEVE THE SAME GROSS.

POPULAR CULTURE
VIDEO GAMES

★ HIGHEST REVENUE GENERATED BY AN ENTERTAINMENT PRODUCT IN 24 HOURS

Call of Duty: Modern Warfare 2 (Activision, 2009) generated $401 million in sales within the first 24 hours of its worldwide launch on November 11, 2009. This is the greatest amount ever generated on a first day of sale by an entertainment product, outstripping any movie, music, or previous video-game launch.

★ BEST-SELLING VIDEO GAME

With lifetime sales of 45.7 million copies between its launch in 2006 and May 2009, the best-selling video game of all time is Nintendo's *Wii Sports*, which came bundled with the Wii console.

★ BEST-SELLING RHYTHM GAME SERIES

Guitar Hero (RedOctane, 2005) had seen total sales of more than 32 million units between November 2005 and June 2009.

★ BEST-SELLING CONSOLE REAL-TIME STRATEGY GAME

Of the current generation of consoles, the best-selling Real-Time Strategy game is *Halo Wars* (Microsoft, 2009), which had achieved global sales of 1.21 million as of May 2009.

★ HIGHEST CASH PRIZE AWARDED IN A FAN MOD TOURNAMENT

The Sendi Mutiara Multimedia Grand National DotA Tournament, which took place in Kuala Lumpur, Malaysia, on November 22–23, 2008, had a prize fund of 120,000 Malaysian ringgits ($35,000). The tournament welcomed competitors from seven countries, who competed on the *Warcraft III* mod "Defense of the Ancients." Team Ehome from China emerged as overall champions of the competition, pocketing RM36,000 ($10,500) in cash along with other prizes.

★ MOST DETAILED VIDEO-GAME CHARACTER

With a character model that consists of 32,816 rendered polygons during gameplay, the most detailed video-game character is Lara Croft in her *Tomb Raider: Underworld* (Eidos Interactive, 2008) incarnation.

World Record attempt 24 hour football gaming marathon

★LONGEST SOCCER GAME MARATHON

A group of gamers, supported by online gaming leagues website Stryxa.com, recorded the longest marathon playing a soccer video game when they played *FIFA 10* (EA Sports, 2009) for 24 hours at Victoria Station, London, UK, on January 27–28, 2009.

★FASTEST-SELLING MULTIPLATFORM ROLE-PLAYING GAME (RPG)

Bethesda's *Fallout 3* sold more than 4.7 million copies in its first week on sale from October 28 to November 4, 2008.

★FASTEST-SELLING PC GAME

Released on November 13, 2008, *World of Warcraft* expansion pack *Wrath of the Lich King* (Activision Blizzard) sold around 2.8 million copies in 24 hours, and 4 million copies in its first month.

★MOST POWERFUL FLIGHT SIMULATOR

Described as "a next generation military simulation synthetic environment," the *Simusphere HD World*, produced by Link Simulation and Training (USA) for clients including the United States Air Force (USAF), is the most powerful flight simulation system in the world. The USAF version simulates an F-16 fighter jet and runs on 120 dual-core PCs, each of which contains a $400 graphics card, allowing for 10,000 onscreen objects to be displayed simultaneously.

★FIRST CONCERT HELD IN A REAL AND A VIRTUAL SPACE SIMULTANEOUSLY

On June 2, 2009, US punk-pop band The Dares (Ben Peterson, Matt Peterson, and Martin Lascano) performed the first music concert to take place in both the real world and in a virtual space. The gig was held on a stage at E3 2009 in the Los Angeles Convention Center, California, USA, and simultaneously online in *Free Realms* (Sony, 2009). The Dares' set list included the *Free Realms* theme "It's Your World."

★LONGEST DRAW DISTANCE IN A RACING GAME

Codemasters' *FUEL* boasts a draw distance of 24.8 miles (40 km), the longest in a simulation racing game. *FUEL*'s racing environment is inspired by the North American wilderness. The landscape, which is modeled from satellite data and rendered by the game engine, is battered by weather effects including blizzards, tsunamis, and tornadoes.

★LARGEST POKÉMON COLLECTION

Lisa Courtney (UK) was found to have 12,113 different items of Pokémon memorabilia when Guinness World Records examined her collection on June 13, 2009.

★LONGEST RACING GAME MARATHON

Rolf Loraas, Hans Moe, Alexander Moerk, Lars-Christian Klingstroem, Per Helge Fagermoen, Benny Charles Fredstad, Benjamin Ward, Jan Dalan, and Joachim Olsen (all Norway) played *Need for Speed Shift* (EA, 2009) for 25 hours at Oslo City, Oslo, Norway, on September 18–19, 2009.

DRAW DISTANCE: The distance in a 3D scene that is still drawn by the game engine.

LONG! SARA LHADI (NETHERLANDS) SPENT A RECORD 16,799 HOURS PLAYING THE MMORPG *RUNESCAPE* BETWEEN NOVEMBER 2004 AND OCTOBER 2009.

SHORT! JUSTIN TOWELL (UK) COMPLETED EMERALD HILL, ZONE 1, ON *SONIC THE HEDGEHOG 2* ON XBOX LIVE ARCADE, IN A RECORD-BRE...

GUINNESS WORLD RECORDS 2011

POPULAR CULTURE
PUBLISHING

★ ★ ★ ★ ★ ★ ★ ★ ★ ★ ★ ★ ★ ★ ☆

★ LARGEST SINGLE-VOLUME BIOGRAPHY

Between 1996 and 2007, Dr A V S Raju (India) wrote a biography chronicling the life of Sri Sathya Sai Baba (India), a popular religious figure and spiritual teacher. The single bound book consists of 32 volumes.

★ MOST BANNED BOOK OF THE YEAR

The book most frequently reported to the American Library Association's (ALA) Office for Intellectual Freedom in 2008 – and each year since 2006 – is *And Tango Makes Three* by Justin Richardson and Peter Parnell (both USA). The award-winning book – which recounts the true tale of two male penguins who raise a baby penguin – attracted the most complaints from parents and school officials for its promotion of a "homosexual lifestyle."

NEW RECORD
UPDATED RECORD

★ LARGEST POP-UP BOOK

The largest pop-up book measures 3 ft 8 in (1.13 m) by 3 ft (92 cm) and weighs 42 lb (19 kg). It is an outsize version of *The Pop-Up Story of Delray Beach* by Roger Culberston (USA) and illustrated by Al Margolis. The book contains six pop-up spreads illustrating the experiences of residents and visitors to the city of Delray Beach, Florida, USA.

★ MOST NOBEL PRIZES FOR LITERATURE (COUNTRY)

The country that claims the most outright or shared Nobel prizes awarded for literature is France, with 13.

★ YOUNGEST RECIPIENT OF THE NOBEL PRIZE FOR LITERATURE

Poet and author Rudyard Kipling (UK, 1865–1936) won the Nobel prize for literature in 1907 at the age of 42, in recognition of his "power of observation, originality of imagination, virility of ideas."

★ FIRST WOMAN TO WIN THE NOBEL PRIZE FOR LITERATURE

Selma Lagerlöf (Sweden, 1858–1940) was awarded the Nobel prize for literature in 1909 for the "lofty idealism, vivid imagination and spiritual perception that characterize her writings."

★ MOST AUDIOBOOKS PUBLISHED FOR ONE AUTHOR

L Ron Hubbard (USA) has had 185 audiobooks published as of April 21, 2009.

★ HIGHEST DAILY ENGLISH-LANGUAGE NEWSPAPER CIRCULATION

The Times of India, owned by the Sahu Jain family (India), has an average daily circulation of 3,146,000 according to the latest figures from the World Association of Newspapers and the Audit Bureau of Circulations.

THICKEST BOOK

The entire collection of Agatha Christie's (UK) *Miss Marple* detective stories – a grand total of 12 novels and 20 short stories – was published as one single volume by HarperCollins on May 20, 2009. The capacious compendium is 12.67 in (322 mm) thick.

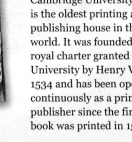

The GREAT GATSBY

F·SCOTT·FITZGERALD

★ OLDEST PLAYBOY MODEL

Model and presenter Patricia Paay (Netherlands, b. April 7, 1949) posed for the Christmas edition of *Playboy Netherlands* on December 10, 2009 at the age of 60.

★ OLDEST PRINTING AND PUBLISHING HOUSE

Cambridge University Press is the oldest printing and publishing house in the world. It was founded on a royal charter granted to the University by Henry VIII in 1534 and has been operating continuously as a printer and publisher since the first Press book was printed in 1584.

★ RICHEST AUTHOR

According to *Forbes*, J K Rowling (UK), author of the Harry Potter series, has grossed more than $1 billion for her novels and from related earnings. Rowling is one of only five self-made female billionaires, and the ★**first billion-dollar author**. The seven Potter books have sold 400 million copies around the world and are published in 55 languages, including Latin and ancient Greek.

★ MOST BOOKS TYPED BACKWARDS

Using a computer and four blank keyboards, and without looking at the screen, Michele Santelia (Italy) has typed backwards 68 books (3,663,324 words; 20,680,060 characters; 24,154 pages; 266,741 paragraphs; 516,498 lines) in their original languages including *The Odyssey*, *Macbeth*, The Vulgate Bible, *Guinness World Records 2002*, and the Dead Sea scrolls (in Ancient Hebrew).

Santelia's most recent book typed backwards and in the English language is the *Life of Abraham Lincoln* (956 pages; 160,311 words; 919,124 characters; 2,810 paragraphs; 16,944 lines). He started typing it on January 20, 2009 and finished it on June 16, 2009.

★ LARGEST ATLAS

The 350-year-old Klencke Atlas was presented to Charles II, King of England, on his restoration in 1660. Created by Dutch merchant Yohannes Klencke, the atlas features 41 maps on 39 sheets, and is 5 ft 10 in (1.78 m) tall, 3 ft 5 in (1.05 m) wide, and 4 in (11 cm) thick.

★ MOST BANNED CLASSIC NOVEL

Topping the American Library Association's list of most banned or "challenged" classic novels is *The Great Gatsby* (1924) by F Scott Fitzgerald. The Baptist College in Charleston, South Carolina, USA, challenged the book because of "language and sexual references" as recently as 1987.

★ LONGEST AUDIOBOOK

Published on August 1, 2008 by Tokyo Shigesato Itoi Office K K (Japan), the audiobook *50 Lectures* by Takaaki Yoshimoto (Japan) has a running time of 115 hr 43 min.

LONGEST NOVEL

A la recherche du temps perdu by Marcel Proust (France) contains around 9,609,000 characters (each letter counts as a character; so do spaces). The title translates as *In Search of Lost Time* and the first of seven volumes appeared in 1913.

DID YOU KNOW?

THE KLENCKE ATLAS WAS GIVEN TO CHARLES II TO WIN HIS FAVOR. CENTURIES AGO, MAPS WERE OFTEN DESIGNED TO INFLUENCE OR FLATTER POWERFUL PEOPLE.

Unseen by the public for 350 years, the pages of the Klencke Atlas went on show at the British Library, London, UK, in 2010.

TRIVIA

NOVA DESCRITTIONE D'ITALIA DI GIOANN. ANTONIO MAGINO

EXTRA! FOR ONLINE FACTS, STATS, AND WORLD RECORDS, TURN TO P.218.

PHOENIX, AZ, USA

Best Western International Inc. is the world's **biggest hotel chain**, with more than 4,000 hotels in 82 countries and territories under its banner. The company, which is based in Phoenix, Arizona, USA, says it has 308,640 rooms available in its establishments which, although part of the Best Western group, are independently owned and operated

33°26'N 112°104'W

POPULAR CULTURE
WHAT'S ON TV

★★★★★★★★★★★★★★★

★ MOST WATCHED TV SERIES (2009)

Global: The most popular TV show continues to be the medical drama *House* (Fox). According to ratings agency Eurodata TV Worldwide, the show – starring Hugh Laurie (UK) as the unconventional, maverick Dr Gregory House – was seen by more than 81.8 million viewers in 66 countries.

UK: The final of *Britain's Got Talent* was seen by nearly 18 million viewers.

Europe: The *Eurovision Song Contest* 2009 clocked up an impressive 122 million viewers.

USA: *NCIS* (NBC) season 7 episode "Reunion" averaged 21.37 million viewers.

MAD
PICTURED ARE *MAD MEN*'S DON AND BETTY DRAPER (JON HAMM AND JANUARY JONES, BOTH USA). THE SHOW FOLLOWS THE RUTHLESSLY COMPETITIVE WORLD OF ADVERTISING IN THE 1960S.

★ LONGEST-RUNNING MEDICAL DRAMA

Casualty (BBC, 1986–present) is the world's most enduring primetime medical drama series. Only the hospital-based soap opera *General Hospital* (ABC, 1963–present) – now the world's ★ **longest-running daytime soap opera** with the demise of *As the World Turns* (CBS, 1956–2010) – has been broadcast for a longer period.

★ MOST WATCHED TV

2009: The funeral of Michael Jackson (USA) on July 7, 2009 was watched by a global audience of 2–3 billion.

Sports event: According to the BBC, English Premier League soccer games are broadcast to more than 600 million homes in 202 countries.

★ MOST TIME-SHIFTED TV SHOW

According to 2009 figures from Nielsen, the most "time-shifted" primetime show of the year was *Battlestar Galactica* (SYFY), which enjoyed a 59.4% increase in viewing figures as a result. Time-shifting involves recording TV shows on digital video recorders (DVRs) or storing them via premium TV services such as Tivo.

★ LONGEST-RUNNING SOAP OPERA ON TV

It was announced in 2009 that *As the World Turns* (CBS, 1956–) would be canceled by September 2010, meaning that the UK's *Coronation Street* (ITV, 1960–) would become the world's longest-running soap opera. Actor William Roach (UK) would then become the ★ **longest-serving soap actor**, having debuted as Ken Barlow in episode 1.

★ HIGHEST-RATED TV SHOWS (CURRENT)

Three shows can boast to be the most critically-acclaimed series currently on TV. The third season of *Mad Men* (Lionsgate/AMC, pictured left), *Sons of Anarchy* (FX), and *Modern Family* (ABC) all scored 86/100 on the critical aggregation site metacritic.com.

75 YEARS OF BROADCAST TV

Although experimental services had operated across the world from the 1920s, the television broadcasting age as we recognize it began at 3 p.m. on November 2, 1936 in London, UK, when the BBC launched the world's **first regular television broadcasts**.

"Good afternoon, ladies and gentlemen. It is with great pleasure that I introduce you to the magic of television..."
Leslie Mitchell, first words spoken on TV

1936: First TV host Radio personality Leslie Mitchell is the first of three TV hosts that also includes Jasmine Bligh and Elizabeth Cowell (all UK), the **first female TV hosts**.

1936: First black performers Buck and Bubbles (USA), an energetic, vaudeville comedy dance act, are guests on *Variety* (UK), one of the shows broadcast on the first day of service.

1936: First magazine show *Picture Page* (UK), a variety and chat show, runs daily from day one, hosted by Joan Millar (Canada), who becomes the world's **first TV star**.

MOST POPULAR SOAP OPERA - CURRENT

In the most recent analysis of viewing habits in 66 countries by Eurodata TV Worldwide (2008), *The Bold and the Beautiful* (CBS) boasted a record 24.5 million viewers.

★ HIGHEST PAID
Actor: Charlie Sheen (USA) was estimated to earn $800,000 per episode of *Two and a Half Men* (CBS, 2003–present).

Actress: Katherine Heigl (USA) – Izzie Stevens in *Grey's Anatomy* (ABC, 2005–present) – earned $200,000 per show.

★ HIGHEST-EARNING PRIMETIME TV STARS

While Oprah reigns supreme as the **highest-earning TV personality** (see above), the Forbes Celebrity 100 list identifies Simon Cowell (UK) and Tyra Banks (USA) as the highest-earning *primetime* celebrities. In the 12 months between June 2009 and June 2010, talent judge Cowell earned an estimated $75 million, while supermodel-turned-host Banks made $30 million.

EMMY AWARDS

★ MOST WINS
The televised Oscars (Academy Awards) ceremony has been nominated for 195 Primetime Emmy awards, winning a record 46 times.

★ MOST WINS FOR A VARIETY, MUSIC, OR COMEDY SERIES
The Daily Show with Jon Stewart (Comedy Central) has won the Emmy for Outstanding Variety, Music, or Comedy series for a record seven consecutive years.

★ YOUNGEST ACTRESS TO WIN A LEAD ACTING EMMY
In 2007, at the age of 23, America Ferrara (USA, b. April 18, 1984) was voted the Outstanding Lead Actress in a Comedy Series for her portrayal of Betty Suarez in *Ugly Betty* (ABC) – the youngest person to win a lead acting Emmy award.

★ HIGHEST-EARNING CELEBRITY

Between June 2009 and June 2010, Oprah Winfrey (USA) earned an estimated $275 million thanks to her monthly magazine, her radio contract, her production company Harpo, and the debut of the Oprah Winfrey Network.

★ NOMINATIONS – MOST IN ONE YEAR
Variety show: *Saturday Night Live* (NBC) – 13 nominations in 2009.
Comedy show: *30 Rock* (NBC) – 22 nominations in 2009.
Drama: *NYPD Blue* (ABC) – 27 nominations in 1994.
Mini-series: *Roots* (ABC) – 37 nominations in 1977.

★ MOST DAYTIME EMMYS WON
The Public Broadcasting Service's *Sesame Street* has won a record 122 Daytime Emmys since 1984.

> *"The only people who never tumble are those who never mount the high wire."*
> **Oprah Winfrey**

IDOL
COWELL PRODUCED THE "GOT TALENT" AND "X FACTOR" FRANCHISES – TWO OF THE FASTEST-SELLING TV FORMATS EVER. "TALENT" WAS THE ONLY SHOW TO BE NO.1 IN THE UK AND USA AT THE SAME TIME.

1936: First TV drama
On day five, excerpts from the West End play *Marigold* by L Allen Harker and F R Pryor (both UK) are broadcast.

1937: First children's series
For the Children (UK) debuts at 3 p.m. on April 24 and runs until 1950 (with a break for World War II); episodes last 10 minutes.

1937: First regular TV chef
Marcel Boulestin (France, left) begins hosting *Dish of the Month* (UK) on October 15.

1938: First TV sci-fi aired – an adaptation of *R.U.R. (Rossum's Universal Robots)*, a play in the Czech language by Karel Čapek; also the world's **first depiction of robots**.

1939: First regular US programming
Franklin D Roosevelt (USA) opens the 1939 New York World's Fair (April 30), relayed to the nation via a high-def telecast.

1939–46: BBC TV suspended for the duration of World War II.

1940: First ice hockey (February 25) and **first basketball game** (February 28) aired.

1941: First TV advert
NBC's WNBT station (USA) promotes a Bulova watch on June 27.

1949: First Emmy Awards
The TV equivalent of the Oscars is first aired on January 25.

POPULAR CULTURE
COP & CRIME SHOWS

★ ★ ★ ★ ★ ★ ★ ★ ★ ★ ★

★FIRST ARMCHAIR DETECTIVE SERIES
The first time the police used TV to appeal for help in a murder case was in Germany in 1938, and the first "missing person" appeal was made on October 3, 1943 by New York police. The first regular series to enlist the help of the public to solve real-life crimes was *Police 5* (LWT, 1962–92), hosted by Shaw Taylor (UK).

★FIRST CRIME SHOW ON TV
Telecrime (BBC, 1938–39) – later known as *Telecrimes* (1946) – challenged TV viewers to unravel crimes before the police and featured the ★**first TV police detective**, Inspector Holt (played by J B Rowe, UK). He was assisted by Sgt Carter (Richard George, UK), ★**TV's first cop sidekick.**

★LONGEST-RUNNING COP SHOW (BY DATE)
Germany's *Der Alte* ("The Old Fox") has run on ZDF since 1977. The UK's longest-running cop shows are ITV's *Taggart* and *The Bill*, which have been running since 1983. The USA's longest-running cop show is *Law & Order* (NBC), which began in 1990.

★MOST SUCCESSFUL COP SHOW FRANCHISE
The Bill (see right) gave rise to a total of three spin-off series. They were:

★LONGEST-RUNNING COP SHOW (BY EPISODE)
At the time of going to press (April 2010), *The Bill* (ITV, 1983–2010) had an episode count of 2,389, with the date of September 30, 2010 slated for its final episode. Despite its various incarnations, *The Bill* is fundamentally a hybrid crime/soap opera, hence the inflated number of episodes.

FRANK COLUMBO
Peter Falk (USA) is the ★**most enduring cop actor**, having portrayed the shambling detective Lieutenant Columbo from *Prescription Murder* (NBC, 1968) to 2003's *Columbo Likes the Nightlife* (ABC).

JANE MARPLE
The ★**most TV depictions of Miss Marple**, Agatha Christie's silver sleuth, is 12, shared by Brit actresses Joan Hickson (*Miss Marple*, BBC, 1984–92, pictured below right) and Geraldine McEwan (*Marple*, ITV, 2004–09, below left).

GEORGE DIXON
The ★**most prolific TV cop** was PC George Dixon (Jack Warner, UK) in *Dixon of Dock Green* (BBC, 1955–76), who appeared in 431 episodes.

FRANK
WHENEVER ASKED FOR HIS FIRST NAME, COLUMBO WOULD ANSWER "LIEUTENANT." BUT LOOK CLOSELY AT HIS WARRANT CARD AND BADGE AND YOU'LL SEE HIS NAME: FRANK!

FIELDS
THE FIRST ACTRESS TO PORTRAY MISS MARPLE WAS THE UK'S GRACIE FIELDS IN THE NBC (USA) *GOODYEAR TV PLAYHOUSE: A MURDER IS ANNOUNCED* IN 1956.

1951: First regular color broadcast
On June 25, CBS broadcast the first color images from five stations on the US east coast... to a virtually nonexistent audience, as so few color TV sets exist!

1951: First use of TV detector vans in the UK to trace TV license evaders.

1952: Longest-running soap opera Procter & Gamble Productions' *Guiding Light* (CBS, USA) first airs on June 30, and is the world's longest-lived soap until it finishes in 2009.

1953: The CBS system fails; RCA's system adopted as industry standard in the USA.

1954: First coast-to-coast color transmission (USA)
RCA's broadcasting wing (NBC) airs first countrywide color transmission on January 1, 1954 with The Tournament of Roses Parade from Pasadena, California.

1954: First network series regularly shown in color: NBC sitcom *The Marriage* debuts.

1954: First in-vision weather report is shown with anchor George Cowling (UK) standing in front of a projected map.

1957: *The Sky at Night* (BBC) introduces the Brits to the monocled Patrick Moore (UK, left), who continues to host the show, making him the **most enduring TV host**.

★ FIRST FEMALE TV COP STAR

Decoy (aka *Police Woman: Decoy*), a US series syndicated in 1957–58, starred Beverly Garland (USA) as undercover policewoman Patricia "Casey" Jones. Britain's first female-led cop show was *The Gentle Touch* (ITV, 1980–84), starring Jill Gascoigne as Detective Inspector Maggie Forbes (pictured left).

Burnside, 2000; *Beech is Back*, 2001; and *MIT: Murder Investigation Team*, 2003–05, giving a combined episode count of 2,413 (as of April 2010).

The **most successful non-soap cop show** ever was *Z-Cars* (BBC, 1962–78), which ran to 799 episodes. With its spin-offs *Softly Softly* (1966–69), *Softly Softly: Task Force* (1969–76), *Barlow at Large* (1971–73), *Barlow* (1974–75), *Jack the Ripper* (1973), and *Second Verdict* (1974), it had a combined episode count of more than 1,100. The **most successful non-soap cop show (current)** is *Law & Order* (see right).

★ HIGHEST-RATED COP SHOW

According to metacritic.com, *The Sopranos* remains the most popular "crime" show among TV reviewers, garnering a score of 96/100; *The Wire*, which could be considered more truly a "cop" show – being more about police than criminals – comes in at second place with a metascore of 89/100.

The cop/crime show that most wowed reviewers in 2009 was the FBI-based *White Collar* (USA Network/Fox) with a score of 78/100.

★ MOST SUCCESSFUL COP FRANCHISE (CURRENT)

While *Z-Cars* holds the absolute record, in terms of shows currently on air, the franchise winner is *Law & Order* (NBC, 1990–present) – which includes *Criminal Intent, Special Victims Unit* (pictured are stars Mariska Hargitay and Ice-T, both USA), and the now defunct *Trial by Jury* and *Conviction*) – with more than 915 episodes to date.

HERCULE POIROT

The ★ **most depictions of Hercule Poirot on TV** is 60 and counting by David Suchet (UK), who has gone on record saying he hopes to film the entire canon (84 stories) by his 65th birthday in May 2011.

PERRY MASON

The ★ **most murders solved on TV** is at least 297 by the defense attorney Perry Mason (Raymond Burr, USA, 1917–93) in *Perry Mason* (CBS, 1957–66) and the *Perry Mason TV Movies* (NBC, 1985–93).

SHERLOCK HOLMES

The **most depictions of Sherlock Holmes on TV** is 41 by Jeremy Brett (UK, pictured) in the ITV series that ran from 1984 to 1994. The **first Holmes TV series** – *Sherlock Holmes* (BBC, 1951) – starred Alan Wheatley (UK).

'ELLO
THE FIRST ACTOR TO PLAY HERCULE POIROT ON TV WAS JAMES L SULLIVAN (UK) IN THE FIRST AGATHA CHRISTIE TV ADAPTATION: *THE WASP'S NEST* (BBC, 1937).

LAW
PERRY MASON WAS THE CREATION OF REAL-LIFE LAWYER ERLE STANLEY GARDNER (USA, 1889–1970), WHO FEATURED HIS FICTIONAL ATTORNEY IN AROUND 80 NOVELS.

ORDER
PERRY MASON HAS APPEARED IN NOVELS, SHORT STORIES, RADIO SERIALS, COMIC BOOKS, TV SERIES, TV MOVIES, DAYTIME SOAPS, AND EVEN A BOOK OF POETRY!

TELE-MENTARY
THE FIRST ACTOR TO PORTRAY SHERLOCK HOLMES ON TV WAS LOUIS HECTOR (USA) IN AN EXPERIMENTAL NBC (USA) PRODUCTION IN 1937.

1958: First actor to die on live TV is Gareth Jones (UK) during an ITV production of *Armchair Theatre*.

1958: *Blue Peter*, the **longest-running children's magazine program**, debuts on BBC1.

1960: Debut of record-breaking soap *Coronation Street* (see p.168).

1963: First murder on live TV takes place as John F Kennedy's assassin, Lee Harvey Oswald (USA), is shot and killed by Jack Ruby (USA).

1963: Longest-running sci-fi show – *Doctor Who* – receives its first airing on November 12.

1965: First use of the f– word on TV is on November 13, 1965 by literary agent Kenneth Tynan (UK) during a satirical discussion show entitled *BBC3*.

1969: The first Moon landing becomes the **most watched live TV event**, drawing in 600 million viewers – a fifth of the world population at the time.

1973: First fly-on-the-wall **documentary series**, *An American Family*, airs to 10 million viewers.

1975: BBC introduces the classic weather symbols as we know them today.

EL PASO, TX, USA

El Paso Diablos Baseball Club, Texas, USA, made the world's **largest pecan pie** on May 22, 1999. The pie weighed 41,586 lb (18.863 tonnes) and measured 50 ft (15.24 m) in diameter when measured at Cohen Stadium.

W.M 81°47'
N. 106°25'

POPULAR CULTURE
SCI-FI & FANTASY TV

★MOST SUCCESSFUL SCI-FI TV ADAPTATION

Paramount's (USA) 2009 movie "rebooting" of the *Star Trek* TV show (NBC, USA, 1966–69, above right) took $385,494,555 globally – the biggest box-office gross for a live-action TV adaptation.

★FIRST SCI-FI SERIAL

The first regular sci-fi serial on TV was *Captain Video and His Video Rangers* (Dumont, USA, June 1949–April 1955). Set in the year 2254, it followed the exploits of Captain Video (played by Richard Coogan, USA), an inventor and "Master of Science." It aired nightly – live – at 7 p.m.

in 1962. *My Favorite Martian* (CBS, USA, 1963–66) was the ★**first live-action sci-fi sitcom**. The show followed the exploits of a Martian "exo-anthropologist" (played by Ray Walston, USA) who crash-lands on Earth and is rescued by a newspaper reporter (played by Bill Bixby, USA), who passes him off to friends and the authorities as his uncle. It ran for three series.

WOOD
THE TORCHWOOD INSTITUTE INVESTIGATES EXTRATERRESTRIAL ACTIVITY ON EARTH AND IS SET IN THE CARDIFF, UK, BRANCH OF THE ORGANIZATION.

★FIRST RECORDED SCI-FI TV SHOW

While early TV shows were broadcast live (see *Captain Video*, above), the first sci-fi series to be prerecorded was *Rocky Jones, Space Ranger* (USA, syndicated, 1953). Recorded shows made for better sets and effects – particularly important for the science-fiction genre.

★FIRST SCI-FI SITCOM ON TV

The animated series *The Jetsons* (ABC, USA) debuted

★HIGHEST-RATED SCI-FI MINISERIES

"Children of Earth" (UK, 2009), the third season of the BBC's sci-fi miniseries *Torchwood* (UK), received a review score of 80/100 on metacritic.com. This made it the highest-rated sci-fi miniseries of 2009, ahead of the reimagined version of *The Prisoner* (AMC/ITV, UK).

LONGEST-RUNNING TV SCI-FI

See Doctor Who, *pp.174–175, and Smallville, opposite.*

TORCH
TORCHWOOD (AN ANAGRAM OF *DOCTOR WHO*) IS A SPIN-OFF SHOW STARRING JOHN BARROWMAN (UK, PICTURED FRONT) AS CAPTAIN JACK HARKNESS.

1976: *The Muppet Show* airs in the UK on September 5, then in the USA on September 27; goes on to become the world's **most popular show**, watched by 300 million viewers in 103 countries.

1976: The BBC formally launches its CEEFAX teletex service.

1977: First "gaffe" show *It'll Be Alright on the Night* (ITV, UK) features host Denis Norden (UK) revealing the gaffes or "bloopers" filmed while making television shows.

1979: First use of satellite data for TV weather reports.

1981: MTV launches in the USA.

1983: Largest TV audience (USA) The final episode of *M*A*S*H* (CBS, left) is transmitted on February 28, 1983 to 60.3% of all households in the USA; it is watched by some 125 million people.

1985: Live Aid takes place in London, UK, and Philadelphia, PA, USA, and is watched by

1.5 billion TV viewers worldwide, making it the world's **largest simultaneous charity rock concert** in terms of viewers.

1986: Over 30 million people tune in as Den divorces Angie in *EastEnders* (BBC, UK) on Christmas Day – the **highest ever viewing figures for a series in the UK.**

PRINCE ALBERT, SK, CANADA

58°12'N 105°45'W

The record for the **most trees planted in a day by an individual** is held by Ken Chaplin (Canada), who single-handedly planted 15,170 red pine seedlings in one day near Prince Albert, Saskatchewan, Canada, on June 30, 2001.

CLONE WARS

Star Wars: The Clone Wars (Lucasfilm Animation/Warner Bros. TV, 2008–present) is the ★**highest-rated sci-fi animation on TV**, with an average review of 64/100 on metacritic.com on its release. The CGI series has expanded the scope of the "galaxy far, far away" and taken the *Star Wars* story in new directions down darker, more mature paths.

★FIRST FANTASY SITCOM

Topper (CBS, then ABC, later NBC; all USA) ran from 1953 to 1956. It was based on Thorne Smith's novels (previously made into movies) about the staid Cosmo Topper, whose life takes an unexpectedly lively turn after he is haunted by a fun-loving couple who had lived in his house before their deaths.

★FIRST SUPERHERO ON TV

Superman was the first comicbook superhero to appear in his own television series. *The Adventures of Superman* (USA, syndicated, 1952) starred George Reeves (USA) as the Man of Steel and was sponsored by Kellogg's.

★MOST PROLIFIC SCI-FI TV WRITERS

Rodman "Rod" Serling (USA) – creator and narrator of *The Twilight Zone* (CBS, USA, 1959–64) – wrote 92 episodes (out of 156) of the successful sci-fi anthology show.

Babylon 5 (PTEN) creator Joe Straczynski (USA) also wrote 92 (out of 110) episodes of his CGI-heavy sci-fi show.

★MOST SCI-FI TV SPIN-OFFS

The Japanese series *Ultraman* (United Artists/Tokyo Broadcasting System, 1966–67) spawned 30 spin-off series and several movies. Unlike *King Kong* (USA, 1933), which used stop-motion animation, *Ultraman* was made using miniature buildings and an actor wearing a monster costume who moved around the diminutive set, creating havoc.

The technique subsequently became a standard for Japanese monster movies (*kaiju*).

★LONGEST-RUNNING SCI-FI TV SHOW (CURRENT)

Smallville (The WB, USA, 2001–), based on the DC Comics character Superman, has aired continuously since October 16, 2001. The last sci-fi show to reach its 10th anniversary was *Stargate SG-1* (Sony/MGM, Canada/USA, 1997–2007).

The original run of *Doctor Who* (BBC, 1963–89) has the absolute record for **most consecutive sci-fi episodes ever**. (For more details, see pp.174–175.)

MOST EXPENSIVE COSTUME FROM A TV SERIES SOLD AT AUCTION

The Superman suit from the 1955 series *The Adventures of Superman* (USA) sold for $129,800 at the Profiles in History auction in Los Angeles, USA, on July 31, 2003. It was one of two costumes from the series worn by George Reeves.

HIGHEST-RATED FANTASY/SCI-FI SHOW

Being Human (BBC) – the tale of a werewolf, vampire, and ghost living together in suburban Britain – was the most critically acclaimed sci-fi show of 2009, according to an average of review scores on metacritic.com.

BEING A DARK COMEDY SERIES BY THE BBC, *BEING HUMAN* ACHIEVED A RATING OF 79/100 ON THE REVIEW AGGREGATION SITE METACRITIC.COM.

HUMAN THE HIT 2009 SHOW STARS RUSSELL TOVEY, AIDAN TURNER, AND LEONORA CRICHLOW (PICTURED LEFT TO RIGHT) AS A WEREWOLF, VAMPIRE, AND GHOST RESPECTIVELY.

★ **NEW RECORD**
★ **UPDATED RECORD**

1993: The **first computer-generated 3D models** on TV are the spacecraft conceived for *Babylon 5* (PTEN, USA).

1996: At its peak of popularity, *Baywatch* (NBC, USA) becomes the **most widely viewed TV series** ever, with an estimated weekly audience of more than 1.1 billion in 142 countries in 1996.

1999: Helen Hunt, the star of *Mad About You* (NBC, USA), becomes the **highest-paid TV actress**, with an estimated salary of $31 million.

2000: Darva Conger (USA) and Rick Rockwell (USA) celebrate the **first reality TV marriage** on *Who Wants to Marry a Multimillionaire?* (Fox, USA).

2004: A four-minute feature film made by director Baz Lurhmann (Australia) advertising Chanel No. 5 perfume becomes the world's **most expensive television advertisement** costing $33 million to produce. It starred Nicole Kidman (Australia) as a Marilyn Monroe-style actress who is pursued by the paparazzi.

2006: The **most watched live sporting event on television** is the 2006 FIFA World Cup held in Germany. FIFA claimed that the tournament was seen by 30 billion (non-unique) viewers.

2009: The **most hours on US television** is 16,343 by presenter Regis Philbin (USA), whose career spans 50 years.

2010: According to *Forbes*, the ★**most powerful person in television** is Oprah Winfrey (USA). Winfrey is also the **highest-paid TV personality**, having earned $275 million in 2008–09 thanks to her extensive media empire. The philanthropist/actress/producer is arguably the most influential woman in the world.

FEATURE
DOCTOR WHO

FREE! WIN!
DOCTOR WHO
NEW DOCTOR!
NEW DANGER!

★ LONGEST-RUNNING TV TIE-IN

Doctor Who Magazine launched (as *Doctor Who Weekly*) on October 11, 1979, and went monthly at issue 44. The magazine's tenure is all the more remarkable for the fact that for 16 years of its 31-year run there was no TV series in production!

★ ★ ★ ★ ★ ★ ★ ★ ★ ★ ★ ★

★ LONGEST-RUNNING SCI-FI TV SHOW

Doctor Who (BBC, UK) has chalked up 769 episodes as of June 2010, encompassing 212 storylines including a full-length TV movie. This total does not include spoofs, spin-offs, or webisodes.

★ MOST SUCCESSFUL SCI-FI TV SHOW

Based on longevity, DVD sales, views on BBC's iPlayer, and publishing spin-offs, *Doctor Who* is the most successful science-fiction program on TV. This eclipses the original *Star Trek* series, which has had numerous spin-offs (such as *The Next Generation* and *Voyager*) that are not a genuine continuation of the same show.

★ MOST PROLIFIC DOCTOR

In terms of the **TV shows**, Tom Baker (UK) starred in 173 episodes (seasons 12–18), more than any other actor. A former monk, Baker was working on a building site when he received the call from the BBC. Famous for his Doctor's lengthy scarf and wild hair, he revitalized the series and lasted seven years.

In terms of **total output** – including audiobooks, TV shows, DVDs, novels, and comics – the busiest Doctor was the tenth (David Tennant, UK), with more than 342 appearances.

TV's ★**least prolific Doctor** was the eighth (Paul McGann, UK), who appeared just once, in a 1996 TV movie. Across all media, the fewest appearances to date were made by the ninth Doctor (Christopher Eccleston, UK), with only 25 outings.

★ YOUNGEST DOCTOR

The latest incarnation of the Doctor is Matt Smith (UK, b. October 28, 1982), who was 26 when he filmed his first scenes as the Time Lord.

The ★**oldest Doctor** was William Hartnell (UK), who played the part from the age of 55 to 57. He last reprised the role in 1973, aged 65.

★ DEAREST DALEK

The most money paid for a Dalek prop at auction was £36,000 ($61,930) by the now-defunct company Indeprod in 2005 for this "Dalek Supreme," first seen on screen in the 1970s.

WHO? PICTURED WITH THE DALEK SUPREME IS JUNE HUDSON (UK), WHO PROVIDED COSTUMES FOR SEVERAL EPISODES OF <u>DOCTOR WHO</u> IN THE 1980s.

★ NEW RECORD ★ UPDATED RECORD

DID YOU KNOW? THE DOCTOR WHO APPRECIATION SOCIETY, WHICH BEGAN IN MAY 1976, IS THE LONGEST-RUNNING DOCTOR WHO FANCLUB.

WHO'S WHO IN DOCTOR WHO?

WILLIAM HARTNELL (1963–66)

PATRICK TROUGHTON (1966–69)

JON PERTWEE (1970–74)

TOM BAKER (1974–81)

PETER DAVISON (1981–84)

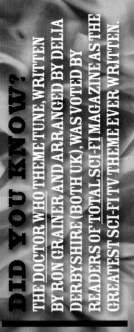

TRIVIA

In *Doctor Who Magazine* polls for **most popular Doctor**, Tom Baker has lost out only three times!

★ LONGEST-SERVING ASSISTANT

James Robert McCrimmon (played principally by Frazer Hines, UK), companion of the second Doctor, appeared in 115 episodes between 1966 and 1969, making him the longest continually serving assistant on screen. The only character to make more appearances other than a Doctor was Brigadier Sir Alistair Gordon Lethbridge-Stewart, portrayed by actor Nicholas Courtney (UK).

TARDIS: The Doctor's means of travel.
Stands for: Time And Relative Dimension(s) In Space.

★ MOST POPULAR STORY

"The Caves of Androzani" (1984) received an average user review of 9.3/10 on imdb.com, and was voted by readers of *Doctor Who Magazine* as the best ever story. The epic tale recounts the last days of the fifth Doctor (Peter Davison, UK), who, by the end of the serial, is poisoned and forced to regenerate – into the sixth Doctor (Colin Baker, UK) – to save his life. The classic four-parter narrowly beat the 2007 episode "Blink," starring tenth Doctor, David Tennant.

★ HUGO AWARDS

The Hugo Awards are presented annually by the World Science Fiction Convention for science fiction and fantasy work (*statue pictured left*). In the category of Best Dramatic Presentation, Short Form – which includes dramatic productions of 90 minutes or less – *Doctor Who* storylines have been nominated 10 times – the ★**most Hugo Award nominations for Best Dramatic Presentation, Short Form**.

In addition, writer Steven Moffat has won a record three awards for his *Doctor Who* stories "The Empty Child"/"The Doctor Dances" (2006), "The Girl in the Fireplace" (2007), and "Blink" (2008). Moffat's three consecutive wins is also a record in this category.

★ LARGEST FICTION SERIES

The official *Doctor Who* books – including novels, novelizations of TV episodes, and "quick reads" – represent the longest licensed fictional series based on one principal character. Some 472 titles have appeared since the mid-1960s.

INTERVIEW MATT SMITH – THE ELEVENTH DOCTOR...

Guinness World Records entered the TARDIS for a chat with the new Doctor and asked how he felt being cast as the eleventh Time Lord.

How does it feel to be the eleventh Doctor?
It's a real privilege to join such a successful show; it's a bit like joining Manchester Utd. It's good to be part of something strong and long may it continue. Plus, I couldn't have inherited the role from a nicer man. I guess it's like anything really – the more you do something the less daunting and intimidating it becomes.

Was there a defining moment during filming when it finally sunk in that you are THE DOCTOR?
I don't know. The Doctor has such a wealth of cultural history and carries such a depth of emotion and duty; initially I didn't know how to digest it all. I just got on with the nuts and bolts of what I had to do... There was a scene when I was standing on the roof in the first episode shouting "I am the Doctor!"...

New Doctor, new TARDIS. What's it like?
It's like a Ferrari, Lamborghini, and Porsche all molded into one! I am quite clumsy though, so I kept breaking parts of the console and the poor production team had to keep fixing it. The TARDIS is a magic concept and it provides a constant source of adventure for both the Doctor and the viewers.

Where would you like the TARDIS to take you if you could go anywhere?
I would definitely travel back in time to see the dinosaurs and then I'd get the TARDIS to take me to the bottom of the sea to the lost city of Atlantis.

FACT: THE 11 DOCTORS HAVE ALL BEEN PORTRAYED BY BRITISH ACTORS...

COLIN BAKER (1984–86)

SYLVESTER McCOY (1987–89, 1996)

PAUL McGANN (1996)

CHRISTOPHER ECCLESTON (2005)

DAVID TENNANT (2005–10)

MATT SMITH (2010–)

POPULAR CULTURE
TOONS & ANIMATION

★HIGHEST-GROSSING 3D ANIMATION

Disney/Pixar's *Up* (USA, 2009) has earned more than $507 million at the global box office from its opening on May 29, 2009. The animated feature tells the story of an old man's dream to visit South America – which he does by tethering thousands of helium balloons to his home and flying there!

FIRST...

ANIMATED MOVIE

The first movie to use the stop-motion technique – to give the illusion of movement to inanimate objects – was Vitagraph's *The Humpty Dumpty Circus* (USA, 1897). Albert E Smith (USA) borrowed his daughter's toy circus and succeeded in animating acrobat and animal figurines by shooting them in barely changed positions one frame at a time.

The ★**first 2D animation** was J Stuart Blackton's (USA, b. UK) *Humorous Phases of Funny Faces* (USA, 1906), a series of caricatures drawn in white chalk on a blackboard, shot one frame at a time, then wiped clean and redrawn.

FIRST PRIME-TIME ANIMATION

The Flintstones (ABC, USA, 1960–66) – a cartoon about a "modern Stone Age family" – premiered on the evening of September 30, 1960. The show was designed to appeal to the entire family, not just children.

FULL-LENGTH FEATURE CARTOON

El Apóstol (Argentina, 1917), a political satire by Quirino Cristiani (Argentina), comprised 58,000 drawings and ran for 70 minutes.

CARTOON "TALKIE"

Max Fleischer's (Austria) animated short *Come Take a Trip in My Airship* (USA, 1924), based on the song of the same name and directed by his brother Dave Fleischer (USA), opened with the animated figure of a woman speaking some patter as the lead-in to the song.

★ FULL-COLOR CARTOON

The first Technicolor cartoon to be commercially released was Disney's *Flowers and Trees* (USA, 1932), a "Silly Symphonies" short that became the ★**first cartoon to win an Oscar**.

CG IMAGES

The Disney movie *Tron* (USA, 1982) was the first major motion feature to fully utilize computer-generated (CG) animation. The movie's setting, inside a video game, was ideal inspiration for computer animators.

CG CHARACTER

The first character in a full-length feature film to be entirely computer-generated was a stained-glass knight that comes to life and steps down from a window in *Young Sherlock Holmes* (USA/UK, 1985). It was designed by John Lasseter (USA), who would later go on to establish Pixar.

★ FEATURE-LENGTH ANIMATED MOVIE

In 1996, animator John Lasseter received a Special Achievement Academy Award for his "inspired leadership of the Pixar *Toy Story* (USA, 1995) team resulting in the first feature-length computer animated film."

> *"I would rather entertain and hope that people learned something than educate people and hope they were entertained."*
> **Walt Disney**

GUINNESS WORLD RECORDS 2011

★ LONGEST-RUNNING SITCOM

The longest-running sitcom by episode count – and the ★longest-running animation series – is *The Simpsons* (Fox, USA), at 452 episodes and counting. It first aired on December 17, 1989 and, during its 20th season (2008–09), overtook the 435 episodes of former record holder *The Adventures of Ozzie and Harriet* (ABC, USA, 1952–66).

ANIME TO WIN AN OSCAR

Sen to Chihiro no Kamikakushi, aka *Spirited Away* (Japan, 2001), is the first anime to win an Oscar, for Best Animated Feature, in 2003. At 124 minutes, Hayao Miyazaki's (Japan) film is also the longest movie to win in this category.

ANIMATION TO BE NOMINATED FOR BEST FOREIGN LANGUAGE FILM

Vals Im Bashir, aka *Waltz with Bashir* (Israel/Germany/France/USA, 2008), was nominated for Best Foreign Language Film at the 2009 Academy Awards.

The movie, directed by Ari Folman (Israel), tells the story of an ex-soldier piecing together his memories of an Israeli Army mission in the first Lebanon war, which began in June 1982.

HIGHEST-GROSSING...

ANIMATION

Shrek 2 (USA, 2004), produced by DreamWorks Animation and directed by Andrew Adamson and Vicky Jenson, took $920.6 million at the global box office, making it the fourth biggest movie of all time. The *Shrek* franchise is also the most successful animated movie series ever.

The **highest-grossing animation adjusted for inflation** is Walt Disney's *Snow White and the Seven Dwarfs* (USA, 1937), which took $184.9 million at the global box office, equivalent to about $1.6 billion in today's money.

★ OPENING WEEKEND

Shrek the Third (USA, 2007) grossed $322,719,944 at the domestic box office over its opening weekend, beginning on May 18, 2007.

Of this total, $47,077,497 was grossed on Saturday, May 19 – the **highest-grossing day for an animation** – and $38,426,991 was earned on Friday, May 18, – the **highest-grossing opening day for an animation**.

★ STOP-MOTION ANIMATION

Chicken Run (UK, 2000), produced by the Bristol, UK-based animation studios Aardman Animations, cost just $67 million to make, but recouped $224.8 million at the international box office.

INSTANT EXPERT

✪ AARDMAN ANIMATIONS' *WALLACE & GROMIT: THE CURSE OF THE WERE-RABBIT* (UK, 2005) USED 6,272 LB (2.84 TONNES) OF PLASTICINE!

✪ *SNOW WHITE AND THE SEVEN DWARFS* (USA, 1937) WAS THE FIRST MOVIE WITH AN OFFICIAL SOUNDTRACK.

✪ THE JAPANESE ANIME *SOREIKE! ANPANMAN*, WRITTEN BY TAKASHI YANASE (JAPAN), BOASTS THE ★MOST CHARACTERS IN AN ANIMATION SERIES, WITH 1,768 DIFFERENT CHARACTERS AS OF JUNE 2009.

✪ *THE JUNGLE BOOK* (USA, 1967) WAS THE LAST MOVIE WALT DISNEY PERSONALLY OVERSAW.

★ MOST "ANNIE" NOMINATIONS

The Annie Awards have been presented by the International Animated Film Association in Los Angeles, California, USA, since 1972 and celebrate the best in animation. Three movies have had a record 16 nominations, each winning 10 awards: *The Incredibles* (USA, 2004), *Wallace & Gromit: The Curse of the Were-Rabbit* (UK, 2005), and *Kung Fu Panda* (USA, 2008).

SAN ANTONIO, TX, USA
The **largest concentration of bats** found anywhere in the world is that of the Mexican free-tailed bat (*Tadarida brasiliensis*) in Bracken Cave, San Antonio, Texas, USA, where up to 20 million females and offspring gather.

29°32'N 98°28'W

POPULAR CULTURE
BLOCK BUSTERS

CINEMA: Short for "cinématographe," derived from the Greek for "movement" and "record." The term was coined by Louis and Auguste Lumière (both France) for their newly invented combined camera and projector – and also the parlor in which their pictures were watched.

SHERLOCK HOLMES

Sherlock Holmes (USA/Germany, 2009), directed by Guy Ritchie (UK), set a new US box-office record for ★**highest-grossing Christmas Day movie**, earning $24.6 million* on Friday, December 25, 2009.

THE DARK KNIGHT

Despite losing almost all of its records to *Avatar* (see p.180), *The Dark Knight* (USA, 2008) is still the ★**highest-grossing movie in its opening weekend**, having taken $158 million from Friday, July 18 to Sunday, July 20, 2008.

THE TWILIGHT SAGA: NEW MOON

In November 2009, the *Twilight* sequel *New Moon* (USA, 2009) eclipsed *The Dark Knight* to achieve the ★**highest opening-day gross** of $72.7 million in the USA.

AVATAR

Now officially the ★**most successful movie** in history – at least in terms of box-office takings – James Cameron's (Canada) *Avatar*

AUSTIN, TX, USA

30°17'N
97°45'W

Rob Williams of Austin, Texas, USA, chose an unconventional method to make a Bologna, cheese, and lettuce sandwich – complete with sliced tomatoes, mustard, mayo, and olives on cocktail sticks – in 1 min 57 sec on November 10, 2000. His record? **The fastest time to make a sandwich using only the feet.**

> "I think the Smurfs thing is funny, personally. Jar Jar is a bit of a low blow."
>
> **Director James Cameron on comparisons between the blue-skinned Na'vi of *Avatar* and Smurfs and Jar Jar Binks**

HOLMES
SHERLOCK HOLMES IS THE *MOST FREQUENTLY RECURRING CHARACTER ON SCREEN. HE HAS BEEN PORTRAYED BY SOME 81 ACTORS IN MORE THAN 217 FILMS.

HORROR
WITH A BOX-OFFICE GROSS OF $296,596,319 TO MARCH 24, 2010, *NEW MOON* (SEE BELOW LEFT) IS THE MOST SUCCESSFUL MOVIE IN BOTH VAMPIRE AND WEREWOLF GENRES.

TAR

THE HANGOVER

SAW·III

HARRY POTTER VI

(USA/UK, 2010) achieved the box-office triple, topping first the foreign chart (January 23, 2010), then the world chart (January 25, 2010) and finally the domestic (February 2, 2010).

The surprise hit of 2009 was Todd Phillips' (USA) road movie *The Hangover* (USA, 2009), which quickly became the ★**highest-grossing R-rated comedy**, grossing $467.3 million at the global box office.

The ★**highest-grossing Halloween** movie is *Saw III* (USA, 2006) the third installment of the Jigsaw Killer franchise, which had taken $33.6 million by October 31, 2006. Globally, the threequel was the most successful of the series.

Harry Potter installment *The Half-Blood Prince* (UK/USA, 2009) had the ★**highest-grossing worldwide opening**, raking in $394 million up to the end of its first domestic weekend in July 2009.

OKLAHOMA CITY, OK, USA

The **longest chain of pipe cleaners** measured 10,459 ft (3.18 km) and was made by Oklahoma Children's Cancer Association at the Children's Hospital OU Medical Center in Oklahoma City, Oklahoma, USA, on February 14, 2007.

35°28'N
97°32'W

POPULAR CULTURE
AT THE MOVIES

★ ★ ★ ★ ★ ★ ★ ★ ★ ★ ★ ★ ★

★ LARGEST MOVIE THEATER SCREEN (DRIVE-IN)

The famous outdoor water-filming facility at Pinewood Studios in Middlesex, UK, was, in 2009, converted into a giant drive-in theater with a screen measuring a record 240 x 60 ft (73.1 x 18.3 m). The screen opened on Halloween 2009.

★ HIGHEST-GROSSING...

Director: Topping the list of Hollywood's highest-grossing directors is Steven Spielberg (USA), whose motion pictures have earned a whopping $3.76 billion in box office receipts.

★ FIRST BEST ACTRESS OSCAR WON FOR DEPICTING A BEST ACTRESS

Cate Blanchett (Australia, pictured) won the 2005 Best Actress Oscar for depicting Best Actress Academy Award winner Katherine Hepburn (USA) in *Aviator* (2004).

As a producer, Spielberg is responsible for generating $5.03 billion, making him the ★ **highest-grossing producer** too.
★ **Screenwriter**: The 15 movies written by George Lucas (USA) have grossed a lifetime combined total of $3.33 billion.

★ HIGHEST EARNER IN HOLLYWOOD

Michael Bay, director of *Transformers: Revenge of the Fallen* (USA, 2009), earned an estimated $125 million in 2009 thanks to his blockbuster movie release, a share of the merchandising and DVD rights, and a few back-end production deals.

★ LEAST BANKABLE ACTOR

Thanks to flop *Land of the Lost* (USA, 2009), Will Ferrell (USA) floats to the top of the list of most overpaid actors. The movie cost $100 million to make but made just $65 million and is the latest in a run of bad luck for Ferrell. On average, for every $1 he is paid, he returns just $3.29 at the box office, according to *Forbes*.

★ LEAST BANKABLE ACTRESS

In the same list is Drew Barrymore (USA), whose $1 fee will see a return of $7.43 (£4.66) – the lowest return on investment for an actress.

★ FIRST WINNER OF A BEST ACTRESS OSCAR AND A WORST ACTRESS RAZZIE IN THE SAME YEAR

Sandra Bullock (USA) won Worst Actress at the 2009 Golden Raspberry Awards for *All About Steve* (USA, 2009) and turned up in person to accept the trophy the day before she won the Academy Award for Best Actress in *The Blind Side* (USA, 2009).

RAZZIES:
The Golden Raspberry Awards, set up in 1981 by John Wilson (USA) to "salute the worst that Hollywood has to offer." The anti-Oscars!

★ MOST BANKABLE STARS

The Hollywood actor giving the best value for money is Shia LaBeouf (USA); in 2009, the star of *Transformers* and *Indiana Jones 4* made $160 for every $1 he was paid. The most bankable actress, according to *Forbes*, is *King Kong* star Naomi Watts (UK), who made $44 per $1 paid.

DID YOU KNOW?

THERE ARE 11 CATEGORIES IN THE GOLDEN RASPBERRY AWARDS (RAZZIES), INCLUDING WORST PICTURE AND WORST NEW STAR.

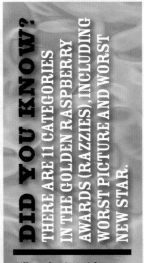

Bill Cosby (USA) became the ★ **first Razzie winner to collect the prize in person** in 1987.

TRIVIA

37°41'N 97°20'W

WICHITA, KA, USA

The **largest stitched teddy bear** measures 55 ft 4 in (16.86 m) in length and was constructed by Dana Warren (USA). The bear was completed on June 6, 2008 and displayed at the Exploration Place in Wichita, Kansas, USA.

QUIZ!
WHO IS *HURT LOCKER*
DIRECTOR KATHRYN
BIGELOW'S FAMOUS EX?
SEE P.278 FOR THE ANSWER.

★FIRST FICTIONAL CHARACTER TO BE OSCAR NOMINATED

Donald Kaufman, a fictitious character in Spike Jonze's (USA) *Adaptation* (USA, 2002), was nonetheless nominated for Best Adapted Screenplay along with his (real) "brother" Charlie Kaufman (USA) at the 2003 Oscars. Both characters appeared in the movie – both played by Nicolas Cage (USA) – and both are credited as writers, yet only Charlie exists!

HIGHEST-EARNING MOVIE STARS

Once again, Harry Potter leads Daniel Radcliffe and Emma Watson top the chart of Hollywood's highest-earning stars. Emma earned $10 million apiece for the last two Potter movies, while Daniel secured $20 million per movie plus a $1 million bonus for licensing and royalties.

★HIGHEST-GROSSING SERIES

The Harry Potter franchise has, in only six movies, earned $5.39 billion at the worldwide box office, ahead of *Star Wars* ($4.32 billion; £2.81 billion) and James Bond ($4.82 billion). The last movie in the series – *Deathly Hallows* – will be delivered in two instalments.

OSCARS

★MOST ACTING NOMINATIONS

With a nomination for her role as cook Julia Child in *Julia & Julie* (USA, 2009), Meryl Streep notched up her 16th Oscars nod (having won two).

WORST OSCAR PERCENTAGE

Sound mixer Kevin O'Connell (USA) has had 20 Oscar nominations without a win – the longest losing streak in Oscars history.

★BEST OSCARS PERCENTAGE

Sound editor Mark Berger (USA) has the best "score" at the Oscars with 100% – he has had four wins from four nominations: *Apocalyse Now*, (USA, 1979), *The Right Stuff* (USA, 1983), *Amadeus* (USA 1984), and *The English Patient* (USA, 1996).

★MOST MULTI-DISCIPLINE TECHNICAL OSCARS

Richard Taylor (NZ), effects supervisor at Weta Workshops in Wellington, New Zealand, has won technical Oscars across a record three disciplines: Visual Effects for *King Kong* (NZ/USA/Ger, 2005), and Costume Design and Make-up for *The Return of the King* (USA/NZ/Ger, 2003).

★FIRST FEMALE TO WIN A BEST PICTURE ACADEMY AWARD

When Kathryn Bigelow's (USA, below) *Hurt Locker* (USA, 2008, below right) won Best Picture at the 2010 Academy Awards ceremony, it marked the first time that a female director had won an Oscar in this category. "There should be more women directing," said Bigelow. "There's just not the awareness that it's really possible. It is."

EXES
THE 2009 OSCARS CEREMONY WAS KNOWN AS THE BATTLE OF THE EXES, AS KATHRYN BIGELOW WAS UP AGAINST EX-HUSBAND JAMES CAMERON FOR BEST DIRECTOR.

SEXIST?
BIGELOW WAS ALSO THE FIRST WOMAN TO BE AWARDED THE DIRECTORS GUILD OF AMERICA AWARD FOR OUTSTANDING ACHIEVEMENT IN FEATURE FILM.

POPULAR CULTURE
3D CINEMA

QUIZ!
WHICH ANIMATED MOVIE WAS THE FIRST TO BE PRODUCED IN STEREOSCOPIC 3D?
FIND OUT THE ANSWER ON P.278.

★★★★★★★★★★★★★★★★

FIRST...

★DEMONSTRATION OF 3D FILM: 1915

An audience at the Astor Theater in New York City, USA, donned red-and-green glasses for the first time to view test reels of 3D footage.

Produced by Edwin S Porter and William E Waddell (both USA), the footage depicted, among other things, dancing girls and the Niagara Falls – the first images seen using the anaglyph 3D process.

TRIVIA

DID YOU KNOW?
IN 1894, WILLIAM FRIESE-GREENE (UK) BECAME THE FIRST TO FILE A PATENT FOR A VIEWING DEVICE THAT COMBINES TWO SEPARATE PICTURES INTO ONE 3D IMAGE.

★MOST ANIMATED 3D FEATURES RELEASED IN A SINGLE YEAR

Hollywood embraced 3D cinema in a big way in 2009, with the major studios releasing a grand total of 10 animated 3D features during the year. While most of these animations were new, *Toy Story 3D* (USA, 2009) was a double feature of the first two movies remastered to be a 3D experience.

SPEX
THE RED-AND-BLUE-LENS 3D GLASSES ARE NOW A THING OF THE PAST. INSTEAD, TODAY'S "POLARIZED" FILTERS SPLIT THE IMAGE INTO HORIZONTAL AND VERTICAL STRIPS.

★3D FEATURE: 1922

Harry K Fairhall and Robert F Elder (both USA) used two cameras and two projectors – "set at a distance from each other equal to the average distance between the human eyes" – to premiere Nat Deverich's (USA) stereoscopic movie *The Power of Love* (USA, 1922) in front of an invited audience at the Ambassador Hotel Theater in Los Angeles, USA, on September 27, 1922. It was the first and only feature-length application of Fairhall and Elder's new technology. The movie is now lost, sadly.

★3D SCREENING TO A PAYING AUDIENCE: 1922

Research by historian Daniel L Symmes suggests that the documentary short *Movies of the Future* (USA, 1922), directed by William Van Doren Kelley (USA), was the first stereoscopic print shown to a paying audience. The 14-minute movie explored this nascent film technology and was shown at the Rivoli Theater in New York City, USA, in 1922.

★3D MOVIE TO BE NOMINATED FOR AN OSCAR: 1936

A short experimental movie entitled *Audioscopiks* (USA, 1935), filmed using the Norling-Leventhal 3-Dimensions process – an anaglyph technique devised by John Norling and Jacob Leventhal (both USA) – received Academy Award recognition in the category "Best Short Subject, Novelty."

The eight-minute reel showcased the 3D effect with a ladder being pushed out of a window, a sliding trombone, a woman on a swing, and someone throwing a baseball.

★MOST EXPENSIVE 3D ANIMATION

The 2009 3D performance-capture version of *A Christmas Carol* (USA), directed by Robert Zemeckis (USA), cost $200 million to produce. One of the first of the new wave of 3D blockbusters, it went on to gross $323,555,899 globally.

45.6 MILLION:
Computing hours required to make *Monsters vs. Aliens* (that's 1.9 million complete days, or 5,205 years!).

3D TALKIE: 1936

Sante Bonaldo's production *Nozze Vagabonde* (*Beggar's Wedding*, Italy, 1936), starring Italians Leda Gloria and Ermes Zacconi, was the first movie to offer 3D polarizing glasses and a synchronized soundtrack.

3D MOVIE IN COLOR: 1952

Bwana Devil (USA, 1952), written and directed by Arch Oboler (USA), promised viewers "The Miracle of the Age!!! A LION in your lap. A LOVER in your arms!" Audiences – who had to wear colored filter glasses – flocked to the cinema to witness the spectacular tale of two man-eating lions.

ASTOUNDING!
NOW WARNER BROS. BRING YOU
Natural Vision **3 DIMENSION**
UNLIKE ANYTHING YOU'VE SEEN BEFORE!
A FEATURE PICTURE! A STORY SENSATION!
HOUSE OF WAX

4D: The fourth dimension – in moviespeak, this refers to the use of water, vibrations, smells, etc., to further enhance your viewing sensation!

★ **NEW RECORD**
★ **UPDATED RECORD**

★ FIRST 3D MOVIE WITH STEREO SOUND

Warner Bros., the second major Hollywood studio to enter the 3D market and the first to do so in full color, released *House of Wax* (1953) with stereo sound.

TOP 10

	MOVIE	WORLDWIDE GROSS TO FEB 2010 (MILLIONS)*	DATE RELEASED
1	*Avatar* (Fox)	$2,376 m	2010
2	*Ice Age: Dawn of the Dinosaurs* (Fox, above)	$884 m	2009
3	*Up* (Buena Vista)	$723 m	2009
4	*Alice in Wonderland* (Walt Disney Pictures)	$660 m	2010
5	*Monsters Vs. Aliens* (Paramount/DreamWorks)	$381 m	2009
6	*A Christmas Carol* (Buena Vista)	$323 m	2009
7	*Chicken Little* (Buena Vista)	$314 m	2005
8	*Bolt* (Buena Vista)	$308 m	2009
9	*G-Force* (Buena Vista)	$285 m	2009
10	*Journey to the Center of the Earth* (Warner Bros./New Line)	$241 m	2009

Source: boxofficemojo.com   *figures as of May 3 2010

Despite a poor critical reception, the movie grossed $95,000 in its first week from just two theaters.

★ 3D MOVIE BY A MAJOR STUDIO: 1953

Columbia Pictures became the first big studio to venture into the 3D movie market with their release of *Man in the Dark* (USA, 1953) on April 9, 1953. The movie – a remake of the 1936 film noir *The Man Who Lived Twice* (USA) – was rushed out to capitalize on the 3D craze, and wowed audiences with scenes in which spiders, fists, and dead bodies loomed out of the screen.

★ 3D MOVIE...

In French (1953): *Soirs de Paris* (France, 1953), directed by Jean Laviron (France), ran for 85 minutes.
In Japanese (1953): *Tobidashita Nichi Yôbi*, aka *Runaway Sunday* (Japan, 1953), was a supporting movie lasting just 11 minutes.
In Indian (1983): *Chhota Chetan* (India, 1983, aka *My Dear Kuttichathan*), a children's fantasy movie.

MISCELLANY

★ HIGHEST BUDGET-TO-BOX-OFFICE RATIO FOR A 3D MOVIE

To date, the most successful 3D movie in terms of its profitability is *The Stewardesses* (USA, 1969), directed by Al Silliman (USA). A pioneering, single-camera 3D system was devised to keep the total budget just over $100,000. An adult movie, it grossed upward of $30 million at the box office.

★ BIGGEST 3D OPENING WEEKEND

Tim Burton's (USA) *Alice in Wonderland* (USA, 2010) grossed an unprecedented $116.1 million in the USA on March 5–7. Its nearest 3D rival, *Avatar* (USA, 2009) took a "mere" £77 million in its opening weekend.

★ FIRST ANIMATED FEATURE PRODUCED IN STEREOSCOPIC 3D

Until *Monsters vs. Aliens* (USA, 2009), animated movies were converted to 3D after completion; *MvA*, however, was "shot" in a stereoscopic format from the beginning, an expensive "premium" process that added $15 million to the budget.

FEATURE
THAT'S
SHOWBIZ

★ ★ ★ ★ ★ ★ ★ ★ ★ ★

Here at *Guinness World Records*, our researchers don't just stick to scientific journals and research papers for record-worthy content – it's also our responsibility to monitor the fashion and celebrity news in order to bring you the most up-to-date showbiz records.

So, what have we discovered this year? Well, Johnny Depp (USA) topped the *People* magazine poll of ★**sexiest men alive** for the second time this year, while the magazine revealed the ★**most beautiful person** to be actress Christina Applegate (USA).

In the power stakes, Brad Pitt (USA) returns as the ★**most powerful actor**, thanks in part to his Oscar-nominated role in *Benjamin Button* (USA, 2008), but largely to endless tabloid news of his family life and stories about his humanitarian activities.

No surprise, then, that 2009's ★**most powerful actress** was Pitt's partner Angelina Jolie (USA)!

The ★**richest fashion designer** is Giorgio Armani (Italy, below). Clothes, watches, perfumes, homeware, and hotels all bear his name… a fantastic achievement for a medical school dropout who's now worth a record $5.3 billion!

In surveys of magazine and online polls regarding the ★**most infamous female celebrity**, one name repeatedly floats to the surface: Lindsay Lohan (USA). *Forbes* and E-Poll named her the "most infamous," while others were less kind, focusing on the troubled actress' private life as well as her unfortunate movie choices. Runners-up included singer Amy Winehouse (UK) and Miss California Carrie Prejean (USA).

MOST INFAMOUS
FEMALE CELEBRITY

Li-lo's movie *I Know Who Killed Me* (USA, 2007) won a record eight Golden Raspberries – including two Worst Actress awards for Lohan's two roles.

> *"You can think you've made it and yet the next day's press will always be waiting for you!"*
> **Giorgio Armani, the world's richest fashion designer**

… AND MALE CELEBRITY

Alex Rodriguez (USA) has had better years. Since his revelations about drug abuse during the 2000s, the New York Yankees No.13 – and multiple world-record holder – has had a bad press. "Slugger turned tabloid tragedy," said *Forbes*, who listed A-Rod as their No.1 ☆**most infamous male celebrity** thanks to his steroid use, his high-profile divorce, and higher-profile affair with Madonna!

PLUS…
A-ROD: THE MANY LIVES OF ALEX RODRIGUEZ, AN UNAUTHORIZED BIOGRAPHY, ALSO ACCUSES THE ST...
OF CHEAT...

POWER COUPLES

	COUPLE	COMBINED EARNINGS (JUNE 1, 2008–JUNE 1, 2009)
1	Shawn "Jay-Z" Carter & Beyoncé Knowles (both USA, right)	$122m
2	Harrison Ford & Calista Flockhart (both USA)	$69m
3	Brad Pitt & Angelina Jolie (both USA)	$55m
4	Will & Jada Pinkett Smith (both USA)	$48m
5	David & Victoria Beckham (both UK, below)	$46m
6	Ellen DeGeneres & Portia de Rossi (both USA)	$36m
7	Tom Hanks & Rita Wilson (both USA)	$35.5m
8	Jim Carrey & Jenny McCarthy (both USA)	$34m
9	Tom Cruise & Katie Holmes (both USA)	$33.5m
10	Chris Martin (UK) & Gwyneth Paltrow (USA)	$22m

Source: *Forbes*

EXTRA! WHO ARE THE BIGGEST RECORD-BREAKERS IN THE MUSIC INDUSTRY? FIND OUT ON PP.186-189.

EXTRA! FOR MORE ONLINE STATS, FACTS, AND WORLD RECORDS, TURN TO P.218.

★ MOST TRUSTED CELEBRITY

In a survey conducted by E-Poll Market Research for business magazine *Forbes*, respondents were asked to rate the "trustworthiness, awareness, and appeal" of celebrities. Top of the list was actor James Earl Jones (USA) – the velvety voice behind NBC's Olympic coverage and the CNN tagline (and *Star Wars'* less-than-trustworthy Darth Vader!).

(5) VID BECKHAM

POSH & THE DOSH

★ MOST SEARCHED-FOR FEMALE

Singer Lady Gaga (USA, aka Stefani Joanne Angelina Germanotta) – was the most searched-for female online in 2009, according to Google, the **largest search engine**.

Did you know: Lady Gaga adapted her stage name from the Queen hit song "Radio Ga Ga."

★ MOST SEARCHED-FOR MALE

The untimely death of Michael Jackson (USA, 1958–2009) – first announced virally – sent you online in your millions, making him the most searched-for male in 2009.

Did you know: Jackson achieved more world records *after* his death than he did when he was alive! See p.189 for more of his posthumous record-breaking feats.

★ HIGHEST-EARNING PRIMETIME TV STAR

From June 1, 2008 to June 1, 2009, *X Factor* and *American Idol* judge Simon Cowell (UK) earned $75 million.

★ MOST POWERFUL SPORTS STAR

Despite the controversial end to his year, golfing legend Tiger Woods (USA) earned an impressive $103 million in 2009, and topped the 2010 *BusinessWeek* Sports Power 100 list.

★ MOST SEARCHED-FOR CELEBRITY WEDDING

The wedding of the year – if Google's hit tracker is anything to go by – was that of reality TV star Khloé Kardashian and the LA Lakers' Lamar Odom (both USA) on September 27, 2009. It ranked the highest on the Google zeitgeist list of celeb weddings.

PLUS... THE REALITY TV SHOW *KEEPING UP WITH THE KARDASHIANS* DEBUTED IN THE USA IN OCTOBER 2007 AND FOLLOWS THE LIVES OF LOS ANGELES SOCIALITES.

CELEBRITY TWEEPS*

Actor Ashton Kutcher (USA, below right) is ahead in the celeb Twitter battle, as the ★**first tweep with over 1 million followers**. The ★**most searched-for tweep of 2009**? Singer/actress Miley Cyrus (USA, below left), according to Google.

234,901 FOLLOWERS

4,649,421 FOLLOWERS

*TWEEPS: PEOPLE (PEEPS) WHO USE TWITTER

POPULAR CULTURE
MUSIC

CHART-TOPPERS

★ MOST SIMULTANEOUS US HOT 100 HITS BY A FEMALE

On November 14, 2009, 19-year-old US country singer Taylor Swift became the first female artist to have eight tracks simultaneously on the US Hot 100. On that chart she also became the first artist to have five tracks simultaneously enter the Top 30.

★ 21st CENTURY'S TOP-SELLING ALBUM ACT (USA)

Rapper Eminem (USA) was the biggest-selling album act in the US in the first 10 years of the century, with sales of 32,241,000.

★ MOST NEW ENTRIES ON UK ALBUM CHART

On the September 19, 2009 chart, 16 albums by The Beatles (UK) entered the UK Top 75. This included four in the Top 10 -- a record for a group.

★ MOST SUCCESSIVE WEEKS AT TOP OF US HOT 100

The Black Eyed Peas (USA) spent 26 successive weeks at No.1 on the US Hot 100 in 2009. After 12 weeks at the summit their "Boom Boom Pow" was replaced by "I Gotta Feeling," which stayed at the top for 14 weeks.

★ MOST CHARTED TEENAGER (USA)

The 16-year-old singer/actor Miley Cyrus (USA) scored her 29th US Hot 100 chart entry on November 7, 2009 with "Party in the USA." She has had hits under her own name and as Hannah Montana.

MOST SUCCESSFUL FIRST WEEK UK ALBUM SALE

Released on November 23, 2009, Susan Boyle's (UK) *I Dreamed a Dream* sold 411,820 copies in its first week in the UK (133,599 on the first day) -- the biggest weekly UK sale by any solo singer's album.

★ MOST SUCCESSIVE ALBUM ENTRIES AT NO.1 (USA)

On June 6, 2009, Eminem's (USA) album *Relapse* gave him his fifth successive US album chart entry at No.1. This equaled the record set between 1998 and 2003 by fellow rapper DMX (USA).

★ FEMALE WITH MOST ALBUM NO.1s (UK)

Madonna (USA) has had 11 UK No.1 albums. Her latest chart-topper came with *Celebration* on October 3, 2009. She is also the **biggest-selling female album act of the 21st century (UK)**, with sales of 6.68 million to October 2009.

★ FEMALE WITH MOST ALBUM NO.1s (USA)

Barbra Streisand (USA) had her ninth No.1 album in the USA on October 17, 2009, aged 67. She is also the first artist to have a No.1 album in five different decades.

★ MOST WEEKS ON UK CHART IN ANY YEAR

In 2009, Lady Gaga (USA) clocked up 154 chart weeks in the UK Top 75 (with 90 of these in the Top 40), mainly thanks to her hits "Just Dance," "Poker Face," "Paparazzi," and "Bad Romance".

Madonna Louise Ciccone was born on August 16, 1958 in Bay City, Michigan, USA. Her first album was *Madonna*, in 1983.

TRIVIA

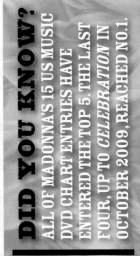

★ BIGGEST JUMP TO NO.1 (UK)

Pixie Lott's (UK) single "Boys and Girls" broke the record for a jump within the Top 75 to the No.1 spot in the UK on September 19, 2009, when it climbed there from No.73.

ALBUM

SUSAN BOYLE WAS AGED 48 WHEN HER ALBUM *I DREAMED A DREAM* DEBUTED AT NO.1 IN THE US AND UK. SHE IS THE **OLDEST ARTIST TO REACH NO.1** ON THESE CHARTS WITH A DEBUT.

★ FASTEST-SELLING ALBUM BY A FEMALE (UK)

Susan Boyle's (UK) debut album *I Dreamed a Dream*, released in November 2009, sold more than a million copies in just 21 days. It was the biggest-selling album in the UK in 2009, and a clip of her singing the title song for the first time on UK TV's *Britain's Got Talent* was the most watched YouTube clip in 2009.

DIGITAL HITS

★ MOST DOWNLOADED ACTS IN A YEAR (USA)

In 2009, Lady Gaga (USA) broke the record for female acts by selling 11.1 million downloads in the USA. The Black Eyed Peas (USA) broke the record for a group, with 10.3 million downloads.

★ FASTEST-SELLING DIGITAL TRACK (UK)

Californian alternative hard rock band Rage Against the Machine's 1993 recording "Killing in the Name" entered the UK singles chart at No.1 on December 26, 2009. It was available only as a download, and in its first week sold 502,672 copies.

★ BIGGEST-SELLING DIGITAL ALBUM ACT (USA)

In July 2009, British band Coldplay became the first act to sell more than a million digital albums in the USA.

★ MOST SIMULTANEOUS TOP 20 ENTRIES ON US DIGITAL CHART

On November 14, 2009, Taylor Swift (USA) became the first act to have five tracks ("Jump Then Fall," "Untouchable," "Other Side of the Door," "Superstar," and "Come in with the Rain") enter the Top 20 of the US digital chart simultaneously.

★ FIRST 3D BROADCAST ON INTERNET

British rock trio Keane were the first act to make a 3D broadcast on the Internet. They sang five songs in a 20-minute set from Studio Two at Abbey Road, London, UK. In 2006, Keane also released the **first USB stick single**, "Nothing in My Way."

★ MOST SIMULTANEOUS HITS ON UK SINGLES CHART DEBUT

On the chart dated January 23, 2010, the cast of the US TV series *Glee* (USA) made their UK chart debut with five tracks simultaneously entering the UK Top 75.

★ NEW RECORD
★ UPDATED RECORD

POPULAR CULTURE

MUSIC

★ ★ ★ ★ ★ ★ ★ ★ ★ ★ ★ ★ ★ ★

"It's a great honor to visit the Guinness World Records offices. I love the book."

Michael Jackson, October 14, 2006

Michael Jackson scored 13 US chart-topping singles as a solo star. The **most US No.1 singles** to date is 20, by The Beatles (UK).

★ MOST SINGLES SOLD IN A YEAR (UK)

In 2009, an unprecedented 152.7 million "singles" were sold in the UK, with a record 98% of them being downloaded tracks. It was the first year since 1967 that more singles were sold in the UK than albums.

TOP EARNERS

★ MOST SUCCESSFUL TOUR (SOLO ARTIST)

Madonna's (USA) Sticky & Sweet tour (August 23, 2008– September 2, 2009) grossed $408 million.

★ TOP-SELLING FEMALE RECORDING ARTIST

Madonna (USA) holds the record for album sales up to December 2009 of 75 million in the USA and 200 million abroad.

★ TOP-GROSSING COUNTRY ACT

Kenny Chesney (USA) is the top-grossing country music performer of the 21st century. Since 2002, he has sold seven million tickets to his shows and grossed almost $500 million.

★ BIGGEST AND MOST EXPENSIVE TOP 40 BOX SET (US & UK)

The 16-CD box set *The Beatles in Stereo*, which sold for $243.98, entered the US album chart at No.15 on September 26, 2009. One

TRIVIA

week earlier, it had entered the UK chart at No.24 – it sold there for £172 ($265).

HIGHEST ANNUAL EARNINGS EVER FOR A POP STAR

In 1989, Michael Jackson (USA) topped the Forbes list as the highest paid entertainer, with annual earnings of $125 million. This record is still unbroken 21 years later.

YOUNG & OLD

★ OLDEST NO.1 SINGLES ACT (UK)

Sir Tom Jones (UK) was 68 years 9 months old when he sang on "Barry Islands in the Stream" with Vanessa Jenkins, Bryn West, and

★ MOST SUCCESSFUL REALITY TV GIRL GROUP

Girls Aloud (UK/Ireland) formed on a reality TV show *Pop Stars: The Rivals* in 2002, and have gone on to have 20 Top 10 singles as of January 2009, including a female record 17 consecutive Top 10 hits from December 2002 to December 2007.

MICHAEL JACKSON, 1958–2009

Before his untimely death on June 25, 2009 at the age of 50, Michael Joseph Jackson (USA) was probably the most famous living human being on the planet. A multiple Guinness World Record holder – he received eight in his lifetime for his chart achievements, album sales, earnings and charity donations – Michael's contribution to the arts was immeasureable. And remarkably, the record breaking continued after his passing.

In the year of his death, a record **11.3 million tracks** by the artist were downloaded in the USA, and **2.8 million albums** were sold in the UK. From his death to the end of November 2009, he sold **7 million albums**, **10.2 million downloaded tracks** and **1.3 million DVDs** in the USA. The first morning after his death saw over **1 million YouTube plays of "Beat It"**, and in the first week **2.6 million Michael Jackson downloads** were sold in the USA.

HIGHEST-GROSSING SOLO TOUR OF AUSTRALIA

US singer P!nk (born Alecia Moore) grossed $80 million for her 58 arena shows in Australia, which were seen by 660,000 people in the summer of 2009.

Robin Gibb (all UK). A charity single, the track topped the UK chart on March 21, 2009.

★ YOUNGEST COUNTRY "ENTERTAINER OF THE YEAR"

In 2009, 19-year-old Taylor Swift (USA) became the youngest artist to receive the Country Music Association's (CMA) highest award, Entertainer of the Year.

In that year, her 43 shows took $23.7 million gross and her album *Fearless* outsold all others in the USA.

★ OLDEST UK CHART-TOPPER AND RECORD SPANS OF NO.1s

On May 9, 2009, Bob Dylan (USA) topped the UK album chart with *Together Through Life*, which made the 67-year-old the oldest act to top the UK chart with

a newly recorded album. It was his first No.1 for 38 years 7 months and increased his span of studio-recorded No.1 albums to 44 years and 1 month – also both records.

★ HIGHEST-GROSSING CONCERT MOVIE

The release of Michael Jackson's rehearsals for the *This Is It* tour on October 28, 2009 grossed $250 million. It opened simultaneously in 250,000 movie theaters around the world and took $200 million in its first two weeks.

HIT! US SALES OF MICHAEL JACKSON'S *THRILLER* ALBUM ARE ESTIMATED AT OVER 55 MILLION; GLOBAL FIGURES ARE IMPOSSIBLE TO CONFIRM BUT WOULD PUSH THIS TO WELL OVER 100 MILLION.

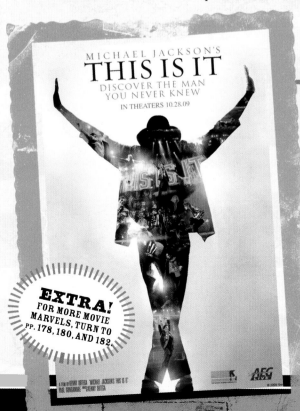

MICHAEL JACKSON'S
THIS IS IT
DISCOVER THE MAN YOU NEVER KNEW
IN THEATERS 10.28.09

EXTRA! FOR MORE MOVIE MARVELS, TURN TO PP. 178, 180, AND 182.

A FILM BY KENNY ORTEGA "MICHAEL JACKSON'S THIS IS IT"
PROD. SONGWRITING PRODUCED BY KENNY ORTEGA
AEG

GUINNESS WORLD RECORDS
CERTIFICATE
The most successful entertainer of all time is Michael Jackson (USA), who in 1989 alone earned $125 million from single and album sales
GUINNESS WORLD RECORDS LTD

GUINNESS WORLD RECORDS
CERTIFICATE
The first entertainer to have officially ratified sales of more than 100 million albums outside the USA is Michael Jackson (USA)
GUINNESS WORLD RECORDS LTD

GUINNESS WORLD RECORDS
CERTIFICATE
The biggest-selling album of all time, with sales of over 104 million, is Michael Jackson's *Thriller* (1982). It remained in the Billboard 200 Top 10 for 80 consecutive weeks
GUINNESS WORLD RECORDS LTD

ST PAUL, MN, USA

The **tallest ice building** was an ice palace completed in January 1992, used 18,000 blocks of ice, at St Paul, Minnesota, USA, during the Winter Carnival. Built by TMK Construction Specialties Inc., it was 50.8 m (166 ft 8 in) high and contained 4,900 tonnes (10.8 million lb) of ice.

44°57'N 93°06'W

POPULAR CULTURE
THEATER & CLASSICAL ARTS

★ ★ ★ ★ ★ ★ ★ ★ ★ ★ ★

★ MOST PROLIFIC THEATER PRODUCER
Theater impresario Howard E Pechet (Canada) produced 485 plays at 10 different venues across Canada, between January 1975 and July 2008.

★ MOST FLAMENCO TAPS IN A MINUTE (MALE)
José Miguel Fernández Pintado (Spain) performed 814 flamenco taps in one minute on the set of *Lo Show dei Record* in Rome, Italy, on April 1, 2010.

FASTEST PANTOMIME HORSE (FEMALE)
Samantha Kavanagh and Melissa Archer (both UK, front and rear, respectively) ran 328 ft (100 m) in 18.13 seconds as a pantomime horse at an event organized by the advertising agency Claydon Heeley Jones Mason at Harrow School, Middlesex, UK, on August 18, 2005.

The record for the ★ **fastest pantomime horse (male)** is held by Shane Crawford and Adrian Mott (both Australia), who ran 100 m in 12.045 seconds outside the set of *The Footy Show* in Melbourne, Victoria, Australia, on 30 July 2009.

SMALLEST PROFESSIONAL THEATER
Founded in 2004, The Theatre Lilli Chapeau, in Miltenberg, Germany, has a maximum capacity of 27 seats. The theater performs around 70 shows per year and the only performer to have graced its stage is Lilli Chapeau, aka Celine Bauer (pictured above right).

The ★ **fastest pantomime horse (mixed)** – Nafi Baram and Kathleen Rice (both UK, front and rear, respectively) – ran 100 m in 16.37 seconds at the Battersea Millennium Arena, London, UK, on November 30, 2006.

★ MOST TONYS FOR A PLAY
The Coast of Utopia by playwright Tom Stoppard (UK) won a record seven Tony Awards in 2007. A trilogy of plays – *Voyage*, *Shipwreck*, and *Salvage* – lasting nine hours in total and embracing a 33-year timespan, *The Coast of Utopia* explores the subject of change as experienced by a huge cast of around 70 real-life Russian writers, politicians, philosophers, and journalists.

EXTRA! TURN BACK TO PP.184-185 FOR ALL THE TOP SHOWBIZ RECORDS.

> *"You can't stop my happiness, 'cuz I like the way I am! And you just can't stop my knife and fork when I see a Christmas ham!"*
> **Edna Turnblad in *Hairspray***

★ MOST TONY AWARDS FOR PLAYING THE OPPOSITE SEX
Only two actors have ever won a Tony Award for playing someone of the opposite sex: Mary Martin (USA) for playing the title role in *Peter Pan* in 1956 and Harvey Fierstein (USA, left) for his depiction of Edna Turnblad in *Hairspray* in 2003.

★ MOST TONY AWARDS WON FOR BEST ACTRESS IN A MUSICAL

Angela Lansbury (UK, above left) has won four Tony Awards (out of four nominations) in the category of Best Performance by a Leading Actress in a Musical for *Mame* (1966), *Dear World* (1969), *Gypsy* (1975), and *Sweeney Todd* (1979). The ★**most Tony awards for a male actor in a musical** is three, by Hinton Battle (USA, above right), who won for *Sophisticated Ladies* (1981), *The Tapdance Kid* (1984), and *Miss Saigon* (1991), all in the category of Featured Role in a Musical.

FASTEST THEATRICAL PRODUCTION

The cast and crew of Dundee University Musical Society in association with Apex Productions produced and performed *Seven Brides for Seven Brothers* at the Gardyne Theatre, Dundee, UK, at 7:30 p.m. on September 27, 2003 – 23 hr 30 min after first receiving the script. The production time included all auditions, casting, rehearsals, publicity, rigging, stage and set design, and construction time.

★ LARGEST SIMULTANEOUS PERFORMANCE OF ONE SHOW

The most widespread simultaneous performance of a show was organized by Stagecoach Theatre Arts and achieved by 66 performances of *Glad Rags* in the UK, Ireland, and Germany at 4:15 p.m. on December 6, 2008.

★ MOST BALLET DANCERS "EN POINTE"

A total of 220 ballet dancers successfully stood "en pointe" (meaning on the tips of their toes) for a minute at the Youth America Grand Prix (USA) 10th Anniversary Gala at New York City Center in Manhattan, New York City, USA, on April 22, 2009.

★ LARGEST AUDIENCE FOR A COMEDIAN

German comedian Mario Barth performed in front of an audience of 67,733 people at the Olympiastadion, Berlin, Germany, on July 12, 2008.

★ MOST THEATRICAL APPEARANCES ON A SINGLE NIGHT

Pendem Krishna Kumar (India) appeared in nine different scripted roles in nine different theater productions in Suryapet, India, on July 9, 2009.

★ NEW RECORD
★ UPDATED RECORD

★ LONGEST-RUNNING PLAY

The longest continuously run show in the world is *The Mousetrap* by Dame Agatha Christie (UK, 1890–1976), with 23,940 performances as of May 10, 2010 at St Martin's Theatre in London, UK. The play opened on November 25, 1952 at the Ambassadors Theatre, London, and moved after 8,862 performances to the St Martin's Theatre next door on March 25, 1974. Pictured below is the cast from the 58th annual performance.

POPULAR CULTURE
ART & SCULPTURE

★LARGEST SAND ART

The largest artwork created from sand – and the ★**largest freehand drawing** – is 3.02 miles (4.86 km) in diameter and contains 1,000 individual circles. Jim Denevan (USA, inset) made the artwork in the Black Rock Desert, Nevada, USA, in May 2009 in seven days, etching the sand with a rake and using chains dragged behind a vehicle.

★LARGEST RUBIK'S CUBE MOSAIC

Five artists from the art collective Cube Works Studio in Toronto, Canada, re-created *The Last Supper* by Leonardo da Vinci... from 4,050 Rubik's cubes! The miraculous "cube-ist" mosaic measures 17 ft (5.18 m) by 8 ft 6 in (2.59 m), weighs 1,102 lb (500 kg), and was finally completed on October 23, 2009.

★ **NEW RECORD**
★ **UPDATED RECORD**

LARGEST...

★DRAWING

The largest pencil drawing by one artist – *My journey of life, where I meet people of different color, birds, trees, etc... and the life goes on* – is 1,500 ft (457.20 m) long and 20 in (50.8 cm) wide, and has an overall surface area of 2,490 ft² (231.33 m²). It was completed by Jainthan Francis (USA) and measured in Sayreville, New Jersey, USA, on June 21, 2009.

ANAMORPHIC:

A work of art that seems distorted from most angles, but will appear normal when seen from a particular viewpoint.

★ANAMORPHIC PAVEMENT ART

To mark the launch of *Ice Age 3* on DVD in the UK in November 2009, Twentieth Century Fox Home Entertainment asked German artist Edgar Mueller to paint a 3,423-ft² (318-m²) anamorphic reproduction of the movie's poster on the pavement outside London's Westfield Shopping Centre. In the USA, Fox promoted the movie with an ice statue of the character Scrat. Its height made it, briefly, a record-holder, but today the world's **tallest ice sculpture** is a 53-ft 2.58-in-tall (16.22-m) piece created by the People's Government of Yichun city, China, on January 19, 2010.

★FINGER PAINTING

A finger painting measuring 22,619.51 ft² (2,101.43 m²) was created by 3,242 students in Hong Kong, China, on November 26, 2009.

★SHUTTLECOCK MOSAIC

A shuttlecock mosaic measuring 326.95 ft² (30.375 m²) was created by Fuqiang Zhao (China) on August 2, 2009. It comprised 5,236 individual shuttlecocks and depicted two interlaced hearts and the words "Show the love with shuttlecocks, be together forever".

★BEAD MOSAIC

The largest bead mosaic measures 72.33 ft² (6.72 m²) and was realized by Cao Zhitao (China) at an event organized by the Fuxin Municipal Government in Fuxin City, Liaoning Province, China, on October 25, 2009. The mosaic contained more than 30,000 agate beads.

★PAINTING BY NUMBERS

The largest painting by numbers measures 26,493 ft² (2,461.3 m²) and was created by 960 students from Mingren Elementary School in Tongliao City, Inner Mongolia, China, on September 30, 2009.

★GROUND-BASED DIGITAL LUNAR MOSAIC

On April 4, 2009, 11 amateur astronomers (all UK) used a telescope owned by broadcaster Patrick Moore (UK) to capture 288 images of the Moon. These were then digitally stitched together to make a lunar mosaic 87.4 megapixels in size.

LONGEST PAINTING BY NUMBERS

The world's longest painting by numbers measures 3,147 ft 5 in (959.35 m) long and is entitled Birds and Wetlands. It was created by 2,041 participants at an event organized by the Hong Kong Wetland Park and was staged at their premises in Hong Kong, China, on October 17, 2009.

EXTRA!
FOR MORE OUTSIZED ENDEAVORS, TURN TO P.200, P.204, AND P.206.

★ PAVEMENT ART

Chalk pavement art measuring 18,372 ft 8 in (5,600 m) long and 6 ft 6 in (2 m) wide was created by 5,000 students from Jena, Germany, on June 5, 2009.

★ CARTOON STRIP

The students, teachers and members of Vasavi Vidhyalaya Matriculation School, Trichy, India, created a continuous 1,971-ft 8-in (601-m) cartoon strip. It was measured in Tamil Nadu, India, on January 25, 2010.

MISCELLANY

★ LEAST VALUABLE ART COLLECTION IN A PUBLIC MUSEUM

The Museum of Bad Art's (MOBA) collection in Boston, Massachusetts, USA, has the lowest value of any public museum's art collection. Its 573 works are worth a total of just $1,197.35.

ACTUAL SIZE

★ OLDEST FIGURATIVE SCULPTURE

The Venus of Hohle Fels is the name given to a female figurine carved from a mammoth tusk and dated to c. 33,000 BC. It was discovered in the Hohle Fels ("Hollow Rock") cave near Ulm in Baden-Württemberg, Germany, in September 2008 by Nicolas Conard and a team from the University of Tübingen, Germany.

★ LARGEST INFLATABLE SCULPTURE

Gulliver has a volume of 63,252.45 ft³ (1,791.11 m³) and measures 196 ft 10 in x 65 ft 7 in x 22 ft 11 in (60 x 20 x 7 m) in size. It was presented and measured in Taipei, Taiwan, on July 20, 2009.

★ LARGEST MODELING BALLOON SCULPTURE

John Cassidy (USA) used 434 modeling balloons to make a biplane that measured 192 in (490 cm) wide and 147 in (375 cm) long on September 25, 2009.

★ CONFETTI MOSAIC

Nikki Douthwaite (UK) made a mosaic consisting of 587,000 hole-punched dots measuring 10 ft 1 in x 6 ft 10 in (3.07 x 2.08 m) in February–June 2008.

★ MURAL (SOLO)

Ernesto Espiridion Rios Rocha (Mexico) single-handedly created a mural covering 18,066 ft² (1,678 m²) in Mazatlán, Mexico, on October 6, 2009.

LONGEST...

★ PAINTING

The longest painting measures 16,256 ft 6 in (4,955 m) long and was created by 8,000 school students (all Bahrain) at an event organized by the Ministry of Education in Manama, Bahrain, on December 13, 2009. The theme of the painting was "life in Bahrain."

★ OLDEST PAINTING ON A WALL

In October 2006, the French archaeological mission at Dja'de al-Mughara – a Neolithic settlement on the Euphrates River near Aleppo, Syria – identified walls of a house that bore a series of geometric paintings. Measuring 25.1 ft² (2 m²), the wall paintings date from c. 9,000 BC.

THUNDER BAY, ON, CANADA
Despite having an artificial leg, Terry Fox (Canada, 1958–81) managed to raise Can$24.7 million (US$20.7 million) on a charity run from St John's, Newfoundland, to Thunder Bay, Ontario. This represents the **largest amount of money raised in a**

8°22'N
89°14'W

ENGINEERING AND TECHNOLOGY

★ ★ ★ ★ ★ ★ ★ ★ ★ ★ ★ ★ ★ ★ ★

★ HEAVIEST LIMOUSINE

The Midnight Rider is a tractor-trailer limousine that weighs 50,560 lb (22,933 kg), is 70 ft (21.3 m) long and 13 ft 8 in (4.1 m) high. This mighty motor features three lounges and a separate bar, and can accommodate 40 passengers served by a crew of four. It was designed by Michael Machado and Pamela Bartholemew (both USA) in California, USA, and began operation on September 3, 2004.

CAR
THE PLUSH INTERIOR DECOR IS BASED ON THE DAYS OF THE RAILROAD PULLMAN CARS, WHICH WERE POPULAR FROM THE MID-19TH CENTURY.

BAR
THE BAR CONTAINS AIR-SUSPENSION SEATS FOR A SMOOTH RIDE, SATELLITE TV AND LARGE MOVIE SCREENS, AND AN INTERNAL PHONE SYSTEM WITH FOUR OUTSIDE LINES!

★ **NEW RECORD**
★ **UPDATED RECORD**

EXTRA!
TURN TO PP. 212–213
FOR MORE VEHICLE
RECORDS.

CONTENTS

ENGINEERING AND TECHNOLOGY
ARCHI-TECTURE

★ NEW RECORD ★ UPDATED RECORD

★HIGHEST OBSERVATION DECK

A glass observation deck 1,568 ft 1 in (477.96 m) above street level is located on the 100th floor of the Shanghai World Financial Center in Pudong, China. The mixed-use skyscraper also houses the world's **highest hotel** – the Park Hyatt Shanghai occupies floors 79 to 93.

★LARGEST REINFORCED CONCRETE CEMENT FLAT ROOF SPAN

The Satsang Hall within the Govind Devji's Temple in Jaipur, India, has a reinforced concrete cement flat roof with a single span of 119 ft (36.27 m). It was designed by N M Roof Designers Ltd, and the hall was dedicated to the public on July 23, 2009.

★LARGEST REVOLVING RESTAURANT

Bellini is an Italian and international cuisine restaurant located on the 45th floor of Mexico City's World Trade Center. The establishment opened in 1994 and has an area of 11,244.58 ft² (1,044.66 m²).

★ LARGEST SHOPPING MALL

The Dubai Mall in Dubai, UAE, has an internal floor area of 5.9 million ft² (548,127 m²) over four levels. It houses 1,200 retail outlets and more than 160 food and drink outlets, and opened on November 4, 2008.

LARGEST HOTEL LOBBY

The lobby at the Hyatt Regency in San Francisco, California, USA, is 350 ft (107 m) long, 160 ft (49 m) wide and, at 170 ft (52 m), is the height of a 15-story building. The lobby has 300,000 cascading lights and features trees, a stream, and a fountain.

★TALLEST BUILDING

The Burj Khalifa (formally Burj Dubai) opened on January 17, 2009 in Dubai, UAE. It topped out at a record-breaking 2,717 ft (828 m), making it not only the tallest man-made structure on Earth but also the **★tallest building ever**.

HIGH!
THE RECORD-BREAKING BURJ KHALIFA ALSO HOLDS THE TITLE FOR THE ★BUILDING WITH THE MOST FLOORS, AT 160 STORYS!

RISE!
DUBAI IS HOME TO A RANGE OF OTHER IMPRESSIVE STRUCTURES, INCLUDING THE ROSE RAYHAAN, THE ★TALLEST HOTEL, STANDING AT 1,092 FT 6 IN (333 M).

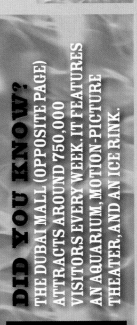

★ LARGEST STEEL STRUCTURE

Designed by Swiss architects Herzog & de Meuron, the Beijing Olympic Stadium, also known as the Bird's Nest, cost $423 million to construct and has a floor space of 2,777,088 ft² (258,000 m²) on a 51-acre (21-ha) site. The main body of the stadium is a saddle-shaped elliptic steel structure weighing 42,000 tons (38,100 tonnes).

HIGHEST CONCENTRATION OF THEME HOTELS

There are more than 16 theme hotels on the Strip in Las Vegas, Nevada, USA. Themes include the skylines of Paris and New York, Treasure Island, and Venetian. Las Vegas boasts an incredible 120,000 hotel rooms, nearly one for every four of its inhabitants.

LARGEST RETRACTABLE STADIUM ROOF

Completed in June 1989, the roof of the SkyDome, home of the Toronto Blue Jays baseball team located near the CN Tower in Toronto, Canada, covers 8 acres (3.2 ha), spans 685 ft (209 m) at its widest, and rises to 282 ft (86 m). It weighs 12,125 tons (11,000 tonnes) and takes 20 minutes to open fully. When retracted, the entire field and 91% of the seats are uncovered.

LARGEST AIRPORT PASSENGER TERMINAL

The Hong Kong International Airport passenger terminal building is 0.8 miles (1.3 km) long and covers 5,920,150 ft² (550,000 m²). It has a capacity of 45 million passengers a year, arriving on 460 flights every day, and cost $20 billion to build. The baggage hall alone is as big as the Yankee Stadium in New York City, USA.

★ TALLEST STEEL STRUCTURE

Willis Tower (formerly Sears Tower) in Chicago, Illinois, USA, is a 1,451-ft-tall (442-m), 108-story office skyscraper constructed from steel. The building's design includes nine steel-unit square tubes in a 3 x 3 arrangement, with a 75 x 75 ft (22 x 22 m) footprint. Completed in 1974, it has 4.56 million ft² (423,637 m²) of floor space.

★ TALLEST CONCRETE STRUCTURE

Completed in 2009, the 92-story Trump International Hotel & Tower in Chicago, Illinois, USA, tops out at 1,170 ft (360 m), or 1,389 ft (423 m) including the building's spire. Designed by Skidmore, Owings, and Merrill, the complex features 486 residential apartments and a 339-room hotel, and is the world's tallest formwork concrete structure.

LARGEST RESIDENTIAL PALACE

The palace (Istana Nurul Iman) of HM the Sultan of Brunei in the capital Bandar Seri Begawan is the largest residence in the world, with a floor space of 2,152,780 ft² (200,000 m²), 1,788 rooms and 257 lavatories.

The Council on Tall Buildings and Urban Habitat provide official guidelines on big structures.

TRIVIA

"In China, a bird's nest is very expensive, something you eat on special occasions."

Architect Li Xinggang explains the origins of the stadium's nickname

★ LARGEST DEPARTMENT STORE

Built by Shinsegae Co. Ltd and opened on June 26, 2009, the Shinsegae ("New World") Centum City Department Store in Busan, South Korea, covers an area of 3.16 million ft² (293,905 m²), beating the previous record holder, the famous Macy's store in New York City, USA, by more than 1.022 million ft² (95,000 m²).

ENGINEERING AND TECHNOLOGY
ROLLER COASTERS

COSTLY THE ★MOST EXPENSIVE ROLLER COASTER JUST IN TERMS OF PURE STEEL IS *STEEL DRAGON 2000* IN MIE, JAPAN, WHICH COST $50 MILLION IN 2000. FOR THE PRICIEST ROLLER COASTER INCLUDING SETS AND EXTRAS, SEE BELOW.

★FASTEST (ABSOLUTE)

The *ring°racer* Formula One-themed coaster at the Nürburgring racetrack in Nürburg, Germany, features a pneumatic launch system that blasts riders to 134.8 mph (216.9 km/h) in a breathtaking 2.5 seconds – twice as fast as a Formula One car.

★MOST TRACK INVERSIONS

Colossus at Thorpe Park, Chertsey, Surrey, UK, turns riders upside down a total of 10 times during each 2,789-ft (850-m) run. The ride has a maximum height of 98 ft (30 m) and a top speed of 40 mph (65 km/h). The inversions include a vertical loop, a twin cobra roll, a twin corkscrew, and five heart rolls. The *Tenth Ring Roller Coaster* of Chimelong Paradise in Guangzhou, China, also holds the record, but is a duplicate of *Colossus*.

FASTEST

★ABSOLUTE

See *ring°racer*, *left*.

★4TH DIMENSION

This type of coaster features cars that sit either side of the track and spin about a horizontal axis. The ★**first 4th dimension coaster** was *X* at Six Flags Magic Mountain, in 2002, but the ★**fastest** is *Eejanaika* at Fuji-Q Highland in Fujiyoshida, Yamanashi, Japan, which reaches 78.3 mph (126 km/h).

FLYING

Tatsu at Six Flags Magic Mountain in Valencia, California, USA, is the fastest flying coaster – that is, its riders travel with their backs parallel to the track to give the impression of flight. It reaches speeds of 62 mph (99.7 km/h). At 170 ft (51.8 m) high, it is also the world's **tallest flying coaster**.

SHUTTLE

A shuttle coaster is one that does not complete a full circuit and must therefore travel out and back. The speed record for this category of coaster is shared by *Superman the Escape* at Six Flags Magic Mountain, Valencia, California, USA, and *Tower of Terror* at Dreamworld, Gold Coast, Australia. Both opened in 1997 and both register a top speed of 100 mph (161 km/h).

★MOST EXPENSIVE

Expedition Everest was opened by Disney for $100 million in 2006 after six years of research and construction. The concept is a train journey through the Himalayas that uses a shortcut via Forbidden Mountain, wherein lies the fearsome Yeti – an enormous 22-ft-tall (6.7-m) audio-animatronic beast controlled by 19 actuators and covered in 1,000 ft² (93 m²) of fur.

TOP 10 FASTEST

	SPEED	COASTER	PARK	LOCATION	DATE
*	134.8 mph	ring°racer	Nürburgring	Nürburg, Germany	2009
1	128 mph	Kingda Ka	Six Flags Great Adventure	Jackson, New Jersey, USA	2005
2	120 mph	Top Thrill Dragster	Cedar Point	Sandusky, Ohio, USA	2003
3	106.9 mph	Dodonp	Fuji-Q Highland	Fujiyoshida, Yamanashi, Japan	2001
4	100 mph	Superman the Escape	Six Flags Magic Mountain	Valencia, California, USA	1997
		Tower of Terror	Dreamworld	Coomera, Australia	1997
5	95 mph	Steel Dragon 2000	Nagashima Spa Land	Nagashima, Kuwana Mie, Japan	2000
6	93 mph	Millennium Force	Cedar Point	Sandusky, Ohio, USA	2000
*	90 mph	Intimidator 305 (above)	Kings Dominion	Doswell, Virginia, USA	2010
7	85 mph	Goliath	Six Flags Magic Mountain	Valencia, California, USA	2000
		Phantom's Revenge	Kennywood	West Mifflin, Pennsylvania, USA	1991
		Titan	Six Flags Over Texas	Arlington, Texas, USA	2001
8	83.9 mph	Furius Baco	PortAventura Park	Salou, Tarragona, Spain	2007
9	82 mph	Xcelerator	Knott's Berry Farm	Buena Park, California, USA	2002
10	80.8 mph	Fujiyama	Fuji-Q Highland	Fujiyoshida, Yamanashi, Japan	1996
		Thunder Dolphin	Tokyo Dome City	Bunkyo Tokyo, Japan	2003

Source: Roller Coaster Database * Unopened at time of going to press

DID YOU KNOW?

THE CONTINENT WITH THE MOST ROLLER COASTERS IS ASIA, WITH 828; NORTH AMERICA IS NEXT, WITH 731.

The longest roller coaster of all is *Steel Dragon 2000*: 8,133 ft 2 in long (2,478.9 m), it opened on August 1, 2000.

TRIVIA

★ UPDATED RECORD ★ NEW RECORD

★ SUSPENDED

The speed record for suspended coasters – in which the riders hang from the track and pivot from side to side, emphasizing the track's banks and turns – is shared between *Vortex* at Canada's Wonderland in Vaughan, Ontario, Canada, and *Ninja* at Six Flags Magic Mountain in Valencia, California, USA. Both can reach 55 mph (88.5 km/h).

FASTEST (WOODEN)

Colossos at Heide-Park Soltau in Lower Saxony, Germany, reaches a peak speed of 74.6 mph (120 km/h). It is also the **tallest operating wooden coaster** at 196 ft 10 in (60 m).

TALLEST

ABSOLUTE

Kingda Ka, see *Tallest absolute* (right).

★ 4TH DIMENSION

At 249 ft 4 in (76 m) tall, *Eejanaika* at Fuji-Q Highland in Yamanashi Prefecture, Japan, is the loftiest of the 4th dimension coasters. The 2-min 10-sec ride opened at a cost of just over Y3.5 billion ($35 million).

FLYING

Tatsu, see *Fastest flying coaster,* opposite page.

SHUTTLE

Superman the Escape at Six Flags Magic Mountain, Valencia, California, USA, opened in 1997 at a height of 415 ft (126.5 m).

★ SUSPENDED

Vortex at Wonderland in Vaughan, Ontario, Canada, reaches a peak of 91 ft (27.7 m), making it the world's tallest suspended ride.

STEEPEST

★ ABSOLUTE

Mumbo Jumbo at Flamingo Land Theme Park & Zoo in Malton, UK, has an angle of descent of 112°. The 98-ft-tall (30-m) ride was opened on July 4, 2009 at a cost of £4 million ($6.3 million). The extreme drop exerts a maximum force of 4 g.

WOODEN

El Toro at Six Flags Great Adventure, New Jersey, USA, has a drop of 76°. The 4,400-ft (1,341-m) ride lasts 1 min 43 sec, reaching speeds of 75 mph (120 km/h). It towers 188 ft (57.3 m) above the theme park at its tallest point.

★ SHUTTLE

The steepest angle of descent on a shuttle-style coaster is 90°, a record currently held by at least 14 different rides. The most recent shuttle-style coaster to open was the 196-ft (60-m) *Aftershock* at the Silverwood Theme Park in Athol, Idaho, USA, which had relocated from Six Flags Great America in Gurnee, Illinois, USA.

TALLEST (ABSOLUTE)

Kingda Ka at Six Flags Great Adventure in New Jersey, USA, reaches a height of 456 ft (139 m). It opened in spring 2005 and at the time was the world's fastest coaster.

ENGINEERING AND TECHNOLOGY
BIG ENGINEERING

★ ★ ★ ★ ★ ★ ★ ★ ★ ★ ★ ★ ★ ★ ☆

★ LARGEST FLOOD DEFENCE

The Delta Works off the coast of Holland is a huge series of dams, locks, sluices, storm surge barriers, and dykes designed to protect low-lying areas of the country from the sea. Construction began in 1950 and ended in 1997 with the completion of the Maeslantkering and the Hartelkering barriers. The Delta Works contain some 10,250 miles (16,495 km) of dykes and around 300 structures.

★ LARGEST MAN-MADE EXCAVATION

The Bingham Canyon Copper Mine near Salt Lake City, Utah, USA, is the world's largest manmade excavation. More than 5.9 billion tons (5.4 billion tonnes) of rock have been excavated from it since 1906. Visible from space, it measures 2.5 miles (4 km) across and 0.75 miles (1.2 km) deep and has been called "the richest hole on Earth." As of 2004, more than 16.9 million tons (15.4 million tonnes) of copper have been produced from the mine, as well as 23 million oz (652 million g) of gold and 190 million oz (5.3 billion g) of silver.

★ HEAVIEST WEIGHT LIFTED BY CRANE

A barge, ballasted with water and weighing a hefty 44,385,667 lb (20,133 tonnes) was lifted by the "Taisun" crane at Yantai Raffles Shipyard, Yantai, China, on April 18, 2008.

★ LONGEST DRILLED OIL WELL

The world's longest drilled oil well is BD-04-A, with a total length of 40,320 ft (12,289 m). It was completed in May 2008 by Maersk Oil Qatar and Qatar Petroleum, in the Al-Shaheen offshore oil field off the coast of Qatar. The well includes a horizontal section measuring 35,770 ft (10,902 m).

★ LARGEST EXCAVATION BY HAND

Jagersfontein Mine near Jagersfontein, South Africa, is an open-pit mine that has provided some of the largest diamonds ever discovered. It operated as a mine from 1888 until 1971, first as an open mine and then as an underground mine. The Jagersfontein Mine was dug by hand to a depth of 660 ft (201 m) between 1888 and 1911. The area of the opening measures 48.55 acres (19.65 ha).

★ FARTHEST MANMADE LEANING TOWER

The "Capital Gate" has an inclination of 18 degrees and is 524 ft 11 in (160 m) high. It was designed by Global Architects RMJM (Dubai) and was completed in Abu Dhabi, United Arab Emirates, on January 4, 2010.

TALLEST BRIDGE

The 8,070-ft-long (2,460-m) Millau Viaduct across the Tarn Valley, France, is supported by seven concrete piers, the tallest of which measures 1,095 ft 4.8 in (333.88 m) from the ground to its highest point.

★ NEW RECORD
★ UPDATED RECORD

PEINER

HIGH THE DELTA WORKS HAS BEEN DECLARED ONE OF THE SEVEN WONDERS OF THE MODERN WORLD BY THE AMERICAN SOCIETY OF CIVIL ENGINEERS.

MIGHTY THE PROJECT WAS FINISHED AFTER ALMOST 50 YEARS IN 1997 WITH THE COMPLETION OF THE MAESLANTKERING AND HARTELKERING BARRIERS.

DID YOU KNOW?

AT 1,181 FT (360 M) LONG AND WEIGHING 225,282 GROSS TONNAGE, MS *OASIS OF THE SEAS* IS THE LARGEST PASSENGER SHIP.

MS *Allure of the Seas*, sister ship to the *Oasis*, is due to launch in 2010.

TRIVIA

★LARGEST LAKE CREATED BY A NUCLEAR EXPLOSION

On January 15, 1965, the Soviet Union detonated a 140-kiloton nuclear device underneath a dry bed of the Chagan River, Kazakhstan. Part of the Soviets' Nuclear Explosions for the National Economy program, the raised rim of the resulting crater dammed the river, allowing the creation of a reservoir, now known as Lake Chagan. It has a volume of around 3,531,000 ft³ (100,000 m³).

TALLEST HOSPITAL

Guy's Tower at Guy's Hospital in London, UK, is 468 ft (142.6 m) tall. It was completed in 1974 and has 34 stories.

★LARGEST AUTOCLAVE

An autoclave is typically used to sterilize medical or laboratory instruments. In August 2006, ASC Process Systems (USA) announced it had built an autoclave with an internal volume of 82,000 ft³ (2,321 m³). It is designed to process components of the Boeing 787 Dreamliner passenger aircraft by subjecting them to temperatures of up to 450°F (232°C) and pressures of up to 10.2 bar.

TALLEST BOAT LIFT

The Strépy-Thieu boat lift on the Canal du Centre, Hainaut, Belgium, uses a counterweight system to carry boats a vertical distance of 240 ft (73.15 m) from its upstream and downstream sections. The two boxes, or caissons, that each boat enters are 367 x 39 ft (112 x 12 m) and weigh between 7,936 and 9,259 tons (7,200–8,400 tonnes), depending on the current water level. It takes seven minutes for the vertical journey to be completed.

★TALLEST TRANSMISSION TOWER

At Jiangyin, Jiangsu Province, China, two electricity transmission towers stand on opposite banks of the Yangtze River at 1,137 ft (346.5 m) tall. Their height allows the power lines to span the river, which is 7,556 ft (2,303 m) wide at this point. Another tower, on the Damaoshan Mountain in Zhoushan city, China, will be 1,213 ft (370 m) tall when it is completed in 2010.

★WIDEST CANAL

The Cape Cod Canal, which crosses the land that connects Cape Cod to mainland Massachusetts, USA, was constructed between 1909 and 1916. It is 17.4 miles (28 km) long and 540 ft (164.6 m) wide. It is a segment of the Atlantic Intracoastal Waterway, which runs for 3,000 miles (4,800 km) along the American east coast.

MOST EXPENSIVE OBJECT ON EARTH

The Itaipu hydroelectric dam on the Paraná River between Brazil and Paraguay cost $27 billion to build in 1984 ($35.93 billion today), which makes it the priciest object on Earth. Only the International Space Station (ISS) has cost more as a single project.

★TALLEST CHIMNEY DEMOLISHED BY EXPLOSIVES

The Westerholt Power Plant in Gelsenkirchen-Westerholt, Germany, was a coal power plant constructed in the 1960s and decommissioned in 2005. Its chimney, or smokestack, was constructed in 1997 and was 1,104 ft (337 m) high – the tallest in Germany at that time. It was demolished using explosives on December 3, 2006.

MOST SPACIOUS BUILDING

The Boeing Company's main assembly plant in Everett, Washington, USA, has a volume of 472 million ft³ (13.4 million m³) and a floor area of 98.3 acres (39.8 ha). Boeing's 747, 767, and 777 aircraft are assembled there.

EXTRA! FOR MORE AERONAUTICAL RECORDS, TURN BACK TO PP.116–117.

Willie Jones (USA) was admitted to Grady Memorial Hospital, Atlanta, Georgia, USA, on July 10, 1980 with heatstroke on a day when the temperature reached 90°F (32.2°C). His temperature was found to be 115.7°F (46.5°C) – the **highest known body temperature**.

33°45'N 84°23'W

ENGINEERING AND TECHNOLOGY
ROAD & RAIL

★ ★ ★ ★ ★ ★ ★ ★ ★ ★ ★ ★ ★

{ *"I don't have to be a potty mouth, chew tobacco, and be 300 pounds to drive a truck."* }

Lisa Kelly, ice road trucker

★ LONGEST ICE ROAD

Canada's Tibbitt to Contwoyto Winter Road was first used in 1982 to supply mines in the Northwest Territories. Open from January to the end of March, the ice road is rebuilt annually. It is 353 miles (568 km) long, 308 miles (495 km) of which traverses frozen lakes.

★ LONGEST UNDERWATER ROAD TUNNEL

The Tokyo Bay Aqua-Line is a combination of bridge and tunnel that spans Tokyo Bay, Japan. The tunnel section is 31,440 ft (9,583 m) long and was opened in 1997.

★ OLDEST "MAGIC ROUNDABOUT"

Ring junctions were first designed by the Road Research Laboratory (UK) in order to ease traffic congestion at busy junctions. The first opened in Swindon, UK, in 1972. Nicknamed the "Magic Roundabout," it consists of five mini-roundabouts connected together in a circle, allowing traffic to move in both directions around the main central island.

★ FASTEST JET-POWERED TRAIN

The M-497 was a prototype experimental train powered by two General Electric J47-19 jet engines. It was developed and tested in 1966 in the USA and was able to reach a top speed of 183 mph (296 km/h).

★ HIGHEST RAILROAD STATION

The Tanggula Railroad Station in Tibet is the highest in the world at 16,627 ft (5,068 m) above sea level. The unstaffed station on the Qingzang Railroad opened on July 1, 2006 and has a 0.77-mile-long (1.25-km) platform.

ROAD

DEADLIEST PLACE TO TRAVEL BY ROAD

According to findings from its first report on global road safety, the World Health Organization states that Eritrea, in Africa, is the deadliest place to travel by road in terms of deaths caused by road traffic accidents. There were 48 deaths per 100,000 people in 2007.

★ LARGEST NATIONAL ROAD NETWORK

The USA has 4,017,661 miles (6,465,799 km) of roads, of which 2,615,870 miles (4,209,835 km) are paved. China is in second place with 2,226,817 miles (3,583,715 km) of roads.

★ OLDEST STACK INTERCHANGE

The Four Level Interchange in Los Angeles, California, USA, features, as its name suggests, four layers of multilane road and was first opened to the public in 1953. The interchange links US Route 101 to State Route 110 using a free-flowing design to help minimize LA's notorious congestion.

★ OLDEST SUBWAY TUNNEL

The Atlantic Avenue Tunnel beneath Brooklyn, USA, was built over a period of seven months in 1844. Running for 2,517 ft (767 m), it is 21 ft (6.4 m) wide and 17 ft (5.2 m) high. The tunnel was the first in the world built underground in order to improve urban congestion, public safety, and rail operations. It operated until 1861, when the ends were sealed off, and was rediscovered in 1981.

SMALLEST ARMORED TRAIN

During World War II, the 15-in-gauge (381-mm) Romney, Hythe & Dymchurch Railway, which runs between Hythe and Dungeness along the coast of Kent, UK, was requisitioned by the British government for use in the war effort. Roughly a quarter of the size of UK standard-gauge trains, a steam locomotive and several passenger cars were given steel armor for wartime use.

FASTEST STEAM LOCOMOTIVE

The London North Eastern Railway "Class A4" No. 4468 *Mallard* hauled seven passenger cars at a speed of 125 mph (201 km/h) between Grantham, Lincolnshire, and Peterborough, Cambridgeshire, UK, on July 3, 1938.

RAIL

★ LONGEST SUBWAY BY TOTAL LENGTH

The London Underground, London, UK, has a combined length of around 250 miles (400 km) of track, as well as 270 stations. Some 45% of it is underground. With its first section opening in 1863, the London Underground is also the **oldest subway system** in the world.

★ LARGEST NATIONAL RAIL NETWORK

The USA has some 140,695 miles (226,427 km) of rail. Second place belongs to Russia, with 54,156 miles (87,157 km) of track.

HEAVIEST HAUL RAILROAD

On April 8, 2008, the Fortescue Metals Group (Australia) completed 155 miles (250 km) of single-track railroad capable of running 1.53-mile-long (2.5-km) trains carrying a gross load of 42,328 tons (38,400 tonnes) of ore.

OLDEST STEAM LOCOMOTIVE IN USE

The *Fairy Queen* was built in 1855 by Kitson Thompson Hewitson of Leeds, UK. Brought back into service in October 1997 hauling a twin-car train between Delhi Cantonment, Delhi, and Alwar, Rajasthan, India, the train now provides a popular service to tourists.

NEW RECORD
★ **UPDATED RECORD**

CHUFF!
THE FAIRY QUEEN WAS RESTORED AND MADE FULLY FUNCTIONAL IN 1966. WHEN NOT IN USE, IT IS KEPT AT THE INDIAN NATIONAL RAILWAY MUSEUM IN NEW DELHI.

CHUFF!
THE OFFICIAL SPEED OF THE FAIRY QUEEN IS 25 MPH (40 KM/H), ALTHOUGH IT IS CAPABLE OF GOING MUCH FASTER THAN THIS.

KNOXVILLE, TN, USA
FORDISC is the world's **most complete database of the human skeleton**. Established by the University of Tennessee's "Body Farm," it allows data captured from decomposing bodies to be organized and analyzed by forensic anthropologists.

35°58'N
83°55'W

ENGINEERING AND TECHNOLOGY
BIG STUFF

★ ★ ★ ★ ★ ★ ★ ★ ★ ★ ★ ★ ★ ★

LARGEST...

★ BACKPACK/RUCKSACK

A backpack/rucksack 9 ft 10 in (3 m) tall and 9 ft 8 in (2.95 m) wide, adorned with the character Lulu Caty, was manufactured by Lulu Caty (Rainbow Max Co., China) and unveiled in Dubai, UAE, on October 10, 2009.

★ CHRISTMAS STAR ORNAMENT

Measuring 103 ft 8 in (31.59 m) tall, the largest Christmas star ornament was constructed by Apple A Day Properties (India) and unveiled in Kochi, Kerala, India, on December 31, 2009. The giant festive decoration was created to celebrate the building of a new music academy in the city.

★ LARGEST SPORTS SHOE

A sports shoe measuring 13 ft 1 in (4 m) long, 5 ft 2 in (1.6 m) wide, and 5 ft 6 in (1.7 m) high was created by Launch Group (UK) in Cardiff, UK, in March 2009. It was made on behalf of supermarket chain Tesco's support for Cancer Research UK's Race for Life.

★ LARGEST SCREWDRIVER

Thomas Blackthorne (UK) owns the world's largest screwdriver. It has an acrylic handle that measures 7.6 in (19.5 cm) at its widest point and is 19.6 in (50 cm) long. The steel shaft is 1 in (25 mm) thick and projects a farther 20 in (51 cm), making the overall length 39.7 in (101 cm).

★ CUP OF TEA

Mercy Health Center of Fort Scott, Kansas, USA, made a cup of tea measuring 7.92 ft (2.41 m) in diameter, 1.96 ft (0.6 m) in height, and with a volume of 660 gal (3,000 liters). The giant cuppa was unveiled on September 26, 2009.

★ FAN

A fan measuring 27 ft 10 in (8.48 m) long and 17 ft (5.18 m) in height when fully opened was created by Goods of Desire (G.O.D.) and was unveiled at the G.O.D. Peak Galleria store in Hong Kong, China, on August 20, 2009. The fan was made from wood and paper and operated just like a standard-size fan of that construction.

★ GLASS OF SPRITZER

A spritzer with a volume of 109 gal (500 liters) was created by the Hungarian Wine Marketing Agency in Budapest, Hungary, on June 20, 2009. It was made by combining 54 gal (250 liters) each of Neszmely Rose wine and soda water.

★ GOLF TEE

Students of Jerry Havill's Team Problem Solving Course at Bay de Noc Community College in Escanaba, Michigan, USA, built a giant golf tee that measured 26 ft 8 in (8.13 m) long with a head diameter of 35 in (88.9 cm), and a shaft width of 13.87 in (35.24 cm). It was unveiled on July 23, 2009.

★ POM-POM

A pom-pom measuring 3 ft (91.4 cm) high and 10 ft 5 in (320 cm) across was created by the creative arts department at Self Unlimited in Kent, UK, on June 30, 2009.

★ LONGEST USABLE GOLF CLUB

Measuring 13 ft 5 in (4.09 m) in length, the longest usable golf club was created and used by Denmark's Karsten Maas. The club was used to drive a ball a distance of 403 ft 6 in (123 m) on a Trackman device at the Bella Center, Copenhagen, Denmark, on January 24, 2009.

EXTRA! CAN'T GET ENOUGH BIG STUFF? NO PROBLEM – JUST TURN THE PAGE TO FIND MORE SCALED-UP RECORDS.

LARGEST BEACH BALL

An inflatable beach ball measuring 41 ft 3 in (12.59 m) in diameter was made by Westtoer (Belgium), and displayed in Liège, Belgium, on August 8, 2009.

LARGEST WARDROBE

Jan Bilý (Czech Republic) and his company Art-Style created a wardrobe that measures 19 ft 10 in (6.06 m) high, 13 ft 4 in (4.07 m) wide, and 4 ft 11 in (1.5 m) deep. The wardrobe, which has two doors, was presented and measured in Prague, Czech Republic, on September 10, 2009.

★ POSTER

A 139-ft 9-in x 207-ft (42.6 x 63.1-m) poster was created by Alpiq (Switzerland) and presented and measured at the Cleuson Dam near Nendaz, Switzerland, on February 8, 2010. The poster is a greeting to Swiss athletes at the Winter Olympics in Vancouver, Canada.

★ SANTA HAT

Measuring a whopping 50 ft 9 in (15.47 m) long and 27 ft (8.23 m) wide, the largest Santa hat was created by children from the Chill Youth Club (all Norway). The festive headgear, which took a total of three months to construct, was presented in Fredrikstad, Norway, on December 9, 2008.

★ TRUMPET

Benny J Mamoto (Indonesia) built a playable trumpet measuring 104 ft 11.8 in (32 m) long with a bell of 17 ft (5.20 m) in diameter, and 22 ft 3.7 in (6.8 m) in circumference. It was displayed in Tondano, North Sulawesi, Indonesia, on October 31, 2009.

LONGEST...

★ ABACUS

An abacus measuring 43 ft 0.14 in (13.11 m) was presented at an event organized by the Development & Reform Commission of Fuxin Municipal Government in Fuxin city, Liaoning province, China, on October 25, 2009.

★ COUCH

Fancy a nice long sit down? You could do worse than choose the world's longest couch, which was measured at 2,920 ft 9 in (890.25 m) in Sykkylven, Norway, on June 14, 2009. The super-size sofa, which was manufactured by 20 local furniture factories, was put together and displayed across the span of the Sykkylven bridge.

★ TABLECLOTH

A tablecloth measuring 3,776 ft 10.74 in (1,151.2 m) long and 5 ft 3 in (1.6 m) wide was made by Green Development Ltd (Poland) and unveiled in Żyrardów, Poland, on June 13, 2009.

★ WALK-THROUGH HORROR HOUSE

The Cutting Edge Haunted House in Fort Worth Texas, USA, had a walk-through measured at 2,261 ft 0.9 in (689.17 m) long on September 12, 2009.

★ WEDDING DRESS TRAIN

Watters Inc. (USA) created a wedding dress train 7,829 ft 6 in (2,386.44 m) long. It was measured in Round Mountain, Texas, USA, on December 19, 2009.

★ WOODEN CHAIN

Markley B Noel (USA) created a wooden chain measuring 487 ft 6 in (148.59 m) long in Kalamazoo, Michigan, USA, on October 2, 2009.

★ LONGEST RIDEABLE SURFBOARD

A surfboard measuring 30 ft 10 in (9.42 m) long was successfully ridden by Rico De Souza (Brazil, pictured) at Solemar Beach, Espirito Santo, Brazil, on June 12, 2009.

The **largest surfboard ever** was made by Nev Hyman (Australia) and is 39 ft 4 in (12 m) long, 9 ft 10 in (3 m) wide, and 11.8 in (30 cm) thick. It was launched in Queensland, Australia, on March 5, 2005.

TRASH

A RECORD 23-FT 4-IN-TALL (7.13-M), 15-FT 7-IN-WIDE (4.76-M) TRASH CAN WAS CREATED BY REALIZAR IMPACT MARKETING AND MODELO (PORTUGAL) IN JUNE 2009.

BRUSH

A WORLD-BEATING PAINTBRUSH MEASURING 14 FT 3 IN (4.35 M) IN LENGTH WAS CREATED BY PRIMAL

ENGINEERING AND TECHNOLOGY
BIG STUFF

★ LARGEST HIGH-DEFINITION TV SCREEN

A Diamond Vision High Definition LED television screen measuring 35 ft 8.4 in x 352 ft 9 in (10.88 x 107.52 m) was unveiled on January 28, 2010 at Meydan Racecourse, Dubai, UAE. The world-beating screen, which has a total surface area of 12,591.83 ft² (1,169.82 m²), was created by the Mitsubishi Electric Corporation (Japan) for the Meydan City Corporation, which is based in Dubai.

★ LONGEST BALLOON CHAIN

A balloon chain measuring 2.92 miles (4.77 km) long was constructed by customers of the shopping mall Belforte (Italy). The chain, which used 42,000 balloons, was displayed and measured in Serravalle, Italy, on July 12, 2009.

★ LONGEST CHAIN OF FIRE HOSES

Verband Bernischer Gemeiden and Gebäudeversicherung Bern organized the connection of the longest chain of fire hoses, which carried water a distance of 34.8 miles (56 km) between Frutigen and Bern, Switzerland, on September 19, 2003.

LARGEST...

	OBJECT	DIMENSIONS	RECORD HOLDER	DATE ACHIEVED
★	Ballpoint pen	11 ft 11 in (3.63 m) long	Biswaroop Roy Chowdhury (India)	March 29, 2009
★	Canned food structure	115,527 cans	Disney VoluntEARS (USA)	February 11, 2010
★	Cardboard box	20 ft 1.2 in (6.12 m) wide; 46 ft 1.2 in (14.05 m) long; 9 ft 0.3 in (2.75 m) tall	Chegg.com (USA)	September 19, 2009
★	Ceramic plate	6,327 lb 4 oz (2,870 kg) in weight; 19 ft (5.8 m) in diameter	Joe Kabalan and the Association of Lebanese Industrialists (both Lebanon)	October 14, 2009
★	Chair	98 ft 5 in (30 m) tall	XXXLutz and Holzleimbauwerk Wiehag GmbH (both Austria)	February 9, 2009
★	Chess set	Board: 19 ft 4 in (5.89 m) on each side King: 47 in (119 cm) tall; 1 ft 2 in (37.4 cm) wide	Medicine Hat Chess Club (Canada)	May 27, 2009
★	Chinowa	36 ft 1 in (11 m) in diameter	Aichiken Gokokujinjya (Japan)	June 28, 2009
★	Chopsticks	27 ft 6 in (8.4 m)	Wakasa Chopsticks Industry Cooperative (Japan)	March 22, 2009
★	Cup of hot chocolate	84.07 gal (318.23 liters)	City of St Thomas (Canada)	December 22, 2009
★	Cup of soft drink	1,213.5 gal (4,593.7 liters)	People's Government of Jiagedaqi District, China	August 6, 2009
★	Cushion	33 ft 0.8 in x 33 ft 0.8 in (10.08 x 10.08 m)	Shanghai Konglong Textile Ornaments Co., Ltd (China)	May 29, 2009
★	Dog biscuit	231 lb 7 oz (105 kg)	Warner Bros. Entertainment UK and the Canine Cookie Company (both UK)	October 5, 2009
★	Flag (draped)	467,206.99 ft² (43,404.95 m²)	Grace Galindez-Gupana (Philippines)	April 11, 2009
★	Flute	10 ft 7 in (3.25 m) long; 1.97 in (5 cm) in diameter	Fushun Youth and Children Palace (China)	July 14, 2009
★	Soccer shirt	234 ft 1 in x 259 ft 8 in (71.35 x 79.15 m)	AVEA (Turkey)	April 5, 2009
★	Fresh flower garland	1.3 miles (2.2 km) long	The people of Peiting (Germany)	July 19, 2009

★ NEW RECORD ★ UPDATED RECORD

★ LARGEST CARD STRUCTURE

Bryan Berg (USA) completed a playing card structure measuring 34 ft 1.05 in (10.39 m) long, 9 ft 5.39 in (2.88 m) tall, and 11 ft 7.37 in (3.54 m) deep at the Venetian Macao-Resort-Hotel in Macau, China, on March 10, 2010. The structure, which was made of 218,792 cards, was a replica of the Macau skyline.

LARGEST... CONT'D

OBJECT	DIMENSIONS	RECORD HOLDER	DATE ACHIEVED
★ Glow stick	9 ft 10 in (3 m) tall; 7.87 in (20 cm) in diameter	KNIXS GmbH (Germany)	June 29, 2009
★ Handwoven carpet	10,279 ft² (955 m²)	Samovar Carpets & Antiques (Kuwait)	November 1, 2009
★ Horseshoe	1 ft 10 in (56 cm) long; 2 ft (61.5 cm) wide	Caritas Tagesstätte Krumbach (Austria)	June 21, 2008
★ Impossible bottle	15.8 gal (60 liters)	Aidano Dallafiora (Italy)	August 24, 2009
★ Inflatable sofa	67 ft 3 in (20.5 m) long; 26 ft 9 in (8.10 m) wide; 26 ft 5 in (8.1 m) tall	Jacobs Krönung (Germany)	April 14, 2009
★ Javelin	94 ft 7 in (28.83 m) long; 11 in (30 cm) in diameter	Vattenfall (Germany)	July 31, 2009
★ Model aircraft by wingspan	49 ft 2 in (15 m) wingspan	Markus Stadelmann (Switzerland)	May 8, 2009
★ Postcard	524.74 ft² (48.75 m²)	Deutsche Post (Germany) and Toyota Cars (Japan)	August 10, 2009
★ Punching bag	22 ft 10 in (6.97 m) tall; 3 ft 2 in (98 cm) wide; 1,763 lb (800 kg) in weight	Helio Dipp, Jr and Cintia Schmitt (both Brazil)	March 28, 2009
★ Scissors	7 ft 7 in (2.31 m) from tip to handle	Neerja Roy Chowdhury (India)	August 16, 2009
★ Sheet of handmade paper	45 ft 7 in x 22 ft 7 in (13.9 m x 6.9 m)	Made for Masaki Takahashi and Kazuki Maeda (both Japan)	August 19, 2009
★ Shopping bag (made from paper)	13 ft 8 in x 21 ft 8 in x 5 ft 10 in (4.18 m x 6.62 m x 1.79 m)	Kaufland (Romania)	May 18, 2009
★ Shower	100 ft (30.48 m) long; 40 ft (12.19 m) wide; 10 ft (3.04 m) tall	PertPlus and Chicago firefighters (both USA)	July 9, 2009
★ Sky lantern	38 ft 3 in (11.68 m) high; 32 ft 9 in (10 m) wide; 30 ft 6 in (9.3 m) deep; 38,360.2 ft³ (1,086.24 m³) in volume	Jhon Freddy Daza, Eyder Burbano, and Rene Muñoz (all Colombia)	January 11, 2009
★ Ten Commandments tablet	700.08 ft² (65.04 m²)	Grace Galindez-Gupana (Philippines)	April 11, 2009
★ Trousers	40 ft (12.19 m) long; 26 ft (7.92 m) waist	Rishi S. Thobhani from R.S.T. International Limited (UK)	May 23, 2009

★ LARGEST SANDAL

Created in December 2003 by Nelson Jimenez Florez (Colombia), the largest sandal measures 21 ft 7 in (6.6 m) long, 6 ft 6 in (2 m) wide, and 11 ft 5 in (3.5 m) high and was designed on behalf of Diseos Ruddy, Bucaramanga, Colombia.

★ LARGEST HANDBAG

A handbag created by Picard and Klar in Offenbach, Germany, measured 16 ft 4 in (5 m) tall, 21 ft 3 in (6.5 m) long, and 8 ft 2 in (2.5 m) deep in June 2001.

★ LARGEST PACKAGED PRODUCT DISPLAY

A display of promotional Kleenex tissue boxes measuring 10,228.54 ft³ (289.64 m³) was constructed by Al-Mansouriya Consumers Trading Co. and Olayan Kimberly-Clark (both Kuwait) at The Sultan Center, Kuwait, on March 7, 2010.

★ LONGEST WOODEN BENCH

A 2,011-ft 6-in-long (613.13-m) bench was built by a group of people from Osieczna (Poland) and unveiled in Szlachta, Poland, on August 27, 2005.

★ LARGEST GARDEN SPADE

An 11-ft 10-in-tall (3.61-m) spade with a 1-ft 11-in-wide (59.8-cm) blade was manufactured by Rollins Bulldog Tools Ltd (UK) and presented in Wigan, UK, on December 7, 2009.

★ LARGEST BUTTON-DOWN SHIRT

On June 25, 2009, Walbusch (Germany) presented a button-down shirt 214 ft 6 in (65.39 m) long, with a chest of 172 ft 11 in (52.72 m), and sleeves of 78 ft 8 in x 51 ft 3 in (23.98 m x 15.64 m). The gargantuan garment was measured at the LTU Arena, in Düsseldorf, Germany.

MITT
THE LARGEST BASEBALL MITT MEASURES 26 FT (8 M) HIGH, 32 FT (9.7 M) WIDE, AND 12 FT (3.6 M) DEEP, AND WEIGHS 20,000 LB (9,070 KG).

★ LARGEST GARDEN GNOME

A giant garden gnome measuring 17 ft 8 in (5.41 m) tall was made by the company PHU MALPOL (Poland) and presented in Nowa Sol, Poland, on June 2, 2009. It was built from fiberglass-covered polystyrene.

MAT
USING 70,000 BEER MATS, SVEN GOEBEL (GERMANY) BUILT A STRUCTURE MEASURING 9 FT 10 IN (3 M) TALL AND 16 FT 4 IN (5 M) WIDE IN GERMANY ON AUGUST 16, 2004.

ENGINEERING AND TECHNOLOGY
ALTERNATIVE ENERGIES

★LARGEST TOKAMAK

With a radius of 9 ft 8.5 in (2.96 m) and a plasma volume of 3,500 ft³ (100 m³), the Joint European Torus in Culham, Oxfordshire, UK, is the largest operating tokamak in the world. Tokamaks use a magnetic field to confine plasma and are used for experiments in nuclear fusion.

★LARGEST PHOTOVOLTAIC POWER PLANT

The Olmedilla Photovoltaic Park in Olmedilla, Spain, uses around 162,000 solar panels to generate a maximum of 60 megawatts on a sunny day. Completed in September 2008, it can provide enough electricity to power around 40,000 homes.

★ **NEW RECORD**
★ **UPDATED RECORD**

★OLDEST ALTERNATIVE FUEL

In medieval Europe, *c.* 1500, the overuse of wood for burning led to general shortages and deforestation. Around this time, Europeans began to burn coal instead of wood, the first time in history that an alternative fuel was adopted because of shortages of conventional fuel.

★LARGEST HYDROELECTRIC WAVE-POWER DEVICE

In November 2009, Aquamarine Power (UK) launched Oyster, a 213-ton (194-tonne) device bolted to the seabed off the Orkney Islands, UK. It consists of a simple mechanical hinged flap that, at 33 ft (10 m) below the sea's surface, oscillates with passing waves and drives hydraulic pistons that power a turbine. This demonstration model is designed to supply around 315 kilowatts of power.

Hydro power remains the **largest contributor to renewable energy**, reaching a capacity of 770 gigawatts in 2007.

★HIGHEST-ALTITUDE WIND GENERATOR

In December 2007, a wind generator designed to supply power to a gold mine became operational in the Veladero mine in San Juan, in the Andes mountain range, Argentina. Built by DeWind (Germany) and owned by Barrick (Canada), the hub of the generator is 13,484 ft (4,110 m) above sea level.

On March 11, 2009, strong winds across Spain allowed the country's wind power infrastructure to generate some 11,180 megawatts, 40% of all of its national electricity requirements – the ★**highest percentage of power generated by wind**.

★LARGEST SOLAR-POWERED BUILDING

In December 2009, China unveiled an office building in Dezhou, Shangdong province, that meets almost all of its energy needs with its solar-paneled roof. The building covers 807,000 ft² (75,000 m²) and contains research facilities, display areas, and a hotel.

Altamont Pas, California, USA, is the **largest wind farm**, with a record 7,300 turbines.

TRIVIA

★ MOST ELECTRICITY PRODUCED FROM A KITE

In 2008, scientists at Delft University of Technology, the Netherlands, successfully tested a kite-powered electricity-generating system known as Laddermill. The concept involves a kite being raised upward by the wind, with the strings of the kite attached to a generator on the ground. The test involved a single kite with an area of 107 ft² (10 m²) that was able to generate 10 kw of electricity while in flight – enough to power approximately 10 homes. The researchers believe that in time they could generate 100 megawatts of electricity

★ FIRST CLEAN COAL POWER STATION

In September 2008, a new prototype power plant went online at The Schwarze Pumpe power station, Spremberg, Germany. It is the first in the world to use the CCS technique – carbon capture and storage, which means it captures the CO_2 emissions produced from burning coal, preventing them from entering the atmosphere.

this way, enough for up to 100,000 homes.

★ LARGEST SOURCE OF HELIUM 3

Helium 3 is an isotope of helium that is a strong candidate as fuel for nuclear fusion. It is produced by the Sun and streams off into space as part of the solar wind. Helium 3 exists only as a trace on Earth but, on the Moon, with its lack of atmosphere and magnetic field, the solar Helium 3 atoms directly strike and embed themselves into the lunar soil. The isotope was discovered on the Moon by Apollo astronauts and scientists estimate there could be 1.1 million tons of it spread across the lunar surface – enough to power the whole world's energy needs for thousands of years.

★ FIRST OSMOTIC POWER PLANT

In November 2009, a prototype osmotic power plant went online on the banks of the Oslo fjord in Norway. It generates power using osmosis, which occurs naturally when two solutions of different concentrations meet each other at a semi-permeable membrane. The pressure difference generated as one liquid passes through the membrane can be converted to electricity.

In this prototype power station, the two liquids used are salt water from the sea and fresh water from runoff into the sea. The station's initial capacity is around 4 kilowatts, enough to heat a large kettle, but scientists hope that this can be increased to 25 megawatts by 2015.

★ FASTEST AUTOMOBILE POWERED BY BIOGAS

Jürgen Hohenester (Germany) reached a speed of 226.55 mph (364.6 km/h) in a biogas-powered automobile at the ATP testing facilities in Papenburg, Germany, on April 3, 2009. The technology was developed by TÜV Rheinland's Competence Center for Alternative Fuels.

★ LARGEST OFFSHORE WIND FARM

The Horns Rev 2 offshore wind farm was officially inaugurated on September 17, 2009. Located in a shallow region of the North Sea, off the coast of Denmark, it comprises 91 turbines, each with a maximum capacity of 2.3 megawatts, giving a total of 209 megawatts at peak production.

POWER THE USA IS THE GREATEST PRODUCER OF WIND POWER, WITH ABOUT 2% OF ITS ELECTRICITY PRODUCED IN THIS WAY. IT IS HOPED THAT THIS FIGURE WILL RISE TO 20% BY 2030.

WIND THE WORLD'S FIRST WIND FARM WAS BUILT IN 1980, AND LOCATED ON CROTCHED MOUNTAIN, NEW HAMPSHIRE, USA. ITS 20 TURBINES COULD PRODUCE 30 KILOWATTS EACH.

The Cleveland Convention Center, Ohio, USA, hosted the White Elephant Sale (instituted 1933) – the **largest ever jumble sale** – on October 18, 19, 1983. In total it raised $427,025.21

ENGINEERING AND TECHNOLOGY

DEFENSE TECHNOLOGY

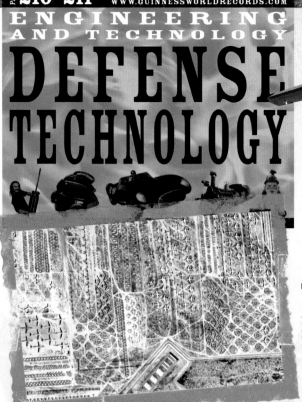

★ LARGEST AIRCRAFT "GRAVEYARD"

The 309th Aerospace Maintenance and Regeneration Group (aka "The Boneyard," above) is a US Air Force storage facility, where old planes are salvaged for parts or made ready for service again. Located on the Davis-Monthan Air Force Base in Tucson, Arizona, USA, the 4-mile² (10.3-km²) site accommodates around 4,000 aircraft.

★ **NEW RECORD** ★ **UPDATED RECORD**

★ LONGEST CONFIRMED SNIPER KILL

Confirmed by GPS, Craig Harrison (UK) of the UK's Household Cavalry killed two Taliban insurgents from a distance of 1.54 miles (2.47 km) in November 2009. It took the 8.59 mm rounds almost three seconds to hit their targets, which were 3,000 ft (914 m) beyond the recommended range of the L115A3 sniper rifle (picture below). A third shot took out the insurgent's machine gun.

RECORD-BREAKING C-5M SUPER GALAXY

The largest aircraft in the US Air Force, the Lockheed Martin C-5M Super Galaxy, set 41 aviation records on September 13, 2009 in a flight from Dover Air Force Base, Delaware, USA. Of these, 33 were new records and eight were updates of existing records. The principle flight record set was a world altitude record of 41,188 ft (12,554 m) obtained in 23 min 59 sec while carrying a 176,610 lb (80,108 kg) payload.

★ FIRST USE OF PLAYSTATIONS AS MILITARY TRAINING EQUIPMENT

The British Royal Navy is the first service organization to use Sony PlayStations for military use. Marine engineering technicians have been provided with the PlayStations to enable them to use study packages produced by the Maritime Warfare School at HMS *Collingwood*, Fareham, UK. So far, the school has bought 230 consoles, in recognition of the arrival of a generation that no longer naturally studies from books.

★ DEADLIEST UAV

The Predator C Avenger Unmanned Aerial Vehicle is capable of 460 mph (740 km/h) at 60,000 ft (18,288 m) for up to 20 hours. The ability to carry 3,000 lb (1,360 kg) of weapons and its stealthy design – there are no sharp angles between surfaces in order to reduce its radar signature – make it the world's deadliest UAV to date. Its first flight was on April 4, 2009.

★ MOST ADVANCED ROBOTIC SNAKE FOR MILITARY OPERATIONS

The Israeli Defense Ministry has developed a 6-ft (1.8-m) robotic snake that can be fitted with video and audio equipment. Operated from a laptop, it is used to advance on the ground into hostile environments to collect information. It also has applications for locating survivors in disaster areas or after terrorist attacks.

★ SMALLEST ROBOTIC MINESWEEPER

Engineers at the Massachusetts Institute of Technology (MIT) in Massachusetts, USA, have designed small robots, smaller than a cigarette lighter, based on the Atlantic razor clam (*Ensis directus*). The clam is one of nature's best diggers, able to burrow about 0.3 in (1 cm) per second. Used in conjunction with seabed-penetrating sonar to locate sea mines, the robotic clam can be deposited next to the mine in order to detonate it.

DID YOU KNOW?

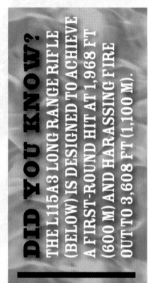

THE L115A3 LONG RANGE RIFLE (BELOW) IS DESIGNED TO ACHIEVE A FIRST-ROUND HIT AT 1,968 FT (600 M) AND HARASSING FIRE OUT TO 3,608 FT (1,100 M).

The rifle's heavy 8.59 mm bullets are less likely to be deflected in flight.

TRIVIA

★ SMALLEST FLIGHT-DECK PRINTER

The world's smallest flight-deck printer is the ToughWriter 5, used to print in-flight text and graphics. It is 7.3 in (185 mm) deep and weighs less than 9 lb (4 kg).

EXTRA!
FOR MORE MILITARY HARDWARE RECORDS, TURN BACK TO PP.128-129.

EXTRA! FOR EPIC-SCALE ENGINEERING RECORDS, TURN BACK TO PP.200-201.

★MOST NUCLEAR WEAPONS

As of May 2010, Russia had 4,650 operational warheads out of a stockpile of 12,000, according to the Federation of American Scientists. Pictured above is a Topol-M intercontinental ballistic missile, displayed in Moscow's Victory Day Parade in May 2009.

★OLDEST SERVING MILITARY WARSHIP

Built in the Netherlands, the VMF *Kommuna* is a 2,500-ton (2,267-tonne) catamaran salvage vessel that entered service in 1915 and is still serving in the Russian Navy today, employed to recover small submarines and submersibles. It is considered more cost-effective to keep the ship operational than to fund and build a replacement.

★LARGEST AIRSHIP

Built by Zeppelin Luftschifftechnik GmbH Germany and owned by the US company Airship Ventures Inc., *Eureka* has a length of 246 ft (75 m). Airships are used nowadays for surveillance, research, sightseeing, and advertising. Plans are underway to make a geostationary airship platform for military intelligence and reconnaissance applications.

★SUBMARINE WITH BIGGEST "EARS"

HMS *Astute* is a nuclear-powered attack submarine currently undergoing sea trials for the UK's Royal Navy. It has the biggest "ears" of any sonar system in service today. The Type 2076 sonar is reported to be able to detect ships leaving New York harbor while lying in the English Channel, 3,452 miles (5,556 km) away.

★LONGEST FLIGHT BY SOLAR-POWERED SPYPLANE

Between July 28 and 31, 2008, *Zephyr*, a solar-powered, high-altitude, long-endurance (HALE) unmanned aerial system (UAS), achieved a record flight of 82 hr 37 min. *Zephyr* is launched by hand, and flies on solar power generated by amorphous silicon arrays that cover the 75-ft (22.8-m) wings. By night, it is powered by a lithium-sulfur battery that is charged during the day. Made of carbon fiber weighing less than 100 lb (30 kg), it is designed to carry military surveillance payloads and operate at altitudes of 60,000 ft (18,288 m) at speeds of up to 70 mph (112 km/h).

★FIRST USE OF QUAD BIKES IN COMBAT

A total of 200 upgraded quad bikes have been ordered for UK forces in Afghanistan. They will be used to deliver vital combat supplies and are fitted with dual stretchers to evacuate two casualties at a time, thereby speeding up emergency treatment.

★NEWEST LITTORAL COMBAT SHIP

The US Navy commissioned the USS *Independence* littoral ("close-to-shore") combat ship, LCS-2, into service on January 16, 2010. Although it is the second vessel in the LCS class, it is the first of a new type of ship based on a three-hulled design and built of aluminum. Manufactured by General Dynamics and Austal (USA), it can carry a crew of 75 and accommodate two MH-60S Seahawk helicopters. It is 379 ft (115.5 m) long and has a top speed of around 44 knots (50.6 mph; 81.4 km/h).

★MOST EXPENSIVE SINGLE WEAPON SYSTEM

The USS *Ronald Reagan*, the CVN 76 class, nuclear-powered aircraft carrier, is, with its crew, armament, 85 aircraft, and other defense and communication systems, the most costly operational weapon system in the world. Its total cost was around $4.5 billion.

DOWN HMS *ASTUTE* CAN PURIFY WATER AND AIR, AND IS THEREFORE ABLE TO CIRCUMNAVIGATE THE GLOBE WITHOUT RESURFACING.

DOWN THE SUBMARINE'S NUCLEAR REACTOR WILL NOT NEED TO BE REFUELED DURING ITS EXPECTED 25-YEAR SERVICE.

ENGINEERING AND TECHNOLOGY

MEGA MOTORS

★ ★ ★ ★ ★ ★ ★ ★ ★ ★ ★ ★ ★

SMALLEST AND LOWEST AUTOMOBILES

The ★smallest automobile is 41 in (104.14 cm) high and 26 in (66.04 cm) wide and was measured on May 8, 2009.

The ★lowest automobile is 19 in (48.26 cm) from the ground. Perry Watkins (UK) created both cars.

★FASTEST 0-60 MPH ACCELERATION BY A FOUR-SEATER PRODUCTION AUTOMOBILE

A Nissan GT-R achieved an acceleration of 0–60 mph in 3.5 seconds while completing a lap of the Nürburgring circuit in Nürburg, Germany, on April 17, 2008.

★HIGHEST VEHICLE MILEAGE

A 1966 Volvo P-1800S owned by Irvin Gordon of East Patchogue, New York, USA, had covered in excess of 2,721,000 miles (4,379,033.78 km) by August 2009. The automobile, still driven on a daily basis, covers more than 100,000 miles (160,000 km) per year, thanks in part to being driven to numerous auto shows and events in the USA and Europe.

★ MOST EXPENSIVE CAR

The greatest price ever paid for a car is $17,275,000 (£12,000,000) for a 1963 Ferrari 250 GT, of which only 36 were ever made. It was sold to TV presenter Chris Evans (UK) on May 14, 2010.

★HIGHEST AVERAGE SPEED IN A STEAM AUTOMOBILE

On August 26, 2009, Don Wales (UK) achieved a Fédération Internationale de l'Automobile (FIA)-approved average speed of 139.84 mph (225.05 km/h) over two one-kilometer runs in the *Inspiration Streamliner* at Edwards Air Force Base in California, USA.

★MOST EXPENSIVE "VETERAN" AUTOMOBILE

The highest amount paid for a London to Brighton Run veteran (i.e., pre-1905) automobile is £3,521,500 ($7,242,916), for the oldest surviving Rolls-Royce, numbered 20154. The two-seater, 10-hp automobile was sold to an anonymous British collector in London, UK, on December 3, 2007.

FASTEST PRODUCTION MOTORCYCLE

The Suzuki GSX1300R Hayabusa is reported to reach speeds of 194 mph (312 km/h), making it the fastest production bike in the world. Named after a Japanese peregrine falcon, the 474-lb (215-kg) Hayabusa is powered by a 1,298 cc (72.2 cu in) engine with four valves per cylinder.

HORSEPOWER: A measurement of power, originally to compare the output of steam engines against the power of draft (heavy labor) horses.

301 VTG

H₂ HYDROGEN Powered

2016

DID YOU KNOW?

IN JULY 2009, DIVERS RECOVERED A 1925 BUGATTI THAT HAD BEEN SITTING ON THE BOTTOM OF LAKE MAGGIORE, ITALY, FOR 73 YEARS. IT COULD FETCH MORE THAN $129,500 AT AUCTION.

The Bugatti was dumped in the water in 1936 by a frustrated Swiss official. The owner had abandoned it still owing import tax.

TRIVIA

★ MOST EXPENSIVE POSTWAR AUTOMOBILE

The most money paid for a postwar automobile is $12,390,000 for a two-seat 1957 Ferrari 250 Testa Rossa. This rare racing car is one of only 22 built and was sold at Ferrari's factory at Maranelo, Italy, on May 17, 2009.

★ FASTEST ELECTRIC CAR

The highest average speed achieved for an electric vehicle is 303.025 mph (487.672 km/h) over a two-way flying kilometer by *Buckeye Bullet 2*, designed and built by engineering students at The Ohio State University (USA) at the university's Center for Automotive Research (CAR) and driven by Roger Schroer (USA) at the Bonneville Salt Flats, Utah, USA, on September 25, 2009. The hydrogen fuel cell streamliner is nicknamed "La Jamais Contente" in tribute to the first vehicle to go faster than 60 mph (100 km/h) in 1899.

FUEL
BB2 IS THE FIRST HYDROGEN FUEL CELL STREAMLINER. IT IS DRIVEN BY A 700-HP ELECTRIC MOTOR FUELED BY ONBOARD HYDROGEN AND OXYGEN.

COOL
A RADIATOR WOULD CAUSE TOO MUCH DRAG TRAVELING AT MORE THAN 300 MPH (480 KM), SO AN ICE BATH WAS USED TO KEEP THE FUEL CELLS COOL.

FASTEST CARAVAN TOW BY A PRODUCTION AUTOMOBILE

A Mercedes Benz S600 driven by Eugene Herbert (South Africa) reached a speed of 139.113 mph (223.881 km/h) towing a standard caravan at Hoedspruit Air Force Base, South Africa, on October 24, 2003.

FASTEST PRODUCTION AUTOMOBILE

The Ultimate Aero TT Super Car, made by Shelby Supercars (USA), achieved two-way timed speeds in excess of 256.14 mph (412 km/h) on Highway 221, Washington, USA, on September 13, 2007. It can go from 0 to 60 mph in just 2.78 seconds.

LIGHTEST CAR

Louis Borsi (UK) has built and driven a 21-lb (9.5-kg) car with a 2.5 cc engine. It is capable of 15 mph (25 km/h) at top speed.

★ FASTEST AMPHIBIOUS CAR

With an engine based on the LS Corvette power train, the WaterCar Python is the fastest amphibious vehicle in the world. It has a top speed of 60 mph (96 km; 52 knots) on water and can perform a 0–60 mph acceleration in 4.5 seconds on land. The Python is hand-built to order and prices start from $200,000.

★ NEW RECORD
UPDATED RECORD

Stillwater TECHNOLOGIES, INC. | DeLILLE Specialty Gases | TRC EWi | Enriching. Expanding. Excelling. A Partnership of Honda and The Ohio State University | BALLARD VENTURI
The MathWorks | Ford
ODYNE, INC.

PITTSBURGH, PA, USA

40°26'N 79°58'W

The **first brain cell transplant** was performed by a team of doctors from the University of Pittsburgh Medical Center, Pennsylvania, USA, on June 23, 1998. The aim of the operation was to reverse the damage that had been caused to 62-year-old Alma Cerasini (USA) by a stroke.

ENGINEERING AND TECHNOLOGY

TOP TECH

EXTRA! EXPERIENCE THE CUTTING-EDGE OF SCIENCE ON PP.216-217.

★ THINNEST x10 ZOOM DIGITAL CAMERA

Casio's 12.1-megapixel Exilim EX-H10 digital camera is, at just under 1 in (24.3 mm) thick, the slimmest digital camera with a x10 optical telephoto zoom. At just 5.78 oz (164 g), it is also among the lightest. It can take 100 pictures a day for 10 days without needing to be charged.

★ **NEW RECORD**
★ **UPDATED RECORD**

★ MOST EXPENSIVE TELEVISION

The PrestigeHD Supreme Rose TV, made from 61 lb (28 kg) of 18-carat rose gold inset with 72 brilliant 1-carat flawless diamonds, costs $2,250,000.

BLING! THE SUPREME ROSE TV WAS DESIGNED BY STUART HUGHES (UK) AND HAS ALLIGATOR SKIN HANDSEWN INTO THE INNER SCREEN LAYER.

★ MOST SECURE MOUSE

The Fujitsu PalmSecure mouse may look like a regular three-button optical mouse, but it features a CIA-level security device to prevent unauthorized use: a palm-vein biometric sensor. As you place your hand over the mouse, the sensor reads the unique pattern of veins on your palm and, if there is a match, grants you access to the cursor. It retails for Y20,500 ($220).

★ LIGHTEST TOUCHSCREEN CELL PHONE

The modu-t (right), which weighs a mere 1.94 oz (55.1 g), is manufactured by modu Ltd (Israel) and was launched at the Mobile World Congress in Barcelona, Spain, on February 15, 2010. The phone is 1.83 x 2.95 x 0.43 in (46.5 x 75 x 11 mm) in size.

ACTUAL SIZE

★ THINNEST LCD TV

LG Korea has created a fully hi-def (1,920 x 1,080 pixel) liquid-crystal display panel that is a mere 0.10 in (2.6 mm) thick. The 42-in (106-cm) screen uses an ultraslim LED backlighting system, and the entire unit weighs just 9 lb 4 oz (4.2 kg).

THIN IN MAY 2009, LG KOREA PRODUCED A 0.2-IN (5.9-MM) LCD PANEL - THEN THE WORLD'S THINNEST. JUST SEVEN MONTHS LATER, THIS NEW PANEL SMASHED THEIR OWN RECORD.

★FIRST 3D CAMCORDER

On January 7, 2010, Panasonic unveiled the world's first professional-use 3D camcorder, equipped with double lenses that can record high-definition movies on an SD memory card. The twin-lens camera was demonstrated during a press preview at the company's plant in Amagasaki city in Hyogo prefecture, western Japan. The retail price? $21,000.

FIRST USB PROSTHETIC

In May 2008, Finnish computer programmer Jerry Jalava lost part of a finger in a motorcycle accident. Instead of a regular fingertip prosthetic, Jalava had a 2-GB USB memory stick made, allowing him to carry data around with him constantly.

★SMALLEST MP3 PLAYER

No bigger than a couple of sugar cubes, the Micro Sport MP3 player (right) boasts a 4-GB memory, full stereo sound through its two earbuds, and a rechargeable battery.

ACTUAL SIZE

★MOST POWERFUL VACUUM CLEANER

The handheld Dyson DC31 vacuum cleaner is powered by a digital motor that spins at 104,000 rpm. That's five times faster than the engine of a Formula One racing car, and ten times faster than a standard commercial airliner!

★FASTEST SMS

Sonja Kristiansen (Norway) wrote a 160-character text message in 37.28 seconds at Oslo City Shopping Center in Oslo, Norway, on November 14, 2009.

★BEST-SELLING iPAD APP

At the time of going to press (April 2010), Apple had just launched their much-anticipated iPad. This tablet computer sold at least 300,000 units on its first day (although some early estimates place this figure as high as 700,000), with 1 million apps downloaded.

To date, the biggest-selling paid-for app is Pages, which is a word-processing program.

The most downloaded free app for the iPad as of April 2010 is iBooks – an ebook reader and shopfront with which the user can browse for (and download) tens of thousands of books, many of them free.

Be sure to look out for **Guinness World Records: At Your Fingertips**, *a free iPad lite app that showcases record-breaking achievements.*

★ MOST COMPACT ELECTRIC BIKE

Weighing in at 22 lb (10 kg), and folding down to just 6 x 23.5 x 23.5 in (15 x 60 x 60 cm) – smaller than most folding bicycles – the YikeBike is the most compact folding electric bicycle on the market. The "mini-farthing" design is based on the "penny farthing" bicycle of c.1870.

ENGINEERING AND TECHNOLOGY
CUTTING-EDGE SCIENCE

EXTRA! PREFER SCIENCE FICTION TO SCIENCE FACT? TURN TO PP.172-173.

★ MOST WATER-REPELLENT MANMADE MATERIAL

In February 2010, scientists at the University of Florida, USA, announced that they had created an almost perfect water-repellent, or hydrophobic, surface. They used sheets of polypropylene and a mold to create tiny irregular "hairs" on the surface of the sheets, which resemble the microscopic structure of hairs on some water-walking arthropods.

★ **NEW RECORD**
★ **UPDATED RECORD**

★ HIGHEST LASER ENERGY SHONE ON TO A SINGLE TARGET

In June 2009, scientists at the National Ignition Facility at Lawrence Livermore National Laboratory in California, USA, began operating the array of 192 powerful lasers designed to research nuclear fusion. The lasers are focused on a fingernail-sized container known as a hohlraum that will eventually contain a pellet of hydrogen fuel for fusion experiments. On January 27, 2010, researchers fired the laser array for a few billionths of a second and delivered one megajoule of energy onto the target. This is equivalent to the explosion caused by 0.44 lb (0.2 kg) of TNT.

★ FIRST EVIDENCE OF EVOLUTION WITHOUT DNA

In January 2010, scientists at the Scripps Research Institute, California, USA, reported that they had witnessed evidence of evolution occurring in the lifeless, DNA-less proteins known as prions (artwork shown above). They exhibited signs of adapting to new environments and following the rules of natural selection. Prions are associated with 20 different diseases of the brain in humans and animals.

★ DEEPEST UNDERGROUND LAB

SNOLAB, 1.2 miles (2 km) below ground in Sudbury, Ontario, Canada, is best known for housing the Sudbury Neutrino Observatory. The observatory was created to study neutrinos -- weakly interacting particles -- using the rock above it to filter out cosmic radiation. This ensured that only neutrinos, which easily penetrate matter, were observed.

★ LARGEST KNOWN PRIME NUMBER

On August 23, 2008, the latest giant number discovered by the Great Internet Mersenne Prime Search project was announced. It is a Mersenne prime, which means it can be written as 2^n-1, where "n" is a power; $2^{43112609}-1$ contains some 12,978,189 digits. As a prime number, it can only be divided by itself and 1.

★ FASTEST COMPUTER

The Jaguar supercomputer at the Oak Ridge National Laboratory in Oak Ridge, Tennessee, USA, became the world's fastest in November 2009 after an upgrade. Built by Cray Inc. (USA), it is capable of 1.759 petaflops (quadrillion floating point operations per second).

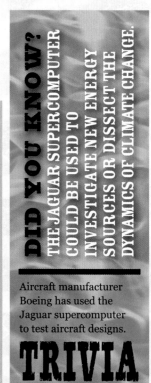

DID YOU KNOW? THE JAGUAR SUPERCOMPUTER COULD BE USED TO INVESTIGATE NEW ENERGY SOURCES OR DISSECT THE DYNAMICS OF CLIMATE CHANGE.

Aircraft manufacturer Boeing has used the Jaguar supercomputer to test aircraft designs.

TRIVIA

★SHORTEST WAVELENGTH LASER

The Linac Coherent Light Source (LCLS) at the SLAC National Accelerator Laboratory, Stanford, California, USA, is an X-ray laser capable of producing X-ray laser radiation at a wavelength of just 0.15 nanometers. Visible light that the human eye can see ranges from around 390 to 750 nanometers.

★HIGHEST ENERGY OPERATIONAL ACCELERATOR

On March 19, 2010, scientists at the Large Hadron Collider in Geneva, Switzerland, announced that they had used the particle accelerator to produce two beams of protons with energies of 3.5 tera electron volts. (One electron volt equals the kinetic energy gained by an electron when it is accelerated by one volt. "Tera" means "trillion.")

★SLOWEST LIGHT

In January 2010, a team of US scientists reported that they had "frozen" light to a standstill for 1.5 seconds using a form of supercold matter known as a Bose–Einstein condensate.

★HIGHEST MANMADE TEMPERATURE

In February 2010, scientists at Brookhaven National Laboratory's Relativistic Heavy Ion Collider on Long Island, New York, USA, announced that they had smashed together gold ions at nearly the speed of light, briefly forming an exotic state of matter known as a quark-gluon plasma. This substance is believed to have filled the universe just a few microseconds after the Big Bang. During the experiment the plasma reached temperatures of around 4 trillion°C, some 250,000 times hotter than the center of the Sun.

★HEAVIEST ELEMENT

Copernicium, with an atomic number of 112, is the heaviest element officially recognized to date. It was first created on February 9, 1996 at the Gesellschaft für Schwerionenforschung (GSI, right) in Darmstadt, Germany, and officially named copernicium on February 19, 2010.

★LOWEST MANMADE TEMPERATURE

A team of scientists at the Massachusetts Institute of Technology (MIT), Cambridge, Massachusetts, USA, led by Professor Aaron E Leanhardt, managed to produce a temperature of 450 picokelvin above absolute zero by cooling down a Bose–Einstein condensate. Details of their research first appeared in *Science* magazine on September 12, 2003.

★FIRST HOMOGENEOUS SELF-RIGHTING SHAPE

The Gömböc is a mathematical shape first theorized in 1996 and proven in 2006 by Hungarian scientists Péter Várkonyi and Gábor Domokos. It is a three-dimensional shape that is mono-monostatic, convex, and homogeneous, i.e. with equal density throughout. It is characterized by its properties of balance in that it has two equilibria, one stable and one unstable.

★FIRST VIRUS-POWERED BATTERY

In April 2009, scientists at MIT in Massachusetts, USA, announced that they had used genetically engineered viruses to build the positive and negative ends of a lithium ion battery. In tests, the new battery technology can be charged up more than 100 times before deteriorating.

LONG
COPERNICIUM WAS CREATED USING GSI'S LINEAR ACCELERATOR, PICTURED RIGHT. THIS DEVICE HAS A TOTAL LENGTH OF 393 FT 8 IN (120 M).

FAST
THIS TYPE OF PARTICLE ACCELERATOR GREATLY INCREASES THE VELOCITY OF CHARGED SUBATOMIC PARTICLES OR IONS.

ENGINEERING
AND TECHNOLOGY
INTERNET

★ ★ ★ ★ ★ ★ ★ ★ ★ ★ ★ ★ ★ ★

★ OLDEST .COM

Symbolics.com was registered by computer manufacturer Symbolics Inc. (USA) on March 15, 1985, making it the world's oldest .com url. Symbolics.com is still registered and active today, and was bought by XF.com in 2009.

★ FIRST TWEET

Twitter was invented by Jack Dorsey (USA) in 2006. Users can post messages ("tweets") of up to 140 characters, which are sent to their subscribers. The first tweet was posted by Dorsey at 9:50 p.m. PST on March 21, 2006, and read "just setting up my twittr."

★ FIRST TWEET FROM SPACE

On October 21, 2009, US astronauts Nicola Stott and Jeff Williams took part in a live "tweetup" from the International Space Station with around 35 members of the public at NASA Headquarters, Washington, DC, USA.

★ LARGEST BOTNET

In December 2009, an operation by Spanish police and the FBI closed down a network of more than 13 million PCs that had been infected with viruses. This so-called "Mariposa botnet" was designed to steal credit card data, passwords, and account information. It had infected machines in 190 countries, spreading via USB sticks, spammed links, and a vulnerability in Internet Explorer.

★ FASTEST-SELLING TOP-LEVEL DOMAIN

The .me domain is the Internet country code for Montenegro, located in southeastern Europe, which first became an independent state in June 2006. Registration for .me domains was made available on July 16, 2008. By January 2010, more than 320,000 .me domains had been sold, making it the fastest-selling top-level domain in the history of the Internet. The suffix is popular due to its attractiveness for social networking websites.

★ GREATEST MEMES

According to MSNBC, the top Internet meme (see left) of 2009 was Kanye West's antics during the MTV Video Music Awards in New York City, USA, on September 13, when he grabbed the mic from award-winner Taylor Swift, announcing Beyoncé should have won. West's outburst led to the "Ima let you finish" meme. In second place was the "Crasher Squirrel," in which Melissa Brandts and her husband, Jackson, were taking a photo of themselves using a timer. During the shot, a squirrel popped up in front of the camera.

MEME
AN IDEA THAT POSSESSES SOME QUALITY THAT MAKES PEOPLE WANT TO SHARE IT WITH EACH OTHER - SUCH AS A JOKE, OR A YOUTUBE VIDEO. ON THE INTERNET, MEMES ARE SAID TO GROW AND BE TRANSMITTED "VIRALLY."

DID YOU KNOW?

WIKIPEDIA IS THE LARGEST ONLINE ENCYCLOPEDIA. IT CONTAINED 19,878,548 PAGES IN NUMEROUS LANGUAGES AS OF MARCH 31, 2010, AND HAS UNDERGONE 377,162,709 PAGE EDITS SINCE ITS LAUNCH ON JANUARY 15, 2000.

WIKIPEDIA
The Free Encyclopedia

★ MOST SONGS DOWNLOADED FROM ONE COMPANY

On February 25, 2010, the 10 billionth song was downloaded from iTunes, Apple's online music store: "Guess Things Happen That Way," a 1958 hit by Johnny Cash. To mark the event, the lucky downloader, Louie Sulcer (USA), received a $10,000 iTunes gift card from Apple.

★ LARGEST INTERNET EXCHANGE

Of the exchanges that make their data public, the largest by traffic is the Deutscher Commercial Internet Exchange in Frankfurt, Germany. As of March 2010, it had a maximum throughput of 1,994 gigabits/sec. (The term "Throughput" refers to the amount of work processed in a given time.)

★ FIRST FLASHMOB

"Flashmobs" are sudden gatherings of people in a public place at a set time to engage in a brief and usually pointless activity. The first notable flashmob, organized by Bill Wasik (USA), occurred in May 2003 in New York City, USA, though police had received a tip-off. The second attempt, also by Wasik, was more successful: on June 3, 2003, nearly 100 people gathered around a $10,000 rug at Macy's department store in New York (below).

★ MOST INTERNET USERS (COUNTRY)

According to www.internetworldstats.com, China had approximately 360,000,000 Internet users by September 2009, 26.9% of its population.

★ MOST VIEWED ONLINE VIDEO AD

As of August 19, 2009, the advertisement for Evian Roller Babies had been watched 25,687,416 times via online video sites.

★ LARGEST ONLINE QUIZ

Five hundred employees of DKV Seguros, Spain, took part in an online quiz in Saragoza, Spain, on September 9, 2009.

★ LONGEST LAN PARTY

On April 11–12, 2009, a nonstop local area network (LAN) party lasting 40 hours was completed by 274 gamers during Cyber Fusion 2009 at the Multimedia University in Cyberjaya, Malaysia.

LARGEST AUDIENCE FOR AN INTERNET CONCERT

On October 25, 2009, U2's set at the Rose Bowl, Pasadena, USA, was streamed live on YouTube. It was watched over the web by nearly 10 million people.

IN SPACE
DURING THE EUROPEAN LEG OF U2'S 360° TOUR THERE WAS A LIVE VIDEO LINK-UP WITH THE CREW OF THE INTERNATIONAL SPACE STATION!

AWARD
U2 (IRELAND) HAVE WON A RECORD 22 GRAMMYS, THE MOST FOR ANY GROUP. THEY HAVE ALSO WON SEVEN BRIT AWARDS, MORE THAN ANY OTHER GROUP.

★ NEW RECORD
★ UPDATED RECORD

RUG COLLECTION

SPORTS

CONTENTS

GRAND!
THE FOUR TENNIS GRAND SLAM TOURNAMENTS ARE THE AUSTRALIAN OPEN, THE FRENCH OPEN, WIMBLEDON, AND THE US OPEN.

SLAM!
SIX PEOPLE HAVE WON ALL FOUR GRAND SLAM TITLES IN THEIR CAREER: FRED PERRY, DON BUDGE, ROD LAVER, ROY EMERSON, ANDRE AGASSI, AND ROGER FEDERER.

★ MOST GRAND SLAM TITLES

When Roger Federer (Switzerland, pictured) clinched his fourth Australian Open title by defeating Andy Murray (UK) 6-3 6-4 7-6 (13-11) on January 31, 2010, he recorded his 16th Grand Slam singles title, the **greatest number of Grand Slam singles tennis titles won by a man**. Federer's first Grand Slam win had come at Wimbledon: he triumphed over Mark Philippoussis (Australia) at the London, UK, tournament on July 6, 2003.

As well as six Wimbledon grass court Slam victories, Federer has won four Australian Open titles, five US Open titles and, in 2009, won his first French Open title, beating Robin Söderling (Sweden) in the final.

SPORTS
ACTION SPORTS

EXTRA! FOR MORE FABULOUS FEATS AND DARING DEEDS, DON'T FORGET STUNTS ON P.88.

★ NEW RECORD
★ UPDATED RECORD

ON A WING AND A PRAYER

With an impressive six titles to his name between 1985 and 1999, Jerzy Makula (Poland) has the ★**most wins of the World Glider Aerobatic Championships**, a competition organized by the Gliding Commission of the Fédération Aéronautique Internationale (FAI).

★FARTHEST DYNO WALL CLIMB

Dynamic ("dyno") moves involve climbers flinging themselves from one handhold to the next. Nicky de Leeuw (Netherlands) achieved a distance of 9 ft 2 in (2.80 m) in Eindhoven, the Netherlands, on June 14, 2009. The ★**farthest distance achieved by a woman in Dyno climbing** is 6 ft 5 in (1.98 m) by Anne-Laure Chevrier (France) on the set of *Lo Show dei Record* in Milan, Italy, on April 17, 2009.

AQUABIKE

• On October 11, 1996, Cory A Wimpheimer (USA) recorded a time of 17.76 seconds to complete an International Jet Sports Boating Association (IJSBA) Pro Runabout 785 slalom course on Lake Havasu, Arizona, USA. This represents the ★**fastest time** in which this course has been completed.

• The ★**most wins of the IJSBA Pro Runabout 1200 World Championships** is five by Chris MacClugage (USA) who claimed titles in 1999, 2001–02, 2004, and 2005.

• Based in Monaco, the Union Internationale Motonautique (UIM) is the governing body for the sports of powerboating and aquabiking. Gimmi Bosio (Italy) holds the record for the ★**most wins of the UIM Aquabike Pro Runabout 1200 World Championship**, with two titles, in 2001–02. The ★**most wins of the UIM Pro Ski World Championship** is also two, with Kevin Laigle (France) claiming the top spot in 2002 and 2004.

PARA-GLIDING

• Nicole Fedele (Italy) paraglided 102.2 miles (164.6 km) from Sorica, Slovenia, to Piombada, Italy, and back on August 19, 2009, to secure the record for the ★**farthest paragliding out-and-return distance (female)**.

• The record for the ★**farthest paragliding out-and-return distance (male)** is held by Aljaz Valic, who flew 161.3 miles (259.7 km), departing from and returning to Soriska Planina, in his Slovenian homeland, on July 20, 2006.

• The team of Toby Colombe and Cefn Hoile (both UK) achieved a distance of 104 miles (167.3 km) in setting the record for the ★**farthest paragliding out-and-return distance by a team** when gliding from Sorica in Slovenia and back on July 26, 2009.

• The ★**farthest flight by a paraglider (male)** was made by Nevil Hulett (South Africa) who paraglided a distance of 312.5 miles (502.9 km) from Copperton, South Africa, on December 14, 2008.

BUNGEE

• The ★**highest bungee dive into water** was recorded by action sports enthusiast Zhang Di (China), who performed a dive into water from a height of 164 ft (50 m) in Quindao city, Shandong province, China, on November 15, 2006.

• The **highest bungee jump from a building** is 652 ft 10 in (199 m) by A J Hackett (New Zealand), who leaped off a platform at 764 ft 5 in (233 m) on the Macau Tower, Macau, China, on December 17, 2006. This meant that Hackett came within 111 ft 6 in (34 m) of the ground at the lowest point of his jump.

AWESOME AQUA-BATICS!

Lee Stone (UK, right) and Alessander Lenzi (Brazil) share the honor of the ★**most wins of the Union Internationale Motonautique (UIM) Aquabike Pro Freestyle Class World Championship**, with three wins apiece. Lenzi won the title from 2003 to 2005 and Stone took the top spot from 2006 to 2008.

★MOST KITE SURFING CHAMPIONSHIPS (FEMALE)

When it comes to kite surfing, few can compare to Kristin Boese (Germany, above). Between 2005 and 2008, she won nine kite surfing world championship titles!

★LONGEST MOUNTAINBOARD RACE

With a course that stretches 6.95 miles (11.18 km) down Palomar Mountain, San Diego County, California, USA, the annual Nate Harrison Grade Race is a true mountainboard endurance test. Four victories over the event's six-year history makes Kris Kidwell (USA) the king of the mountain.

Tournament at Smith Mountain Lake, Virginia, USA, on July 25, 2009, Linda Brown (USA, b. December 10, 1945) is the ★oldest competitive wakeboarder.

AERO-BATICS

• Daredevil pilot Joann Osterud (Canada) flew upside down for 4 hr 38 min 10 sec on a flight from Vancouver to Vanderhoof, Canada, on July 24, 1991, to record the longest inverted flight (aerobatics).
• Svetlana Kapanina (Russia) has recorded the ★most wins of the women's Aerobatics World Championships, having won the women's overall competition an unprecedented six times, in 1996, 1998, 2001, 2003, 2005, and 2007.
• No single male pilot has dominated the World Championships in quite the way that Svetlana Kapanina has in the women's event. The ★most wins of the men's Aerobatics World Championships is two, achieved by two pilots, Petr Jirmus (Czechoslovakia) in 1984 and 1986; and Sergei Rakhmanin (Russia) in 2003 and 2005.

KITE SURFING

• The ★longest journey kite surfing (male) is 178.50 nautical miles (205.41 miles; 330.58 km) by Steen Carstens (Denmark), who traveled from Sprogo, Denmark, to Lysekil, Sweden, on August 17, 2009. The longest continuous kite surfing journey (female) was 115.4 nautical miles (132.80 miles; 213.72 km) by Andreya Wharry (UK) between Watergate Bay, UK, and Dungarven, Ireland, on September 7, 2005.
• The youngest kite surfing world champion (female) is Gisela Pulido (Spain, b. January 14, 1994) who won her first Kiteboard Pro World Tour (KPWT) world title on November 4, 2004 aged 10 years 294 days.

★MOST SURFERS ON A WAVE

A total of 110 surfers rode a single wave at the Earthwave Beach Festival, Muizenberg Beach, Cape Town, South Africa, on October 4, 2009 at an event to raise awareness of climate change.

WAKE-BOARDING

• The ★longest wakeboarding ramp jump (male) is a 49-ft 2-in (15-m) attempt by Jérôme Macquart (France), which was filmed as part of L'Été De Tous Les Records, in Argelès-Gazost, France, on July 14, 2004.
• In wakeboarding, the term "superman" describes the situation when boarders are completely lifted off the surface of the water, higher than head height, and assume a stretched pose (with the wakeboard attached to their feet). Jérôme Macquart performed an unprecedented five "supermans" in 30 seconds at Biscarrosse, France, on July 14, 2005. This feat represents the ★most wakeboarding "supermans" in 30 seconds.
• Aged 63 years 227 days when she competed in the Battle of Bull Run Wakeboard

DID YOU KNOW?
ALTHOUGH OFTEN USED GENERICALLY FOR ALL SINGLE-SEATER WATER VEHICLES, THE TERM "JET SKI" IS ACTUALLY A BRAND NAME OWNED BY KAWASAKI HEAVY INDUSTRIES OF JAPAN.

The farthest distance covered on a jet ski in 24 hours is 1,019.94 miles (1,641.43 km) by Ivan Otulic (Croatia).

TRIVIA

AIR
IAN METCHER (AUSTRALIA) WAS 85 YEARS OLD WHEN HE WON AN AEROBATICS TITLE IN 2001, MAKING HIM THE OLDEST COMPETITIVE AEROBATIC PILOT.

WATER
NUNO GOMES (SOUTH AFRICA) PERFORMED A RECORD 1,044-FT-DEEP (318.25-M) SCUBA DIVE IN THE RED SEA OFF DAHAB, EGYPT, ON JUNE 10, 2005.

SPORTS
AMERICAN FOOTBALL

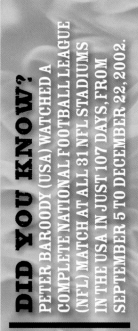

★ HIGHEST PUNTING AVERAGE (CAREER)

Shane Lechler (USA) has played for the Oakland Raiders (USA) in the NFL since the 2000 season, in which time he has attained the highest career punting average of 47.3 yards per game.

★ MOST KICKOFF RETURNS FOR TOUCHDOWNS IN AN NFL GAME

There have been seven occasions on which an NFL player has scored two touchdowns from a kickoff return: Timmy Brown for Philadelphia Eagles against Dallas Cowboys on November 6, 1966; Travis Williams for Green Bay Packers against Cleveland Browns on November 12, 1967; Ron Brown for LA Rams against Green Bay Packers on November 24, 1985; Tyrone Hughes for New Orleans Saints against LA Rams on October 23, 1994; Chad Morton for New York Jets against Buffalo Bills on September 8, 2002; Devin Hester for Chicago Bears against St Louis Rams on December 11, 2006; Andre Davis for Houston Texans against Jacksonville Jaguars on December 30, 2007; and Ted Ginn, Jr. for Miami Dolphins against New York Jets (all teams and players USA) on November 1, 2009.

★ MOST CATCHES IN AN NFL GAME

Brandon Marshall (USA) made a record 21 catches in a single NFL game, playing as wide receiver for the Denver Broncos against the Indianapolis Colts (both USA) in Indianapolis, Indiana, USA, on December 13, 2009. Marshall totaled 200 yards across his 21 receptions, two of which were for touchdowns.

★ MOST COMBINED YARDS FROM SCRIMMAGE IN AN NFL SEASON

Chris Johnson (USA) recorded 2,509 combined yards from scrimmage playing for the Tennessee Titans (USA) from September 10, 2009 to January 3, 2010.

★ HIGHEST COMPLETION PERCENTAGE IN AN NFL GAME

Kurt Warner (USA) recorded a completion percentage of 92.3% playing as quarterback for the Arizona Cardinals (USA) in a 31-17 win over the Jacksonville Jaguars (USA) on September 20, 2009.

★ MOST PASS COMPLETIONS IN AN NFL CAREER

Brett Favre (USA) has made 6,083 pass completions in his career playing for the Atlanta Falcons, Green Bay Packers, New York Jets, and Minnesota Vikings (all USA) between 1992 and 2009, the most pass completions in an NFL career by a quarterback.

Favre's career has also seen him record the ★ most postseason passing yards in an NFL career with 5,855 yards. He broke the record with 310 passing yards on January 24, 2010 while quarterbacking the Minnesota Vikings in a 31-28 loss to the New Orleans Saints (both USA) in the NFC Championship Game.

Neil Rackers (USA) scored a record 40 field goals playing for the Arizona Cardinals in the 2005 NFL season.

TRIVIA

★ MOST TOUCHDOWN PASSES IN ONE QUARTER OF A GAME

Tom Brady (USA) made the most touchdown passes in one quarter of an NFL game when he threw for five touchdowns playing for the New England Patriots against the Tennessee Titans (both USA) at Gillette Stadium, Foxborough, Massachusetts, USA, on October 18, 2009. Brady also holds the record for the **most touchdown passes in a season**, with 50 touchdown passes thrown during the 2007 season.

EXTRA! TO CHECK OUT FOOTBALL WITH A ROUND BALL, JUST TURN TO SOCCER ON P.250.

POOCH KICK: A punt or kickoff that is deliberately kicked with less than full force. Often used to try to prevent the opposition from returning the ball.

★ OLDEST SUPER BOWL PLAYER

Aged 42 years 11 days, placekicker Matt Stover (USA) became the oldest player in Super Bowl history when he made an appearance for the Indianapolis Colts (USA) in Super Bowl XLIV on February 7, 2010. The game, which was played at the Sun Life Stadium, Miami Gardens, Florida, USA, saw the Colts lose to the New Orleans Saints (USA) 31–17.

★HIGHEST COMPLETION PERCENTAGE (SEASON)

Quarterback Drew Brees (USA) registered a 70.62% completion percentage playing for the New Orleans Saints (USA) in the 2009 season, an NFL record.

A DECADE OF SUCCESS

Peyton Manning (USA) was one of the standout American sportsmen of the Noughties, a decade in which he racked up a host of world records. Playing for the Indianapolis Colts (USA) from 2000 to 2009, Manning achieved the ★most passing touchdowns in a decade, with 314, and also the ★most passing yards in a decade, with 42,254. In that period, Manning also achieved the ★most wins of the NFL Most Valuable Player award, with four wins, in 2003, 2004, 2008, and 2009.

Despite posting the best start in the history of the Super Bowl, the Bears went on to lose the game 29-17.

Hester also jointly holds the record for the ★longest play in NFL history, which he set when he returned a missed field goal 108 yards for a touchdown playing for the Chicago Bears against the New York Giants (both USA) on November 12, 2006. The score equaled the feat of Hester's Chicago Bears teammate Nathan Vasher (USA), who returned a missed field goal 108 yards for a touchdown against the San Francisco 49ers (USA) at Soldier Field, Chicago, Illinois, USA, on November 13, 2005.

★MOST TOUCHDOWNS BY A TIGHT END IN AN NFL SEASON

Vernon Davis (USA) scored 13 touchdowns playing for the San Francisco 49ers (USA) as tight end in the 2009 season, matching the 2004 record set by Antonio Gates (USA) of the San Diego Chargers (USA).

MOST POINTS SCORED BY AN INDIVIDUAL IN A SINGLE GAME

Ernie Nevers (USA) scored 40 points for the Chicago Cardinals v. the Chicago Bears (both USA) on November 28, 1929. Nevers scored six touchdowns and kicked four extra points in a game that the Cardinals won 40-6. The next highest individual total is 36 points.

★FIRST PERSON TO RETURN AN OPENING KICKOFF FOR A TOUCHDOWN IN THE SUPER BOWL

Playing for the Chicago Bears against the Indianapolis Colts (both USA) in Super Bowl XLI, Devin Hester (USA) became the first player in Super Bowl history to return the opening kickoff for a touchdown, at Dolphin Stadium in Miami Gardens, Florida, USA, on February 4, 2007.

★ NEW RECORD
★ UPDATED RECORD

MOST KICKOFF RETURNS FOR TOUCHDOWNS (CAREER)

Wide receiver/return specialist Joshua Cribbs (USA) has made eight returns for touchdowns in his NFL career playing for the Cleveland Browns (USA) since 2005.

PUNT
STEVE O'NEAL (USA) PUNTED A BALL 98 YARDS PLAYING FOR THE NEW YORK JETS [...] DENVER

HIGH
ON NOVEMBER 26, 2006, THE TENNESSEE TITANS MADE THE LARGEST COMEBACK IN THE LAST 10 MINUTES OF AN NFL GAME. HAVING TRAILED 21-0 IN THE 4TH QUARTER, THEY CAME BACK TO BEAT THE NEW YORK GIANTS 24-21.

SPORTS

AMERICAN FOOTBALL

EXTRA!
FLIP FORWARD TO P.232 FOR ALL THE LATEST BASEBALL RECORDS.

★ MOST REGULAR SEASON WINS

The Chicago Bears (USA) have won 693 regular season games, the most by a team in NFL history, since competing in the inaugural NFL season in 1920.

★ **FIRST NFL TEAM TO SCORE TOUCHDOWNS ON INTERCEPTION, KICKOFF, AND PUNT RETURNS IN THE SAME GAME**

The Minnesota Vikings (USA) became the first NFL team in history to score touchdowns on interception, kickoff, and punt returns in the same game, against the New York Giants (USA), in Giants Stadium, New York, USA, on November 13, 2005.

HIGHEST SUPER BOWL ATTENDANCE

A crowd of 103,985 saw Super Bowl XIV between the Pittsburgh Steelers and the LA Rams (both USA) at the Rose Bowl, Pasadena, California, USA, on January 20, 1980.

FIRST UNDEFEATED REGULAR SEASON

The New England Patriots (USA) scored a 16-0 record in 2007, becoming the first NFL team to achieve an undefeated regular season since the league went to a 16-game schedule in 1978.

HIGHEST REGULAR SEASON SCORE

The Washington Redskins (USA) scored 72 points against the New York Giants' (USA) 41 at Washington, USA, on November 27, 1966. The aggregate score of 113 is also a record.

★ **MOST CONSECUTIVE NFL GAME WINS TO START A CAREER (HEAD COACH)**

Jim Caldwell (USA) started his career as head coach with the Indianapolis Colts (USA, see also below left) with 14 consecutive wins from September 13, 2009 to December 17, 2009, the best start to a coaching career in NFL history.

HIGHEST AGGREGATE SCORE IN A SUPER BOWL

When the San Francisco 49ers beat the San Diego Chargers (both USA) 49-26 in Super Bowl XXIX, they posted the highest aggregate score of any Super Bowl. The game, which was played on January 29, 1995 at Joe Robbie Stadium in Miami, Florida, saw the 49ers become the first team to win five Super Bowls. It was also the first Super Bowl between two teams from the same state.

COLTS CLASSICS

The Indianapolis Colts (USA) recorded 23 consecutive wins from November 2, 2008 to December 17, 2009, the ★ **most consecutive wins in NFL history**. The winning streak came at the end of a successful 10-year period for the Colts, whose 115 wins from 2000 to 2009 stand as the ★ **most NFL game wins in a single decade**.

> "The great thing about this game is that it requires an immense amount of authenticity."
> **Indianapolis Colts head coach Jim Caldwell**

DID YOU KNOW?

SOME MASSIVE INTERNATIONAL MUSIC STARS HAVE PROVIDED THE HALFTIME ENTERTAINMENT AT THE SUPER BOWL OVER THE YEARS, INCLUDING MICHAEL JACKSON, PAUL MCCARTNEY, AND U2.

The Rolling Stones played "Start Me Up," "Rough Justice," and "Satisfaction" at Super Bowl XL in 2006.

TRIVIA

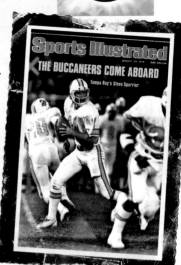

THE BUCCANEERS COME ABOARD

Tampa Bay's Steve Spurrier

★LARGEST NFL ATTENDANCE

An unprecedented crowd of 105,121 spectators watched the Dallas Cowboys play the New York Giants (both USA) at the Cowboys Stadium in Arlington, Texas, USA, on September 20, 2009. The game, which marked the opening of the stadium, saw the Giants win 33-31.

★HIGHEST POSTSEASON WINNING PERCENTAGE BY AN NFL HEAD COACH

NFL coaching legend Vince Lombardi (USA) registered a postseason mark of nine wins and one loss as coach of the Green Bay Packers (1961–67) -- a .900 win percentage.

LARGEST COMEBACK IN A CHAMPIONSHIP GAME

On January 21, 2007, the Indianapolis Colts (USA) overcame a 21-3 deficit and won the American Football Conference championship game over the New England Patriots (USA) 38-34, pulling off the biggest comeback in conference championship game history.

WORST START BY AN NFL FRANCHISE

In 1976, the Tampa Bay Buccaneers (USA) marked their first year in the NFL by losing their first 26 regular games, over two seasons. The streak was ended by a 33-14 win over the New Orleans Saints (USA) on December 11, 1977.

HIGHEST SCORE IN A NON-NFL GAME

Georgia Tech from Atlanta, Georgia, USA, scored 222 points, including a record 32 touchdowns, against Cumberland University, Lebanon, Tennessee, USA, on October 7, 1916. Georgia Tech is one of the most successful college football teams.

MOST CONSECUTIVE POSTSEASON VICTORIES BY AN NFL TEAM

The New England Patriots (USA) won 10 consecutive NFL postseason games from 2001 to 2006. During this time, they captured three Super Bowls in four seasons.

★MOST POINTS SCORED IN AN NFL REGULAR SEASON BY A TEAM

In 2007, the New England Patriots (USA) scored 589 points, topping the 556 points by the Minnesota Vikings (USA) in 1998.

In that same season, the Patriots scored the **most touchdowns by a team in an NFL season** with 75, surpassing the previous high of 70 by the Miami Dolphins (USA) in 1984.

FIRST NFL REGULAR SEASON GAME PLAYED IN EUROPE

On October 28, 2007, the New York Giants beat the Miami Dolphins (both USA) 13-10 at Wembley Stadium in London, UK, in the first NFL regular season game to be played in Europe.

★HIGHEST-SCORING POSTSEASON NFL GAME

On January 10, 2010, a play-off game between the Arizona Cardinals and the Green Bay Packers (both USA) ended in a 51-45 victory to the Cardinals. The 96-point total is an NFL postseason record.

ROBINSON

IWEBEM   DANSBY

WON
THE PITTSBURGH STEELERS HAVE WON THE SUPER BOWL ON A RECORD SIX OCCASIONS, AT SUPER BOWLS IX, X, XIII, XIV, XL, AND XLIII.

LOST
THREE TEAMS HAVE RUN OUT LOSERS IN THE SUPER BOWL ON FOUR OCCASIONS - THE MINNES...

SPORTS
AUTO-SPORTS

★MOST FORMULA ONE GRANDS PRIX

The greatest number of Formula One (F1) Grand Prix wins by a driver is 91, by Michael Schumacher (Germany) between August 30, 1992 and October 1, 2006. Schumacher also holds the record for the ★**most points scored in a Formula One career**: he amassed 1,377 points from races between August 25, 1991 and March 14, 2010.

★MOST NASCAR TRUCK SERIES CHAMPIONSHIPS

Ron Hornaday, Jr (USA) has been National Association for Stock Car Auto Racing (NASCAR) Truck Series champion four times, 1996–2009.

CARS

DAKAR RALLY

The ★**most consecutive Dakar rallies completed** is 20, by Yoshimasa Sugawara (Japan), from 1983 to 2009.

He also holds a record for the ★**most consecutive Dakar rallies raced**, having entered 26 competitions during the same time period.

★MOST F1 FASTEST LAPS IN A CAREER

The greatest number of fastest laps achieved by one driver in a Formula One career is 76 by Michael Schumacher (Germany)

between August 25, 1991 and October 22, 2006.

The ★**most fastest laps by one driver in a Formula One season** is 10, by Michael Schumacher in 2004 and Kimi Raikkonen (Finland) in 2005 and 2008.

MOST F1 POLE POSITIONS

The prolific Michael Schumacher also holds the record for the ★**most Formula One pole positions**: 68, achieved while he was driving for the Benetton and Ferrari teams between 1991 and 2006.

The ★**most consecutive Formula One pole positions** is eight, by Ayrton Senna (Brazil) for McLaren between the 1988 Spanish Grand Prix and the 1989 USA Grand Prix.

★MOST F1 WINS BY A MANUFACTURER

Ferrari (Italy) won 211 Formula One Grands Prix between 1961 and 2010, the greatest number of Grand Prix wins by a manufacturer.

Ferrari has also achieved the ★**most Formula One Constructors' World Championship titles**, with 16, in 1961, 1964, 1975–77, 1979, 1982–83, 1999–2004, and 2007–08.

★MOST F1 GRAND PRIX STARTS

Rubens Barrichello (Brazil) had 284 Formula One Grand Prix starts from 1993 to 2009.

★YOUNGEST DRIVER TO FINISH AN F1 RACE

Jaime Alguersuari (Spain, b. March 23, 1990) was aged just 19 years 125 days when he completed the Hungarian Grand Prix in Budapest, Hungary, on July 26, 2009.

WORLD RALLY CHAMPIONSHIPS

The ★**most FIA World Rallying Championship title wins** is six and was achieved by Sebastien Loeb (France) in 2004–09. This achievement also gives Loeb the record for the ★**most consecutive FIA World Rally Championship titles**, with six titles between 2004 and 2009. He won his sixth title on October 25, 2009 by just one point (93 points to 92) over his Finnish rival, Mikko Hirvonen.

The ★**most World Rally Championship race wins** is 53 and was achieved – yes, you've guessed it – by Sebastien Loeb, in 2002–09.

★MOST MOTO GRAND PRIX CHAMPIONSHIPS

Valentino Rossi (Italy) has won six Moto Grand Prix championships, in 2002–05 and 2008–09. Racing for the FIAT Yamaha Team, he acquired 306 points, winning six of the 17 races he took part in. The Moto GP was instituted in 2002, replacing the World Motorcycling Championship 500 cc Grand Prix.

★ MOST E1 CLASS ENDURO WORLD CHAMPIONSHIPS

Two riders have won the E1 class Enduro World Championships on two occasions: Ivan Cervantes (Spain), in 2005–06, and Mika Ahola (Finland, pictured above), in 2008–09.

QUIZ!
MICHAEL SCHUMACHER IS AN F1 LEGEND, BUT HE IS NOT THE YOUNGEST DRIVER TO FINISH AN F1 RACE. WHO IS?
SEE P.278 FOR THE ANSWER.

BIKES

★ MOST WINS AT THE LE MANS 24-HOUR RACE

The greatest number of wins by a driver at the Le Mans 24-hour race is eight, by Tom Kristensen (Denmark), in 1997, 2000–05, and 2008.

★ MOST CONSECUTIVE SPRINT CUP SERIES CHAMPIONSHIPS

Jimmie Johnson (USA) won four consecutive National Association for Stock Car Racing (NASCAR) Sprint Cup Series championships, from 2006 to 2009.

SUPERBIKE CHAMPIONSHIPS

The ★most American Motorcyclist Association (AMA) Superbike titles won by an individual rider is seven, by Matt Mladin (Australia), in 1999–2001, 2003–05, and 2009.

Between 1979 and 2009, Suzuki and Kawasaki (both Japan) won the championship 13 times, the **most AMA Superbike titles won by a manufacturer**.

The **most Superbike world championship manufacturer's titles won** is 16 by Ducati, in 1991–96, 1998–2004, 2006, and 2008–09.

ISLE OF MAN TT RACES

The ★**fastest average speed by a rider at the Isle of Man TT** is 131.578 mph (211.754 km/h) by John McGuinness (UK) on a Honda CBR1000RR in 2009.

The ★**fastest lap recorded by a rider at the Isle of Man TT in the Superbike TT class** is 17 min 21.29 sec, also by John McGuinness, on a Honda CBR1000RR, in 2009.

John McGuinness also recorded the ★**fastest time by a rider in an Isle of Man TT Superbike race (six laps)**. Riding a 1000 HM Plant Honda, he registered a time of 1 hr 46 min 7.16 sec in 2009.

★ MOST WORLD TOURING CAR CHAMPIONSHIPS BY A DRIVER

Guernsey-born racer Andy Priaulx has won three World Touring Car Championships driving for BMW Team UK, from 2005 to 2007.

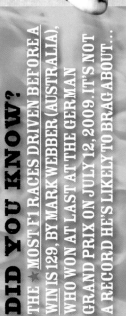

F1!
THE TERM "FORMULA ONE" REFERS TO RULES (THE "FORMULA") TO WHICH ALL DRIVERS AND MANUFACTURERS TAKING PART IN THE RACE MUST AGREE.

The ★**fastest lap by a woman** on the 37.73-mile (60.75-km) Isle of Man TT course is 19 min 22.6 sec at an average speed of 116.83 mph (188.02 km/h) and was achieved by Jenny Tinmouth (UK) on June 12, 2009.

★ MOST MOTOCROSS DES NATIONS WINS

The Motorcross des Nations, also known as the "Olympics of Motocross," has been contested annually since 1947. The national team with the greatest number of wins is the USA, with 20 between 1981 and 2009.

DID YOU KNOW?
THE ★MOST F1 RACES DRIVEN BEFORE A WIN IS 129, BY MARK WEBBER (AUSTRALIA), WHO WON AT LAST AT THE GERMAN GRAND PRIX ON JULY 12, 2009. IT'S NOT A RECORD HE'S LIKELY TO BRAG ABOUT...

★ NEW RECORD · ★ UPDATED RECORD

André Lagache and René Léonard (both France) won the first Le Mans race, staged in 1923.

TRIVIA

IMPALA SS

Ashrita Furman (USA) simultaneously balanced 700 eggs vertically on one end at the Rhode Island School of Design in Providence, Rhode Island,

SPORTS

BALL SPORTS

MOST ALL-IRELAND FINAL WINS

Kerry (Ireland) have won Gaelic football's All-Ireland Senior Football Championships, the sport's premier knockout competition, 36 times between 1903 and 2009.

★MOST POINTS IN A PRO BEACH VOLLEYBALL MATCH

When Larissa Franca and Juliana Felisberta Silva (Brazil, pictured) defeated Misty May-Treanor and Kerri Walsh (USA) 28-26, 40-42, 15-13 in Acapulco, Mexico, on October 30, 2005, the two teams clocked up a record 164 points in the match.

AUSSIE RULES

★MOST LEIGH MATTHEWS TROPHIES

Gary Ablett, Jr (Australia) has been awarded a record three Leigh Matthews Trophies, the highly coveted award presented to the most valuable player in the Australian Football League over a season. Ablett earned the awards playing for Geelong in 2007–09.

★MOST PLAYERS USED IN AN AFL SEASON

In 1911, St Kilda used 62 players over the course of the season, a record for the Australian Football League (then Victorian Football League).

CANADIAN FOOTBALL

★LARGEST GREY CUP TV AUDIENCE

The Canadian Football League's (CFL) Grey Cup is the biggest TV sports event in Canada. A total of 6.1 million viewers watched the Grey Cup match between the Montreal Alouettes and Saskatchewan Roughriders at Calgary, Canada, on November 29, 2009. The Alouettes won the game 28-27.

EXTRA!
PREFER BATS TO BALLS?
CHECK OUT TENNIS
& RACKET SPORTS
ON P.254.

★MOST VOLLEYBALL GRAND PRIX WINS

Brazil's female volleyball team has won the Grand Prix event eight times: in 1994, 1996, 1998, 2004–06, and 2008–09.

MIKASA

FIVB

CASH!
MISTY MAY-TREANOR (USA) HAS WON A RECORD $1,833,658 IN BEACH VOLLEYBALL EARNINGS THROUGH TO THE END OF THE 2009 SEASON.

"I'm 5'9"... For indoor volleyball I'd be short but for beach I'm average. People say I play tall."
Beach volleyball star Misty May-Treanor

★MOST NETBALL GOALS SCORED IN ONE HOUR (TEAM)

A record 257 netball goals were scored in one hour at an event organized by The Co-operative World Netball Series, at Piccadilly Gardens, Manchester, UK, on September 16, 2009.

HURLING

★MOST WINS OF ALL-IRELAND FINALS

Between 1904 and 2009, Kilkenny won a total of 32 All-Ireland Hurling Championships, the most wins by one team.

Part of Kilkenny's success included the **greatest number of successive wins in the All-Ireland Hurling Final**, with four in a row from 2006 to 2009, equaling Cork's run from 1941 to 1944.

KORFBALL

★MOST INDOOR EUROPEAN CUPS

Dutch korfball club Papendrechtse have won the indoor Korfball European Cup five times, in 1985, 1990, 1999–2000, and 2002.

★MOST WORLD GAMES WINS

The Netherlands holds the record for the most wins of the korfball tournament at the World Games with seven victories, in 1985, 1989, 1993, 1997, 2001, 2005, and 2009.

VOLLEY-BALL

★MOST WOMEN'S BEACH VOLLEYBALL WORLD CHAMPIONSHIPS

The world championships were first staged for both men and women in 1997. The USA women's pair has won the title four times, in 2003, 2005, 2007, and 2009.

★MOST MEN'S WORLD LEAGUE TITLES

Two national sides have each won eight gold medals in the World League: Italy were victorious in 1990–92, 1994–95, 1997, and 1999–2000, while Brazil won in 1993, 2001, 2003–07, and 2009.

★MOST TOUCH-DOWN PASSES IN A CFL SEASON (BY A QUARTER-BACK)

Doug Flutie (USA) threw 48 touchdown passes playing for the Calgary Stampeders in the Canadian Football League in 1995.

CUP! THE LARGEST BEACH VOLLEYBALL TOURNAMENT, THE HOSVI CUP, FEATURED 1,448 PARTICIPANTS AT THE HOSVI BEACH RESORT, ITALY, ON MAY 24, 2009.

HANDBALL

★HIGHEST COMBINED SCORE IN A WORLD CHAMPIONSHIP FINAL

The 2005 Men's Handball World Championship final between Spain and Croatia saw an aggregate of 74 points scored. Spain won 40-34.

★The highest combined score recorded in a Women's Handball World Championship final

is 61 points, in the match between France and Hungary in 2003. France won the match 32-29.

★FIRST NETBALL WORLD SERIES WINNERS

The inaugural Netball World Series was played in 2009 at Manchester, UK, and was won by New Zealand. This international competition features modified rules and will be played every year by the top six teams in the world.

DID YOU KNOW? THE MOST CONSECUTIVE VOLLEYBALL PASSES IS 92 AND WAS SET BY SV BAYER WUPPERTAL (GERMANY) IN THE BAYERHALL, WUPPERTAL, GERMANY, ON NOVEMBER 25, 2006.

The Brazil men's pair has won the beach volleyball World Championships title four times, in 1997, 1999, 2003, and 2005.

TRIVIA

BOSTON, MA, USA

The **first telephone call** was made in March 1876 in Boston, Massachusetts, USA, when Alexander Graham Bell (UK) phoned his assistant in a nearby room and said "Come here Watson, I want you."

SPORTS
BASEBALL

★ ★ ★ ★ ★ ★ ★ ★ ★ ★ ★ ☆

WORLD SERIES

★MOST GAMES PITCHED IN THE WORLD SERIES IN A CAREER

Mariano Rivera (Panama) of the New York Yankees (USA) pitched a record 24 games in World Series play in 1996, 1998, 1999, 2000, 2001, 2003, and 2009. The right-handed relief pitcher has won five World Series with the Yankees (1996, 1998, 1999, 2000, and 2009).

MOST HOME RUNS IN A WORLD SERIES GAME

Two batters have hit three home runs in a World Series game: Reggie Jackson (USA) of the New York Yankees (USA) in Game 6 of the 1977 World Series against the Los Angeles Dodgers (USA) on October 18, 1977; and Babe Ruth (USA) of the New York Yankees in Game 4 of the 1926 World Series against the St Louis Cardinals (USA) on October 6, 1926 and in Game 4 of the 1928 World Series, also against the St Louis Cardinals, on October 9, 1928.

★MOST STRIKEOUTS BY A BATTER IN A SINGLE WORLD SERIES

Ryan Howard of the Philadelphia Phillies (both USA) holds the unfortunate record for the most strikeouts by a batter in a World Series, with 13 in the 2009 World Series against the New York Yankees (USA).

WOW!
LAWRENCE PETER "YOGI" BERRA (USA) PLAYED IN A RECORD 14 WORLD SERIES FOR THE NEW YORK YANKEES (USA) BETWEEN 1947 AND 1963.

★MOST RUNS BATTED IN A WORLD SERIES GAME

Hideki Matsui (Japan) equaled the record for most runs batted in a World Series game when he hit six, playing for the New York Yankees against the Philadelphia Phillies (both USA) in Game 6 of the 2009 World Series on November 4, 2009. Matsui equaled the record of Robert C Richardson (USA) of the New York Yankees against the Pittsburgh Pirates (USA) in Game 3 of the 1960 World Series on October 8, 1960.

★LARGEST TELEVISION AUDIENCE FOR A WORLD SERIES

The highest average viewing figures per game for a baseball World Series is 44,278,950 viewers for the 1978 World Series between the New York Yankees and the LA Dodgers (both USA), on October 10–17, 1978. The games were broadcast on NBC and averaged a 56% share, meaning that they reached around 24.5 million homes.

★MOST WINS OF THE WORLD SERIES

The New York Yankees (USA) have won the World Series on 27 occasions: 1923, 1927–28, 1932, 1936–39, 1941, 1943, 1947, 1949–53, 1956, 1958, 1961–62, 1977–78, 1996, 1998–2000, and 2009.

MOST HOME RUNS IN A SINGLE WORLD SERIES

Chase Utley of the Philadelphia Phillies (both USA) hit five home runs in the 2009 World Series against the New York Yankees (USA), equaling the record set by Reggie Jackson (USA) of the New York Yankees in the 1977 World Series against the Los Angeles Dodgers (USA).

STRIKEOUT: When a batter has three strikes and does not manage to reach first base. This is a good stat for the pitcher, but bad for the batter!

★MOST CONSECUTIVE 200-HIT SEASONS

Playing for the Seattle Mariners (USA) from 2001 to 2009, Ichiro Suzuki (Japan) became the first player in Major League Baseball history to record 200 or more hits in nine straight seasons.

OWW!
GUS WEYHING (USA) HIT A RECORD 277 BATSMEN DURING HIS CAREER AS A PITCHER BETWEEN 1887 AND 1901. DESPITE THIS, HE WAS KNOWN AS A DECENT PITCHER!

★MOST GAMES PLAYED AT CATCHER

In 2009, Ivan Rodriguez (Puerto Rico) celebrated his 2,288th career game as catcher with the Texas Rangers, Florida Marlins, Detroit Tigers, New York Yankees, and Houston Astros (all USA) since he made his Major League debut on June 20, 1991.

★MOST GAMES PLAYED AT SHORTSTOP

Omar Vizquel (Venezuela) set a Major League Baseball record by playing 2,681 games in the shortstop position. Since 1989, he has played for the Seattle Mariners, Cleveland Indians, San Francisco Giants, Texas Rangers, and Chicago White Sox (all USA).

The venerable Vizquel also tops the list for ★**most double-plays by a shortstop**, having participated in a record 1,720 double-plays during a 20-year career in which he has received 11 Gold Glove awards in recognition of his fielding expertise.

★MOST POSTSEASON WINS BY A MANAGER

Joe Torre (USA) has achieved a record 84 postseason wins as a manager while at the helm of the Atlanta Braves, New York Yankees, and Los Angeles Dodgers (all USA) from 1982 to 2009.

★MOST HOME RUNS IN POSTSEASON

The Dominican Republic's Manny Ramirez has hit a record 29 postseason home runs playing for the Cleveland Indians, Boston Red Sox, and Los Angeles Dodgers (all USA) from 1995 to 2009.

★MOST HOME RUNS SCORED UNDER ONE MANAGER

Chipper Jones (USA) has hit 426 home runs playing for the Atlanta Braves under manager Robert J Cox (both USA) from 1993 to 2009.

★MOST STRIKEOUTS BY A LEFT-HANDED PITCHER

Left-handed pitcher Randy Johnson (USA) has recorded 4,875 strikeouts playing for the Montreal Expos (Canada), Seattle Mariners, Houston Astros, Arizona Diamondbacks, and New York Yankees (all USA) from 1988 to 2009.

★MOST COMBINED WINS AND SAVES

Andy Pettitte (USA) and Mariano Rivera (Panama) have combined for a win and a save on 59 occasions pitching for the New York Yankees (USA) from 1996 to 2009. Pettitte and Rivera surpassed the previous mark of 57 by Bob Welch and Dennis Eckersley (both USA) playing for the Oakland Athletics (USA) in the 1980s and 1990s.

MLB CAREER RECORDS

★MOST EJECTIONS FROM A GAME

Robert J Cox (USA) has been ejected from an MLB game 150 times while managing the Toronto Blue Jays (Canada) and Atlanta Braves (USA) from 1978 to 2009.

★MOST ASSISTS BY A FIRST BASEMAN IN A SEASON

Albert Pujols (Dominican Republic) achieved 185 assists as first baseman for the St Louis Cardinals (USA) during the 2009 season.

"There is no pressure. I just concentrate and do the best I can."
Albert Pujols, St Louis Cardinals' first baseman

EXTRA! FOR MORE DISPLAYS OF STRENGTH AND BALANCE, PITCH INTO P.90.

★ **NEW RECORD**
UPDATED RECORD

SPORTS
BASEBALL

★ MOST STRIKEOUTS IN AN MLB SEASON BY A BATTER

Playing for the Arizona Diamondbacks (USA) in 2009, Mark Reynolds (USA) scored a Major League Baseball record 223 strikeouts in the season.

PHEW!
THE FASTEST RECORDED BASEBALL PITCH IS 100.9 MPH (162.3 KM/H) AND WAS ACHIEVED BY LYNN NOLAN RYAN (USA) ON AUGUST 20, 1974.

MLB MILESTONES

FIRST PROFESSIONAL FRANCHISE TO LOSE 10,000 MATCHES

The Philadelphia Phillies (USA) became the first professional sports franchise ever to lose 10,000 games, dropping a 10-2 decision to the St Louis Cardinals (USA) on July 15, 2007. The franchise has a long history of losing, having played – and lost – its first game in May 1883.

★ FIRST PERSON WITH 2,000 WINS AS A MANAGER AND 2,000 HITS AS A PLAYER

Joe Torre (USA) is the only person in baseball history to record at least 2,000 games as a manager and 2,000 hits as a player.

FIRST PERSON TO RECORD 500 SAVES IN A CAREER AS A RELIEF PITCHER

The first relief pitcher in Major League Baseball (MLB) history to record 500 saves in a career is Trevor Hoffman (USA), playing for the Florida Marlins and San Diego Padres (both USA) from 1993 to 2007.

EXTRA!
FOR BATS OF A WINGED NATURE, GO LOOK AT MAMMALS ON P.65.

★ FEWEST GAMES TO REACH 200 HOME RUNS

Ryan Howard of the Philadelphia Phillies (both USA) needed just 658 games to reach 200 career home runs, achieving the feat on July 17, 2009.

★ FIRST TEAM WITH 500 CONSECUTIVE SELLOUTS

The Boston Red Sox (USA) recorded 500 consecutive regular-season sellout crowds at Fenway Park from May 15, 2003 to June 16, 2009.

MOST SEASONS WITH 40 OR MORE SAVES

Trevor Hoffman (USA) has recorded at least 40 saves in nine seasons for the San Diego Padres (USA) in 1996, 1998–2001, and 2004–07.

YOUNGEST PERSON TO HIT 50 HOME RUNS IN A SEASON

At 23 years 139 days, Prince Fielder (USA, b. May 9, 1984) became the youngest Major League player ever to hit 50 home runs in a season, when he homered while playing for the Milwaukee Brewers against the St Louis Cardinals (both USA) at Miller Park in Milwaukee, Wisconsin, USA, on September 25, 2007.

YOUNGEST PERSON TO HIT 500 HOME RUNS

At the age of just 32 years 8 days, Alex Rodriguez (USA, b. July 27, 1975) became the youngest player in baseball history to reach 500 career home runs when he homered off Kyle Davies (USA) – who was pitching for the Kansas City Royals (USA) against Rodriguez's New York Yankees (USA) team – at Yankee Stadium in the Bronx, New York City, USA, on August 3, 2007.

NEW RECORD
UPDATED RECORD

MOST IN A ROW

★ POSTSEASON GAMES DRIVING IN A RUN

Three players have recorded eight consecutive postseason games with at least one run batted in. Alex Rodriguez of the New York Yankees (both USA) achieved the feat between October 8, 2007 and October 20, 2009, just one day after Ryan Howard of the Philadelphia Phillies (both USA) had completed his own eight-game sequence on October 7–19, 2009. The first player to set the mark was Lou Gehrig (USA) while playing for the New York Yankees between October 4, 1928 and October 2, 1932.

★ MOST CAREER HOME RUNS BY A DESIGNATED HITTER

David Ortiz (Dominican Republic) hit a grand total of 274 home runs during a career in which he played for the Minnesota Twins and Boston Red Sox (both USA). Ortiz achieved his record playing between 1997 and 2009.

10°30'N 66°55'W

CARACAS, VENEZUELA
The **longest regularly scheduled bus route**, known as the "Liberator's Route," is 6,003 miles (9,660 km) long and is operated by Expreso Internacional Ormeño S.A. of Lima, Peru. It links Caracas, Venezuela and Buenos Aires, Argentina, passing through the capitals of six South American countries.

★ LONGEST BASEBALL MARATHON

The Jonny G Foundation Cardinals and the Edward Jones Browns (both USA) played baseball for 48 hr 9 min 27 sec at the T R Hughes Ballpark in St Louis, Missouri, USA, on October 9–11, 2009. Money raised by the event was donated to the SSM Cardinal Glennon Children's Medical Center.

★ LOSING SEASONS BY A TEAM

The Pittsburgh Pirates (USA) recorded 17 consecutive losing seasons from 1993 to 2009, surpassing the 16 straight losing seasons by the Philadelphia Phillies (USA) from 1933 to 1948.

HITS IN MLB

On June 19–21, 1938, right-handed third baseman Michael Franklin "Pinky" Higgins (USA) recorded 12 consecutive hits playing for the Boston Red Sox (USA). Walter "Moose" Dropo (USA) equaled this on July 14–15, 1952, playing for the Detroit Tigers (USA).

GAMES BATTED SAFELY

Joseph Paul DiMaggio (USA), playing for the New York Yankees (USA), safely batted in 56 consecutive games between May 15 and July 16, 1941.

DiMaggio played for nine World Series champions, but this was deemed his greatest feat and elevated him to the ranks of celebrity.

★ GAMES WITHOUT AN ERROR

The New York Yankees (USA) recorded 18 consecutive games without error from May 14, 2009 to June 1, 2009.

★ MOST BATTERS CONSECUTIVELY RETIRED BY A PITCHER

Mark Buehrle (USA) set a Major League Baseball record when he retired 45 batters in a row pitching for the Chicago White Sox (USA) on July 18–28, 2009.

THROUGH THE GATE

LARGEST ATTENDANCE AT A WORLD SERIES

A record 420,784 people attended the six-match series between the Los Angeles Dodgers and the Chicago White Sox (both USA) on October 1–8, 1959. The **largest attendance for a single World Series game** is 92,706 for the fifth game of the series, at the Memorial Coliseum in Los Angeles, USA, on October 6, 1959.

LARGEST ATTENDANCE AT A BASEBALL CLUB IN ONE YEAR

The record for annual attendance at an individual team is 4,483,350, for the home games of the Colorado Rockies (USA) at Mile High Stadium, Denver, Colorado, USA, in 1993.

Formed in 1993, the Colorado Rockies originally played at the Mile High Stadium, which had a capacity of 76,100. In 1995, they relocated to the Coors Field, with a smaller capacity of 50,381.

★ LARGEST ATTENDANCE AT A BASEBALL GAME

A 115,300-strong crowd attended an exhibition game played between the Los Angeles Dodgers and the Boston Red Sox (both USA) at the Los Angeles Memorial Coliseum, California, USA, on March 29, 2008.

INSTANT EXPERT

★ THE FIRST OFFICIALLY RECORDED BASEBALL GAME IN US HISTORY TOOK PLACE ON JUNE 19, 1846, IN HOBOKEN, NEW JERSEY, USA. THE "NEW YORK NINE" DEFEATED THE NEW YORK KNICKERBOCKERS, 23-1, IN FOUR INNINGS.

★ THE NATIONAL ASSOCIATION OF BASEBALL PLAYERS (NABBP) WAS THE FIRST GOVERNING ORGANIZATION IN US BASEBALL. IT WAS FOUNDED IN 1857.

★ IN 1903, BOSTON PLAYED THE PITTSBURGH PIRATES IN THE FIRST WORLD SERIES, WHICH BOSTON WON.

DID YOU KNOW?

TAKEYOSHI TOMINAGA AND HIKARU ADACHI (BOTH JAPAN) ACHIEVED 21 BASEBALL HITS IN ONE MINUTE ON THE SET OF *ZHENG DA ZONG YI* IN BEIJING, CHINA, ON NOVEMBER 14, 2008.

TRIVIA

Lou Gehrig's (USA) glove from his last baseball game on April 30, 1939 sold for $389,500 on September 29, 1999.

SAN JUAN, PUERTO RICO
Wilfred Benitez (b. New York, 12 September 1958) of Puerto Rico, was 17 years 176 days old when he won the WBA light welterweight title in San Juan,

18°27'N
66°04'W

SPORTS

BASKETBALL

NBA

★HIGHEST MARGIN OF VICTORY IN A PLAY-OFF GAME

On April 27, 2009, the Denver Nuggets (USA) beat the New Orleans Hornets (USA) by 58 points in a play-off game that they won 121-63, matching the Minneapolis Lakers' (USA) 133-75 win over the St Louis Hawks (USA) in 1956.

★HIGHEST 3-POINT FIELD GOAL PERCENTAGE (CAREER)

Steve Kerr (USA) recorded a 3-point field goal percentage of .454 playing for six different teams from 1988–89 to 2002–03.

HIGH
EPIPHANNY PRINCE (USA), FROM MURRY BERGTRAUM HIGH SCHOOL IN NEW YORK CITY, USA, SCORED A HIGH SCHOOL RECORD 113 POINTS AGAINST BRANDEIS HIGH IN 2006.

SCHOOL
THE MOST FREE THROWS IN ONE MINUTE IS 50 BY BOB J. FISHER (USA) AT VALLEY HEIGHTS HIGH SCHOOL, BLUE RAPIDS, KANSAS, USA, ON JANUARY 9, 2010.

QUIZ!
HOW MANY COUNTRIES HAVE THE HARLEM GLOBETROTTERS PLAYED IN TO DATE?
SEE P.278 FOR THE ANSWER.

★YOUNGEST INDIVIDUAL TO SCORE 25,000 POINTS IN AN NBA CAREER

Kobe Bryant (USA, b. August 23, 1978) was 31 years 151 days old when he reached the landmark of 25,000 National Basketball Association (NBA) career points. He achieved this feat playing for the Los Angeles Lakers (USA) on January 21, 2010.

★YOUNGEST INDIVIDUAL TO SCORE 12,000 POINTS IN A CAREER

At 24 years 35 days, Lebron James (USA, b. December 30, 1984) is the youngest player in NBA history to score 12,000 career points. James reached the mark playing for the Cleveland Cavaliers (USA) on February 3, 2009.

★MOST PLAY-OFF GAMES WON BY A COACH

As coach of the Chicago Bulls (USA) between 1989 and 1997 and the Los Angeles Lakers (USA) during two stints in charge, 1999–2003 and 2005–10, Phil Jackson (USA) won an unprecedented 219 play-off games.

★MOST ASSISTS IN ONE QUARTER

Steve Blake (USA) of the Portland Trail Blazers (USA) recorded 14 assists in the first quarter of a game against the Los Angeles Clippers (USA) on February 22, 2009. Blake matched the mark set by John Lucas (USA) of the San Antonio Spurs (USA) during the second quarter of a game against the Denver Nuggets (USA) on April 15, 1984.

★MOST CONSECUTIVE LOSSES TO START A SEASON

The New Jersey Nets (USA) started the 2009–10 season with a record 18 defeats in a row from October 28 to December 3, 2009.

★ NEW RECORD
★ UPDATED RECORD

★MOST BLOCKED SHOTS IN AN NBA FINALS GAME

Dwight Howard (USA) holds the record for the most blocked shots in an NBA Finals game with nine, playing for the Orlando Magic (USA) in Game 4 of the NBA Finals against the Los Angeles Lakers (USA) on June 11, 2009.

★HIGHEST 3-POINT FIELD GOAL PERCENTAGE (WNBA)

The highest 3-point field goal percentage (minimum 100 attempts) in Women's National Basketball Association (WNBA) games is .458 by Jennifer Azzi (USA) for the Detroit Shock (1999), the Utah Starzz (2000–02) and the San Antonio Silver Stars (all USA) in the 2003 season.

MOST NBA CHAMPIONSHIP TITLES WON BY A COACH

In 2009, Phil Jackson (USA) won his 10th NBA title as head coach, surpassing Red Auerbach's (USA) nine titles. Jackson won six NBA titles with the Chicago Bulls (USA) in 1991–93 and 1996–98, and four with the Los Angeles Lakers (USA) in 2000–02 and 2009.

★MOST FIELD GOALS IN A CAREER

Lisa Leslie (USA) scored 2,332 field goals in a 12-year career playing for the Los Angeles Sparks (USA) between 1997 and 2009.

WNBA

★HIGHEST FREE THROW PERCENTAGE

Eva Nemcova (Czech Republic) made a free throw percentage of .897 playing for the Cleveland Rockers (USA) from 1997 to 2001.

★HIGHEST REBOUNDS PER GAME AVERAGE

Cheryl Ford (USA) averaged 9.7 rebounds per game playing for the Detroit Shock (USA) since 2003.

★HIGHEST POINT-SCORING AVERAGE IN A CAREER

Seimone Augustus (USA) has scored 2,230 points in 105 games for the Minnesota Lynx (USA) since 2006, giving her a record point-scoring average of 21.2.

SKILLS

★MOST BASKETBALL BOUNCES IN ONE MINUTE

Kiran Harpal (Netherlands) made 384 bounces of a basketball in one minute at the Hiernasst Youth Center in Wijchen, the Netherlands, on Guinness World Records Day, November 12, 2009.

★FARTHEST SLAM DUNK USING A TRAMPOLINE

Jordan Ramos (UK) set the record for the farthest slam dunk from a trampoline with a 23-ft 5-in (7.15-m) effort on the set of *Blue Peter*, at BBC Television Studios, UK, on March 30, 2010.

★MOST FREE THROWS IN ONE HOUR

Perry Dissmore (USA) made an incredible 1,926 basketball free throws in one hour at Chipola College's Milton Johnson Health Center in Marianna, Florida, USA, on October 9, 2009.

★MOST CONSECUTIVE LOSSES BY AN NBA TEAM

The National Basketball Association (NBA) record for most consecutive losses by a team is 24 by the Cleveland Cavaliers (USA). The Cavaliers' record stretched over two seasons, 1981–82 and 1982–83.

DID YOU KNOW? BETWEEN JANUARY 1926 AND MAY 2010, LEGENDARY EXHIBITION TEAM THE HARLEM GLOBETROTTERS (USA) PLAYED IN A RECORD 120 COUNTRIES.

The Harlem Globetrotters claim to have played more than 25,000 games in their 84-year history.

TRIVIA

EXTRA! WANT TO FIND OUT ABOUT THE NBA

SPORTS
COMBAT SPORTS

LONG
BOXERS BOB FITZSIMMONS (UK, 1863–1917) AND JACK JOHNSON (USA, 1878–1946) SHARE THE LONGEST BOXING CAREER TITLE, WITH 31 YEARS IN THE RING EACH.

★OLDEST FEMALE PRO BOXER

Kazumi Izaki (Japan, b. March 2, 1963) was 46 years 304 days old when she fought Naoko Fujioka (Japan) in a flyweight bout in Tokyo, Japan, on November 30, 2009, although she was defeated by her younger opponent with a Technical Knockout (TKO) in round two.

★MOST FULL-CONTACT KICKS IN AN HOUR BY A TEAM

A team of 36 members of the Cobh Martial Arts Academy performed a total of 12,428 contact kicks in one hour in Cobh, Cork, Ireland, on April 22, 2009.

★MOST WRESTLING CHOKESLAMS IN ONE MINUTE

A chokeslam is a move in which a wrestler grasps an opponent's neck and slams him or her down. Italian wrestlers Nury Ayachi (aka Kaio), Carlo Lenzoni (aka Charlie Kid), and Mariel Shehi performed 34 chokeslams in a minute on the set of *Lo Show dei Record* in Rome, Italy, on February 25, 2010.

SHORT
TONY CANZONERI (USA, 1908–59) WAS WORLD LIGHT-WELTERWEIGHT BOXING CHAMPION FOR JUST 33 DAYS, FROM MAY 21, TO JUNE 23, 1933.

★ NEW RECORD
★ UPDATED RECORD

★MOST COMPETITIVE FULL-CONTACT ROUNDS

Between February 1993 and November 12, 2009, Paddy Doyle (UK) achieved 6,324 competitive full contact rounds in boxing and other martial arts.

★MOST MARTIAL ARTS KICKS IN ONE MINUTE (ONE LEG, FEMALE)

Chloe Bruce (UK) performed 212 martial arts kicks in a minute using just her right leg on the set of *Zheng Da Zong Yi – Guinness World Records Special* in Beijing, China, on June 19, 2009. Chloe's kicks were so swift that slow-motion footage was required to verify her feat.

★MOST MARTIAL ARTS THROWS IN ONE MINUTE

Veteran television comedian Joe Pasquale (UK) performed 29 martial arts throws in one minute on the set of *Guinness World Records – Smashed* at Pinewood Studios, UK, on April 15, 2009.

DID YOU KNOW?

ON MAY 13, 2000, *RIKISHI* ASANOKIRI LOST HIS SUMO BOUT DURING A TOURNAMENT AT THE KOKUGIKAN, SUMIDA-KU, TOKYO, JAPAN, BECAUSE HIS BELT FELL OFF DURING THE CONTEST.

John Ozuna (USA) threw a 43.3-mph (69.6-km/h) martial arts punch at KO Kung Fu Karate, San Jose, California, USA, on June 14, 2008.

TRIVIA

QUIZ!
WHO WROTE THE MARQUESS OF QUEENSBURY RULES?

SEE P.278 FOR THE ANSWER.

★MOST UFC MIDDLEWEIGHT CHAMPIONSHIP WINS

Lean, keen fighting machine Anderson Silva (Brazil) won a total of seven Ultimate Fighting Championship (UFC) Middleweight Championship bouts between 2006 and 2009.

Foil fencer Valentina Vezzali (Italy) cut
out a niche for herself in the world of fencing
with three consecutive individual Olympic gold
medals in foil fencing to her name, achieved
in 2000, 2004, and 2008.

MOST BOXING WORLD TITLES IN DIFFERENT WEIGHT DIVISIONS

Two men have held boxing titles at five
different weight divisions. Thomas Hearns
(USA) established his record between 1980
and 1988 while Manny Pacquiao (Philippines)
recently equaled the feat with titles in the WBO
Welterweight, WBC Lightweight, WBC Super
Featherweight, IBF Super Bantamweight,
and WBC Flyweight divisions.

★MOST PUNCHES LANDED IN A CHAMPIONSHIP BOXING MATCH

Troy Dorsey (USA) landed
a bone-shaking 620 punches
during the course of a
12-round IBF Featherweight
title match against Jorge
Paez (Mexico) in Las Vegas,
Nevada, USA, on February 4,
1990. Perhaps surprisingly,
this feat of fast-flying fists
didn't result in Dorsey's
victory. He eventually lost
the fight in a split decision,
despite the fact that Paez
landed only 340 punches
in reply.

★MOST PUNCHES THROWN IN A CHAMPIONSHIP BOXING MATCH

Antonio Margarito (Mexico)
threw 1,675 punches in a
12-round WBO Welterweight
title match victory against
Joshua Clottey (Ghana) in
Atlantic City, New Jersey,
USA, on December 2, 2006.

★MOST MARTIAL ARTS THROWS OF THE SAME PERSON IN ONE MINUTE

Martial artist Vito Zaccaria
(Italy) performed a total of
30 martial arts throws on his
fellow countryman Michele
Vallierion in one minute
on the set of *Lo Show dei
Record* in Milan, Italy, on
April 25, 2009.

★MOST SUMO TOP DIVISION WINS

The most Makunouchi wins
in Sumo wrestling by an
individual *rikishi* is 815
by Kaio (Japan, born
Hiroyuki Koga) from
1993 to 2010.

★TALLEST UFC FIGHTER

In the world of
UFC fighting there
is no one taller
than Stefan Struve
(Netherlands), who
measures 6 ft 11 in
(2.11 m). The
**★shortest UFC
fighters** are the
5-ft 6-in (1.65-m)
Manny Gamburyan,
Tyson Griffin,
Matt Serra, and Sean
Sherk (all USA).

INSTANT EXPERT

☢ THERE ARE FOUR OFFICIAL
SANCTIONING BODIES FOR THE
SPORT OF BOXING – THE WORLD
BOXING ASSOCIATION (WBA), THE
WORLD BOXING COUNCIL (WBC),
THE INTERNATIONAL BOXING
FEDERATION (IBF), AND THE WORLD
BOXING ORGANIZATION (WBO).

☢ DESPITE BEING NAMED
AFTER THE NINTH MARQUESS
OF QUEENSBURY, THE FAMOUS
RULES THAT BEAR HIS NAME WERE
ACTUALLY WRITTEN BY WELSHMAN
JOHN GRAHAM CHAMBERS.

☢ BOXING FIRST BECAME AN
OLYMPIC SPORT AT THE 1904
OLYMPIC GAMES HELD IN ST LOUIS,
MISSOURI, USA.

★MOST JUDO WORLD CHAMPIONSHIP WINS

Ryoko Tani (Japan) won
a record seven women's
World Judo Championship titles
in the 48 kg (105 lb) category
between 1993 and 2007 –
her first win came when she
was just 18 years and
27 days old.

EXTRA!
FOR SPORTS OF A MORE
X-TREME NATURE,
HEAD FOR X GAMES,
STARTING ON P.264.

RIKISHI:
The Japanese word for a professional
Sumo wrestler.

SPORTS
CYCLING

★FASTEST 3 KM TEAM PURSUIT (WOMEN'S TEAM)

The Great Britain trio of Elizabeth Armitstead, Wendy Houvenagel, and Joanna Rowsell set a new record for the women's 3 km team pursuit of 3 min 21.875 sec in Manchester, UK, on November 1, 2009.

MOST WINS...

★UCI TIME TRIAL WORLD CHAMPIONSHIPS (FEMALE)

France's Jeannie Longo-Ciprelli has won four Time Trial World Championships, in 1995–97 and 2001.

She also holds the record for the ★**most UCI Road Race World Championships won by a female**, with five wins in 1985–87, 1989, and 1995.

UCI TIME TRIAL WORLD CHAMPIONSHIPS (MALE)

Two men have won the Time Trial World Championships on three occasions: Michael Rogers (Australia) triumphed in 2003–05, and Fabian Cancellara (Switzerland) in 2006–07 and 2009.

★TRIALS CYCLING WORLD CHAMPIONSHIPS (TEAM)

Spain is the only team to have won the Trials Cycling World Championships twice, in 2008 and 2009.

★UCI PROTOUR

Spain's Alejandro Valverde is the only rider to have won the UCI ProTour on two occasions, in 2006 and 2008.

★UCI WOMEN'S ROAD WORLD CUPS

Four women have won the UCI Road World Cup on two occasions: Diana Ziliute (Lithuania) in 1998 and 2000; Nicole Cooke (UK) in 2003 and 2006; Oenone Wood (Australia) in 2004 and 2005; and Marianne Vos (Netherlands) in 2007 and 2009.

TRIALS CYCLING WORLD CHAMPIONSHIPS – ELITE CLASS (MALE)

Benito Ros Charral (Spain) has won the Elite Men's Trials World Championships a record six times, in 2003–05 and 2007–09.

UCI TRIALS CYCLING WORLD CHAMPIONSHIPS (FEMALE)

Switzerland's Karin Moor has won the Trials Cycling World Championships title on eight occasions, in consecutive years from 2001 to 2007 and again in 2009.

★MOUNTAIN BIKE WORLD CHAMPIONSHIPS (MARATHON, MALE)

Only two male riders have secured the UCI Mountain Bike Marathon World Championships on two occasions: Thomas Frischknecht (Switzerland), in 2003 and 2005, and Roel Paulissen (Belgium), in 2008–09.

The most wins of the **Mountain Bike World Championships marathon by a female rider** is four by Gunn-Rita Dahle Flesjå (Norway), in 2004–06 and 2008.

MOUNTAIN BIKE WORLD CUPS (FOUR-CROSS, FEMALE)

Anneke Beerten (Netherlands) has won the women's Four-Cross Mountain Bike World Cup on three occasions, in 2007–09.

Brian Lopes (USA) has won three Four-Cross World Cups, in 2002, 2005 and 2007, the greatest number by a male rider.

★ NEW RECORD
★ UPDATED RECORD

MOST MOUNTAIN BIKE CROSS-COUNTRY WORLD CUPS (MALE)

Julien Absalon (France) has won more mountain bike cross-country World Cup titles than any other man. His record five victories came in 2003 and from 2006 to 2009. Absalon has also won two Olympic gold medals in the discipline, in 2004 and 2008.

"It's about winning gold medals and I'd rather have one gold than three silvers."
Sir Chris Hoy displays the mentality of a winner

★ MOST GIRO D'ITALIA FEMMINILE WINS

Fabiana Luperini (Italy) has won the Tour of Italy women's race (Giro d'Italia Femminile) on five occasions, consecutively from 1995 to 1998 and again in 2008.

FASTEST...

★ UNPACED 500 M, STANDING START (WOMEN'S TEAM)

The Australia team of Kaarle McCulloch and Anna Meares set the team record for the women's unpaced 500 m cycle from a standing start with a time of 33.149 seconds at Pruszkow, Poland, on March 26, 2009.

The day before, Simona Krupeckaite (Lithuania) had set the individual female fastest time for the discipline, with 33.296 seconds at the same event in Poland.

★ UNPACED 750 M, STANDING START (MEN'S TEAM)

The Great Britain team of Chris Hoy, Jason Kenny, and Jamie Staff recorded a time of 42.950 seconds for the unpaced 750 m cycle from a standing start at Beijing, China, on August 15, 2008. The time came en route to the trio winning the team sprint gold medal at the Beijing Olympic Games, in which they beat France in the final in a time of 43.128 seconds.

DID YOU KNOW?

THE UNION CYCLISTE INTERNATIONALE (UCI) IS THE WORLD GOVERNING BODY FOR THE SPORT OF CYCLING.

The ★ greatest distance cycled on a static bike in a minute is 1.27 miles (2.04 km), by Miguel Angel Castro (Spain).

TRIVIA

LAND'S END TO JOHN O'GROATS

A classic cycling challenge, the 874-mile (1,407-km) route from Land's End in Cornwall, England, UK, to John O'Groats in Caithness, Scotland, UK, requires riders to travel the length of Great Britain between its two most distant points.

The ★ fastest time by a male rider to cycle from Land's End to John O'Groats is 44 hr 4 min 19 sec, by Gethin Butler (UK) in September 2001.

The ★ fastest time by a female rider to cycle from Land's End to John O'Groats is 52 hr 45 min 11 sec, set by Lynne Taylor (UK) on October 3, 2002.

Lynne is also the co-holder of the ★ fastest time to cycle from Land's End to John O'Groats on a tandem bicycle (mixed team), having achieved a time of 51 hr 19 min 23 sec with Andy Wilkinson (UK) in 2000.

★ MOST UCI MEN'S ROAD WORLD CUPS

Paolo Bettini (Italy) has won the UCI Road World Cup three times, which is a record for a male rider. The wins came in 2002–04. This competition was replaced by the UCI ProTour in 2005.

★ UNPACED 200 M FLYING START (MALE)

Kevin Sireau (France) set a new record of 9.572 seconds for the unpaced 200 m flying start sprint in Moscow, Russia, on May 30, 2009.

SPORTS

GOLF

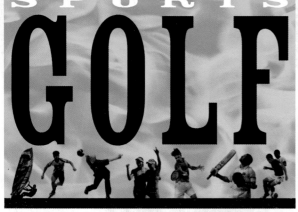

★ ★ ★ ★ ★ ★ ★ ★ ★ ★ ★ ★ ★ ★

"Records are made to be broken. Could somebody make 10 [birdies] in a row? Sure."

Birdie king Mark Calcavecchia (USA)

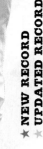

★ **MOST BIRDIES RECORDED IN A US MASTERS ROUND**

Anthony Kim (USA) scored 11 birdies in his second round at The Masters tournament at Augusta National, Augusta, Georgia, USA, on April 10, 2009. The previous record of 10 birdies had been set by Nick Price (Zimbabwe) in 1986.

EXTRA!
FOR A DIFFERENT KIND OF BIRDIE, SPREAD YOUR WINGS AND FLY OVER TO P. 62.

★ **LOWEST SCORE BELOW PAR IN 72 HOLES IN A PGA TOUR EVENT**

Ernie Els (South Africa) had a score of -31 (31 under par) after 72 holes of the 2003 Mercedes Championships, Maui, Hawaii, USA, on January 9–12, 2003.

★ NEW RECORD
★ UPDATED RECORD

★ HIGHEST PRIZE MONEY FOR A GOLF TOURNAMENT

The Professional Golfer's Association (PGA) tour Players Championships contested at Sawgrass, Florida, USA, in 2008 and 2009 had a total prize pool of $9,500,000 each year – with a spectacular $1,710,000 going to the winner.

★ HIGHEST COMBINED PRIZE MONEY FOR THE WGC MATCH PLAY CHAMPIONSHIP

The World Golf Championships (WGC) Match Play Championship played at the Ritz-Carlton Golf Club, Marana, Arizona, USA, in 2009 had a total prize pool of $8,500,000.

★ LOWEST SCORE IN 72 HOLES IN A PGA TOUR EVENT

Tommy Armour III (USA) posted a four-round score of 254 (26 strokes under par) at the 2003 Valero Texas Open, San Antonio, Texas, USA, on September 25–28, 2003.

★ MOST BIRDIES IN A 72-HOLE GOLF PGA TOUR EVENT

Mark Calcavecchia (USA) hit 32 birdies in 72 holes at the 2001 Phoenix Open in Phoenix, USA, on January 25–28, 2001. The feat was equaled by Paul Gow (Australia) at the 2001 B.C. Open, in New York, USA, on July 19–22, 2001.

★ MOST CONSECUTIVE BIRDIES IN A PGA TOUR EVENT

Playing "preferred lies" on a rain-sodden course, US PGA tour veteran Mark Calcavecchia (USA) scored nine consecutive birdies in the third round of the Canadian Open at Oakville, Ontario, Canada, on July 25, 2009.

★ MOST CONSECUTIVE US AMATEUR GOLF TITLES

Before embarking on a stellar professional career, Tiger Woods (USA) recorded three consecutive US Amateur Championship wins between 1994 and 1996.

MOST CURTIS CUP APPEARANCES

Carole Semple-Thompson (USA) played in 12 ties and won a record 18 matches from 1974 to 2002.

★ MOST SOLHEIM CUP APPEARANCES

Laura Davies (UK) has played for Europe in every Solheim Cup from 1990 to 2009, making 11 appearances.

MORE!
A RECORD 632 PEOPLE TOOK PART IN A GOLF LESSON TAUGHT BY ZHANG LIANWEI (CHINA) IN HAINAN PROVINCE, CHINA, ON DECEMBER 11, 2009.

FORE!
IN FEBRUARY 1971, ASTRONAUT ALAN SHEPARD (USA) STRUCK TWO GOLF BALLS ON THE SURFACE OF THE MOON, THE MOST REMOTE GOLF SHOTS EVER.

★ LONGEST SEATED GOLF SHOT

Dale Sheppard (Australia) hit a golf ball 372 ft 6 in (113.55 m), while seated, on the Moonah Links Golf Club's Open Course 11th hole in Mornington Peninsula, Victoria, Australia, on November 27, 2009.

before sunset at 5:30 p.m. They were raising money for the Grafton Oncology Ward. The final score after 10-and-a-half rounds was 952 (206 over par).

★ MOST HOLES PLAYED BY FOURBALL TEAMS IN 24 HOURS

In an event organized by PGA Design Consulting Ltd, MBC ESPN, and AHA Golf Inc. at Gunsan Country Club, South Korea, 93 fourball teams played 6,974 holes of golf in 24 hours on June 28, 2009.

★ OLDEST GOLFER TO WIN A CLUB CHAMPIONSHIP

Tom S Bennett (USA, b. January 26, 1934) won the Valencia Golf and Country Club championship aged 75 years 56 days in Naples, Florida, USA, on March 23, 2009.

★ FEWEST STROKES TO COMPLETE A MARATHON DISTANCE

Jake Sand (USA) took 494 strokes to complete the marathon distance of 26 miles 385 yd (42.195 km) playing golf at Desert Mountain Golf Resort, Arizona, USA, on May 28, 2009. Sand averaged a very creditable 93.4 yd (85.4 m) per shot and completed the marathon distance in a time of 9 hr 57 min 25.14 sec.

YOUNGEST WINNER ON THE PGA EUROPEAN TOUR

Danny Lee (New Zealand, b. July 24, 1990) was aged just 18 years 213 days when he won the Johnnie Walker Classic at The Vines Resort and Country Club, Perth, Australia, on February 22, 2009.

★ LARGEST ONE-DAY GOLF TOURNAMENT

A one-day golf tournament featuring 1,019 participants was held by Golfers512 Fund Raising Campaign (China) at Mission Hills Golf Club in Shenzhen, China, on June 12, 2009.

★ MOST 18-HOLE GOLF COURSES PLAYED IN ONE YEAR

Cathie and Jonathan Weaver (both Canada) played a total of 449 different 18-hole golf courses in one year. Their golfing bonanza was staged at a variety of locations across Canada and the USA, from April 1, 2008 to March 31, 2009.

★ LONGEST 19TH HOLE

The "Extreme 19th" at the Legend Golf and Safari Resort, South Africa, measures 1,312 ft 4 in (400 m) in horizontal distance, with the tee and hole separated by a 1,410-ft 9-in (430-m) drop. The tee is located on Hanglip Mountain.

★ MOST SOLHEIM CUP POINTS SCORED

Sweden's Annika Sorenstam scored 24 Solheim Cup points playing for the Europe team in the biennial event from 1994 to 2007.

Sorenstam also holds the record for the **highest career earnings on the US LPGA Tour**, with $22,573,192 between 1993 and 2009.

★ MOST HOLES PLAYED BY A PAIR IN 12 HOURS (CART)

Using a golf cart to speed their progress, Jason Casserly and Chris Woods (both Australia) played 189 holes of golf in 12 hours at Grafton District Golf Club, Grafton, Australia, on April 26, 2009. The golfers used foursome rules (taking alternate shots), starting at 5:30 a.m., just before sunrise, and finishing just

★ HIGHEST WINNING US MASTERS SCORE

The highest score recorded by a golfer to win The Masters golf tournament is 289, by three golfers: Sam Snead (USA) in 1954, Jack Burke, Jr (USA) in 1956, and Zach Johnson (USA, far left) in 2007.

The longest golf course in British Open history was Carnoustie, Scotland, which measured 7,421 yd (6,785 m) in 2007.

TRIVIA

SPORTS
ICE HOCKEY

★ EXTRA!
FOR WARMER, MORE RELAXING PASTIMES, TRY OUT SOME TOYS & GAMES ON P.146.

★ NEW RECORD
★ UPDATED RECORD

★ MOST REGULAR-SEASON GOALS CONCEDED BY A GOALTENDER

Gilles Meloche (Canada) has allowed more regular-season goals in his career than any other NHL goaltender, having conceded 2,756 goals playing for the Chicago Black Hawks, California Golden Seals, Cleveland Barons, Minnesota North Stars, and Pittsburgh Penguins (all USA) from the 1970–71 season to 1987–88.

GOALIES

★ MOST MATCHES WON BY AN NHL GOALTENDER

Martin Brodeur is no stranger to these pages, but as the Canadian netminder's career goes on and on, the records just keep tumbling. Brodeur has now recorded 598 regular-season wins in his career playing for the New Jersey Devils (USA) since the 1993–94 season to January 2010.

• Brodeur also holds the NHL record for ★ **most regular-season games played by a goaltender**, having played 1,069 times for the Devils in his career.

• Such career longevity has seen Brodeur take the records for ★ **most regular-season minutes played**, with 63,091, and also the ★ **most regular-season shutouts by a goaltender**, with 108 career clean sheets.

★ MOST STANLEY CUP PLAYOFF GAMES PLAYED BY A GOALTENDER

Retired goaltending great Patrick Roy (Canada) still holds the NHL record for most games played by a goaltender in the Stanley Cup playoffs, having featured in 247 matches playing for the Montreal Canadiens (Canada) and Colorado Rockies (USA) from 1985–86 to 2002–03.

• Having played in so many playoff games for two exceptional teams, it's perhaps no surprise that Roy, dubbed "St Patrick" by fans, holds the NHL record for **most wins by a goaltender in the Stanley Cup playoffs** with 151 career victories.

• Roy is the **only player to have won the Conn Smythe Trophy on three occasions**, in 1986, 1993, and 2001. The prestigious trophy is awarded each year to the Most Valuable Player in the Stanley Cup playoffs.

★ MOST REGULAR SEASON LOSSES BY A GOALTENDER

In a career that stretched from 1989 to 2009, Curtis Joseph (Canada) tied the unfortunate record for most regular-season career losses by an NHL goaltender, which had been set by Lorne "Gump" Worsley (Canada) between 1952 and 1974. Both long-playing netminders have experienced 352 defeats.

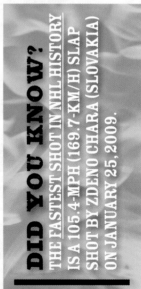

DID YOU KNOW?
THE FASTEST SHOT IN NHL HISTORY IS A 105.4-MPH (169.7-KM/H) SLAP SHOT BY ZDENO CHARA (SLOVAKIA) ON JANUARY 25, 2009.

Per Olsen (Denmark) hit the **fastest goal**, 2 seconds into a game in the Danish First Division on January 14, 1990.

TRIVIA

★ YOUNGEST CAPTAIN OF A STANLEY CUP-WINNING TEAM

At 21 years 10 months 5 days, Sidney Crosby (Canada, b. August 7, 1987) became the youngest captain of a Stanley Cup-winning team when the Pittsburgh Penguins defeated the Detroit Red Wings (both USA) in the 2009 finals.

★FIRST TEAM TO WIN 3,000 REGULAR-SEASON GAMES

The Montreal Canadiens (Canada) beat the Florida Panthers (USA) 5-2 on December 29, 2008, in Sunrise, Florida, USA – their 3,000th regular-season victory. The Canadiens are the first team in NHL history to achieve the feat.

SCORING

FASTEST GOALS SCORED IN AN NHL MATCH

The quickest goals in an NHL match came five seconds after the opening whistle.

This record is held jointly by three players. Doug Smail (Canada), for the Winnipeg Jets (Canada) against the St Louis Blues (USA) at Winnipeg, Manitoba, Canada, on December 20, 1981; Bryan John Trottier

(Canada), for the New York Islanders against the Boston Bruins (both USA) at Boston, USA, on March 22, 1984; and Alexander Mogilny (Russia), for the Buffalo Sabres (USA) against the Toronto Maple Leafs (Canada) at Toronto, Ontario, Canada, on December 21, 1991.

ONLY PLAYERS TO SCORE IN THEIR FIRST SIX GAMES

Joe Malone, Newsy Lalonde, and Cy Denneny (all Canada) each scored in their first six games during the NHL's inaugural season way back in 1917–18.

On November 1, 2006, Evgeni Malkin (Russia) became the first NHL player in 89 years to score in his first six games while playing for the Pittsburgh Penguins (USA). His scoring streak had begun on October 18, 2006.

★MOST SHOOTOUT GOALS

As of March 2010, Vyacheslav Kozlov (Russia) has scored 27 NHL ice hockey shootout goals in his career, playing for the Detroit Red Wings, Buffalo Sabres, and Atlanta Thrashers, from 1991 to 2010.

★MOST CONSECUTIVE SEASONS SCORING MORE THAN 100 POINTS

The Detroit Red Wings (USA) became the first team in the history of the NHL to top 100 points in 10 straight seasons, from 1999–2000 to 2009–10.

★MOST CONSECUTIVE GAMES IN WHICH AN NHL DEFENSEMAN HAS SCORED

Mike Green (Canada) set a record for defensemen by scoring a goal in eight consecutive games for the Washington Capitals (USA) during the 2008–09 season, his last goal coming in a 5-1 win over the Tampa Bay Lightning (USA) on February 14, 2009.

"Try to just carry a positive attitude and try to be a good teammate every day."

Mike Sillinger on playing for a number of teams (see left)

★MOST TRADED PLAYERS

Mike Sillinger (right) and Brent Ashton (both Canada) have each been traded (sold to another team) a record nine times during their careers playing in the NHL.

OLD! THE OLDEST REGULAR ICE HOCKEY PLAYER IS KLAUS SIMON (GERMANY), WHO CURRENTLY PLAYS FOR CLUB OSTERODE (GERMANY) AGED 69.

YOUNG! ON NOVEMBER 12, 1942, AGED 16 YEARS 11 MONTHS, BEP GUIDOLIN (CANADA) BECAME THE YOUNGEST NHL PLAYER WHEN HE PLAYED FOR THE BOSTON BRUINS (USA).

SPORTS
MARATHONS

AMAZING AUSSIE

The ★**most wins of the wheelchair event at the New York Marathon by a male athlete** is four by Kurt Fearnley (Australia) in 2006–09. Kurt also holds the record for the ★**fastest time to complete the London Marathon by a male wheelchair athlete** with 1 hr 28 min 57 sec on April 26, 2009.

FAST
THE FASTEST TIME TO COMPLETE THE LONDON MARATHON BY A FEMALE WHEELCHAIR ATHLETE IS 1 HR 48 MIN 4 SEC BY SANDRA GRAF (SWITZERLAND) IN 2008.

★ **NEW RECORD**
★ **UPDATED RECORD**

FASTEST TIME TO RUN THE LONDON MARATHON (MALE)

Kenya's Samuel Wanjiru recorded the fastest time to complete the London Marathon by a male athlete when he completed the 26-mile 385-yard (42.195-km) course, which winds through the streets of London, UK, in 2 hr 5 min 10 sec on April 26, 2009.

★FASTEST MARATHON ON CRUTCHES (ONE LEG)

Simon Baker (UK) completed the fastest marathon on crutches using one leg when he crossed the finish line at the 2008 Dublin City Marathon in Dublin, Ireland, in 6 hr 42 min 47 sec on October 27, 2008.

★FASTEST MARATHON BY A RELAY TEAM

The fastest time in which a relay team has completed a marathon is 2 hr 10 min 50 sec, by the Team Jack & Adam's Bicycles/Zapata Roadrunners (USA), formed by Rueben Ondari, Stephen Ariga, Kibet Cherop, Scott Kimbell, and Derek Yorek (Kenya/USA), in the Silicon Laboratories Austin Marathon Relay, at Auditorium Shores in Austin, Texas, USA, on September 27, 2009.

★FASTEST MARATHON WEARING ARMOR

On September 21, 2008, Peter Pedersen (Denmark) completed the HC Andersen Marathon in Odense, Denmark, in 6 hr 46 min 59 sec wearing a full suit of armor for the entire run.

APPLY!
FANCY TRYING FOR A GUINNESS WORLD RECORD AT THE VIRGIN LONDON MARATHON 2011? APPLY ONLINE AT:
WWW.GUINNESSWORLD
RECORDS.COM/VIRGIN

★MOST SIBLINGS TO COMPLETE A MARATHON

An incredible 16 siblings from the Kapral family – Chris, Vince, Steve, Tony, Joe, Doug, Angela, Allison, Theresa, Phil, Michelle, Mary, Nick, Mike, David, and Sarah (all USA) – ran the Community First Fox City Marathon, Appleton, Wisconsin, USA, on September 20, 2009.

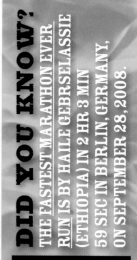

DID YOU KNOW? THE FASTEST MARATHON EVER RUN IS BY HAILE GEBRSELASSIE (ETHIOPIA) IN 2 HR 3 MIN 59 SEC IN BERLIN, GERMANY, ON SEPTEMBER 28, 2008.

Haile Gebrselassie's marathon world record run had an average speed of 12.6 mph (20.4 km/h).

TRIVIA

VIRGIN LONDON MARATHON 2010

On April 25, 2010, an incredible 36,549 runners completed the Virgin London Marathon (UK), a record for this great city marathon, which was celebrating its 30th anniversary. Once again Guinness World Records was proud to be involved, with 75 runners competing in 27 record categories and an astounding 19 new Guinness World Records awarded on the day. Well done, everyone!

LONDON MARATHON RECORDS

RECORD TITLE	RECORD RESULT & RUNNER	RECORD TITLE	RECORD RESULT & RUNNER	RECORD TITLE	RECORD RESULT & RUNNER
★Fastest marathon carrying a 60-lb pack	5 hr 28 min 53 sec by Benjamin Harrop (UK)	★Fastest marathon in a firefighter's uniform	5 hr 32 min 55 sec by Nigel Addison-Evans (UK)	★Fastest marathon in school uniform (female)	4 hr 14 min 46 sec by Louise Winstanley (UK)
★Fastest marathon in an animal costume (male)	3 hr 30 min 10 sec by Kevin Robins (UK) dressed as a tiger	★Fastest marathon dressed as a golfer (male)	3 hr 43 min 20 sec by Bertrand Bodson (Belgium)	★Fastest marathon in a superhero costume (female)	3 hr 8 min 55 sec by Jill Christie (UK)
★Fastest marathon dressed as a baby	3 hr 13 min 30 sec by Tony Audenshaw (UK)	★Fastest marathon dressed as a jester	3 hr 33 min 55 sec by David Smith (UK)	★Fastest marathon dressed as a television character (male)	4 hr 1 min 40 sec by Paul Franks (UK) dressed as a Dalek
★Fastest marathon dressed as a bottle (female)	4 hr 54 min 36 sec by Gill Begnor (UK)	★Fastest marathon dressed as a leprechaun	3 hr 9 min 40 sec by Ben Afforselles (UK)	★Tallest costume worn running in a marathon (See picture, right)	23 ft 1 in (7.04 m) by Jean Paul Delacy (UK)
★Longest crochet chain while running a marathon	253 ft (77.4 m) by Susie Hewer (UK)	★Fastest marathon in a martial arts suit	3 hr 39 min 20 sec by Peter Kelly (UK)	★Fastest marathon dressed as a cartoon character	3 hr 7 min 34 sec by David Ross (UK) dressed as Fred Flintstone
★Fastest marathon dressed as a doctor (male)	4 hr 21 min 9 sec by Tom Solomon (UK)	★Fastest marathon in a nurse's uniform (male)	3 hr 46 min 27 sec by Andrew White (UK)	★Fastest marathon dressed as a book character	4 hr 1 min 47 sec by Ian Young (UK) dressed as Sherlock Holmes

TEAM CATERPILLAR

The ★most runners linked to complete a marathon is 34, by Team Caterpillar at the Virgin London Marathon, London, UK, on April 25, 2010. The team, organized by Phil Nevin (UK), included Princess Beatrice (UK), the first royal to run the London Marathon, and Virgin boss Richard Branson (UK) and finished in a time of 5 hr 13 m 3 sec.

SPORTS
NBA JAM

★ ★ ★ ★ ★ ★ ★ ★ ★ ★ ★ ★ ★

ALL★STAR JAM SESSION DALLAS★2010 PRESENTED BY adidas

★LARGEST SPORTS TRADING CARD

At the NBA All-Star Jam Session in Dallas, Texas, USA, on February 13, 2010, a sports trading card measuring 59.75 x 84 in (151 x 213 cm) was unveiled by Panini (USA). The colossal card featured LA Lakers star Kobe Bryant (USA).

★MOST POINTS SCORED AS KOBE BRYANT ON THE NBA 2K10 VIDEO GAME

At the NBA All-Star Jam Session, fans and players get the chance to show off their skills on the latest NBA video game. On February 13, 2010, Chico Kora (USA) scored 29 points playing as Kobe Bryant on 2K Sports *NBA 2K10* (playing a four-minute game, with one minute per quarter).

Several other video-game records were set at the NBA All-Star Jam Session.

★MOST FREE THROWS MADE IN TWO MINUTES WHILE ALTERNATING HANDS

Jeff Harris (USA) made 44 basketball free throws in two minutes using alternate hands at the NBA All-Star Jam Session in Dallas, Texas, USA, on February 10, 2010.

The ★**most steals on 2K Sports *NBA 2K10* (playing a four-minute game, with one minute per quarter)** is seven by Wesley Parker (USA), on February 10, 2010. The ★**most assists**, within the same parameters, is 16 by Andrew Frost and J R Wildly (both USA), on February 11, 2010.

The ★**most points scored in the first half of a 2K Sports *NBA 2K10* video game**, within the same parameters, is 17 by Cody Redrick and Brandon McJunlain (both USA), on February 12, 2010.

HIGHEST SLAM DUNK WITH A BACKFLIP

Jerry Burrell (USA) made a slam dunk having performed a backflip from a 15-ft 4-in-tall (4.67-m) platform. Burrell achieved the feat during the NBA All-Star Jam Session in Phoenix, Arizona, USA, on February 16, 2009.

ALL
THE RECORD FOR THE MOST CONSECUTIVE ALL-STAR GAME SELECTIONS IS 14, JOINTLY HELD BY SHAQUILLE O'NEAL, JERRY WEST AND KARL MALONE (ALL USA).

★FARTHEST SHOT MADE WHILE SITTING ON COURT

Orlando Magic (USA) center Dwight Howard (USA) made a shot measured at 52 ft 6 in (15.99 m) while sitting on the court at the NBA All-Star Jam Session in Dallas, Texas, USA, on February 13, 2010.

STAR
MICHAEL JORDAN (USA) SCORED 262 POINTS IN NBA ALL-STAR GAMES, INCLUDING 20 POINTS IN HIS 14TH AND FINAL GAME IN ATLANTA, GEORGIA, USA, ON FEBRUARY 9, 2003.

DID YOU KNOW?

THE ★FARTHEST SIX-PERSON TANDEM BEFORE A DUNK USING A TRAMPOLINE IS 20 FT (6 M) AND WAS ACHIEVED BY TEAM ACRODUNK (USA).

The **most consecutive three-pointers scored** on *NBA 2K9* is eight by Marcus Platt (USA).

TRIVIA

FARTHEST HOOK SHOT

Special K Daley (USA) of the Harlem Globetrotters recorded a hook shot measured at 46 ft 6 in (14.15 m) at the NBA All-Star Jam Session, Dallas, Texas, USA, on February 13, 2010.

108,713

★ LARGEST ATTENDANCE FOR A BASKETBALL GAME

The NBA All-Star Game played at Cowboys Stadium in Arlington, Texas, USA, on February 14, 2010 was watched by 108,713 fans, the largest ever basketball crowd. The game saw the East beat the West 141–139.

one hand for 32.88 seconds. Baker achieved the record by spinning one ball on top of the other. At the same event, Baker also performed the **most headers while spinning two basketballs**, with 40 bounces of the ball on his forehead.

LONGEST TIME SPINNING TWO BASKETBALLS USING ONE HAND

During the NBA All-Star Jam Session held in Phoenix, Arizona, USA, on February 14, 2009, professional basketball freestyler Tommy Baker (UK) spun two basketballs using

LONGEST TIME SPINNING A BASKETBALL ON ONE TOE

Jack Ryan (USA) spun a basketball on his toe for 9.53 seconds at the NBA All-Star Jam Session in New Orleans, Louisiana, USA, on February 13, 2008.

★ LONGEST TIME SPINNING A BASKETBALL ON THE NOSE

Harlem Globetrotter Scooter Christensen (USA) kept a ball spinning on his nose for 5.1 seconds during the NBA All-Star Jam Session in Dallas, Texas, USA, on February 13 2010.

LONGEST TIME SPINNING A BASKETBALL ON ONE FINGER

Joseph Odhiambo (USA) span a basketball continuously for 4 hr 15 min on February 19, 2006 in Houston, Texas, USA.

MOST FREE THROWS

At the NBA All-Star Jam Session in New Orleans, Louisiana, USA, on February 16, 2008, Becky Hammon of the San Antonio Silver Stars (both USA) made the **most free throws in one minute by a female player**: 38.

At the same event three days earlier, NBA Hall of Famer Rick Barry (USA) had recorded the **most underhanded free throws in one minute**: 24. National Wheelchair Basketball Association (NWBA) player Jeff Griffin (USA) scored the **most consecutive free throws from a wheelchair**, with three successful throws in a row, on February 12, 2009 at the NBA All-Star Jam Session in Phoenix, Arizona, USA.

MOST THREE-POINTERS IN TWO MINUTES

On February 17, 2008, Jason Kapono (USA) of the Toronto Raptors (Canada) scored 43 three-pointers in two minutes at the NBA All-Star Jam Session in New Orleans, Louisiana, USA.

MOST UNDERHANDED HALF-COURT SHOTS IN ONE MINUTE

Only two people have achieved two underhanded half-court shots in one minute: Jason Kidd (USA) of the Dallas Mavericks (USA) and Bucket Blades (USA, pictured) of the Harlem Globetrotters. Kidd set the record during the NBA All-Star Jam Session in New Orleans, Louisiana, USA, on February 16, 2008 and Blades equaled it during the NBA All-Star Jam Session in Dallas, Texas, USA, on February 13, 2010.

EXTRA! FOR MORE ALL-COURT ACTION, TRACK BACK TO THE BASKETBALL SPREAD ON PP.230–231.

★ NEW RECORD
★ ★ UPDATED RECORD

SPORTS
SOCCER

★ ★ ★ ★ ★

★ MOST WINS OF THE BEACH SOCCER WORLD CUP

Brazil have won the FIFA Beach Soccer World Cup on four of the five occasions it has been held (2006–09). Before it became officially recognized by FIFA in 2005, a version of the Beach Soccer World Cup had been running since 1995, and Brazil had won nine out of the 10 events.

★ LOWEST GOAL AVERAGE IN FIFA WORLD CUP FINALS

The goal average at the 1990 FIFA World Cup Finals in Italy was just 2.21 per game, the lowest since the competition began in 1930. The overall average for the 18 World Cup Finals to Germany 2006 is 2.91 goals per match.

★ MOST GOALS SCORED IN A WORLD CUP FINALS

A record 171 goals were scored by the 32 teams in the FIFA World Cup Finals held in France in 1998.

★ MOST FIFA FAIR PLAY TROPHY WINS

Brazil have won the FIFA Fair Play Trophy four times, in 1982, 1986, 1994, and 2006. The trophy is awarded to the team with the best record of fair play during a World Cup Final.

★ LONGEST UNBEATEN RUN IN INTERNATIONAL SOCCER

Two international soccer teams have achieved unbeaten runs stretching to the 35-game mark: Brazil were the first team to set the record, between December 16, 1993 and January 18, 1996, and Spain from October 11, 2006 until June 20, 2009.

In this period, Brazil won the 1994 World Cup, reached the 1995 Copa America final, and reached the final of the 1996 Gold Cup. Their run was ended with a 2-0 defeat in the Gold Cup final to Mexico. During the 35-game run Brazil did lose one game by penalty shoot-out (the 1995 Copa America final to hosts Uruguay), but were still unbeaten after extra-time.

Spain's undefeated sequence, meanwhile, saw them win the 2008 European Championships and reach the semifinals of the 2009 Confederations Cup before losing to the USA.

★ MOST GOALS SCORED IN A FIFA BEACH SOCCER WORLD CUP CAREER

Madjer (Portugal) is the most prolific goalscorer in FIFA Beach Soccer World Cups, with 67 goals between 2005 and 2009. Madjer also has the **most FIFA Beach Soccer World Cup Golden Shoe awards**, having won three times.

MOST WINS OF THE CONFEDERATIONS CUP

When Brazil came back from a 0-2 halftime deficit to beat the USA 3-2 in the final of the 2009 Confederations Cup in South Africa on June 28, 2009, it saw the South American country register its third victory in the competition. Previous wins had occurred in 1997 and 2005.

EXTRA!
TURN TO P.138 TO FIND OUT WHO'S THE MOST EXPENSIVE SOCCER PLAYER OF ALL TIME.

SOCCER: It is widely believed that the word "soccer" is a contraction of "Association" from "Association Football."

MOST AFRICA CUP OF NATIONS WON BY A PLAYER

Ahmed Hassan has played in eight Africa Cup of Nations tournaments for Egypt between 1996 and 2010. During that period he has been on the winning side a record four times, in 1998, 2006, 2008, and 2010.

MOST GOALS SCORED IN FIFA WOMEN'S WORLD CUP MATCHES

Brigit Prinz (Germany) has scored a total of 14 goals in FIFA Women's World Cup matches. Her latest goal was scored in the FIFA World Cup Final at the Hongkou Stadium in Shanghai, China, on September 30, 2007.

on February 16, 2000. Nakayama netted on 1 min, 2 min, and 3 min 15 sec, beating the 62-year-old mark set by George William Hall (England), who scored three goals in 3 min 30 sec against Ireland at Old Trafford, Manchester, UK, on November 16, 1938.

HIS
THE MOST INTERNATIONAL CAPS WON BY A MALE SOCCER PLAYER IS 181 BY MOHAMED AL-DEAYEA FOR SAUDI ARABIA BETWEEN 1990 AND 2006.

NEW RECORD
**UPDATED RECORD*

AFRICA CUP OF NATIONS

The ★most consecutive matches played in Africa Cup of Nations tournaments is 34, by Rigobert Song (Cameroon) between 1996 and 2010. During his run, Song was part of the victorious Cameroon teams of 2000 and 2002.

★MOST GOALS SCORED IN AFRICA CUP OF NATIONS

Cameroon's Samuel Eto'o has scored a total of 18 goals in Africa Cup of Nations tournaments from 1996 to 2010. He has also won the African Footballer of the Year award three times, a record he shares with Abedi Pelé (Ghana) and George Weah (Liberia).

FASTEST HAT TRICK IN INTERNATIONAL SOCCER

Japanese international Masashi "Gon" Nakayama scored a hat trick in 3 min 15 sec against Brunei during an Asian Cup qualifying match played

MOST GOALS SCORED IN A COPA AMERICA TOURNAMENT

Three soccer players have scored nine goals in a single Copa America tournament: Jair Rosa Pinto (Brazil) in 1949; and Humberto Maschio (Argentina) and Javier Ambrois (Uruguay), both in 1957.

MOST APPEARANCES AS CAPTAIN IN FIFA WORLD CUP FINALS

Argentina's Diego Maradona captained his country in 16 World Cup Finals matches between 1982 and 1994. Maradona's tenure as captain included leading his country to World Cup victory in the 1986 final against West Germany.

★MOST GOALS SCORED IN INTERNATIONAL SOCCER (MALE OR FEMALE)

The record for most career international goals scored, by a man or woman, is 158 by Mia Hamm (USA) from 1987 to 2004. Hamm's stellar career included 275 appearances for the USA national team and two Women's World Cup titles, in 1991 and 1999.

★MOST CONSECUTIVE WINS IN INTERNATIONALS

Between June 26, 2008 and June 20, 2009, Spain won 15 consecutive international soccer matches. The sequence began when they beat Russia 3-0 in the semifinals of the 2008 European Championships. Their 15th consecutive win came with a 2-0 victory over South Africa in their final group game in the 2009 Confederations Cup.

HERS
THE MOST INTERNATIONAL CAPS WON BY A FEMALE SOCCER PLAYER IS 342 BY KRISTINE LILLY FOR THE USA IN A CAREER THAT BEGAN IN 1987.

DAKAR, SENEGAL
Ari Vatanen (Finland) has won the Dakar Rally four times, first in 1987 and then on three more occasions from 1989 to 1991 inclusively – the **most Dakar Rally wins**.

14°41'N
17°26'W

SPORTS
SOCCER

EXTRA!
PREFER TO PLAY SOCCER WITH A CONTROLLER IN YOUR HAND? GO TO VIDEOGAMES ON p.162.

PREMIER LEAGUE BAD BOYS

The ★**most yellow cards received by a player in the English Premier League** is 93 by Lee Bowyer (UK, above right) between 1996 and 2010. The **most red cards received by a player in the English Premier League** is eight, by three players: Richard Dunne (Ireland, above left), between 1996 and 2008; Duncan Ferguson (UK), between 1994 and 2006; and Patrick Vieira (France), between 1996 and 2005.

★MOST WINS OF BUNDESLIGA BY A PLAYER

Two players have won Germany's Bundesliga title on eight occasions: Mehmet Scholl (Germany, pictured) in 1994, 1997, 1999–2001, 2003, and 2005–06; and Oliver Kahn (Germany) in 1997, 1999–2001, 2003, 2005–06, and 2008. Both players were part of the Bayern Munich team.

> "I don't try to favor the foreign players."
> **Arsenal manager Arsène Wenger (France)**

★YOUNGEST SOCCER PLAYER IN A TOP DIVISION

Mauricio Baldivieso (Bolivia) was aged 12 years 362 days when he represented Aurora FC against La Paz in the Clausura competition of the Liga de Fútbol Profesional Boliviano at Estadio Hernando Siles, La Paz, Bolivia, on July 19, 2009.

★YOUNGEST GOALSCORER IN LA LIGA

The youngest goalscorer in the top division of Spanish soccer is Iker Muniain (Spain), who was 16 years 289 days old when he scored for Athletico Bilbao in a 2-2 draw with Real Valladolid, in Valladolid, Spain, on October 4, 2009.

★MOST BUNDESLIGA TITLES WON BY A COACH

Udo Lattek (Poland) secured eight Bundesliga titles in his career as a soccer coach. Six titles came in his two spells as coach of Bayern Munich, winning in 1972–74 and 1985–87, and two with the Borussia Mönchengladbach team in 1976–77.

★FIRST ALL-FOREIGN PREMIER LEAGUE MATCH SQUAD

The squad selected by Arsenal (UK) for the match against Crystal Palace (UK) on February 14, 2005 was the first all-foreign lineup to play in an English Premier League match. The squad consisted of: Jens Lehmann (Germany); Lauren (Cameroon); Kolo Touré (Ivory Coast); Pascal Cygan, Gaël Clichy, Robert Pirès, Patrick Vieira, and Thierry Henry (all France); Edu (Brazil); Jose-Antonio Reyes (Spain); and Dennis Bergkamp (Netherlands). Subs: Manuel Almunia and Cesc Fàbregas (both Spain); Philippe Senderos (Switzerland); Mathieu Flamini (France); and Robin van Persie (Netherlands). Arsenal won 5-1.

RICH!
THE HIGHEST ANNUAL REVENUE FOR A SOCCER CLUB IS 401,400,000 EUROS ($544,699,707) BY REAL MADRID (SPAIN) IN 2008-09.

TOP!
THE ★MOST DOMESTIC LEAGUE TITLES WON BY A SOCCER CLUB IS 53, BY RANGERS FC (UK), IN THE SCOTTISH DIVISION 1 AND PREMIER DIVISION BETWEEN 1891 AND 2010.

LISBON, PORTUGAL

The **shortest reign ever** was that of Crown Prince Luis Filipe of Portugal, who was King of Portugal for about 20 minutes on February 1, 1908. His father, the King, was shot dead in Lisbon, and he was mortally wounded at the same time.

LONGEST HOME UNBEATEN STREAKS IN THE TOP DIVISION OF THE LEADING DOMESTIC LEAGUES

SOURCE: INFOSTRADA SPORTS

NUMBER	CLUB	START DATE	END DATE	WON	DRAWN	LEAGUE
121	Real Madrid	February 17, 1957	February 21, 1965	112	9	La Liga (SPA)
93	PSV	February 17, 1983	March 4, 1989	77	16	Eredivisie (NED)
92	FC Nantes	June 4, 1976	March 14, 1981	80	12	Ligue 1 (FRA)
88	Torino	January 31, 1943	October 23, 1949	78	10	Série A (ITA)
86	Chelsea	March 20, 2004	October 5, 2008	62	24	Premier League (ENG)
73	Bayern Munich	April 11, 1970	September 14, 1974	62	11	Bundesliga (GER)
68	Palmeiras*	February 23, 1986	September 2, 1990	45	23	Série A (ITA)
49	Banfield**	May 7, 1950	May 24, 1953	35	14	Primera División (ARG)
25	Urawa Red Diamonds	September 24, 2005	April 7, 2007	22	3	J-League (JPN)
25	Gamba Osaka	March 29, 2006	August 11, 2007	20	5	J-League (JPN)
24	Columbus Crew	June 28, 2008	September 26, 2009	18	6	MLS (USA)

Notes:

*Palmeiras streak also includes São Paulo Championship (Paulista);

**Banfield streak does not include 1951 championship decider against Racing, which was played on a neutral pitch.

Jeff Cunningham (USA) has scored a record 36 match-winning goals in his MLS career.

TRIVIA

★ MOST COPPA ITALIA WINS

Two teams have won the Coppa Italia, the premier cup competition in Italian soccer, on a record nine occasions: Juventus in 1938, 1942, 1959–60, 1965, 1979, 1983, 1990, 1995; and Roma in 1964, 1969, 1980–81, 1984, 1986, 1991, 2007–08.

★ MOST WINS OF THE TIPPELIGAEN

The Tippeligaen is the top division of league soccer competition in Norway. The most successful team in the league, in terms of titles won, is Rosenborg, who have been league champions a record 21 times between 1967, when they won their first title, and 2009, when they won their latest.

★ MOST GOALS SCORED IN A PREMIER LEAGUE MATCH BY AN INDIVIDUAL PLAYER

Three players have scored five goals in a single English Premier League match: Andy Cole (UK) for Manchester United versus Ipswich at Old Trafford, Manchester, UK, on March 4, 1995; Alan Shearer (UK) for Newcastle United versus Sheffield Wednesday at St James' Park, Newcastle, UK, on September 19, 1999; and most recently Jermain Defoe (UK) for Tottenham Hotspur versus Wigan Athletic at White Hart Lane, London, UK, on November 22, 2009.

★ MOST DURABLE SOCCER REFEREE

Hungary's Csernyi Géza (b. March 25, 1932) has been an active soccer referee for 57 years. Géza gained his refereeing qualification on June 7, 1950 and officiated his last match in Hungary in February 2007.

★ MOST SOCCER MANAGEMENT REJECTION LETTERS

Between 2000 and 2010, Patrick Rielly (UK) has received 46 rejection letters from soccer clubs to whom he has applied to be manager. His first rejection came from Millwall FC, others include Celtic, Manchester City, and West Ham United (all UK).

FASTEST SPOT KICK

Francisco Javier Galan Màrin (Spain, above) spot-kicked a ball at 80.1 mph (129 km/h) for *El Show de los Récords* in Madrid, Spain, on October 29, 2001. The **fastest known shot on goal** was by David Hirst (UK) for Sheffield Wednesday v. Arsenal on September 16, 1996. It clocked in at 114 mph (183 km/h) – but hit the bar!

★ NEW RECORD ★ UPDATED RECORD

SPORTS
TENNIS & RACKET SPORTS

★ ★ ★ ★ ★ ★ ★ ★ ★ ★

★ **NEW RECORD**
★ **UPDATED RECORD**

TENNIS

★ MOST ACES SERVED IN A DAVIS CUP MATCH

Ivo Karlovic (Croatia) served 78 aces against Radek Stepanek (Czech Republic) in the semifinal of the Davis Cup, held at Porec, Croatia, on September 18, 2009. Sadly, Karlovic's serving power was not enough to grant him victory – he lost the match 7-6, 6-7, 6-7, 7-6, 14-16.

★ MOST CONSECUTIVE GRAND SLAM TOURNAMENTS PLAYED

From her first appearance at Wimbledon on June 20, 1994 to her first match at the 2009 US Open on August 31, 2009, Ai Sugiyama (Japan) played 62 consecutive Grand Slam tournaments.

★ LARGEST SINGLE-DAY ATTENDANCE AT WIMBLEDON

A total of 45,955 people watched the second day of the Wimbledon tournament, at London, UK, on June 23, 2009.

★ MOST TENNIS CLUB CHAMPIONSHIPS (MALE)

Stuart Foster (UK) secured 55 championships at Leverstock Green Lawn Tennis Club in Hemel Hempstead, Hertfordshire, UK, from 1985 to 2009.

Stuart also holds the record for the ★ **most tennis club men's doubles championships with multiple partners**, with 24 titles won from 1985 to 2009 at the same club.

★ HIGHEST EARNINGS IN A SEASON (FEMALE)

Serena Williams (USA) earned a whopping $6,545,586 in 2009. This is just a small chunk of the $30,491,460 she earned in her career between 1997 and 2009. While this gives her the record for the ★ **highest earnings in a professional career (female)**, her wealth is a fraction of the $55,350,788 Roger Federer (Switzerland) won between 1998 and 2010 – the ★ **highest earnings in a tennis career (male)**.

★ TALLEST GRAND SLAM WINNER

Juan Martín del Potro (Argentina) measured 6 ft 6 in (198 cm) when he won the 2009 US Open in Flushing Meadows, New York City, USA, on September 14, 2009.

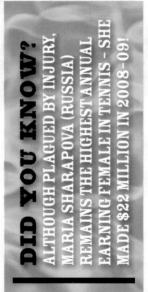
The goal for top tennis players is to get a "Grand Slam" – victories in all four Majors (see p.221). An even harder feat is to win all four in one year!

TRIVIA

EXTRA!
FOR MORE OF ROGER FEDERER'S TENNIS RECORDS, TURN TO PP.220-221.

★ MOST GAMES IN A WIMBLEDON FINAL

The Wimbledon final held on July 5, 2009 was a particularly punishing affair, with Andy Roddick (USA) forcing Roger Federer (Switzerland) to play 77 games before the Swiss tennis legend finally claimed a 5-7, 7-6, 7-6, 3-6, 16-14 victory.

THE BODY-SLAMMING BRYANS

Twins Bob and Mike Bryan (both USA, aka "the Bryans") scored the ★**most wins of the International Tennis Federation Men's Doubles World Championship by the same pair** with six, in 2003–07 and 2009.

RACQUET-BALL

★**MOST MEN'S TEAM WINS AT THE WORLD RACQUETBALL CHAMPIONSHIPS**

Instituted in 1984 and based on the US game of racquetball, the World Racquetball Championships has been won a total of eight times by the US men's team, between 1984 and 2008.

The achievements of the men's team pale in comparison to those of the US women's team, however, which has won the competition on 13 occasions. This represents the record for the ★**most women's team wins at the World Racquetball Championships**.

TABLE TENNIS

★**MOST MEN'S TEAM EUROPEAN TABLE TENNIS CHAMPIONSHIPS**

Sweden's table tennis team won a total of 14 European Table Tennis Championship team titles between 1964 and 2002.

BADMINTON WORLD CHAMPIONSHIPS

In the struggle for the ★**most Badminton World Championships men's singles titles**, Lin Dan (China) takes the honors, with wins in 2006, 2007, and 2009. His latest victory saw Lin finally take the record from his fellow countryman, Yang Yang.

BADMINTON

★**MOST WORLD TEAM BADMINTON CHAMPIONSHIP APPEARANCES**

The men's team from Denmark has put in 25 appearances at the final stage of the World Team Badminton Championships, otherwise known as the Thomas Cup, between 1949 and 2008.

★**LONGEST BADMINTON DOUBLES MARATHON**

Dedicated sportsmen Joost Berkelmans, Rick Blok, Thijs Maassen, and Steven van Puffelen (all Netherlands) played an extended doubles badminton marathon lasting 27 hours at De Toekomstgroep badminton sports center, Almere, the Netherlands, on February 27–28, 2009.

POWER PLAYER

Squash maestro Jonathon Power (Canada) claimed the record for the ★**most wins of the Professional Squash Association Masters singles tournament** with a total of three victories, in 2001–02 and 2005. Shortly after his last win, Jonathon announced his retirement from the sport.

IN!
AUSTRALIAN ROD LAVER WAS THE FIRST MAN TO WIN TWO SINGLE-SEASON GRAND SLAMS, FIRST AS AN AMATEUR IN 1962, AND THEN AS A PRO IN 1969.

OUT!
ALTHOUGH HE WAS THE FIRST MAN TO WIN A GRAND SLAM (ALL FOUR MAJORS), FRED PERRY (UK) NEVER MANAGED THE FEAT IN A SINGLE YEAR.

SPORTS
TRACK & FIELD

★ **NEW RECORD**
★ **UPDATED RECORD**

MOST IAAF WORLD ATHLETE OF THE YEAR AWARDS

The IAAF World Athlete of the Year Award is organized by the International Association of Athletics Federations, and given annually to the most outstanding global track and field athlete. The ★**most Men's IAAF World Athlete of the Year Trophies** won is three by Hicham El Guerrouj (Morocco), each year from 2001 to 2003. The ★**most Women's IAAF World Athlete of the Year Trophies** won is also three, by Yelena Isinbayeva (Russia) in 2004–05 and 2008.

HIGHEST POLE VAULT (FEMALE)

Despite missing out in the 2009 World Championships, Yelena Isinbayeva (Russia) has continued to break records in women's pole-vaulting over the past year, both indoors and outdoors.

The **highest pole vault (female) (indoors)** now stands at 5.00 m (16 ft 4 in) and was set in Donetsk, Ukraine, on February 15, 2009, While on August 29, 2009, in Zurich, Switzerland, Isinbayeva extended the record for the ★ **highest pole vault (female)** to 5.06 m (16 ft 7 in) on her first attempt at the height at the Zurich Weltklasse event.

FASTEST MAN

Usain Bolt's (Jamaica) incredible career continues, quite literally, apace. In 2009, his amazing form saw him break the following sprint records: ★**Fastest run 100 m (male)** in 9.58 seconds in Berlin, Germany, on August 16, 2009; ★**Fastest run 150 m (male)** in 14.35 seconds in Manchester, UK, on May 17, 2009; ★**Fastest run 200 m (male)** in 19.19 seconds in Berlin, Germany, on August 20, 2009.

FAST
THE FASTEST 400 M EVER RUN IS 43.18 SECONDS BY MICHAEL JOHNSON (USA) IN SEVILLE, SPAIN, ON AUGUST 26, 1999. USA IN BOLT'S FASTEST 400 M IS 45.28 SECONDS, SO FAR...

VAST
ARVIND PANDYA (INDIA) RAN BACKWARD ACROSS THE USA FROM LOS ANGELES TO NEW YORK CITY IN 107 DAYS IN 1984.

SEIKO NEW WR
SEIKO
9.58

DID YOU KNOW?

ON NOVEMBER 15, 2009, TIRUNESH DIBABA (ETHIOPIA) COMPLETED A 15-KM (9.32-MILE) ROAD RUN IN 46 MIN 28 SEC AT THE ZEVENHEUVELENLOOP EVENT IN NIJMEGEN, THE NETHERLANDS.

Eleanor Robinson (UK) ran 1,000 km in 7 days 1 hr 28 min 29 sec on March 18, 1998.

TRIVIA

★ FARTHEST HAMMER THROW (FEMALE)

Poland's Anita Wlodarczyk threw the hammer an unprecedented distance of 77.96 m (255 ft 9 in) to win the gold medal at the 12th IAAF World Championships in Berlin, Germany, on August 22, 2009.

★ FASTEST RUN 5,000 M (FEMALE) (INDOORS)

Meseret Defar (Ethiopia) ran 5,000 m in 14 min 24.37 sec at the GE Galan Meeting in Stockholm, Sweden, on February 18, 2009.

★ FASTEST RELAY RUNNING 100 MILES BY A TEAM OF 10

The fastest time to complete 100 miles (160.9 km) by a team of 10 runners in relay is 8 hr 19 min 53 sec by members of the ECU Cross-Country Alumni (USA). The record-breaking relay took place at Ada High School Track, Ada, Oklahoma, USA, on December 31, 2009.

★ FASTEST RELAY 100 X 10 KILOMETERS

The record for the fastest 100 x 10-km (6.2-mile) relay is 77 hr 17 min 25 sec and was set by the Florida Striders Track Club (USA) at Bishop John J Snyder High School, Jacksonville, Florida, USA, on December 3–6, 2009.

★ FASTEST 100 KM ULTRA DISTANCE TRACK (WOMEN)

Norimi Sakurai (Japan) ran 100 km (62.1 km) in 7 hr 14 min 6 sec in Verona, Italy, on September 27, 2003.

MOST MOUNTAIN RUNNING TITLES

The ★most wins of the Mountain Running World Championship (male) is six by Jonathan Wyatt (New Zealand), who was victorious in 1998, 2000, 2002, 2004–05, and 2008.

The ★most wins of the Mountain Running World Championship (female) is four, which has been achieved by two runners: Isabelle Guillot (France) in 1989, 1991, 1993, and 1997; and Gudrun Pfluger (Austria) in 1992, 1994, 1995, and 1996.

MOST EUROPEAN ATHLETE OF THE YEAR AWARDS

The ★most Men's European Athlete of the Year Trophies won by an individual athlete is two, by three different athletes: Jonathan Edwards (UK) in 1995 and 1998; Jan Železný (Czech Republic) in 1996 and 2000; and Christian Olsson (Sweden) in 2003–04. Similarly, the ★most Women's European Athlete of the Year Trophies won by an individual athlete is also two, by Carolina Klüft (Sweden) in 2003 and 2006; and Yelena Isinbayeva (Russia) in 2005 and 2008. This annual award is decided by votes from members of the European Athletic Association, media, and fans.

LONGEST TRIPLE JUMP (MALE) (INDOORS)

Teddy Tamgho (France) jumped 17.9 m (58 ft 9 in) in Doha, Qatar, on March 14, 2010. Tamgho set the mark on his last jump of the competition to surpass the record of 17.83 m (58 ft 5.96 in) held jointly by Aliecer Urrutia (Cuba) and Christian Olsson (Sweden).

EXTRA! FOR MORE EXCEPTIONAL TRACK & FIELD RECORDS, GO TO OUR SPORTS REFERENCE SECTION, STARTING ON P.268.

★ FASTEST RUN 4 X 1,500 M RELAY

On September 4, 2009, in Brussels, Belgium, William Biwott Tanui, Gideon Gathimba, Geoffrey Kipkoech Rono, ansd Augustine Kiprono Choge, representing Kenya, ran the 4 x 1,500 m relay in 14 min 36.23 sec. The time was almost two seconds better than the previous best set by West Germany in 1977.

SPORTS
WACKY WORLD CHAMPIONSHIPS

★ ★ ★ ★ ★ ★ ★ ★ ★

FASTEST SNAIL

The annual World Snail Racing Championships is held in July outside St Andrew's Church in Congham, Norfolk, UK. Races are conducted on a 13-in (33-cm) circular course, on which the snails race from the center to the perimeter. The all-time record holder is a snail named Archie, trained by Carl Bramham (UK), who "sprinted" to the winning post in 2 min 20 sec in 1995.

OLDEST SHIN-KICKING CHAMPIONSHIPS

Competitive shin-kicking is known to have been taking place since 1636 as part of Robert Dover's Cotswold Olimpicks, held in England since 1612. These Olimpicks were hosted continually until 1644, then again from 1660 to 1852, revived in 1951, and then held annually from 1965. Competitors must wear soft shoes and can protect their shins with straw.

★ FIRST REDNECK GAMES

In 1996, radio DJ Mac Davis (USA) of station Y-96 of East Dublin, Georgia, USA, conceived the Redneck Games as an antidote to that year's Olympic Games in nearby Atlanta. "The media kept saying that the Olympics were going to be run by a bunch of rednecks," said Davis, "so we figured if that's what the world expects, we'll give it to them." The Games feature events such as the cigarette flip, bobbing for pig's trotters, and the mud-pit belly flop.

LARGEST AUDIENCE AT A CAMEL WRESTLING FESTIVAL

At the 1994 Camel Wrestling Festival in Selçuk, Turkey, 20,000 people watched 120 dromedaries wrestle in a 2,000-year-old stadium in the city of Ephesus.

★ MOST WORMS CHARMED

Sophie Smith (UK) charmed a record 567 worms in 30 minutes from a 9.84-ft^2 (3-m^2) plot at the 2009 World Worm Charming Championships, held in Willaston, Cheshire, UK, on June 17, 2009.

MOST ELEPHANT POLO WORLD CHAMPIONSHIPS

The Tiger Top Tuskers team (Nepal) have won the World Elephant Polo Association Championships in Nepal on eight occasions, in 1983–85, 1987, 1992, 1998, 2000, and 2003.

SPLASH! IN THE MUD-PIT BELLY FLOP AT THE REDNECK GAMES, POINTS ARE AWARDED FOR BEAUTY OF FORM AND THE SIZE OF THE SPLASH.

CRUSH! WINNERS OF EVENTS AT THE REDNECK GAMES WIN A HIGHLY COVETED TROPHY – A HALF-CRUSHED, EMPTY, MOUNTED BEER CAN!

MOST TIDDLY-WINKS TITLES

Larry Khan (USA) won 19 singles titles at the Tiddlywinks World Championships between 1983 and 2003. He also won 10 pairs titles between 1978 and 1998.

occasions: Dennis Minett (UK) in 1971–73, Mike Fordham (UK) in 1983–85, and David Hollis (UK) in 1999–2001. Hollis was also the **youngest World Pea Shooting champion** when he scooped the title in 1999 aged just 13 years old.

FASTEST WIFE CARRYING

Margo Uusarj and Sandra Kullas (both Estonia) completed the 831-ft 8-in (253.5-m) obstacle course at the World Wife-Carrying Championships, held annually in Sonkajärvi, Finland, in 56.9 seconds on July 1, 2006. This is the fastest time achieved since the rule for a minimum wife weight of 108 lb (49 kg) was introduced in 2002.

World Championships in the Men's category, in 1989, 1993, 1995–99, 2001, and 2003–09. Historically the championships have been played at irregular intervals, but have been held every year since their inception in 1909.

MOST CONSECUTIVE WORLD PEA SHOOTING CHAMPIONSHIPS

Three people have won the World Pea Shooting Championships, held annually in Witcham, Cambridgeshire, UK, on three consecutive

★MOST HORSESHOE PITCHING WORLD CHAMPIONSHIPS (MALE)

Alan Francis (USA) has won a record 15 Horseshoe Pitching

★MOST WINS OF THE SAUNA WORLD CHAMPIONSHIPS

The Sauna World Championships is held in Heinola, Finland, each year. The title is awarded to the person who stays in the sauna for the longest time. Timo Kaukonen (Finland) has won the event five times, in 2003, 2005–07, and 2009.

MOST WORLD CONKER CHAMPIONSHIPS WON (MALE)

Two men have won the World Conker Championship in Ashton, Northamptonshire, UK, on three occasions: P Midlane (UK) in 1969, 1973, and 1985 and J Marsh (UK) in 1974, 1975, and 1994.

QUIZ! WHAT NUMBER DO YOU GET IF YOU ADD TOGETHER THE <u>MOST WORMS CHARMED</u> AND THE <u>MOST HORSESHOE PITCHING TITLES WON</u>? SEE p.278 FOR THE ANSWER.

SPORT STACKING

Sport stacking involves stacking plastic cups in specific sequences in the fastest time possible. The current master of sport stacking is Steven Purugganan (USA), who holds many world records including:
• The ★**fastest sport stacking individual cycle stack**, in 5.93 seconds on January 3, 2009.
• On April 19, 2009 at the WSSA World Sport Stacking Championships in Denver, Colorado, USA, Team USA (comprising Purugganan along with Joel Brown, Luke Myers, and Alex Schumann, all USA) completed the ★**fastest sport stacking 3-6-3 timed relay** in 12.72 seconds.
• At the same event, Steven Purugganan and his brother Andrew Purugganan (USA) completed the ★**fastest sport stacking doubles cycle stack** in 7.58 seconds.

In tiddlywinks, the large disk, which is used to flip the smaller disks into the air, is called a "squidger."

TRIVIA

SPORTS
WATER-SPORTS

★ ★ ★ ★ ★ ★ ★ ★ ★ ★ ★ ★ ★

DIVING

★MOST GOLD MEDALS WON AT A SINGLE EUROPEAN CHAMPIONSHIP

Tania Cagnotto (Italy) won an impressive three golds at the 2009 European Diving Championships in Turin, Italy, on April 5, 2009.

★MOST WORLD CHAMPIONSHIPS

Jingjing Guo (China) won a grand total of 10 FINA diving world titles, in the women's 3 m springboard, individual, and synchronized categories in 2001, 2003, 2005, 2007, and 2009.

CANOEING

★OLDEST OLYMPIC MEDALIST (FEMALE)

Josefa Idem (Italy, b. September 23, 1964) was aged 43 years 335 days when she won silver in the K1 class 500 m flatwater event at the 2008 Olympic Games in Beijing, China, on August 23, 2008.

GREATEST DISTANCE ON FLOWING WATER IN 24 HOURS

Ian Adamson (USA) paddled 261.6 miles (421 km) down the Yukon River, Canada, on June 20–21, 2004.

★FASTEST LONG COURSE 100 M FREESTYLE (MALE)

Brazilian Cesar Cielo Filho completed the 100 m freestyle event in 46.91 seconds on July 30, 2009 at the Fédération Internationale de Natation (FINA) World Championships in Rome, Italy. The event was the last before FINA's new guidelines on swimsuits came into effect in January 2010.

FASTEST LONG COURSE 100 M BACKSTROKE (FEMALE)

Gemma Spofforth (UK) claimed her first World Championship title, and a world record into the bargain, with her 58.12-second swim in Rome, Italy, on July 28, 2009.

SCUBA DIVING

★LONGEST DIVE IN AN ENCLOSED ENVIRONMENT

Cem Karabay (Turkey) spent 135 hr 2 min 19 sec inside a water tank, breathing via scuba equipment, at the Beylikduzu Migros Shopping Mall in Istanbul, Turkey, from August 30 to September 5, 2009.

SWIMMING

The Marathon Swimming World Cup was an endurance swimming event organized by FINA and held between 1993 and 2006. Petar Stoychev (Bulgaria) holds the record for the ★most men's Marathon Swimming World Cups, with six wins from 2001 to 2006.

The ★most women's Marathon Swimming World Cups is the three wins racked up by Edith van Dijk (Netherlands) in 2000–01 and 2005.

In 2007, the event was superseded by the FINA 10 km Marathon Swimming World Cup. Three swimmers share the record for the ★most FINA 10 km Marathon Swimming World Cups (male) – Vladmir Dyatchin (Russia), Valerio Cleri (Italy), and Thomas Lurz (Germany) for their respective victories in 2007, 2008, and 2009.

EXTRA! FOR MORE SWIMMING RECORDS, DIVE INTO OUR SPORTS REFERENCE SECTION, STARTING ON P.268.

BRILLIANT BJÖRN

World-beating windsurfer Björn Dunkerbeck (Switzerland) has the ★**most Professional Windsurfers Association (PWA) World Championship titles**, with 33 wins between 1988 and 2001, including a PWA Freestyle World Championship victory in 1998 and a PWA Speed World Championship title in 1994.

WIND
BJÖRN DUNKERBECK ALSO HOLDS THE RECORDS FOR ★MOST WAVE WINDSURFING TITLES (SEVEN WINS) AND ★MOST RACE WINDSURFING TITLES (12 WINS).

★ MOST WOMEN'S WATER POLO WORLD CHAMPIONSHIPS

Since the introduction of the women's Water Polo World Championships in 1986, the USA women's team has won the event three times, in 2003, 2007, and 2009.

Angela Maurer (Germany) has earned the distinction of winning the **most FINA 10 km Marathon Swimming World Cups (female)**, with a total of two victories, in 2007 and 2008.

★ LARGEST RACE (OPEN WATER)

A total of 13,755 participants swam the 2009 Midmar Mile at Midmar Dam, Howick, near Pietermaritzburg, South Africa, on February 7–8, 2009.

UNIVERSITY BOAT RACE

The annual Boat Race held each spring between teams from the UK universities of Oxford and Cambridge was inaugurated on June 10, 1829 with a race from Hambledon Lock to Henley Bridge on the River Thames; Oxford won. Outrigged eights boats were first used in 1846 and have since been adopted as the standard vessel for the event.

In the 156 races to 2010, Cambridge has won a total of 80 times, Oxford 75 times and there was a dead heat on March 24, 1877, handing Cambridge the record for the ★**most wins**.

Cambridge also hold the record for the ★**most consecutive wins**, with a series of 13 victories from 1924 to 1936.

The ★**oldest rower** was Mike Wherley (USA, Oxford) at 36 years 14 days, in the 2008 race, although cox Andrew Probert (UK, Cambridge) was aged 38 years 3 months for the 1992 race.

Finally, the **lightest individual oarsman** was Alfred Higgins (UK), who weighed 132 lb 6 oz (60.1 kg) for the April 1, 1882 race.

★ FASTEST 2,000 M ROWING SINGLE SCULLS (MEN)

New Zealand rower Mahe Drysdale completed the 2,000 m course in the men's sculls in 6 min 33.35 sec at Poznań, Poland, on August 29, 2009.

BAGGED
IN THE COURSE OF HIS WINDSURFING CAREER, BJÖRN HAS PICKED UP AN IMPRESSIVE TOTAL OF SIX GUINNESS WORLD RECORDS ACHIEVEMENTS.

SPORTS

WHEEL SKILLS

MISTY FLIP: Front flip with a 180° twist. The skater (or rider) either goes off the jump backward or lands backward.

★MOST 180° JUMPS (SWITCHES) ON A BICYCLE IN ONE MINUTE

Kenny Belaey (Belgium) performed 35 jumps of 180° at the Safety Jogger Classic bike festival held in Belgium, on September 20, 2009.

> "Our goal is to make this as authentic as possible... Just a full-on, old-school stunt."
>
> **Travis Pastrana keeps rally-car-jumping real**

BICYCLE

• Xavi Casas (Andorra) recorded the ★**most people stepped over by bicycle in two minutes** when he cleared 97 people on the set of *Guinness World Records*, Madrid, Spain, on January 14, 2009.

• Benito Ros Charral (Spain) recorded the ★**highest bunny hop on a bicycle**, achieving a hop of 4 ft 8 in (1.42 m) at the 2009 Bike the Rock festival in Heubach, Germany, on May 17, 2009.

• Charral has also accomplished the ★**fastest time to bunny-hop 15 hurdles on a trials bicycle**, with a time of 26.08 seconds on the set of *Zheng Da Zong Yi – Guinness World Records Special* in Beijing, China, on November 20, 2009.

• Also on the set of *Zheng Da Zong Yi – Guinness World Records Special*, the UK's Ben Wallace recorded the ★**highest bicycle backflip** with a flip of 8 ft 6 in (2.60 m).

• Austria's Thomas Öhler completed the ★**highest bicycle wall climb** with a 9-ft 5.9-in (2.89-m) climb at the MTB Freestyle night, Kaprun, Austria, on August 7, 2009.

• Lance Trappe (USA) executed the ★**most continuous front wheel hops on a bicycle**, with 108 hops at Lake Buena Vista, Florida, USA, on June 16, 2009.

INLINE SKATES

• Steve Swain (UK) completed the ★**highest misty flip on inline skates** with a 6-ft 10-in (2.08-m) attempt in London, UK, on April 23, 2009.

★MOST WORLD UNICYCLE HOCKEY TITLES

UNICON, the world championships of unicycling, has been held biennially since 1984. Unicycle hockey was added to the programme of events in 1994, since when nine tournaments have been contested. The Swiss Power Team (Switzerland) has won the title a record three times, in 2004, 2006 and 2010 (pictured, in red).

• The ★**highest ramp jump on inline skates** is 15 ft 5 in (4.7 m) and was achieved by Zhang Baoxiang (China) in Beijing, China, on November 5, 2009.

• Paul Randles (UK) completed the ★**fastest 20-cone backward slalom on inline skates** in 5.62 seconds on the set of *Guinness World Records*, in Madrid, Spain, on January 23, 2009.

QUIZ!
JUST HOW HIGH IS THE HIGHEST WALL CLIMB ON A BICYCLE?

SEE P.278 FOR THE ANSWER.

★MOST DOWNHILL SKATEBOARD CHAMPIONSHIPS (FEMALE)

Three women have won the International Gravity Sports Association Women's Downhill Championships on two occasions: Angelina Nobre (Switzerland) in 2004–05, Jolanda Vogler (Switzerland) in 2006–07, and Brianne Davies (Canada, pictured) in 2008–09.

★FASTEST INLINE SPEED SKATER OVER 300 M

On September 19, 2009, Joey Mantia (USA) set the fastest track 300 m by an individual male inline speed skater, as ratified by the sport's governing body, the Fédération Internationale de Roller Sports, when he recorded a time of 24.25 seconds in Haining, China.

MOTORCYCLE

• The **longest motorcycle ramp jump** is 351 ft (106.98 m), achieved by Robbie Maddison (Australia) at the Crusty Demons Night of World Records at Calder Park Raceway in Melbourne, Victoria, Australia, on March 29, 2008.

• Minibike master Ricardo Piedras (Spain) set the ★**longest jump with a backflip performed on a minimoto** with his 41-ft 9-in (12.72-m) attempt on the set of *Lo Show dei Record* in Milan, Italy, on April 11, 2009.

• Michele Pradelli (Italy) performed the **longest standing jump on a motorcycle** with an attempt measuring 13 ft 11 in (4.26 m) on the set of *Lo Show dei Record* in Milan, Italy, on April 25, 2009.

★LONGEST JUMP IN A RALLY CAR

On December 31, 2009 in Long Beach, California, USA, Travis Pastrana (USA) made a record leap of 269 ft (81.9 m) in his Subaru rally car. The ramp-to-ramp jump was made off the Pine Street Pier onto a floating barge anchored in Long Beach's Rainbow Harbor as part of the "RedBull: New Year. No Limits" event.

SKATEBOARD

• The UK's Alex DeCunha recorded the ★**most skateboarding no-comply flips in one minute** by achieving 56 flips in 60 seconds on the set of *Guinness World Records Smashed* at Pinewood Studios, UK, on April 15, 2009.

• Rob Dyrdek (USA) recorded the ★**most skateboard 720 kick flips in one minute** – a total of seven – on MTV's *The Rob & Big Show* in Los Angeles, California, USA, on September 17, 2007.

• On the same show, Dyrdek recorded the ★**most heel-flip shove-its in one minute** with 10.

• With an effort of 4 ft 11 in (1.5 m), Terence Bougdour (France) set the record for the **highest skateboard 540 McTwist off a halfpipe** on the set of *L'Été De Tous Les Records* in La Tranche-sur-Mer, France, on July 27, 2005.

WOW! STEFAN AKESSON (SWEDEN) SKATEBOARD WHEELIED FOR A RECORD 224 FT 10 IN (68.54 M) IN STOCKHOLM, SWEDEN, ON NOVEMBER 2, 2007.

LOW! THE LOWEST MOTORCYCLE BACKFLIP EVER WAS 3 FT (91 CM) OFF THE GROUND, ACHIEVED BY TRAVIS PASTRANA (USA) ON NOVEMBER 17, 2008.

EXTRA! FOR MORE FUN ON WHEELS, TAKE A LONG RUN AND JUMP OVER TO AUTOSPORTS ON P.228.

SPORTS
X GAMES

★ ★ ★ ★ ★ ★ ★ ★ ★ ★ ★ ★ ★ ★ ★

"Back when I was a kid, even if I made it to the highest level, I didn't think it could take me this far."
X Games icon Dave Mirra

★ FIRST AMPUTEE TO WIN A SUMMER X GAMES GOLD MEDAL

Riding a 2009 Suzuki RMZ450F, Chris Ridgway (USA) won gold in the X Games adaptive Moto X class at X Games 15 in Los Angeles, California, USA, on July 31, 2009.

EXTRA!
FOR WORLD CHAMPIONSHIP GAMES OF A TRULY WACKY NATURE, FLIP BACK TO P.258.

SUMMER

LONGEST SKATEBOARD RAMP JUMP

Pro skateboarder Danny Way (USA) performed a skateboard ramp jump with a 79-ft (24-m) 360 air on his Mega Ramp at X Games 10 in Los Angeles, California, USA, on August 8, 2004.

YOUNGEST X GAMES GOLD MEDALIST

On August 17, 2003, Ryan Sheckler (USA, b. December 30, 1989) won the Skateboard Park gold medal at ESPN X Games 9 in Los Angeles, California, USA. He was 13 years 230 days old.

Lyn-z Adams Hawkins (USA, b. September 1, 1989) became the **youngest female to win a gold medal at the X Games** in any discipline when she won the Skateboard Vert competition aged 14 years 321 days at X Games 10, Los Angeles, California, USA, on August 7, 2004.

★ MOST MEDALS

Dave Mirra (USA), who competes in BMX Freestyle, has won a total of 24 ESPN X Games medals. Mirra also holds the record for the ★ **most BMX Freestyle**

MOST SUMMER X GAMES SKATE MEDALS

The greatest number of ESPN Summer X Games Skateboard medals is 19 and was achieved by Andy Macdonald (USA) between 1999 and 2009.

medals, with 23. Fourteen of those are gold, giving Mirra another record for the **most ESPN Summer X Games gold medals won**.

MOST MOTO X MEDALS AT SUMMER X GAMES

As of ESPN Summer X Games 12, held in 2006, Travis Pastrana (USA) had won 11 Moto X medals, including seven gold.

GREATEST ATTENDANCE FOR A SUMMER ACTION SPORTS EVENT

ESPN Summer X Games Five, held in San Francisco, California, USA, were attended by 268,390 visitors over its 10-day duration

YOUNGEST X GAMES ATHLETE

Nyjah Huston (USA, b. November 30, 1994) was 11 years 246 days old when he made his debut at X Games 12 (August 3–6, 2006). He competed in the Men's Skateboard Street event.

LONGEST MOTO X
DIRT-TO-DIRT BACK FLIP

Jeremy Stenberg, pictured, and Nate Adams (both USA) completed a Moto X dirt-to-dirt back flip of 100 ft (30.48 m) during the Moto X Freestyle Finals at X Games 11 in Los Angeles, California, USA, on August 6, 2005.

WINTER X

WINTER

★ MOST GOLD MEDALS

Shaun White (USA) has won 10 ESPN Winter X Games gold medals. White's tally of gold medals all come from the snowboard Superpipe and Slopestyle disciplines. He won his 10th gold medal at Winter X Games 14 in 2010.

★ MOST MEDALS

Prolific X Games star Shaun White also holds the record for the most ESPN Winter X Games medals won, with 15. His 15th medal came at Winter X Games 14 in 2010.

★ MOST SKIER X MEDALS

The largest medal haul for Skier X Men's is six by Enak Gavaggio (France). He took gold in 1999, four bronze in 2001–04, and a fifth at ESPN

SUMMER
THE FIRST X GAMES WAS HOSTED IN RHODE ISLAND, USA, IN 1995. THEN, AS NOW, THE SPONSOR WAS AMERICAN SPORTS BROADCASTER ESPN.

WINTER
TWO YEARS AFTER THE INAUGURAL SUMMER X GAMES, THE WINTER EQUIVALENT KICKED OFF AT MOUNTAIN RESORT IN CALIFORNIA'S BIG BEAR LAKE.

★ MOST SNOWSKATE KICK FLIPS IN 30 SECONDS

Max Hilty (USA) completed a total of 14 kick flips on his snowskate board in 30 seconds at Winter X Games 14 in Aspen, Colorado, USA, on January 29, 2010.

Winter X Games 11 in Aspen/Snowmass, Colorado, USA, on January 28, 2007.

Aleisha Cline (Canada), Magdalena Jonsson (Sweden), and Ophélie David (France) have all won five medals for Skier X, the ★ **most Skier X Women's medals**. Out of that total, both Cline and David have won four golds.

★ MOST SKIING MEDALS

Tanner Hall (USA) has won 11 ESPN Winter X Games medals in skiing disciplines, as of the ESPN Winter X Games 11 in Aspen/Snowmass, Colorado, USA, on January 28–31, 2007. Hall has won a gold for Big Air, three golds and one silver for Slopestyle, and three golds and three silvers for SuperPipe Men's.

Jon Olsson (Sweden) holds the record for the ★ **most skiing Slopestyle medals**, with five: bronze in 2002–05 and 2008.

★ MOST SNOCROSS MEDALS

Tucker Hibbert (USA) has won nine SnoCross medals since 1999, comprising five golds, three silvers and one bronze.

Hibbert also holds the record for the ★ **most consecutive gold medals won in Winter X Games snowmobile SnoCross**, with four. He won his last gold at Winter X Games 14 in 2010. It was the first "four-peat" (four gold medals) in snowmobile history.

GREATEST ATTENDANCE FOR A WINTER ACTION SPORTS EVENT

A total of 85,100 spectators attended Winter X Games 5 in 2001 at Mount Snow, Vermont, USA.

WINTER OLLIE DAYS

Phil Smage (USA) is ollie royalty! He holds records for the **highest ollie** (27.75 in; 70.5 cm), **longest ollie** (11 ft 4 in; 3.45 m), and **most ollies** (14) on a snowskate board.

★ NEW RECORD
★ UPDATED RECORD

STIRLING, UK

N7°04°6
3°56'W

During an excavation project at Stirling Castle, Scotland, UK, in the mid-1970s, a gray leather ball was discovered behind oak paneling in a bedroom once used by Mary, Queen of Scots, during her reign in the 16th century. It is the world's **oldest soccer ball**.

SPORTS
X GAMES

★ ★ ★ ★ ★ ★ ★ ★ ★ ★ ★

★ MOST BMX WHEELIE HOPS

Manuel Torres (USA) performed 62 wheelie hops in 30 seconds at X Games 15 in Los Angeles, California, USA, on July 30, 2009. A wheelie hop consists of lifting only the front wheel of a bike off the ground.

DID YOU KNOW?

THE ★ MOST BUNNY HOPS ON A BMX BICYCLE IN 30 SECONDS IS 41 BY BRYAN VENTURA (USA) AT X GAMES 15, ON JULY 30, 2009.

★ MOST HEELFLIPS AND NOLLIES IN 30 SECONDS

Ivan Sebastian Cordova (USA) performed a record nine skateboard heelflips in 30 seconds at X Games 15 in Los Angeles, California, USA, on August 1, 2009. At the same event, Ivan performed the ★ most nollies in 30 seconds: 15.

EXTRA! ARE YOU MAD FOR MEGAMOTORS? THEN PUT YOUR FOOT DOWN AND HEAD FOR P.212.

★ HIGHEST OLLIE ON A SNOWSKATE BOARD

Phil Smage (USA) achieved a 28.5-in (72.4-cm) ollie on a snowskate board at Winter X Games 14 in Aspen, Colorado, USA, on January 29, 2010.

★ MOST GOLD MEDALS IN WOMEN'S SKIER X

Ophélie David (France) has won a record four individual Winter X Games women's Skier X medals, a feat that represents the first "four-peat" in Winter X Games skiing history.

★ HIGHEST AIR ON SKIS ON A SUPERPIPE

At Winter X Games 14 in Aspen, Colorado, USA, on January 31, 2010, Peter Olenick (USA) managed a 24-ft 11-in (7.58-m) air on skis on a superpipe.

SKATEBOARD

★ MOST BACKSIDE GRINDS IN 30 SECONDS

On July 31, 2009, Terrance Covington (USA) achieved 17 backside grinds in 30 seconds at X Games 15 in Los Angeles, California, USA.

★ MOST ROCK AND ROLLS IN 30 SECONDS

Terrance Covington and Dalton Price (both USA) achieved a total of 16 rock and rolls in 30 seconds at X Games 15 in Los Angeles, California, USA, on July 31, 2009.

★ MOST 360 FRONTSIDE SPINS IN 30 SECONDS

Lunati Hamilton (USA) performed six 360 frontside spins in 30 seconds at X Games 15 in Los Angeles, California, USA, on July 30, 2009.

SNOWBOARD

★ HIGHEST AIR ON A SNOWBOARD ON A SUPERPIPE

On January 30, 2010, at Winter X Games 14 in Aspen, Colorado, USA, Shaun White (USA) performed a 23-ft (7-m) air on a snowboard on a superpipe.

★ MOST SKATEBOARD SHOVE-ITS IN 30 SECONDS

The greatest number of skateboard shove-its achieved in 30 seconds is 14 by Eddie Davis (USA), at X Games 15 in Los Angeles, California, USA, on July 30, 2009.

★ NEW RECORD
★ UPDATED RECORD

GAMES

OLLIE: A no-hands aerial skateboard trick, named after skateboard legend Alan "Ollie" Gelfand.

GUINNESS WORLD RECORDS
CERTIFICATE
Winter X Games 14
Aspen, Colorado, USA
January 28-31, 2010

★ MOST OLLIES IN 30 SECONDS

Sten Carr (USA) performed a total of 34 ollies in 30 seconds at X Games 15 in Los Angeles, California, USA, on August 2, 2009.

★ MOST CONSECUTIVE SNOWBOARDER X GOLD MEDALS

Nate Holland (USA) had won five consecutive gold medals at the Winter X Games Snowboarder X competition as of January 2010. Holland won his fifth gold medal (an achievement known as the "five-peat") – the first in the history of the tournament – at Winter X Games 14 in 2010.

★ MOST SNOWBOARDER X MEDALS

Seth Wescott (USA) has won an unprecedented seven medals for Snowboarder X Men's: he picked up four silvers in 2002, 2004, 2005, and 2010 and three bronzes in 1998, 2001, and 2007.

The ★ **most medals for Snowboarder X Women's** won at Winter X Games competitions is seven by Lindsey Jacobellis (USA), who won six golds in 2003–05 and 2008–10 and silver at Winter X Games 11 in Aspen/Snowmass, Colorado, USA, in January 2007.

★ MOST SLOPESTYLE MEDALS

Shaun White (USA) has picked up an unprecedented eight snowboard Slopestyle Winter X Games medals. He won five golds in 2003–06 and 2009, a silver in 2002, and two bronze medals in 2007–08.

The ★ **most women's snowboard Slopestyle medals** won at the Winter X Games is six by Janna Meyen-Weatherby (USA). She collected four gold medals in 2003–06, a silver medal in 2002, and a bronze medal in 2010.

★ MOST SUPERPIPE MEDALS

Shaun White has seven medals in the men's snowboard SuperPipe at the Winter X Games: five gold medals (2003, 2006, and 2008–10) and two silvers (2002 and 2007).

He has also won the most ★ **medals overall** (14) and the ★ **most gold medals** (10) in Winter X Games history.

Kelly Clark (USA) has won the ★ **most women's snowboard SuperPipe medals**, with seven: gold in 2002 and 2006, silver in 2003–04 and 2009–10, and bronze in 2008.

★ HIGHEST HIPPY JUMP ON A SNOWSKATE

Kyle Williams (USA) achieved an 18.5-in (47-cm) hippy jump on a snowskate at Winter X Games 14 in Aspen, Colorado, USA, on January 31, 2010.

WINTER X GAMES

WINTER WINNERS

GWR truly established a presence at Winter X Games 14 in January 2010, carrying out a host of record attempts with skating, biking, snowboarding kids. Pictured below are some of those who set new records.

HIGH! DANNY WAY (USA) PERFORMED THE HIGHEST SKATEBOARD AIR OFF A QUARTERPIPE – 23 FT 6 IN (7.1 M) – OFF A 27-FT (8.2-M) RAMP ON JUNE 19, 2003.

HIGHER! THE HIGHEST AIR ON A BMX BIKE IS 26 FT 6 IN (8.07 M) BY MAT HOFFMAN (USA), ON MARCH 20, 2001. HE WAS TOWED BY A MOTORCYCLE IN THE RUN-UP.

CARDIFF, UK

On November 29, 2005, scientists at Cardiff University in Wales, UK, announced the development of machinery that can drill holes just 22 microns (0.0008 inches) across, making them the **smallest holes ever drilled**

SPORTS
SPORTS REFERENCE

★ ★ ★ ★ ★ ★ ★ ★ ★ ★ ★ ★

MEN'S OUTDOOR 1,500 M

In a record that has stood for more than 12 years, Hicham El Guerrouj (Morocco) won the 1,500 m event at the IAAF Golden League Golden Gala in Rome, Italy, in a time of 3 min 26 sec on July 14, 1998. He also holds the world records for the mile and the 2,000 m.

★ **NEW RECORD**
− **UPDATED RECORD**

TRACK & FIELD – OUTDOOR TRACK EVENTS

MEN	TIME/DISTANCE	NAME & NATIONALITY	LOCATION	DATE
★ 100 m	9.58	Usain Bolt (Jamaica)	Berlin, Germany	Aug 16, 2009
★ 200 m	19.19	Usain Bolt (Jamaica)	Berlin, Germany	Aug 20, 2009
400 m	43.18	Michael Johnson (USA)	Seville, Spain	Aug 26, 1999
800 m	1:41.11	Wilson Kipketer (Denmark)	Cologne, Germany	Aug 24, 1997
1,000 m	2:11.96	Noah Ngeny (Kenya)	Rieti, Italy	Sep 5, 1999
1,500 m	3:26.00	Hicham El Guerrouj (Morocco)	Rome, Italy	Jul 14, 1998
1 mile	3:43.13	Hicham El Guerrouj (Morocco)	Rome, Italy	Jul 7, 1999
2,000 m	4:44.79	Hicham El Guerrouj (Morocco)	Berlin, Germany	Sep 7, 1999
3,000 m	7:20.67	Daniel Komen (Kenya)	Rieti, Italy	Sep 1, 1996
5,000 m	12:37.35	Kenenisa Bekele (Ethiopia)	Hengelo, the Netherlands	May 31, 2004
10,000 m	26:17.53	Kenenisa Bekele (Ethiopia)	Brussels, Belgium	Aug 26, 2005
20,000 m	56:26.00	Haile Gebrselassie (Ethiopia)	Ostrava, Czech Rep	Jun 16, 2007
1 hour	21,285 m	Haile Gebrselassie (Ethiopia)	Ostrava, Czech Rep	Jun 27, 2007
25,000 m	1:13:55.80	Toshihiko Seko (Japan)	Christchurch, NZ	Mar 22, 1981
30,000 m	1:29:18.80	Toshihiko Seko (Japan)	Christchurch, NZ	Mar 22, 1981
3,000 m steeplechase	7:53.63	Saif Saaeed Shaheen (Qatar)	Brussels, Belgium	Sep 3, 2004
110 m hurdles	12.87	Dayron Robles (Cuba)	Ostrava, Czech Rep	Jun 12, 2008
400 m hurdles	46.78	Kevin Young (USA)	Barcelona, Spain	Aug 6, 1992
4 x 100 m relay	37.10	Jamaica (Asafa Powell, Nesta Carter, Michael Frater, Usain Bolt)	Beijing, China	Aug 22, 2008
4 x 200 m relay	1:18.68	Santa Monica Track Club, USA (Michael Marsh, Leroy Burrell, Floyd Heard, Carl Lewis)	Walnut, USA	Apr 17, 1994
4 x 400 m relay	2:54.29	USA (Andrew Valmon, Quincy Watts, Harry Reynolds, Michael Johnson)	Stuttgart, Germany	Aug 22, 1993
4 x 800 m relay	7:02.43	Kenya (Joseph Mutua, William Yiampoy, Ismael Kombich, Wilfred Bungei)	Brussels, Belgium	Aug 25, 2006
★ 4 x 1,500 m relay	14:36.23	Kenya (Geoffrey Kipkoech Rono, Augustine Kiprono Choge, William Biwott Tanui, Gideon Gathimba)	Brussels, Belgium	Sep 4, 2009

WOMEN	TIME/DISTANCE	NAME & NATIONALITY	LOCATION	DATE
100 m	10.49	Florence Griffith-Joyner (USA)	Indianapolis, USA	Jul 16, 1988
200 m	21.34	Florence Griffith-Joyner (USA)	Seoul, South Korea	Sep 29, 1988
400 m	47.60	Marita Koch (GDR)	Canberra, Australia	Oct 6, 1985
800 m	1:53.28	Jarmila Kratochvílová (Czechoslovakia)	Munich, Germany	Jul 26, 1983
1,000 m	2:28.98	Svetlana Masterkova (Russia)	Brussels, Belgium	Aug 23, 1996
1,500 m	3:50.46	Qu Yunxia (China)	Beijing, China	Sep 11, 1993
1 mile	4:12.56	Svetlana Masterkova (Russia)	Zurich, Switzerland	Aug 14, 1996
2,000 m	5:25.36	Sonia O'Sullivan (Ireland)	Edinburgh, UK	Jul 8, 1994
3,000 m	8:06.11	Wang Junxia (China)	Beijing, China	Sep 13, 1993
5,000 m	14:11.15	Tirunesh Dibaba (Ethiopia)	Oslo, Norway	Jun 6, 2008
10,000 m	29:31.78	Wang Junxia (China)	Beijing, China	Sep 8, 1993
20,000 m	1:05:26.60	Tegla Loroupe (Kenya)	Borgholzhausen, Germany	Sep 3, 2000
1 hour	18,517 m	Dire Tune (Ethiopia)	Ostrava, Czech Republic	Jun 12, 2008
25,000 m	1:27:05.90	Tegla Loroupe (Kenya)	Mengerskirchen, Germany	Sep 21, 2002
30,000 m	1:45:50.00	Tegla Loroupe (Kenya)	Warstein, Germany	Jun 6, 2003
3,000 m steeplechase	8:58.81	Gulnara Samitova-Galkina (Russia)	Beijing, China	Aug 17, 2008
100 m hurdles	12.21	Yordanka Donkova (Bulgaria)	Stara Zagora, Bulgaria	Aug 20, 1988
400 m hurdles	52.34	Yuliya Pechonkina (Russia)	Tula, Russia	Aug 8, 2003
4 x 100 m relay	41.37	GDR (Silke Gladisch, Sabine Rieger, Ingrid Auerswald, Marlies Göhr)	Canberra, Australia	Oct 6, 1985
4 x 200 m relay	1:27.46	United States "Blue" (LaTasha Jenkins, LaTasha Colander-Richardson, Nanceen Perry, Marion Jones)	Philadelphia, USA	Apr 29, 2000
4 x 400 m relay	3:15.17	USSR (Tatyana Ledovskaya, Olga Nazarova, Maria Pinigina, Olga Bryzgina)	Seoul, South Korea	Oct 1, 1988
4 x 800 m relay	7:50.17	USSR (Nadezhda Olizarenko, Lyubov Gurina, Lyudmila Borisova, Irina Podyalovskaya)	Moscow, Russia	Aug 5, 1984

OFF THE TRACK?
ASIDE FROM USAIN BOLT'S REMARKABLE 100 M AND 200 M RUNS (SEE ABOVE), VERY FEW TRACK & FIELD RECORDS HAVE BEEN BROKEN THIS YEAR.

55°57'N 3°09'W

EDINBURGH, UK

The world's **largest performing arts festival** is the annual Edinburgh Festival Fringe, instituted in 1947. Between August 7 and 31, 2009, its record year, there were 18,901 artists, 34,265 performances of 2,265 shows and the box office sold no less than 1,859,235 tickets.

TRACK & FIELD - INDOOR TRACK EVENTS

MEN	TIME/DISTANCE	NAME & NATIONALITY	LOCATION	DATE
50 m	5.56	Donovan Bailey (Canada)	Reno, USA	Feb 9, 1996
60 m	6.39	Maurice Greene (USA)	Madrid, Spain	Feb 3, 1998
	6.39	Maurice Greene (USA)	Atlanta, USA	Mar 3, 2001
200 m	19.92	Frank Fredericks (Namibia)	Liévin, France	Feb 18, 1996
400 m	44.57	Kerron Clement (USA)	Fayetteville, USA	Mar 12, 2005
800 m	1:42.67	Wilson Kipketer (Denmark)	Paris, France	Mar 9, 1997
1,000 m	2:14.96	Wilson Kipketer (Denmark)	Birmingham, UK	Feb 20, 2000
1,500 m	3:31.18	Hicham El Guerrouj (Morocco)	Stuttgart, Germany	Feb 2, 1997
1 mile	3:48.45	Hicham El Guerrouj (Morocco)	Ghent, Belgium	Feb 12, 1997
3,000 m	7:24.90	Daniel Komen (Kenya)	Budapest, Hungary	Feb 6, 1998
5,000 m	12:49.60	Kenenisa Bekele (Ethiopia)	Birmingham, UK	Feb 20, 2004
50 m hurdles	6.25	Mark McKoy (Canada)	Kobe, Japan	Mar 5, 1986
60 m hurdles	7.30	Colin Jackson (GB)	Sindelfingen, Germany	Mar 6, 1994
4 x 200 m relay	1:22.11	Great Britain & Northern Ireland (Linford Christie, Darren Braithwaite, Ade Mafe, John Regis)	Glasgow, UK	Mar 3, 1991
4 x 400 m relay	3:02.83	USA (Andre Morris, Dameon Johnson, Deon Minor, Milton Campbell)	Maebashi, Japan	Mar 7, 1999
4 x 800 m relay	7:13.94	Global Athletics & Marketing, USA (Joey Woody, Karl Paranya, Rich Kenah, David Krummenacker)	Boston, USA	Feb 6, 2000
5,000 m walk	18:07.08	Mikhail Shchennikov (Russia)	Moscow, Russia	Feb 14, 1995

WOMEN	TIME/DISTANCE	NAME & NATIONALITY	LOCATION	DATE
50 m	5.96	Irina Privalova (Russia)	Madrid, Spain	Feb 9, 1995
60 m	6.92	Irina Privalova (Russia)	Madrid, Spain	Feb 11, 1993
	6.92	Irina Privalova (Russia)	Madrid, Spain	Feb 9, 1995
200 m	21.87	Merlene Ottey (Jamaica)	Liévin, France	Feb 13, 1993
400 m	49.59	Jarmila Kratochvílová (Czechoslovakia)	Milan, Italy	Mar 7, 1982
800 m	1:55.82	Jolanda Ceplak (Slovenia)	Vienna, Austria	Mar 3, 2002
1,000 m	2:30.94	Maria de Lurdes Mutola (Mozambique)	Stockholm, Sweden	Feb 25, 1999
1,500 m	3:58.28	Yelena Soboleva (Russia)	Moscow, Russia	Feb 18, 2006
1 mile	4:17.14	Doina Melinte (Romania)	East Rutherford, USA	Feb 9, 1990
3,000 m	8:23.72	Meseret Defar (Ethiopia)	Stuttgart, Germany	Feb 3, 2007
5,000 m	14:24.37	Meseret Defar (Ethiopia)	Stockholm, Sweden	Feb 18, 2009
50 m hurdles	6.58	Cornelia Oschkenat (GDR)	Berlin, Germany	Feb 20, 1988
60 m hurdles	7.68	Susanna Kallur (Sweden)	Karlsruhe, Germany	Feb 10, 2008
4 x 200 m relay	1:32.41	Russia (Yekaterina Kondratyeva, Irina Khabarova, Yuliya Pechonkina, Yulia Gushchina)	Glasgow, UK	Jan 29, 2005
4 x 400 m relay	3:23.37	Russia (Yulia Gushchina, Olga Kotlyarova, Olga Zaytseva, Olesya Krasnomovets)	Glasgow, UK	Jan 28, 2006
4 x 800 m relay	•8:12.41	Moscow 1 (Tatyana Andrianova, Oksana Sukhachova-Spasovkhodskaya, Elena Kofanova, Yevgeniya Zinurova)	Moscow, Russia	Feb 28, 2010
3,000 m walk	11:40.33	Claudia Stef (Romania)	Bucharest, Romania	Jan 30, 1999

• Still awaiting ratification at the time of going to press

TRACK & FIELD - ULTRA LONG DISTANCE (TRACK)

MEN	TIME/DISTANCE	NAME & NATIONALITY	LOCATION	DATE
50 km	2:48.06	Jeff Norman (GB)	Timperley, UK	Jun 7, 1980
100 km	6:10.20	Donald Ritchie (GB)	London, UK	Oct 28, 1978
100 miles	11:28.03	Oleg Kharitonov (Russia)	London, UK	Oct 20, 2002
1,000 km	5 days 16:17.00	Yiannis Kouros (Greece)	Colac, Australia	Nov 26–Dec 1, 1984
1,000 miles	11 days 13:54.58	Peter Silkinas (Lithuania)	Nanango, Australia	Mar 11–23, 1998
6 hours	97.2 km (60.4 miles)	Donald Ritchie (GB)	London, UK	Oct 28, 1978
12 hours	162.4 km (100.91 miles)	Yiannis Kouros (Greece)	Montauban, France	Mar 15–16, 1985
24 hours	303.506 km (188.59 miles)	Yiannis Kouros (Greece)	Adelaide, Australia	Oct 4–5, 1997
48 hours	473.495 km (294.21 miles)	Yiannis Kouros (Greece)	Surgères, France	May 3–5, 1996
6 days	1,038.851 km (645.51 miles)	Yiannis Kouros (Greece)	Colac, Australia	Nov 20–26, 2005

WOMEN	TIME/DISTANCE	NAME & NATIONALITY	LOCATION	DATE
50 km	3:18.52	Carolyn Hunter-Rowe (GB)	Barry, UK	Mar 3, 1996
100 km	7:14.06	Norimi Sakurai (Japan)	Verona, Italy	Sep 27, 2003
100 miles	14:25.45	Edit Berces (Hungary)	Verona, Italy	Sep 21–22, 2002
1,000 km	7 days 1:28.29	Eleanor Robinson (GB)	Nanango, Australia	Mar 11–18, 1998
1,000 miles	13 days 1:54.02	Eleanor Robinson (GB)	Nanango, Australia	Mar 11–23, 1998
6 hours	83.2 km (57.7 miles)	Norimi Sakurai (Japan)	Verona, Italy	Sep 27, 2003
12 hours	147.6 km (91.71 miles)	Ann Trason (USA)	Hayward, USA	Aug 3–4, 1991
24 hours	250.106 km (155.40 miles)	Edit Berces (Hungary)	Verona, Italy	Sep 21–22, 2002
48 hours	385.130 km (239.31 miles)	Mami Kudo (Japan)	Surgères, France	May 22–24, 2009
6 days	883.631 km (549.06 miles)	Sandra Barwick (New Zealand)	Campbelltown, Australia	Nov 18–24, 1990

INDOOR 5,000 M

Meseret Defar (Ethiopia) is elated after winning the women's 5,000 m in a time of 14 min 24.37 sec at the Stockholm Globe Arena, Sweden, on February 18, 2009.

SPORTS
SPORTS REFERENCE

★ ★ ★ ★ ★ ★ ★ ★ ★ ★ ★

★ MEN'S HALF MARATHON

On March 21, 2010, Zersenay Tadese (Eritrea) won the 20th Lisbon Half Marathon in Portugal. He did so in a time of 58 min 23 sec, and during the same race ran 20 km in a record 55 min 21 sec.

★ **NEW RECORD**
★ **UPDATED RECORD**

★ HEPTATHLON

Ashton Eaton (USA) is shown below during the pole vault competition of the heptathlon in Fayetteville, USA, on March 13, 2010. He set a new mark of 6,499 points, thereby breaking Dan O'Brien's 17-year-old record.

OFFICIAL WEBSITES
TRACK & FIELD & RACE WALKING:
WWW.IAAF.ORG
CYCLING:
WWW.UCI.CH

TRACK & FIELD - ROAD RACE

MEN	TIME	NAME & NATIONALITY	LOCATION	DATE
★ 10 km	27:01	Micah Kipkemboi Kogo (Kenya)	Brunssum, the Netherlands	Mar 29, 2009
15 km	41:29 41:29	Felix Limo (Kenya) Deriba Merga (Ethiopia)	Nijmegen, the Netherlands Ras Al Khaimah, UAE	Nov 11, 2001 Feb 20, 2009
★ 20 km	55.21	Zersenay Tadese (Eritrea)	Lisbon, Portugal	Mar 21, 2010
★ Half marathon	58.23	Zersenay Tadese (Eritrea)	Lisbon, Portugal	Mar 21, 2010
★ 25 km	•1:11:50	Samuel Kiplimo Kosgei (Kenya)	Berlin, Germany	May 9, 2010
★ 30 km	1:27:49	Haile Gebrselassie (Ethiopia)	Berlin, Germany	Sep 20, 2009
Marathon	2:03:59	Haile Gebrselassie (Ethiopia)	Berlin, Germany	Sep 28, 2008
100 km	6:13:33	Takahiro Sunada (Japan)	Tokoro, Japan	Jun 21, 1998
Road relay	1:57:06	Kenya (Josephat Ndambiri, Martin Mathathi, Daniel Mwangi, Mekubo Mogusu, Onesmus Nyerere, John Kariuki)	Chiba, Japan	Nov 23, 2005

WOMEN	TIME	NAME & NATIONALITY	LOCATION	DATE
10 km	30:21	Paula Radcliffe (GB)	San Juan, Puerto Rico	Feb 23, 2003
★ 15 km	46:28	Tirunesh Dibaba (Ethiopia)	Nijmegen, the Netherlands	Nov 15, 2009
20 km	1:02:57	Lornah Kiplagat (Netherlands)	Udine, Italy	Oct 14, 2007
Half marathon	1:06:25	Lornah Kiplagat (Netherlands)	Udine, Italy	Oct 14, 2007
25 km	1:22:13	Mizuki Noguchi (Japan)	Berlin, Germany	Sep 25, 2005
30 km	1:38:49	Mizuki Noguchi (Japan)	Berlin, Germany	Sep 25, 2005
Marathon	2:15:25	Paula Radcliffe (GB)	London, UK	Apr 13, 2003
100 km	6:33:11	Tomoe Abe (Japan)	Tokoro, Japan	Jun 25, 2000
Road relay	2:11:41	China (Jiang Bo, Dong Yanmei, Zhao Fentgting, Ma Zaijie, Lan Lixin, Li Na)	Beijing, China	Feb 28, 1998

• Still awaiting ratification at the time of going to press

TRACK & FIELD - RACE WALKING

MEN	TIME	NAME & NATIONALITY	LOCATION	DATE
20,000 m	1:17:25.6	Bernardo Segura (Mexico)	Bergen, Norway	May 7, 1994
20 km (road)	1:17:16	Vladimir Kanaykin (Russia)	Saransk, Russia	Sep 29, 2007
30,000 m	2:01:44.1	Maurizio Damilano (Italy)	Cuneo, Italy	Oct 3, 1992
50,000 m	3:40:57.9	Thierry Toutain (France)	Héricourt, France	Sep 29, 1996
50 km (road)	3:34:14	Denis Nizhegorodov (Russia)	Cheboksary, Russia	May 11, 2008

WOMEN	TIME	NAME & NATIONALITY	LOCATION	DATE
10,000 m	41:56.23	Nadezhda Ryashkina (USSR)	Seattle, USA	Jul 24, 1990
20,000 m	1:26:52.3	Olimpiada Ivanova (Russia)	Brisbane, Australia	Sep 6, 2001
20 km (road)	1:25:41	Olimpiada Ivanova (Russia)	Helsinki, Finland	Aug 7, 2005

TRACK & FIELD - INDOOR FIELD EVENTS

MEN	RECORD	NAME & NATIONALITY	LOCATION	DATE
High jump	2.43 m (7 ft 11.66 in)	Javier Sotomayor (Cuba)	Budapest, Hungary	Mar 4, 1989
Pole vault	6.15 m (20 ft 2.12 in)	Sergei Bubka (Ukraine)	Donetsk, Ukraine	Feb 21, 1993
Long jump	8.79 m (28 ft 10.06 in)	Carl Lewis (USA)	New York City, USA	Jan 27, 1984
★ Triple jump	17.90 m (58 ft 9 in)	Teddy Tamgho (France)	Doha, Qatar	Mar 14, 2010
Shot	22.66 m (74 ft 4.12 in)	Randy Barnes (USA)	Los Angeles, USA	Jan 20, 1989
★ Heptathlon*	•6,499 points	Ashton Eaton (USA)	Fayetteville, USA	Mar 13, 2010

WOMEN	RECORD	NAME & NATIONALITY	LOCATION	DATE
High jump	2.08 m (6 ft 9.8 in)	Kajsa Bergqvist (Sweden)	Arnstadt, Germany	Feb 4, 2006
Pole vault	5.00 m (16 ft 4 in)	Yelena Isinbayeva (Russia)	Donetsk, Ukraine	Feb 15, 2009
Long jump	7.37 m (24 ft 2.15 in)	Heike Drechsler (GDR)	Vienna, Austria	Feb 13, 1988
Triple jump	15.36 m (50 ft 4.72 in)	Tatyana Lebedeva (Russia)	Budapest, Hungary	Mar 6, 2004
Shot	22.50 m (73 ft 9.82 in)	Helena Fibingerová (Czechoslovakia)	Jablonec, Czechoslovakia	Feb 19, 1977
Pentathlon†	4,991 points	Irina Belova (EUN)	Berlin, Germany	Feb 15, 1992

* 60 m 6.71 seconds; long jump 7.73 m; shot 13.12 m; high jump 2.11 m; 60 m hurdles 7.77 seconds; pole vault 5.10 m; 1,000 m 2 min 32.67 sec

† 60 m hurdles 8.22 seconds; high jump 1.93 m; shot 13.25 m; long jump 6.67 m; 800 m 2 min 10.26 sec

• Still awaiting ratification at the time of going to press

TRACK & FIELD - OUTDOOR FIELD EVENTS

MEN	RECORD	NAME & NATIONALITY	LOCATION	DATE	
High jump	2.45 m (8 ft 0.45 in)	Javier Sotomayor (Cuba)	Salamanca, Spain	Jul 27, 1993	*100 m 10.64 seconds; long jump 8.11 m; shot 15.33 m; high jump 2.12 m; 400 m 47.79 seconds; 110 m hurdles 13.92 seconds; discus 47.92 m; pole vault 4.80 m; javelin 70.16 m; 1,500 m 4 min 21.98 sec
Pole vault	6.14 m (20 ft 1.73 in)	Sergei Bubka (Ukraine)	Sestriere, Italy	Jul 31, 1994	
Long jump	8.95 m (29 ft 4.36 in)	Mike Powell (USA)	Tokyo, Japan	Aug 30, 1991	
Triple jump	18.29 m (60 ft 0.78 in)	Jonathan Edwards (GB)	Gothenburg, Sweden	Aug 7, 1995	
Shot	23.12 m (75 ft 10.23 in)	Randy Barnes (USA)	Los Angeles, USA	May 20, 1990	
Discus	74.08 m (243 ft 0.53 in)	Jürgen Schult (USSR)	Neubrandenburg, Germany	Jun 6, 1986	
Hammer	86.74 m (284 ft 7 in)	Yuriy Sedykh (USSR)	Stuttgart, Germany	Aug 30, 1986	
Javelin	98.48 m (323 ft 1.16 in)	Jan Železný (Czech Republic)	Jena, Germany	May 25, 1996	
Decathlon*	9,026 points	Roman Šebrle (Czech Republic)	Götzis, Austria	May 27, 2001	
WOMEN	**RECORD**	**NAME & NATIONALITY**	**LOCATION**	**DATE**	
High jump	2.09 m (6 ft 10.28 in)	Stefka Kostadinova (Bulgaria)	Rome, Italy	Aug 30, 1987	† 100 m hurdles 12.69 seconds; high jump 1.86 m; shot 15.80 m; 200 m 22.56 seconds; long jump 7.27 m; javelin 45.66 m; 800 m 2 min 8.51 sec
★Pole vault	5.06 m (16 ft 7.21 in)	Yelena Isinbayeva (Russia)	Zurich, Switzerland	Aug 28, 2009	
Long jump	7.52 m (24 ft 8.06 in)	Galina Chistyakova (USSR)	St Petersburg, Russia	Jun 11, 1988	
Triple jump	15.50 m (50 ft 10.23 in)	Inessa Kravets (Ukraine)	Gothenburg, Sweden	Aug 10, 1995	
Shot	22.63 m (74 ft 2.94 in)	Natalya Lisovskaya (USSR)	Moscow, Russia	Jun 7, 1987	** 100 m 12.49 seconds; long jump 6.12 m; shot 16.42 m; high jump 1.78 m; 400 m 57.19 seconds; 100 m hurdles 14.22 seconds; discus 46.19 m; pole vault 3.10 m; javelin 48.78 m; 1,500 m 5 min 15.86 sec
Discus	76.80 m (252 ft)	Gabriele Reinsch (GDR)	Neubrandenburg, Germany	Jul 9, 1988	
★Hammer	77.96 m (255 ft 9 in)	Anita Wlodarczyk (Poland)	Berlin, Germany	Aug 22, 2009	
Javelin	72.28 m (253 ft 6 in)	Barbora Spotáková (Czech Republic)	Stuttgart, Germany	Sep 13, 2008	
Heptathlon†	7,291 points	Jacqueline Joyner-Kersee (USA)	Seoul, South Korea	Sep 24, 1988	
Decathlon**	8,358 points	Austra Skujyte (Lithuania)	Columbia, USA	Apr 15, 2005	

CYCLING - ABSOLUTE TRACK

MEN	TIME/DISTANCE	NAME & NATIONALITY	LOCATION	DATE
★200 m (flying start)	9.572	Kevin Sireau (France)	Moscow, Russia	May 30, 2009
500 m (flying start)	24.758	Chris Hoy (GB)	La Paz, Bolivia	May 13, 2007
1 km (standing start)	58.875	Arnaud Tournant (France)	La Paz, Bolivia	Oct 10, 2001
4 km (standing start)	4:11.114	Christopher Boardman (GB)	Manchester, UK	Aug 29, 1996
Team 4 km (standing start)	3:53.314	Great Britain (Ed Clancy, Paul Manning, Geraint Thomas, Bradley Wiggins)	Beijing, China	Aug 18, 2008
1 hour	*49.7 km	Ondrej Sosenka (Czech Republic)	Moscow, Russia	Jul 19, 2005
WOMEN	**TIME/DISTANCE**	**NAME & NATIONALITY**	**LOCATION**	**DATE**
200 m (flying start)	10.831	Olga Slioussareva (Russia)	Moscow, Russia	Apr 25, 1993
500 m (flying start)	29.655	Erika Salumäe (USSR)	Moscow, Russia	Aug 6, 1987
★500 m (standing start)	33.296	Simona Krupeckaite (Lithuania)	Pruszków, Poland	Mar 25, 2009
3 km (standing start)	3:24.537	Sarah Ulmer (New Zealand)	Athens, Greece	Aug 22, 2004
1 hour	*46.065 km	Leontien Zijlaard-Van Moorsel (Netherlands)	Mexico City, Mexico	Oct 1, 2003

Some athletes achieved better distances within an hour with bicycles that are no longer allowed by the Union Cycliste Internationale (UCI). The 1-hour records given here are in accordance with the new UCI rules.

★**WOMEN'S POLE VAULT**
Russia's Yelena Isinbayeva is regarded by many as the greatest female pole vaulter of all time. She holds 27 world records (15 outdoor and 12 indoor). Here she celebrates after breaking her own outdoor record by clearing 16 ft 7.21 in (5.06 m) at the IAAF Golden League Athletics meeting in Zurich, Switzerland, on August 28, 2009.

MEN'S CYCLING 500 M FLYING START
Chris Hoy (UK) celebrates breaking the world 500 m altitude record at the Alto Irpavi Velodrome on May 13, 2007 in La Paz, Bolivia. He achieved a time of 24.758 seconds.

TRIVIA

DID YOU KNOW?
TRACK RACING DATES BACK TO THE END OF THE 19TH CENTURY. THE FIRST TRACK WORLD CHAMPIONSHIPS WERE HELD IN 1895. CYCLING WAS ALSO INCLUDED AS AN EVENT IN THE FIRST MODERN OLYMPIC GAMES OF 1896.

★**WOMEN'S CYCLING 500 M STANDING START**
Simona Krupeckaite (Lithuania) rode the women's 500 m in a time of 33.296 seconds at the UCI Track Cycling World Championships held at the BGZ Arena in Pruszków, Poland, on March 25, 2009.

SPORTS

SPORTS REFERENCE

FREEDIVING

MEN'S DEPTH DISCIPLINES	DEPTH/TIME	NAME & NATIONALITY	LOCATION	DATE
★ Constant weight with fins	•124 m (406 ft 9 in)	Herbert Nitsch (Austria)	The Bahamas	Apr 22, 2010
★ Constant weight without fins	•95 m (311 ft 8 in)	William Trubridge (New Zealand)	The Bahamas	Apr 26, 2009
★ Variable weight	142 m (465 ft 10 in)	Herbert Nitsch (Austria)	The Bahamas	Dec 7, 2009
No limit	214 m (702 ft)	Herbert Nitsch (Austria)	Spetses, Greece	Jun 14, 2007
★ Free immersion	•120 m (393 ft 8 in)	Herbert Nitsch (Austria)	The Bahamas	Apr 25, 2010
MEN'S DYNAMIC APNEA	**DEPTH/TIME**	**NAME & NATIONALITY**	**LOCATION**	**DATE**
With fins	250 m (800 ft 2 in)	Alexey Molchanov (Russia)	Lignano, Italy	Oct 5, 2008
Without fins	213 m (698 ft 9 in) 213 m (698 ft 9 in)	Tom Sietas (Germany) Dave Mullins (New Zealand)	Hamburg, Germany Wellington, New Zealand	Jul 2, 2008 Aug 12, 2008
MEN'S STATIC APNEA	**DEPTH/TIME**	**NAME & NATIONALITY**	**LOCATION**	**DATE**
★ Duration	11 min 35 sec	Stephane Mifsud (France)	Hyères, France	Jun 8, 2009
WOMEN'S DEPTH DISCIPLINES	**DEPTH/TIME**	**NAME & NATIONALITY**	**LOCATION**	**DATE**
Constant weight with fins	96 m (314 ft 11 in)	Sara Campbell (UK)	The Bahamas	Apr 2, 2009
★ Constant weight without fins	62 m (203 ft 5 in)	Natalia Molchanova (Russia)	The Bahamas	Dec 3, 2009
Variable weight	122 m (400 ft 3 in)	Tanya Streeter (USA)	Turks and Caicos Islands	Jul 19, 2003
No limit	160 m (524 ft 11 in)	Tanya Streeter (USA)	Turks and Caicos Islands	Aug 17, 2002
Free immersion	85 m (278 ft 10 in)	Natalia Molchanova (Russia)	Crete, Greece	Jul 27, 2008
WOMEN'S DYNAMIC APNEA	**DEPTH/TIME**	**NAME & NATIONALITY**	**LOCATION**	**DATE**
★ With fins	225 m (738 ft 2 in)	Natalia Molchanova (Russia)	Moscow, Russia	Apr 25, 2010
★ Without fins	160 m (524 ft 11 in)	Natalia Molchanova (Russia)	Aarhus, Denmark	Aug 20, 2009
WOMEN'S STATIC APNEA	**DEPTH/TIME**	**NAME & NATIONALITY**	**LOCATION**	**DATE**
★ Duration	8 min 23 sec	Natalia Molchanova (Russia)	Aarhus, Denmark	Aug 21, 2009

★ ★ ★ ★ ★ ☆

★ MEN'S STATIC APNEA

On June 8, 2009 in Hyères, France, freediver Stephane Mifsud (France) held his breath underwater in the men's static apnea event, clocking a time of 11 min 35 sec.

ROWING

MEN	TIME	NAME & NATIONALITY	LOCATION	DATE
★ Single sculls	6:33.35	Mahe Drysdale (New Zealand)	Poznan, Poland	Aug 29, 2009
Double sculls	6:03.25	Jean-Baptiste Macquet, Adrien Hardy (France)	Poznan, Poland	Jun 17, 2006
Quadruple sculls	5:36.20	Christopher Morgan, James McRae, Brendan Long, Daniel Noonan (Australia)	Beijing, China	Aug 10, 2008
Coxless pairs	6:14.27	Matthew Pinsent, James Cracknell (GB)	Seville, Spain	Sep 21, 2002
Coxless fours	5:41.35	Sebastian Thormann, Paul Dienstbach, Philipp Stüer, Bernd Heidicker (Germany)	Seville, Spain	Sep 21, 2002
Coxed pairs*	6:42.16	Igor Boraska, Tihomir Frankovic, Milan Razov (Croatia)	Indianapolis, USA	Sep 18, 1994
Coxed fours*	5:58.96	Matthias Ungemach, Armin Eichholz, Armin Weyrauch, Bahne Rabe, Jörg Dederding (Germany)	Vienna, Austria	Aug 24, 1991
Eights	5:19.85	Deakin, Beery, Hoopman, Volpenhein, Cipollone, Read, Allen, Ahrens, Hansen (USA)	Athens, Greece	Aug 15, 2004
LIGHTWEIGHT	**TIME**	**NAME & NATIONALITY**	**LOCATION**	**DATE**
Single sculls*	6:47.82	Zac Purchase (GB)	Eton, UK	Aug 26, 2006
Double sculls	6:10.02	Mads Rasmussen, Rasmus Quist (Denmark)	Amsterdam, the Netherlands	Jun 23, 2007
Quadruple sculls*	5:45.18	Francesco Esposito, Massimo Lana, Michelangelo Crispi, Massimo Guglielmi (Italy)	Montreal, Canada	Aug 1992
Coxless pairs*	6:26.61	Tony O'Connor, Neville Maxwell (Ireland)	Paris, France	1994
Coxless fours	5:45.60	Thomas Poulsen, Thomas Ebert, Eskild Ebbesen, Victor Feddersen (Denmark)	Lucerne, Switzerland	Jul 9, 1999
Eights*	5:30.24	Altena, Dahlke, Kobor, Stomporowski, Melges, März, Buchheit, Von Warburg, Kaska (Germany)	Montreal, Canada	Aug 1992
WOMEN	**TIME**	**NAME & NATIONALITY**	**LOCATION**	**DATE**
Single skulls	7:07.71	Rumyana Neykova (Bulgaria)	Seville, Spain	Sep 21, 2002
Double skulls	6:38.78	Georgina and Caroline Evers-Swindell (New Zealand)	Seville, Spain	Sep 21, 2002
Quadruple skulls	6:10.80	Kathrin Boron, Katrin Rutschow-Stomporowski, Jana Sorgers, Kerstin Köppen (Germany)	Duisburg, Germany	May 19, 1996
Coxless pairs	6:53.80	Georgeta Andrunache, Viorica Susanu (Romania)	Seville, Spain	Sep 21, 2002
Coxless fours*	6:25.35	Robyn Selby Smith, Jo Lutz, Amber Bradley, Kate Hornsey (Australia)	Eton, UK	Aug 26, 2006
Eights	5:55.50	Mickelson, Whipple, Lind, Goodale, Sickler, Cooke, Shoop, Francia, Davies (USA)	Eton, UK	Aug 27, 2006
LIGHTWEIGHT	**TIME**	**NAME & NATIONALITY**	**LOCATION**	**DATE**
Single skulls*	7:28.15	Constanta Pipota (Romania)	Paris, France	Jun 19, 1994
Double skulls	6:49.77	Dongxiang Xu, Shimin Yan (China)	Poznan, Poland	Jun 17, 2006
Quadruple skulls*	6:23.96	Hua Yu, Haixia Chen, Xuefei Fan, Jing Liu (China)	Eton, UK	Aug 27, 2006
Coxless pairs*	7:18.32	Eliza Blair, Justine Joyce (Australia)	Aiguebelette-le-Lac, France	Sep 7, 1997

*Denotes non-Olympic boat classes

MANCHESTER, UK

53°28'N 2°14'W

Liverpool Road station in Manchester, UK, is the **oldest railroad station**. It was first used on September 15, 1830 and was finally closed on September 30, 1975.

SPEED SKATING - LONG TRACK

MEN	TIME/POINTS	NAME & NATIONALITY	LOCATION	DATE
500 m	34.03	Jeremy Wotherspoon (Canada)	Salt Lake City, USA	Nov 9, 2007
2 x 500 m	68.31	Jeremy Wotherspoon (Canada)	Calgary, Canada	Mar 15, 2008
1,000 m	1:06.42	Shani Davis (USA)	Salt Lake City, USA	Mar 7, 2009
★1,500 m	•1:41.04	Shani Davis (USA)	Salt Lake City, USA	Dec 11, 2009
3,000 m	3:37.28	Eskil Ervik (Norway)	Calgary, Canada	Nov 5, 2005
5,000 m	6:03.32	Sven Kramer (Netherlands)	Calgary, Canada	Nov 17, 2007
10,000 m	12:41.69	Sven Kramer (Netherlands)	Salt Lake City, USA	Mar 10, 2007
500/1,000/500/1,000 m	137.230 points	Jeremy Wotherspoon (Canada)	Calgary, Canada	Jan 18–19, 2003
500/3,000/1,500/5,000 m	146.365 points	Erben Wennemars (Netherlands)	Calgary, Canada	Aug 12–13, 2005
500/5,000/1,500/10,000 m	145.742 points	Shani Davis (USA)	Calgary, Canada	Mar 18–19, 2006
Team pursuit (eight laps)	3:37.80	Netherlands (Sven Kramer, Carl Verheijen, Erben Wennemars)	Salt Lake City, USA	Mar 11, 2007

WOMEN	TIME/POINTS	NAME & NATIONALITY	LOCATION	DATE
★500 m	•37.00	Jenny Wolf (Germany)	Salt Lake City, USA	Dec 11, 2009
2 x 500 m	74.42	Jenny Wolf (Germany)	Salt Lake City, USA	Mar 10, 2007
1,000 m	1:13.11	Cindy Klassen (Canada)	Calgary, Canada	Mar 25, 2006
1,500 m	1:51.79	Cindy Klassen (Canada)	Salt Lake City, USA	Nov 20, 2005
3,000 m	3:53.34	Cindy Klassen (Canada)	Calgary, Canada	Mar 18, 2006
5,000 m	6:45.61	Martina Sáblíková (Czech Republic)	Salt Lake City, USA	Mar 11, 2007
500/1,000/500/1,000 m	149.305 points 149.305 points	Monique Garbrecht-Enfeldt (Germany) Cindy Klassen (Canada)	Salt Lake City, USA Calgary, Canada	Jan 11–12, 2003 Mar 24–25, 2006
500/1,500/1,000/3,000 m	155.576 points	Cindy Klassen (Canada)	Calgary, Canada	Mar 15–17, 2001
500/3,000/1,500/5,000 m	154.580 points	Cindy Klassen (Canada)	Calgary, Canada	Mar 18–19, 2006
★Team pursuit (six laps)	2:55.79	Canada (Kristina Groves, Christine Nesbitt, Brittany Schussler)	Calgary, Canada	Dec 6, 2009

•Still awaiting ratification at the time of going to press

SPEED SKATING - SHORT TRACK

MEN	TIME/POINTS	NAME & NATIONALITY	LOCATION	DATE
★500 m	•40.651	Sung Si-Bak (South Korea)	Marquette, USA	Nov 14, 2009
1,000 m	1:23.454	Charles Hamelin (Canada)	Montreal, Canada	Jan 18, 2009
1,500 m	2:10.639	Ahn Hyun-Soo (South Korea)	Marquette, USA	Oct 24, 2003
3,000 m	4:32.646	Ahn Hyun-Soo (South Korea)	Beijing, China	Dec 7, 2003
5,000 m relay	6:38.486	South Korea (Kwak Yoon-Gy, Lee Ho-Suk, Lee Jung-Su, Sung Si-Bak)	Salt Lake City, USA	Oct 19, 2008

WOMEN	TIME/POINTS	NAME & NATIONALITY	LOCATION	DATE
500 m	42.609	Wang Meng (China)	Beijing, China	Nov 29, 2008
★1,000 m	•1:29.049	Zhou Yang (China)	Vancouver, Canada	Feb 26, 2010
1,500 m	2:16.729	Zhou Yang (China)	Salt Lake City, USA	Feb 9, 2008
3,000 m	4:46.983	Jung Eun-Ju (South Korea)	Harbin, China	Mar 15, 2008
★3,000 m relay	•4:06.610	China (Sun Linlin, Wang Meng, Zhang Hui, Zhou Yang)	Vancouver, Canada	Feb 24, 2010

•Still awaiting ratification at the time of going to press

★ **NEW RECORD**
★ **UPDATED RECORD**

★WOMEN'S 3,000 M SHORT TRACK RELAY

China's gold medalists Sun Linlin, Wang Meng, Zhang Hui, and Zhou Yang (from left to right) attend the medal ceremony at the Vancouver Winter Olympics in Canada. They skated the women's 3,000 m relay in a time of 4 min 6.61 sec on February 24, 2010.

MEN'S 1,500 M LONG TRACK

Shani Davis (USA) skates during the ISU World Cup Speed Skating Championships at the Utah Olympic Oval in Kearns, Salt Lake City, USA. Here he finished the 1,500 m in a time of 1 min 41.04 sec. He holds two more records: the "big combination" (with 145.742 points), which he has held since March 2006, and the 1,000 m (in 1 min 6.42 sec).

GUINNESS WORLD RECORDS 2011

SPORTS
SPORTS REFERENCE

★MEN'S 200 M BREASTSTROKE

Christian Sprenger (Australia) competes in the 200 m breaststroke final during the 13th Fédération Internationale de Natation (FINA) World Championships on July 30, 2009 in Rome, Italy. He finished in 2 min 7.31 sec.

★ **NEW RECORD**
★ **UPDATED RECORD**

SWIMMING – LONG COURSE (50 M POOL)

MEN	TIME	NAME & NATIONALITY	LOCATION	DATE
★50 m freestyle	20.91	Cesar Cielo Filho (Brazil)	Sao Paulo, Brazil	Dec 18, 2009
★100 m freestyle	46.91	Cesar Cielo Filho (Brazil)	Rome, Italy	Jul 30, 2009
★200 m freestyle	1:42.00	Paul Biedermann (Germany)	Rome, Italy	Jul 28, 2009
★400 m freestyle	3:40.07	Paul Biedermann (Germany)	Rome, Italy	Jul 26, 2009
★800 m freestyle	7:32.12	Zhang Lin (China)	Rome, Italy	Jul 29, 2009
1,500 m freestyle	14:34.56	Grant Hackett (Australia)	Fukuoka, Japan	Jul 29, 2001
4 x 100 m freestyle relay	3:08.24	USA (Michael Phelps, Garrett Weber-Gale, Cullen Jones, Jason Lezak)	Beijing, China	Aug 11, 2008
4 x 200 m freestyle relay	6:58.55	USA (Michael Phelps, Ricky Berens, David Walters, Ryan Lochte)	Rome, Italy	Jul 31, 2009
50 m butterfly	22.43	Rafael Muñoz (Spain)	Malaga, Spain	Apr 5, 2009
100 m butterfly	49.82	Michael Phelps (USA)	Rome, Italy	Aug 1, 2009
200 m butterfly	1:51.51	Michael Phelps (USA)	Rome, Italy	Jul 29, 2009
50 m backstroke	24.04	Liam Tancock (UK)	Rome, Italy	Aug 2, 2009
100 m backstroke	51.94	Aaron Peirsol (USA)	Indianapolis, USA	Jul 8, 2009
200 m backstroke	1:51.92	Aaron Peirsol (USA)	Rome, Italy	Jul 31, 2009
50 m breaststroke	26.67	Cameron van der Burgh (South Africa)	Rome, Italy	Jul 29, 2009
100 m breaststroke	58.58	Brenton Rickard (Australia)	Rome, Italy	Jul 27, 2009
200 m breaststroke	2:07.31	Christian Sprenger (Australia)	Rome, Italy	Jul 30, 2009
200 m medley	1:54.10	Ryan Lochte (USA)	Rome, Italy	Jul 30, 2009
400 m medley	4:03.84	Michael Phelps (USA)	Beijing, China	Aug 10, 2008
4 x 100 m medley relay	3:27.28	USA (Aaron Peirsol, Eric Shanteau, Michael Phelps, David Walters)	Rome, Italy	Aug 2, 2009

WOMEN	TIME	NAME & NATIONALITY	LOCATION	DATE
★50 m freestyle	23.73	Britta Steffen (Germany)	Rome, Italy	Aug 2, 2009
★100 m freestyle	52.07	Britta Steffen (Germany)	Rome, Italy	Jul 31, 2009
★200 m freestyle	1:52.98	Federica Pellegrini (Italy)	Rome, Italy	Jul 29, 2009
★400 m freestyle	3:59.15	Federica Pellegrini (Italy)	Rome, Italy	Jul 26, 2009
800 m freestyle	8:14.10	Rebecca Adlington (UK)	Beijing, China	Aug 16, 2008
1,500 m freestyle	15:42.54	Kate Ziegler (USA)	Mission Viejo, USA	Jun 17, 2007
4 x 100 m freestyle relay	3:31.72	Netherlands (Inge Dekker, Ranomi Kromowidjojo, Femke Heemskerk, Marleen Veldhuis)	Rome, Italy	Jul 26, 2009
4 x 200 m freestyle relay	7:42.08	China (Yang Yu, Zhu Qian Wei, Liu Jing, Pang Jiaying)	Rome, Italy	Jul 30, 2009
★50 m butterfly	25.07	Therese Alshammar (Sweden)	Rome, Italy	Jul 31, 2009
★100 m butterfly	56.06	Sarah Sjostrom (Sweden)	Rome, Italy	Jul 27, 2009
★200 m butterfly	•2:01.81	Liu Zige (China)	Jinan, China	Oct 21, 2009
★50 m backstroke	27.06	Zhao Jing (China)	Rome, Italy	Jul 30, 2009
★100 m backstroke	58.12	Gemma Spofforth (UK)	Rome, Italy	Jul 28, 2009
★200 m backstroke	2:04.81	Kirsty Coventry (Zimbabwe)	Rome, Italy	Aug 1, 2009
★50 m breaststroke	29.80	Jessica Hardy (USA)	Federal Way, USA	Aug 7, 2009
★100 m breaststroke	1:04.45	Jessica Hardy (USA)	Federal Way, USA	Aug 7, 2009
★200 m breaststroke	2:20.12	Annamay Pierse (Canada)	Rome, Italy	Jul 30, 2009
★200 m medley	2:06.15	Ariana Kukors (USA)	Rome, Italy	Jul 27, 2009
400 m medley	4:29.45	Stephanie Rice (Australia)	Beijing, China	Aug 10, 2008
4 x 100 m medley relay	3:52.19	China (Zhao Jing, Chen Huijia, Jiao Liuyang, Li Zhesi)	Rome, Italy	Aug 1, 2009

• *Still awaiting ratification at the time of going to press*

MEN'S 50 M BACKSTROKE

Great Britain's Liam Tancock stands on the podium after winning the 50 m backstroke at the FINA World Championships in Rome, Italy, on August 2, 2009. Tancock won gold and set a new world record of 24.04 seconds.

SWIMMING – SHORT COURSE (25 M POOL)

MEN	TIME	NAME & NATIONALITY	LOCATION	DATE
★50 m freestyle	20.30	Roland Schoeman (South Africa)	Pietermaritzburg, South Africa	Aug 8, 2009
100 m freestyle	44.94	Amaury Leveaux (France)	Rijeka, Croatia	Dec 13, 2008
★200 m freestyle	1:39.37	Paul Biedermann (Germany)	Berlin, Germany	Nov 15, 2009
★400 m freestyle	3:32.77	Paul Biedermann (Germany)	Berlin, Germany	Nov 14, 2009
800 m freestyle	7:23.42	Grant Hackett (Australia)	Melbourne, Australia	Jul 20, 2008
1,500 m freestyle	14:10.10	Grant Hackett (Australia)	Perth, Australia	Aug 7, 2001
★4 x 100 m freestyle relay	3:03.30	USA (Nathan Adrian, Matt Greves, Garrett Weber-Gale, Michael Phelps)	Manchester, UK	Dec 19, 2009
★4 x 200 m freestyle relay	6:51.05	Canada (Colin Russel, Stefan Hirniak, Brent Hayden, Joel Greenshields)	Leeds, UK	Aug 7, 2009
★50 m butterfly	21.80	Steffen Deibler (Germany)	Berlin, Germany	Nov 14, 2009
★100 m butterfly	48.48	Evgeny Korotyshkin (Russia)	Berlin, Germany	Nov 15, 2009
★200 m butterfly	1:49.11	Kaio Almeida (Brazil)	Stockholm, Sweden	Nov 10, 2009
★50 m backstroke	22.61	Peter Marshall (USA)	Singapore, Singapore	Nov 22, 2009
★100 m backstroke	48.94	Nick Thoman (USA)	Manchester, UK	Dec 18, 2009
★200 m backstroke	1:46.11	Arkady Vyatchanin (Russia)	Berlin, Germany	Nov 15, 2009
★50 m breaststroke	25.25	Cameron van der Burgh (South Africa)	Berlin, Germany	Nov 14, 2009
★100 m breaststroke	55.61	Cameron van der Burgh (South Africa)	Berlin, Germany	Nov 15, 2009
★200 m breaststroke	•2:00.67	Daniel Gyurta (Hungary)	Istanbul, Turkey	Dec 13, 2009
★100 m medley	•50.76	Peter Mankoc (Slovenia)	Istanbul, Turkey	Dec 12, 2009
★200 m medley	1:51.55	Darian Townsend (South Africa)	Berlin, Germany	Nov 15, 2009
★400 m medley	•3:57.27	Laszlo Cseh (Hungary)	Istanbul, Turkey	Dec 11, 2009
★4 x 100 m medley relay	3:19.16	Russia (Stanislav Donets, Sergey Geybel, Evgeny Korotyshkin, Danila Izotov)	St Petersburg, Russia	Dec 20, 2009

WOMEN	TIME	NAME & NATIONALITY	LOCATION	DATE
50 m freestyle	23.25	Marleen Veldhuis (Netherlands)	Manchester, UK	Apr 13, 2008
★100 m freestyle	51.01	Lisbeth Trickett (Australia)	Hobart, Australia	Aug 10, 2009
★200 m freestyle	•1:51.17	Federica Pellegrini (Italy)	Istanbul, Turkey	Dec 13, 2009
★400 m freestyle	3:54.92	Joanne Jackson (UK)	Leeds, UK	Aug 8, 2009
800 m freestyle	8:04.53	Alessia Filippi (Italy)	Rijeka, Croatia	Dec 12, 2008
★1,500 m freestyle	15:28.65	Lotte Friis (Denmark)	Birkerod, Denmark	Nov 28, 2009
4 x 100 m freestyle relay	3:28.22	Netherlands (Hinkelien Schreuder, Inge Dekker, Ranomi Kromowidjojo, Marleen Veldhuis)	Amsterdam, the Netherlands	Dec 19, 2008
4 x 200 m freestyle relay	7:38.90	Netherlands (Inge Dekker, Femke Heemskerk, Marleen Veldhuis, Ranomi Kromowidjojo)	Manchester, UK	Apr 9, 2008
★50 m butterfly	24.38	Therese Alshammar (Sweden)	Singapore, Singapore	Nov 22, 2009
★100 m butterfly	•55.05	Diane Bui-Duyet (France)	Istanbul, Turkey	Dec 12, 2009
★200 m butterfly	2:00.78	Liu Zige (China)	Berlin, Germany	Nov 15, 2009
★50 m backstroke	•25.70	Sanja Jovanovic (Croatia)	Istanbul, Turkey	Dec 12, 2009
★100 m backstroke	55.23	Sakai Shiho (Japan)	Berlin, Germany	Nov 15, 2009
★200 m backstroke	2:00.18	Sakai Shiho (Japan)	Berlin, Germany	Nov 14, 2009
★50 m breaststroke	28.80	Jessica Hardy (USA)	Berlin, Germany	Nov 15, 2009
★100 m breaststroke	1:02.70	Rebecca Soni (USA)	Manchester, UK	Dec 19, 2009
★200 m breaststroke	2:14.57	Rebecca Soni (USA)	Manchester, UK	Dec 18, 2009
★100 m medley	57.74	Hinkelien Schreuder (Netherlands)	Berlin, Germany	Nov 15, 2009
★200 m medley	2:04.60	Julia Smit (USA)	Manchester, UK	Dec 19, 2009
★400 m medley	4:21.04	Julia Smit (USA)	Manchester, UK	Dec 18, 2009
★4 x 100 m medley relay	3:47.97	USA (Margaret Hoelzer, Jessica Hardy, Dana Vollmer, Amanda Weir)	Manchester, UK	Dec 18, 2009

• Still awaiting ratification at the time of going to press

OFFICIAL WEBSITE
SWIMMING:
WWW.FINA.ORG

★MEN'S 50 M BUTTERFLY

Steffen Deibler (Germany) swimming in a men's 50 m butterfly heat at the FINA short course World Cup in Berlin, Germany, on November 14, 2009. He set a record 21.80 seconds in the event.

★WOMEN'S 1,500 M FREESTYLE

Lotte Friis (Denmark) swam the women's 1,500 m short course freestyle in a time of 15 min 28.65 sec in Birkerod, Denmark, on November 28, 2009.

EXTRA!
FOR TALES OF RECORD-BREAKING ACHIEVEMENTS ON THE WORLD'S OCEANS, TURN TO P.118.

SPORTS
SPORTS REFERENCE

★ ★ ★ ★ ★

MEN'S 77 KG SNATCH

Lu Xiaojun (China) lifts 174 kg in the snatch in the men's 77 kg category at the World Weightlifting Championships in Goyang, South Korea, on November 24, 2009. Xiaojun also holds the record for the total, having successfully lifted 378 kg at the same event.

★ WOMEN'S 75+ KG CLEAN & JERK

Jang Mi-Ran (South Korea) celebrates after lifting 187 kg in the clean and jerk in the women's 75+ kg category at the World Weightlifting Championships in Goyang, South Korea, on November 28, 2009. She also holds the records for the snatch and the total in this category.

OFFICIAL WEBSITES
WEIGHTLIFTING:
WWW.IWF.NET

WATERSKIING:
WWW.IWSF.COM

WEIGHTLIFTING

MEN	CATEGORY	WEIGHT	NAME & NATIONALITY	LOCATION	DATE
56 kg	Snatch	138 kg	Halil Mutlu (Turkey)	Antalya, Turkey	Nov 4, 2001
	Clean & jerk	168 kg	Halil Mutlu (Turkey)	Trencín, Slovakia	Apr 24, 2001
	Total	305 kg	Halil Mutlu (Turkey)	Sydney, Australia	Sep 16, 2000
62 kg	Snatch	153 kg	Shi Zhiyong (China)	Izmir, Turkey	Jun 28, 2002
	Clean & jerk	182 kg	Le Maosheng (China)	Busan, South Korea	Oct 2, 2002
	Total	326 kg	Zhang Jie (China)	Kanazawa, Japan	Apr 28, 2008
69 kg	Snatch	165 kg	Georgi Markov (Bulgaria)	Sydney, Australia	Sep 20, 2000
	Clean & jerk	197 kg	Zhang Guozheng (China)	Qinhuangdao, China	Sep 11, 2003
	Total	357 kg	Galabin Boevski (Bulgaria)	Athens, Greece	Nov 24, 1999
77 kg	★Snatch	174 kg	Lu Xiaojun (China)	Goyang, South Korea	Nov 24, 2009
	Clean & jerk	210 kg	Oleg Perepetchenov (Russia)	Trencín, Slovakia	Apr 27, 2001
	★Total	378 kg	Lu Xiaojun (China)	Goyang, South Korea	Nov 24, 2009
85 kg	Snatch	187 kg	Andrei Rybakou (Belarus)	Chiang Mai, Thailand	Sep 22, 2007
	Clean & jerk	218 kg	Zhang Yong (China)	Ramat Gan, Israel	Apr 25, 1998
	Total	394 kg	Andrei Rybakou (Belarus)	Beijing, China	Aug 15, 2008
94 kg	Snatch	188 kg	Akakios Kakhiasvilis (Greece)	Athens, Greece	Nov 27, 1999
	Clean & jerk	232 kg	Szymon Kolecki (Poland)	Sofia, Bulgaria	Apr 29, 2000
	Total	412 kg	Akakios Kakhiasvilis (Greece)	Athens, Greece	Nov 27, 1999
105 kg	Snatch	200 kg	Andrei Aramnau (Belarus)	Beijing, China	Aug 18, 2008
	Clean & jerk	237 kg	Alan Tsagaev (Bulgaria)	Kiev, Ukraine	Apr 25, 2004
	Total	436 kg	Andrei Aramnau (Belarus)	Beijing, China	Aug 18, 2008
105+ kg	Snatch	213 kg	Hossein Rezazadeh (Iran)	Qinhuangdao, China	Sep 14, 2003
	Clean & jerk	263 kg	Hossein Rezazadeh (Iran)	Athens, Greece	Aug 25, 2004
	Total	476 kg	Hossein Rezazadeh (Iran)	Sydney, Australia	Sep 26, 2000
WOMEN	CATEGORY	WEIGHT	NAME & NATIONALITY	LOCATION	DATE
48 kg	Snatch	98 kg	Yang Lian (China)	Santo Domingo, Dominican Republic	Oct 1, 2006
	Clean & jerk	120 kg	Chen Xiexia (China)	Taian City, China	Apr 21, 2007
	Total	217 kg	Yang Lian (China)	Santo Domingo, Dominican Republic	Oct 1, 2006
53 kg	Snatch	102 kg	Ri Song-Hui (North Korea)	Busan, South Korea	Oct 1, 2002
	Clean & jerk	129 kg	Li Ping (China)	Taian City, China	Apr 22, 2007
	Total	226 kg	Qiu Hongxia (China)	Santo Domingo, Dominican Republic	Oct 2, 2006
58 kg	Snatch	111 kg	Chen Yanqing (China)	Doha, Qatar	Dec 3, 2006
	Clean & jerk	141 kg	Qiu Hongmei (China)	Taian City, China	Apr 23, 2007
	Total	251 kg	Chen Yanqing (China)	Doha, Qatar	Dec 3, 2006
63 kg	Snatch	116 kg	Pawina Thongsuk (Thailand)	Doha, Qatar	Nov 12, 2005
	Clean & jerk	142 kg	Pawina Thongsuk (Thailand)	Doha, Qatar	Dec 4, 2006
	Total	257 kg	Liu Haixia (China)	Chiang Mai, Thailand	Sep 23, 2007
69 kg	Snatch	128 kg	Liu Chunhong (China)	Beijing, China	Aug 13, 2008
	Clean & jerk	158 kg	Liu Chunhong (China)	Beijing, China	Aug 13, 2008
	Total	286 kg	Liu Chunhong (China)	Beijing, China	Aug 13, 2008
75 kg	★Snatch	132 kg	Svetlana Podobedova (Kazakhstan)	Goyang, South Korea	Nov 28, 2009
	★Clean & jerk	160 kg	Svetlana Podobedova (Kazakhstan)	Goyang, South Korea	Nov 28, 2009
	★Total	292 kg	Svetlana Podobedova (Kazakhstan)	Goyang, South Korea	Nov 28, 2009
75+ kg	Snatch	140 kg	Jang Mi-Ran (South Korea)	Beijing, China	Aug 16, 2008
	★Clean & jerk	187 kg	Jang Mi-Ran (South Korea)	Goyang, South Korea	Nov 28, 2009
	Total	326 kg	Jang Mi-Ran (South Korea)	Beijing, China	Aug 16, 2008

WATERSKIING

MEN	RECORD	NAME & NATIONALITY	LOCATION	DATE
Slalom	1.5 buoy | 9.75-m line | 58 km/h	Chris Parrish (USA)	Trophy Lakes, USA	Aug 28, 2005
Barefoot slalom	20.6 crossings of wake in 30 seconds	Keith St Onge (USA)	Bronkhorstspruit, South Africa	Jan 6, 2006
Tricks	12,400 points	Nicolas Le Forestier (France)	Lac de Joux, Switzerland	Sep 4, 2005
★Barefoot tricks	11,250 points	Keith St Onge (USA)	Maize, USA	Aug 15, 2009
★Jump	75.2 m (246 ft 8 in)	Freddy Krueger (USA)	Seffner, USA	Nov 2, 2008
Barefoot jump	27.4 m (89 ft 11 in)	David Small (GB)	Mulwala, Australia	Feb 8, 2004
Ski fly	91.1 m (298 ft 10 in)	Jaret Llewellyn (Canada)	Orlando, USA	May 14, 2000
Overall	2,818.01 points*	Jaret Llewellyn (Canada)	Seffner, USA	Sep 29, 2002

WOMEN	RECORD	NAME & NATIONALITY	LOCATION	DATE
Slalom ★	1 buoy | 10.25-m line | 55 km/h	Kristi Overton Johnson (USA) Karina Nowlan (Australia) Regina Jaquess (USA)	West Palm Beach, USA Sacramento, USA Santa Rosa, USA	Sep 14, 1996 Sep 22, 2008 Jul 4, 2009
Barefoot slalom	17.0 crossings of wake in 30 seconds	Nadine de Villiers (South Africa)	Witbank, South Africa	Jan 5, 2001
★Tricks	9,080 points	Natallia Berdnikava (Belarus)	Polk City, USA	Oct 31, 2009
★Barefoot tricks	4,400 points	Nadine de Villiers (South Africa)	Witbank, South Africa	Jan 5, 2001
★Jump	56.6 m (186 ft)	Elena Milakova (Russia)	Rio Linda, USA	Jul 21, 2002
Barefoot jump	20.6 m (67 ft 7 in)	Nadine de Villiers (South Africa)	Pretoria, South Africa	Mar 4, 2000
Ski fly	69.4 m (227 ft 8.2 in)	Elena Milakova (Russia)	Pine Mountain, USA	May 26, 2002
★Overall	2,934.36 points**	Regina Jaquess (USA)	Santa Rosa, USA	Jul 17, 2009

*5@11.25 m, 10,730 tricks, 71.7 m jump   **4@10.75 m, 8,180 tricks, 52.2 m jump; calculated with the 2006 scoring method*

★WOMEN'S OVERALL
Waterskier Regina Jaquess (USA) in action on July 17, 2009 at Santa Rosa, California, USA. She achieved an overall score of 2,934.36 points.

LONGEST SPORTS MARATHONS

SPORT	TIME	NAME & NATIONALITY	LOCATION	DATE
★Aerobics	26 hours	Dinaz Vervatwala (India)	Secunderabad, India	Jan 9–10, 2010
★Baseball	48 hr 9 min 27 sec	Jonny G Foundation Cardinals and Edward Jones Browns (USA)	St Louis, Missouri, USA	Oct 9–11, 2009
★Basketball	82 hours	Treverton College (South Africa)	Mooi River, South Africa	Aug 7–10, 2009
Basketball (wheelchair)	26 hr 3 min	University of Omaha students and staff (USA)	Omaha, Nebraska, USA	Sep 24–25, 2004
Bowling (tenpin)	120 hours	Andy Milne (Canada)	Mississauga, Ontario, Canada	Oct 24–29, 2005
Bowls (indoor)	36 hours	Arnos Bowling Club (UK)	Southgate, London, UK	Apr 20–21, 2002
★Bowls (outdoor)	170 hr 3 min	Goulburn Railway Bowling Club (Australia)	Goulburn, NSW, Australia	Jan 19–26, 2009
★Cricket	67 hr 9 min	New South Wales Police Force officers (Australia)	Bateau Bay, NSW, Australia	Feb 8–11, 2009
★Curling	54 hr 1 min	The Burlington Golf and Country Club (Canada)	Burlington, Ontario, Canada	Mar 12–14, 2010
★Darts (doubles)	30 hours	Richard Saunders, Lee Hannant, Andrew Brymer, Paul Taylor (UK)	Twyford, Berkshire, UK	Jan 9–10, 2009
Darts (singles)	26 hr 42 min	Stephen Wilson and Robert Henderson (UK)	Palnackie, Scotland, UK	Jun 20–21, 2008
Floorball	24 hr 15 min	TRM Floorball and Hornets Regio Moosseedorf Worblental (Switzerland)	Zollikofen, Switzerland	Apr 27–28, 2007
★Soccer	37 hours	TSV Mutlangen & FC Raron II (Germany)	Mutlangen, Germany	Jul 16–17, 2009
★Soccer (five-a-side)	27 hr 15 min	Collingwood College Challengers & Radio Basingstoke Bandits (UK)	Camberley, Surrey, UK	Oct 17–18, 2009
Hockey (ice)	241 hr 21 min	Brent Saik and friends (Canada)	Strathcona, Alberta, Canada	Feb 8–18, 2008
Hockey (indoor)	50 hours	Bert & Macs and Mid-Town Certigard teams (Canada)	Lethbridge, Alberta, Canada	Mar 25–27, 2008
Hockey (inline/roller)	24 hours	8K Roller Hockey League (USA)	Eastpointe, Michigan, USA	Sep 13–14, 2002
Hockey (street)	105 hr 17 min	Molson Canadian and Canadian Tire teams (Canada)	Lethbridge, Alberta, Canada	Aug 20–24, 2008
Korfball	30 hr 2 min	Kingfisher Korfball Club (UK)	Larkfield, Kent, UK	Jun 14–15, 2008
Netball	58 hours	Sleaford Netball Club (UK)	Sleaford, Lincolnshire, UK	Jul 25–27, 2008
★Pétanque (boules)	52 hours	Gilles de B'Heinsch (Belgium)	Arlon, Belgium	Sep 18–20, 2009
Pool (singles)	53 hr 25 min	Brian Lilley and Daniel Maloney (USA)	Spring Lake, North Carolina, USA	Oct 10–12, 2008
Skiing	202 hr 1 min	Nick Willey (Australia)	Thredbo, NSW, Australia	Sep 2–10, 2005
Snowboarding	180 hr 34 min	Bernhard Mair (Austria)	Bad Kleinkirchheim, Austria	Jan 9–16, 2004
Table soccer	51 hr 52 min	Alexander Gruber, Roman Schelling, Enrico Lechtaler, Christian Nägele (Austria)	Bregenz, Austria	Jun 27–29, 2008
Table tennis (doubles)	101 hr 1 min 11 sec	Lance, Phil, and Mark Warren, Bill Weir (USA)	Sacramento, California, USA	Apr 9–13, 1979
Table tennis (singles)	132 hr 31 min	Danny Price and Randy Nunes (USA)	Cherry Hill, New Jersey, USA	Aug 20–26, 1978
Tennis (doubles)	50 hr 0 min 8 sec	Vince Johnson, Bill Geideman, Brad Ansley, Allen Finley (USA)	Hickory, North Carolina, USA	Nov 7–9, 2008
★Tennis (singles)	36 hr 36 min 36 sec	Jeroen Wagenaar and Serge Fernando (Netherlands)	Hellevoetsluis, the Netherlands	Sep 11–12, 2009
Volleyball (beach)	24 hr 10 min	Krzysztof Garbulski, Michal Fuks, Adam Jankowski, Tomasz Konior (Poland)	Ustka, Poland	Jun 27–28, 2008
Volleyball (indoor)	76 hr 30 min	Zespól Szkól Ekonomicznych students (Poland)	Sosnowiec, Poland	Dec 4–7, 2009

★ NEW RECORD ★ UPDATED RECORD

CREDITS & ACKNOWLEDGMENTS

★ ★ ★ ★ ★ ★ ★ ★ ★ ★

Quiz answers

Q1, p.29. What was the name given to NASA's first space shuttle?
A: *Columbia*

Q2, p.47. No tall tales – how long is the aye aye's tale?
A: 20 in (50.5 cm)

Q3, p.54. To which group do the following creatures belong, mollusk or crustacean?
A: Crab; B: Octopus; C: Slug
A: A) Crustacean; B) Mollusk and C) Mollusk

Q4, p.56. Of all the fish in the sea, which is the largest?
A: The whale shark

Q5, p.58. Which classic arcade video game features an amphibian attempting to cross a busy road and a fast-flowing river?
A: *Frogger*

Q6, p.80. Which of these measures the most: the longest beard, longest mustache or the highest hairstyle?
A: Longest mustache at 14 ft (4.29 m), held by Ram Singh Chauhan (India)

Q7, p.92. Anssi Vanhala solved a Rubik's cube in 36.77 seconds using which bodypart?
A: The feet

Q8, p.112. What was the name of the vehicle that first broke the speed of sound on land and who was its pilot?
A: *Thrust SSC*, driven by Andy Green (UK)

Q9, p.117. In 1911, Norway's Roald Amundsen became the first man to reach the South Pole. What other polar record did he achieve 15 years later?
A: The first flight over the North Pole, in the airship *Norge*

Q10, p.124. On average, how many graves did Johann

Heinrich Karl Thime dig every year throughout his 50-year career?
A: Over 466 graves – that's more than one a day!

Q11, p.131. How old is the oldest person accused of murder?
A: 98 years old

Q12, p.132. Who did Carlos Slim Helu replace as the world's richest man?
A: Bill Gates

Q13, p.140. On May 2, 2007, Lup Fun Yau set a new record for the most jam doughnuts eaten in three minutes. But how many did he eat?
A: Six

Q14, p.181. Who is *Hurt Locker* director Katheryn Bigelow's famous Ex?
A: James Cameron

Q15, p.182. Which animated movie was the first to be made in stereoscopic 3D?
A: *Monsters Vs Aliens*

Q16, p.229. Michael Schumacher is an F1 legend, but he is not the youngest driver to finish an F1 race. Who is?
A: Jaime Alguersuari

Q17, p.236. How many countries have the Harlem Globetrotters played in to date?
A: 120 countries

Q18, p.238. Who wrote the Marquess of Queensbury rules?
A: John Graham Chambers

Q19, p.259. What number do you get if you add the most worms charmed to the most horseshoe pitching titles won?
A: 582 (567 worms + 15 horseshoe titles)

Q20, p.263. Just how high is the highest wall climb on a bicycle?
A: 9 ft 5.9 in (2.89 m)

Guinness World Records would like to thank the following individuals, companies, groups, websites, societies, schools, colleges and universities for their help in the creation of the 2011 edition:
Academy of Motion Picture Arts & Sciences, Oscar Rogelio Antillon Aceituno, Heather Anderson, Ulla Anlander, Roberta Armani, Arriva London, All at Ascent Media, Astoria Park (Queens, NYC), Ted Batchelor and family, Bender Media Services (Sally Treibel, Susan Bender), Beano Max, British Film Institute, Robert Bierfreund, Oliver Blair (Dyson), Bleedingcool.com (Rich Johnston), Luke and Joseph Boatfield, Brian Bolland, Boostamonte Mountainboarding (Brad Beren), Richard Booth, Olivia and Alexander Boulton, Ceri, Katie, Georgie and Emily Boulton, Alfie Boulton-Fay, Victor Bourdariat, Pete Bouvier, Box Office Mojo, Jason Bradbury, Matthew R I Bradford, Bragster team (Dan Barrett, Andy Dust, Luke Forsythe, Adam Moore, Peter Vandenberk), British Waterways Scotland (Donald Macpherson), Sarah Brown, Vittorio 100% Brumotti, Rachel Buchholz (NGK Magazine), Business Week, Kirk, Beth and Gavin Butterfield, CCTV (Guo Tong, Wang Wei and Tony), Kwang-Sung Chun, Simone Ciancotti, Cinefex, Adam Cloke, Mark Collins, Columbus Zoo, Ohio, USA, Commission for the Geological Map of the World, Connexion Cars (Rob and Tracey), Julia Cottrell, Gerard Danford, Debby DeGroot, Deno's Wonder Wheel Amusement Park, Coney Island, USA, Jose Torres Diaz, Doctor Who (BBC America, Russell T Davies, Stephen Moffat, Matt Smith and David Tennant), Doctor Who Magazine, Electric Sky (Jakki Hart and David Pounds), Louis Epstein, ESPN X Games (Marc Murphy, Dan Gordner, Valerie Benardinelli, Katie Moses Swope, Danny Chi, Crystal Yang and Amy Lupo), Eurodata TV Worldwide, Europroducciones TV, Europroducciones, Europroduzzione and Veralia (Renato Vacatello, Stefano Torrisi, Carlo Boserman, Marco Fernandez De Araoz, Gabriela Ventura, Marco Boserman, Mar Izquierdo, Maria Ligues, Dario Viola, Amato Penasilico and Chiara Duranti), Amelia Ewen, Toby Ewen, Eyeworks Australia & New Zealand (Julie Christie, Joanne Law, Philippa Rennie, Erin Downton, Georgina Sinclair, Marc Ellis and James Kerley), Eyeworks Europe (Wim, Kathe, Oliver and Pian), Molly & Isobel Fay, Finnish Naval Academy (Sr lt Tero Hanski), First News (Serena Lacy, Kelane Henderson and the team), FJT Logistics Limited, Forbes, Formulation Inc, The Gadget Show, Alfons Gidlöf, Vilgot Gidlöf, Karen Gillen, Go' Morgen Danmark/Go' Aften Danmark, Google, Alan Green (International Regulations Commission, International Sailing Federation), Jordan, Ryan and Brandon Greenwood, Victoria Grimsell, Kris Growcott, GXT (Paula, Giuliano and Francesco), Haaga-Helia University of Applied Sciences, Hachette Book Group (Craig Young, Vanessa Vasquez and Todd McGarity), Kari Haering (Zone Living), Dan Hall, Hampshire Sports and Prestige Cars, Ray Harper, Roger Hawkins, Merja Hedman and the Finnish Sauna Society, Stuart Hendry, Gavin Hennessey, Tamsin Holman, Hollywood Press Association, Marsha K Hoover, Alistair Humphreys, ICM (Michael Kagan and Greg Lipstone), I Gri.siani hair salon, Rome, Italy, Infomag (Emin Gorgun and Ipek Hazneci), Infostrada Sports (Philip Hennemann and Erik Kleinpenning), INP Media (Bryn Downing), International Commission on Stratigraphy, Internet Movie Database, The Irish Sun (Helen Morrogh), ITV Productions (Jeremy Philips, Caz Stuart and Bernard Kelly), Melanie Johnson, Richard Johnston, Andy Jones, Todd Klein, Dr Erwin J.O. Kompanje and family, Sultan and Hasan Kösen, Kathrine Krone, Olaf Kuchenbecker, Josh Kushins (Lucasfilm), Orla and Thea Langton, Jony Levi, Paul Levitz, Carey Low, Jim Lyngvild, Sean Macaulay, Manda, Macmillan Distribution, Norman D Mangawang, Médiamétrie, Melia White House Hotel, London, Clare Merryfield, Mark Messenger, Dan Meyer, Millennium Seed Bank (Sarah Moss), Steven Moffat, Sophie and Joshua Molloy, Monte-Carlo Television Festival, National Geographic Kids, NBA (Gail Hunter, Patrick Sullivan, Jason Lodato and Karen Barberan), David Nelson, New York City Police Department, The Nielson Company, Jan Nielsen, Norddeich (York and Jurgen), Andrea Oddone, Outline Productions (Laura Mansfield, Diana Hunter and Helen Veale), Andres Ostrofsky, Paley Center for Media, New York, USA (Ron Simon), Eddie Palmer, Dan Phillips, Stuart Phillips, POD Worldwide (Christy Chin, Alex Iskandar Liew and Yip Cheong), Rob Pullar, Queen's Head and Artichoke, RCAF Trenton, Ontario, Canada, Ryan Reiter (Hollywood Almost Free Outdoor Cinema), R&G Productions (Stephane Gateau, Jerome Revon, Patrice Parmentier, Vanina Latcheva and Deborah Amar), Martyn Richards Research (Martyn Richards), Ristorante Sant'Eustorgio (Paolo e Filippo Introini), Stephen Rodriguez (MLS), Jimmy Rollins, Roma Medical (John Pitt and John Dalton), Edward Russell, Eric Sakowski, Scottish Canoe Association (Margaret Winter), The Scottish Sun (Gill Smith and Graeme Donohue), Screecher's Pix (Hayma, Monique and Ryan), Secondskin Makeup Artist, Alex Segura (DC Comics), Victor Hugo Camacho Sedano, Joshua Selinger, Tom Sergeant, SET Japan (Adrian Grey), Dean Shaw (Game Stores Group), Chris Sheedy, The Simpsons (Matt Groening, Antonia Coffman and Art Villanueva), Richard Sisson, Sky 1 (James Townley), Glori Slater (K9 Storm Inc), Carlton J Smith, Matt Smith, Nick Smith, Phee Smith, Sean Sorensen (Motion Theory), Southern California Steampunks, Tom Spilsbury, Ian Starr, Start Licensing (Ian Downes), Daniel Stolar, St Pancras International (Kate Fisher), Nick Steel, Ri Streeter (Weta Workshop), Seyda Subasi-Gemici, The Sultan's Tent restaurant, Toronto, Canada, The Sun (Caroline Iggulden and Dave Masters), Atichart Tavornmard, Charlie Taylor, Holly Taylor, Stephen Taylor, Torfaen County Borough Council (Ben Payne, communications officer), TNR (Claire, Sophie and Tessa), Virgin London Marathon (Natasha Grainger, Nicola Okey and Tiffany Osborne), UCLH (Sharon Spiteri), Maria Vivas, Wandsworth Film Office, Louisa, Jessica, Isabel and Sam Way, Westminster City Council (Francesca Pipe), Adam Wide, Dan Woods, World Health Organization, World Health Statistics, Oz Wright, David Wyatt, X Games, Zippy Productions.

IN MEMORIA
Henry Allingham (**oldest living man**), Gertrude Baines (**oldest living woman**), Melvin Boothe (**longest fingernails - male**), Terry Calcott (**fastest motocycle wheelie**), Chanel and Otto (**oldest dogs**), Gibson (**tallest dog**), Michael Jackson (**most successful pop artist**), Lurch (**largest horn circumference - steer**), He Pingping (**shortest living man (mobile)**), Tomoji Tanabe (**oldest living man**), Helen Wagner (**longest serving soap star**), Don Vesco (**fastest wheel-driven vehicle**)

PICTURE CREDITS
2 Ranald Mackechnie/GWR; Tristan Savatier; Takezo2000 **3** Robert Vos/Photoshot **5** Paul Michael Hughes/GWR **6** *NASA John Wright/GWR; John Wright/GWR* **7** Marc Henrie/Getty Images; Paul Michael Hughes/GWR

USA INTRO 8 Nate Christenson; Rob Fraser/GWR; Paul Michael Hughes/GWR **9** Joe Murphy/Getty Images; Paul Michael Hughes/GWR **11** Adam Bouska

CANADA INTRO 8 Ranald Mackechnie/GWR **11** Ken Ardill; Richard Wahab

12 Paul Michael Hughes/GWR **13** *Adam Bouska*; Paul Michael Hughes/GWR **14** Paul Michael Hughes/GWR; Getty Images **15** Paul Michael Hughes/GWR; John Wright/GWR **16** Paul Michael; Hughes/GWR **17** Paul Michael Hughes/GWR **18** Paul Michael Hughes/GWR **19** Paul Michael Hughes/GWR **20** Tim Anderson/GWR; Yuri Ceschin/GWR; Press Eye **21** Tim Anderson/GWR; Hakan Eijkenboom; Yuri Ceschin/GWR **22** NASA **24** NASA; Robert Gendler/Science Photo Library **25** Steve A. Munsinger/Science Photo Library; NASA/Science Photo Library; David Ducros/Science Photo Library **26** NASA **27** NASA **28** Getty Images; NASA **29** Lori Losey/Getty Images; NASA **30** NASA **31** Dorling Kindersley; G Scharmer; L Rouppe van der Voort (KVA)/Reel EFX Inc. **32** Getty Images **33** M. Timothy O'Keefe/Alamy **34** Daniel Riordan Tom Fox/Corbis **35** Corbis; Grant Dixon/Getty Images **36** Alamy Eitan; Simanor/Getty Images **37** Kevin Schafer/Getty Images; Getty Images; John Beatty/Getty Images **38** Paul Nicklen/Getty Images; NASA; Stephen Belcher/FLPA **39** Steven Miller/NRL NOAA/National Science Foundation **40** Reuters; Jeff Hunter/Getty Images **41** Alamy; Albert Moldvay/Getty Images **42** NOAA; Merrick Davies **43** Radek Dolecki; Simon Battensby/Getty Images **44** Michael Appleton/Getty Images; Rex Features; Colin Braley/Reuters **45** John Russell/Getty Images; Rex Features; Ricardo Mazalan/AP/PA **46** Getty Images **47** H. Schmidbauer/Still Pictures **48** BBC/Random House; Ron Blakey **49** BBC/Random House **50** BBC/Random House **51** BBC/Random House; BBC

INDEX

★ ★ ★ ★ ★ ★ ★ ★ ★ ★ ★ ★

This year's index is organized into two parts: by subject and by superlative. Bold entries in the subject index indicate a main entry on a topic, and entries in BOLD CAPITALS indicate an entire chapter. Neither index lists personal names.

INTRODUCTION
STOP PRESS

★★★★★

★ FASTEST VIOLIN PLAYER

Ben Lee (UK), of violin duo FUSE, played "Flight of the Bumblebee" in 1 min 4.21 sec in London, UK, on April 7, 2010. The quality of the performance was verified by Rodney Friend, the leader/concert master who has performed with the London Symphony Orchestra, New York Philharmonic Orchestra and the BBC Symphony Orchestra in a career spanning 30 years.

★ OLDEST LIVING PERSON

Just as we were going to press we received this image of Eugénie Blanchard (St Barts, France, b. February 16, 1896), who became the oldest person on the planet upon the death of the previous record holder, Kama Chinen (Japan), on May 2, 2010. Eugénie shares her nationality with the **oldest person ever**; *see p.83 for details.*

★ MOST PORK SCRATCHINGS EATEN

Scott Dustan (UK) ate 0.95 oz (27 g) of deep-fried cured pork rind in one minute at The Union, London, UK, on April 30, 2010. At the same event, Courtney Shapiro (USA/UK) consumed 0.74 oz (21 g) in 30 seconds.

★ FASTEST TIME TO KAYAK/CANOE LOCH NESS

A team of 26 Asda employees and suppliers led by senior meat buyer Jim Viggars (all UK) kayaked the length of Loch Ness, Scotland, UK, from Fort Augustus to Dores (a distance of 17.9 nautical miles; 20.59 miles; 33.15 km) in 5 hr 19 min 17 sec on May 18, 2010. The record attempt was organized to raise funds for the Tickled Pink breast cancer charity. All of the team members lined up to cross the finish line together and therefore achieved the same time.

★ LARGEST GAME OF MUSICAL STATUES

A total of 1,079 participants took part in a game of musical statues at an event organized by Danone Finland in Helsinki, Finland, on April 25, 2010.

★ GREATEST PRIZE MONEY FOR A HORSE RACE

The largest prize fund for a single horse race is $10 million for the Dubai World Cup, held at Meydan Racecourse in Dubai, United Arab Emirates (UAE), on March 27, 2010.

SHORTEST PERSON TO PERFORM A WING WALK

The **shortest professional stuntman**, Kiran Shah (UK), stands at 4 ft 1.7 in (1 m 26.3 cm) and performed his first wing walk in Cirencester, Gloucestershire, UK, on April 30, 2010.

★ LARGEST PASTA BOWL

Buca di Beppo Italian Restaurant (USA) served up a 13,786-lb (6,253-kg) bowl of pasta at the chain's Anaheim restaurant, Garden Grove, California, USA, on March 12, 2010.

VW

THE ★ LARGEST CAR MOSAIC WAS CREATED WITH 460 VOLKSWAGEN AUTOMOBILES IN AN EVENT ORGANIZED BY VOLKSWAGEN DO BRASIL IN SÃO PAULO, BRAZIL, ON APRIL 10, 2010.

EXTRA!
IS IT ART YOU ARE LOOKING FOR? IF SO, TURN TO PP.190-191.

APNEA: The suspension of breathing, particularly that practised by divers, from the Greek verb "to breathe."

LARGEST ICE MAZE

The Arctic Glacier Ice Maze (USA) at the Buffalo Powder Keg Festival in Buffalo, New York, USA, featured an ice maze measuring 12,855.68 ft² (1,194.33 m²) on February 26, 2010. The maze was constructed using 2,171 blocks of ice, each weighing 300 lb (36.08 kg).

★ LARGEST SCULPTURE MADE FROM RECYCLED MATERIAL

Under the auspices of RESUR, the local government consortium for the recycling of solid waste materials, a team of students from the Granada School of Architecture in Granada, Spain, designed and built a castle measuring 95 ft 1.7 in (29 m) long, 46 ft 1.9 in (14.07 m) wide and 22 ft 11.5 in (7 m) tall from approximately 50,000 tetra pak milk cartons on May 17, 2010. The cartons were collected by students at the primary schools in the Granada region in the weeks before to the record attempt. The structure had no internal frame and was held together with staples and string.

★ MOST CANS CRUSHED WITH A VEHICLE IN THREE MINUTES

Ian Batey crushed 61,106 cans in three minutes driving a 10-ton (9-tonne) monster truck for Burn Energy Drink (UAE) at the Jumeirah Beach Residence, in Dubai, UAE, on March 6, 2010.

★ FREEDIVING/ DYNAMIC APNEA WITH FINS (WOMEN)

Natalia Molchanova (Russia) dived to a depth of 738 ft 2 in (225 m) without an external oxygen supply in Moscow, Russia, on April 25, 2010, breaking her own record.

★ LONGEST BUBBLE CHAIN

Just as we were finishing off this year's book, bubble blower Sam Heath (aka Sam Sam the Bubbleman) popped into the GWR offices in London, UK, where he created a chain of 26 bubbles. Sam used a standard drinking straw and bubble wand to make the chain.

SHAVES
BARBER JOHN McGUIRE (IRELAND) SHAVED A RECORD 60 HEADS IN ONE HOUR ON THE THE RAY D'ARCY SHOW ON TODAY FM IN DUBLIN, IRELAND, ON FEBRUARY 18, 2010.

WAVES
RTÉ'S THE AFTERNOON SHOW ORGANIZED 414 SWIMMING CLASSES ACROSS IRELAND TO CLAIM THE RECORD FOR THE ★LARGEST SWIMMING LESSON OVER MULTIPLE LOCATIONS ON MAY 21, 2010.

★ NEW RECORD
★ UPDATED RECORD